VANISHING INTO THINGS

VANISHING

— *into* —

THINGS

Knowledge in Chinese Tradition

BARRY ALLEN

———

Harvard University Press

Cambridge, Massachusetts

London, England

2015

First printing

Library of Congress Cataloging-in-Publication Data

Allen, Barry, 1957–

Vanishing into things : knowledge in Chinese tradition / Barry Allen.

pages   cm

ISBN 978-0-674-33591-2 (hardcover)

1. Knowledge, Theory of—China.   I. Title.

BD168.C5A45 2015

121.0951—dc23   2014035114

For Jeanne

翁 海 貞

Don't you remember, Oh Zarathustra, how once your
bird called out above you, as you stood in the forest,
indecisive, not knowing which way to turn?
—NIETZSCHE, *Thus Spoke Zarathustra*

Contents

VANISHING INTO THINGS

Introduction: To Really See the Little Things

> What makes knowledge a thing of beauty is that it benefits life
> and does not go beyond that.
>
> —JI KANG

Duke Huan, ambitious ruler of Qi during China's tumultuous Spring and Autumn period, and his chief adviser, the sage statesman Guan Zhong, had met in secret to plan an attack on the state of Jü. Before they could make their first move, however, they discovered that everybody knew their plan, leaving them defeated before they even began.

The Duke said to Guan Zhong, "You and I closed the doors and planned an attack on Jü. Although the plan has not yet been put into action everybody knows all about it! How can that be?" Guan Zhong replied, "There must be a sage in the state." But how could even a sage penetrate so closely guarded a secret? The Duke thought back to the day of their planning. "On that day there was an attendant who in placing the mat and serving the food looked up at us. It must be him!"

The Duke reassembled the servants. Recognizing the attendant, he had the chief of protocol bring him forward, respectfully seating him in the place for honored guests. He asked, "Are you the one who revealed our plan to attack Jü?" The servant replied, "Yes." "I didn't speak publically about attacking Jü," the Duke said, "yet you have informed the world. How did you know?" He gets a cheeky answer: "I have heard that the perfected man is good at making plans, and the common man is good at figuring them out. I figured it out." *But how could you? How could anyone?* Eventually he gives this explanation: "Happiness and joy are the appearance of bells and drums. Profundity and quietness are the appearance of mourning attire. Effusive fullness with the fingers and toes moving is the appearance of military affairs. On that day when I saw you two in the tower, your mouths were open and not closed. This was talking about Jü. You raised your hand and

1

pointed, your power will be inflicted on Jü. Moreover I have observed that among the minor feudal lords only Jü is not submissive, so I said you would attack it."

With no weapons or troops, this mere servant defeats the Duke's plans and preserves the peace, sparing the people a war. Guan Zhong called him a sage. What makes him sagacious is the canny knowledge by which he sees what is coming and modifies its course with near-invisible subtlety. Hearing the man's explanation the Duke exclaims, "Excellent! 'From the inconspicuous he hits upon brightness'—that's what the saying refers to!"[1]

This proverb, "From the inconspicuous he hits upon brightness" (*yi wei she ming*), epitomizes what Chinese tradition tends to expect and esteem in wise knowledge. It is the cognitive accomplishment of a sage. Highly effective yet infinitely subtle, there is almost nothing to it. A variation on the proverb occurs in the *Daodejing*: "To really see the little things is called enlightenment" (*jian xiao yue ming*). To really see the little things is to see the big things they betoken, and see them well before their development becomes obvious. Such seeing penetrates to the virtual depth of the world, perceiving incipient mutation, recognizing opportunities to align and transform with the changes. In the words of the *Huainanzi* (*Book of the Huainan Masters*): "Since the beginnings of good and bad fortune are tiny as a sprout, people overlook them. Only sages see their beginnings and know their ends. . . . The sages' perception of outcomes at their origin is subtle!"[2]

No one keeps a secret from a sage. Kongzi (Confucius) says, "Look at the means a man employs, observe the basis from which he acts, and discover where it is that he feels at ease. Where can he hide? Where can he hide?" The knowledge is not an oracular premonition, but a canny presagement from inconspicuous indications. "The sage does not value foreknowledge," says Ming dynasty thinker Wang Yangming. "When blessings and calamities come, even a sage cannot avoid them. He only knows the incipient activating force of things and handles it in accordance with the circumstance." The small and inconspicuous are resources to the keen and alert, who discern the mutations they discreetly herald. Mere dust speaks volumes to the wise, as this Chinese general explains:

When the enemy first approaches, if the dust rises in streams but is dispersed, they are dragging brushwood. If it rises up like ears of grain and jumps about chaotically, chariots are coming. If the dust is thick and heavy, swirling and turbulent as it rises up, cavalry are coming. If it is low and broad, spreading and diffuse as it rises, infantry are advancing. When the army is small and the dust is scattered and chaotic, it means the units are not closely ordered. If the troops are numerous but the dust clear, it means the units are well ordered and the general's commands systematic. If the dust rises to the front and rear, left and right, it means they are employing their troops without any consistent method. When the army moves and the dust rises in streaks without dispersing, or when the army halts and the dust also stops, it is because the general's awesomeness and virtue have caused the units to be strictly ordered. If when they decamp or set out their deployments dust rises up and flies off, mount defenses against those places where it originated because enemy forces will certainly be approaching in ambush there. Observing the enemy through rising dust is thus a technique for estimating the enemy's forces and seizing victory.[3]

Such knowledge belongs to what this general calls "the acumen of strategists," which, he says, "[lies] in penetrating the subtle amid unfolding change, and discerning the concordant and contrary."

Penetrating the subtle—seeing a lot in little things. *Discerning the concordant and contrary*—knowing the resonance among things, and how to amplify or dampen emerging tendencies. This commander is not alone in esteeming such knowledge. It is the ecumenical understanding of sage knowledge in Chinese tradition; it is not strictly universal—there are exceptions—but it is the leading idea. In the words again of the *Huainan Masters*, "The commander must see singularly and know singularly. Seeing singularly is to see what is not seen. Knowing singularly is to know what is not known. To see what others do not is called enlightenment" (*jian ren suo bu jian wei zhi ming*).[4]

The problems of knowledge that philosophers tend to be familiar with—problems of justification, skepticism, and the possibility of truth—depend on seldom-articulated assumptions concerning the value of knowledge: for instance, that the best knowledge, the knowledge that matters most to philosophy, has to be true; that this "truth" should be understood ontologically, in terms of adequacy to its object; and that the secure enjoyment of knowledge and truth are conditions on virtue and happiness. Without these assumptions the textbook problems of epistemology are difficult to motivate. Yet the assumptions are not without difficulties of their own, which has made the problems of epistemology increasingly hard to take seriously.

Chinese tradition does not share the problems of epistemology because it does not share the evaluation of knowledge that makes those problems perplexing. Knowledge poses different questions—not about essence or conditions of possibility, but about point and value. What makes knowledge wise and worth pursuing? What is its relationship to other values—good government, say, or ritual, or war? The questions Chinese tradition poses about knowledge respond to different problems, arising from different imperatives in their thought. This is a book about those differences. What makes them interesting, at least to me, is that they emerge at points where Western thinking has proved unexpectedly problematic.

For instance, Western theories of knowledge tend to fix on statements and beliefs—symbolic, linguistic, propositional entities—and have developed highly technical concepts of evidence, warrant, and justification, all to explain a preposterously small fragment of knowledge—the part that is true, "the truth." This contemplative, logocentric approach, much favored in antiquity and never really shaken from later tradition, is counterproductive for understanding the contribution knowledge makes to the technical accomplishment of our civilization. The ingenuity of the inventions, the range and density of technical mediation, the multiplicity of artifactual interfaces in a global technoscientific economy attest to the reach and depth of contemporary knowledge. But this knowledge resists logical analysis into simpler concepts, seldom climaxes in demonstrable truth, and does not stand to pure theory as mere application or derivative "how-to" knowledge. Thus does the best knowledge of our civilization become unaccountable in the epistemologies of the epistemologists.[5]

The exorbitant attachment to theory and truth attends an indifference to art, or what Greeks called *techne.* For all the leading schools of ancient philosophy, theoretical knowledge is the preeminent value, science is the noblest aspiration, and demonstrable truth is the solution to all uncertainty. To know such truth requires clarity and certainty on a level discontinuous with the immanent, empirical, and ordinary. Knowledge becomes a problem of access. There are two levels: the one we live on, a level of everyday experience and opinion, and the transcendent level we have to access if we want to know the truth. The problem of access arises from the decision to make knowledge of truth the best, most prestigious knowledge, and to explain this truth as reality made present to an intellectual soul.

These decisions are taken over by later tradition with little dissent. Not until Nietzsche at the end of the nineteenth century does thinking begin to change. Nietzsche initiates the now-prevalent skepticism about the "correspondence theory of truth." The American pragmatists, especially William James, independently raise similar doubts. Today, most philosophers have abandoned the correspondence theory, though not always for the same reasons. What lesson should we take from the collapse of this ancient expectation concerning the nature of truth?

Nietzsche thought that without the ontological idea of truth (truth as true to beings) the value of knowledge becomes dramatically problematic. Why should we care about knowledge if it is not "the truth"? The question is not put derisively, as if he expects no answer. He poses it to show that it *is* a question, that once-satisfying answers are untenable, and to stimulate a new philosophy of knowledge. He expects reflection on the question to show that philosophical rationalism participates in the irrationality it claims to overcome. Valuing truth above all else is a way for atheists to still believe in God. To turn away from religion because it is not scientific and not true is not the triumph of reason over superstition. It is a new superstition, or one whose superstitious quality is newly apparent, except to those who still think truth is divine. Critical rationalists must awaken to the unreason of their rationalism, as they dutifully demystify demystification, and discover that "truth" is a name for the will to power.

Nietzsche called this predicament "European nihilism." "Why has the advent of nihilism become *necessary?* Because the values we have had hitherto thus draw this final consequence; because nihilism represents the ultimate logical conclusion of our great values and ideals." The death of God is just the beginning. Nietzsche foresees a violent self-overcoming of Western reason, pushing modern culture to the edge of the nihilism that has haunted the West since antiquity. Plato sowed the seed of this nihilism when he taught us to need something transcendent. Without it, all the good things about us seem threatened by metaphysical failure. The merely human, tainted with the stigma of contingency, is worthless. Having inherited this onto-theological expectation, we tend to assume that without a transcendent reference (reason, logic, being), knowledge collapses into relativism, with no real difference between true and false. In the face of modern disbelief about the supernatural, philosophy falls short of a convincing response to its own nihilistic implications.[6]

Hence the postmodern, or perhaps post-Western, problem of knowledge: how to acknowledge the self-destruction of Western rationalism and get beyond the obvious relativistic, nihilistic implications. How to understand the point and value of knowledge when we do not believe in a thing-in-itself. How to remain cheerful and creative in the pursuit of knowledge, when truth, as philosophy has understood it, does not exist. Such problems disclose a new horizon. Epistemology may be passé, but the philosophy of knowledge has never confronted more interesting questions. What is the value of knowledge, if not truth? What is the value of truth, if not adequation or correspondence? What is the relationship between knowledge and technical accomplishment? What is the relationship between knowledge and wisdom? What makes technical, technological knowledge wise?

These are not classical questions. I am not suggesting that we *have* to go to China for an answer, but the excursion may appeal to those who like to see unexpected alternatives in philosophy and to experiment with concepts. However, there is disagreement among scholars about whether such a thing as "Chinese philosophy" even exists, whether it is comparable to Western philosophy, or what should count as "philosophical" in Chinese tradition. Some scholars think Chinese thought is so alien, its language so distant from Western experience, that it is untenable to expect significant conceptual exchange between the two traditions. Others take the view that with due caution philosophy can enter into the movement of Chinese concepts and capture some of their tendency.

Needless to say I favor the latter view. While I try to avoid gratuitously reading Western assumptions into cryptic ancient texts, I do ask them questions their authors never heard of. Some scholars think that is a mistake. They would restrict scholarly usage to *emic* categories, meaning those consistent with the viewpoint of the culture under study. They disavow *etic* categories, or concepts meaningful to the community that studies the culture, as if the only way to discuss Chinese ideas rigorously is in terms the ancient Chinese might recognize as their own. That norm may be appropriate for some types of scholarship, but in philosophy it seems to me a case of the tail wagging the dog. I think we should have as many ways of reading the Chinese as we can invent. There should be a place for conversations that forget whether they are emic or etic, that no longer know whether they are Western or Modern (or Analytic or Continental), that seek a hybrid quality consistent with experimentation in concepts. Only by creative, restive venturesomeness, not by disciplinary specialization however global, will Chinese tradition begin to make a difference to the philosophy of the future.[7]

It is not important whether we call the ancient Chinese thinkers (Confucius and others) *philosophers*. We need not assume they are engaged in any project similar to that of Western philosophers. We do not require comparable intentions at all, and they are obviously lacking. There is no word of ancient Chinese we can translate as "philosophy." Such a word did not exist until the nineteenth century, when the word *zhexue*, combining two Chinese characters, "wisdom" and "study," was coined by a Japanese scholar to refer to the philosophy of Western antiquity. Thus it was only in response to Western problems that philosophical ideas were first identified in Chinese classics, constructing "Chinese philosophy" according to familiar Western models (idealism, realism, and so on). Chinese scholars themselves think the results were not all bad. Some issues were clarified and concepts acquired new precision. But the unrestrained construal of Chinese thought on Western models and the simplistic equation of terms from the classics with concepts of Western theory are obviously untenable.[8]

The Chinese themselves faced a version of the comparative problem in their own history with the introduction of Buddhism, a new religion in China after the first century CE. How should they translate the formidable corpus of Indian thought, whose terse abstraction has nothing in common with Chinese tradition? They did not try to think like Indians, and did not scruple over etic categories—in fact, they used almost nothing else. The result was not naive scholarship. It was the invention of Chinese Buddhism. This need for experimental creativity in the face of cultural discontinuity parallels the challenge to comparative philosophy today, which is to invent the contexts and experiment with the terms in which philosophy is becoming global. Philosophy is not or is no longer "Western," or at least it does not have to be. It may have begun in the West (even that is disputable), but it cannot be reduced to its history. Philosophy has never ceased to question its own conditions, and is now obviously global, or at least working through a new relationship to territory and the earth.

Dissatisfaction with epistemology is a part of that change. There are by now many lines of flight from epistemology—feminist, pragmatist, postpositivist, and poststructuralist, to name a few. I propose an even more literal deterritorialization. We do not need the Chinese problems to be our own for us to learn from how they respond to them. Their innocence of epistemology is what makes their thought interesting for the philosophy of knowledge. Innocence of epistemology does not mean indifference to problems of knowledge. The Chinese have ideas about knowledge because as they thought about the other problems that compelled them, they became perplexed by knowledge—by its difference from ignorance and error; by its relationship to wisdom and virtue; by its effectiveness and irreplaceable contribution to civilization. And they were perplexed for a reason philosophers above all should appreciate, since, as sinologist Angus Graham explains, the "derivation of all value from the value of knowledge" is "one of the constants of Chinese thought." *To know* is for them "the supreme imperative."[9]

Innocence of epistemology also does not mean innocent epistemology, as when scholars speak of China's "epistemological optimism." Supposedly the Chinese innocently, naively rely on lower standards than Western theories of knowledge and science. One has to wonder, though, whether it is really lower standards or different priorities, different standards? If you expect veridical knowledge of things in themselves, or the apodictic demonstration of truth, or even just a robust experimental result, your standard cannot be too high. But certainty is not the only value knowledge serves, and other values can be satisfied without fixing on theory and truth. The notion of epistemological optimism comes from Karl Popper, for whom it is no less a mistake than a corresponding pessimism. The optimists believe that truth is manifest and always recognized. Pessimism is a disbelief in humanity's power to discern the truth, associated with tolerance of doubt and willingness to accept obscurity. Thomas Metzger uses Popper's terms to argue that Chinese tradition is extravagantly optimistic in its epistemology. But how can traditional Chinese thinkers be extravagantly optimistic about a truth they do not recognize and a knowledge they do not value?

The idea that knowledge requires truth—or that truth is objectivity or involves a tricky correspondence to reality about which one could be optimistic or pessimistic—is not a neutral norm suitable for comparing China and the West. Yet that seems to be Metzger's assumption. He refers to what he calls the Great Modern Western Epistemological Revolution, more conveniently, GMWER. China missed it. "The vast majority of the Chinese, including many intellectuals, remained simply unaware of or unresponsive to the GMWER." Even after enlightenment through Western contact they resisted its truth, tending "to ignore the GMWER as unworthy of serious discussion," and "reaffirming [their] epistemological optimism." What looks to Metzger like indifference to the methodological difficulty of knowing the truth might also be the response of people less impressed than he thinks they should be by this Great Revolution. He believes the modern West really knows and China merely believes. *Our* norms are rational and objective, not mere cultural artifacts, like everybody else's. Or they would be if we really had been modern, which we never were, and if the Great Modern

Western Epistemological Revolution were not a myth of demythification that should be hard to fall for any more.[10]

Chinese tradition is bullish on knowledge, which is obviously worth while, certainly better than ignorance, but also elusive and not without dangers of its own. With the notable exception of the Mohists, however, we nowhere find Western philosophy's rationalistic preoccupations. Ideas of truth and representation play no part in understanding what knowledge is or its value. Nor do the perplexities knowledge poses depend on problematic dichotomies like mind and body or appearance and reality. We already glimpsed what the Chinese value in knowledge. The best knowledge, the wise knowledge of a sage, knows the evolution of circumstances from an early point, when their development is not so settled that it cannot be diverted, making highly effective action practically effortless (provided you know how). A servant foils a great duke and prevents a war merely by starting a rumor. Wisps of dust convey strategic opportunities to a commander who can really see the little things. Such knowledge is not deduced from principles or held in the mind as a representation or theory. The expression of the knowledge is action, a response to circumstances that is effortless yet highly effective.

The Chinese describe such action as *wu wei,* which literally means "no action" or "not doing," but in philosophy refers to inaction that is paradoxically active and highly effective. The value of the best, most sagacious knowledge is to fund such action. We meet this idea at the beginning of Chinese reflection with the Confucians, that is, Kongzi and his followers in classical (pre-Qin) times (sixth to third century BCE), where Chapter 1 begins. Chapter 2 introduces the Daoists, principally the works known as *Zhuangzi* and the *Daodejing.* We shall see little difference with Confucians about what knowledge is or why it is valuable. The difference lies in the conditions thought conducive to *wu wei* effectiveness, the way to cultivate it, how to train it for wisdom. Confucians want to do *wu wei* to be good, meaning benevolent, humane, righteous. Daoist authors mock these values. For them the point of effortless effectiveness and the knowledge that makes it possible is to nourish one's vitality, replenishing vital *qi,* extending life to the utmost limit.

A new voice enters in Chapter 3 with Sunzi and the Chinese art of war. The understanding of knowledge in China's military philosophy—how to recognize it, what it does, why it is worth caring for—largely agrees with Confucians and Daoists. The military philosophers esteem knowledge more highly than Western theorists of war, for instance Machiavelli or Clausewitz.

Military victory is a problem not of force but knowledge. That is especially true of the most desirable victory, one that comes without a battle. This art of war concentrates on the problem of how a conventionally weak opponent can triumph over a stronger one. Really, there is only one way: by the knowledge that transforms strength into weakness and weakness into strength. With that you reverse the strategic situation and the enemy's resources become your own. Actual victory in the field is a mere fruit of this intensive transformation.

Another new voice appears in Chapter 4, on Chan (Zen) Buddhism. This was for a time the most influential sect of Buddhism in China, installed in something like 90 percent of the temples. Of all China's Buddhisms, Chan has the most give and take with Daoism, which it deliberately imitates and paradoxically reverses, for instance on the value of knowledge. Chan enlightenment is not an accomplishment of knowledge. On the contrary, knowledge is an obstacle and a kind of suffering. Yet only knowledge can take one to the threshold of enlightened emptiness—an argument Chan adapts from Daoism. The challenge of enlightenment is to get beyond the intentionality and objectivity of knowledge, which is an accomplishment of the very knowledge it leaves behind.

Chan also parallels the rise of medieval Neoconfucianism, the topic of Chapter 5. The philosophers associated with this movement all study Chan, and allow it to discreetly infuse traditional thought. For them, wisdom, the best knowledge, is knowing how to use things well, how to handle them in the right way, meaning the way that advances rather than frustrates their idea of benevolent humanity. A motif of their work is the urgency of what they call "the investigation of things" and "the extension of knowledge." That sounds like empiricism, a comparative proposition we shall examine in detail.

Throughout this book we see that knowledge is more like knowing how to find game than ocular knowledge of presence; more like knowing a territory than seeing an object, more like knowing the relations of things in an environment than contemplating a finished form; and it raises no problem of transcendent access. The problem of knowledge is not how to get beyond perspective, a view from nowhere. The problem is to see deeper into the world, to know it more intimately than concepts and language allow—to know not what is in the world, but what the world is becoming. The Chinese worry is not access, but getting stuck. What we call objects are processes and constantly changing. We must unlearn objectivity, not fixate on forms. Impartiality is its own reward. The point of detachment is not ocular, to see better what was always there anyway. Detachment is good as a means to the desired flexibility, overcoming differences that separate us from the *dao,* the spontaneous flow of changes. Instead of transcending perspectives we become skilled at never getting stuck in one, vanishing into things.

— 1 —

Confucians

The Master said: "Zilu, remark well what I am about to teach you!
This is wisdom: to recognize what you know as what you know,
and recognize what you do not know as what you do not know."

—*ANALECTS OF CONFUCIUS*

The oldest written sources hold few hints about knowledge before Kongzi (Confucius) and the beginning of classical Chinese philosophy. Verifiably pre-Confucian passages of the *Book of History* describe the virtuous ruler's knowledge in terms of enlightened intelligence (*ming*), wisdom (*zhi*), and knowing others (*zhi ren*), that is, knowing how to recognize and use people's abilities. This knowledge may contrast with skillful artifice (*qiao*) and trickery (*jian*). Virtuous rulers are not only wise, they protect people against clever language and beguiling appearances and use their knowledge to regulate the ten thousand things. The *Erya,* a late-Zhou text glossing words of the classics, explains *zhi* (knowledge, wisdom) as "every principle arranged in proper order." The *Book of Songs* praises wisdom, intelligence, and foresight, but also deplores their capacity for deception and disorder. Words for the wisdom of ancient sage emperors also describe the destruction wreaked by cunning ministers, deceptive speakers, and clever women.[1]

A prominent quality in the early vocabulary of knowledge is effectiveness, or more precisely amplified effectiveness. The point of knowledge is the productiveness it enhances, preternatural efficacy being the proof of knowledge, distinguishing it from commonplace cognition. Sometimes there is a connotation of learning and scholarship, as in the explanation of knowledge as "every principle arranged in proper order." There may be an association of knowledge with virtue (*de*), but also worry about artful deviousness. And we see the early priority of knowing others, knowing people, their strength and weakness, especially when they have something to hide.

12

Most of my discussion in this book concerns one or the other of two closely related words, *zhī* 知 and *zhì* 智. They are close in use, in pronunciation, and in written character, and are sometimes explained in terms of each other, for example in *Xunzi*: "Of the means of knowing (*zhī*), those that are in people we call *zhī*. Knowledge (*zhī*) having its union we call *zhì*." Graphically these are the same character, with *zhì* adding the "sun" radical. The graph both words share is a binome formed from the radical *shi* 矢 (arrow) on the left and *kou* 口 (mouth) on the right, prompting the *Shuo Wen*, a Han etymological dictionary, to gloss *zhī* (to know) as "to speak so as to hit the mark." Modern scholars find a tendency to use *zhī* as a verb ("to know") while *zhì* is apparently uncommon as a verb, but freely alternates with *zhī* in the nominal sense of "knowledge" or "wisdom" or sometimes "intelligence." Unless something seems to depend on it I will not always indicate which of these two words an author is using.[2]

Kongzi

The Confucian *Book of Rites* (*Liji*) recounts how, long ago, everything was good. People were good, treating everyone as family. There were no thieves, doors went unlocked, weapons were unknown. This was the time of Grand Unity (*datong*). Then things changed, people became selfish, and unity fell apart. Fortunately, just then a number of profound persons appeared and devised means to mend the shattered harmony. The centerpiece of their solution is the *li*, a word variously translated as rites, rituals, or ceremonies. These function like knots to hold the people together. "Ritual is the knot (*ji*) of the people. If the knot loosens the people will be scattered." Back in the day of Grand Unity, outsiders were not differentiated from neighbors, or older children from younger, offspring from other children, and so on. Rising prosperity challenged this dearth of distinctions, threatening chaos. Instituting the *li* effectively countered the threat, transforming a too-simple primitive harmony into a modest prosperity compatible with social complexity.[3]

Rituals work by shaping people's untaught dispositions (*renqing*). We need no instruction to feel joy, anger, or fear, but do require teaching to express these feelings in a way that enhances solidarity rather than jeopardizing it. At the beginning of life a person is like an uncultivated field. Training in ritual is like tilling. It manages and directs the heart's untaught dispositions.

Rituals do not merely restrain excessive sentiment but collect and channel all our feelings so that they flow in the right course, as a dike safely conveys floodwater. The *Book of Rites* compares the *li* to such things: "Rites are meant to rid the world of evils and scourges just like dams and dikes, which are built up to prevent floods." The rites work inconspicuously on people, unnoticeably transforming them, shaping and polishing them like jade. "The converting power of rites is imperceptible, but it can prevent evils before they are actually done, and can gradually transform the people from bad into good unknowingly."[4]

This account accords with a sociological understanding of rituals as codified performances that focus emotion and attention to create a shared reality, with feelings of solidarity and symbols of group membership. Eventually the *li* prescriptions covered a wide range of social behavior, from solemn rites reserved to the king, to a boy's manners among family and friends. They include ceremonies that reinforce hierarchy, sympathy, and fairness within the clan, such as rites for ancestors and rituals of filial piety, and collective festivals where music may add to the occasion. By Kongzi's time in the late Spring and Autumn period, the *li* formed a vast code of social behavior. Writers refer to the three hundred rules of ceremony and the three thousand rules of conduct. No important social interaction lacks a scripted, normative form. Practically everything one does, especially among others, is to some degree ceremonial.[5]

These *li* are not formulas to be adhered to grimly. The Chinese show a sophisticated recognition that their rites are not foolproof. Ritual practitioners have to know that the *li* may not always work, whether due to incompetence, people lacking the skill to follow the ritual script, or an inadequacy of the ritual itself to the complexity of a given situation. Anticipating and coping with potential dysfunction requires more than rote learning of ritual's textual tradition. It requires experts trained to adapt the tradition to living circumstances. A fluent ritual practitioner "knows ritual" (*zhili*), an expression that implies recognition of potential failure and knowing how to modify an inherited script in accordance with context, to preserve the spirit of the ceremony with the material at hand.

Kongzi, a master of such fluency, has a high opinion of the *li*. According to the *Book of Rites*, "The Master said, 'Sit, you three, and I will tell you about ritual, so that by means of ritual you will flow (*liu*) around the world and there will be no area that you will not cover.'" In *Analects* he mentions something called the *di* sacrifice, an ancient Zhou ritual performed by the king to honor his first ancestor. By Kongzi's time it had fallen into disuse and was no longer understood. Apparently someone asked him about it. "The Master said, 'I do not understand it. One who understood it could handle the world as if he had it right here,' and he pointed to the palm of his hand" (A 3.11).[6]

The early Zhou dynasty saw the last of the sage kings, who brought the *li* to perfection. To Kongzi this is the Golden Age (A 3.14). All the problems of the present trace back to a decline from this summit of ceremonial culture. Rulers have lost the *dao,* the way given to people by the ancient sages. *Analects* is the earliest Chinese text to prominently feature this fascinating word *dao.* "The *dao* does not prevail" (A 5.7); "The world has lost the *dao*" (A 16.2); "In the morning hear the *dao,* in the evening die content" (A 4.8). For the *dao* to prevail is for ceremonial practice to rule in life. The Confucian scholar (*ru*) is a custodian of the *li.* At the time, being a master of rites was a useful occupation. Every court needed several, and those are the men whom Kongzi and his disciples teach.[7]

This need for experts arises not merely from the prolixity of ritual tradition. The *li* are not empty formalities. A compelling performance requires a practitioner who is sincere, authentic, truthful—in Chinese *cheng,* the opposite of fake or counterfeit, acting without calculation or ulterior motive. To be effective in the ritual one has to be sincere, and to be sincere one must know oneself. That is not a given. Most people know themselves poorly. To know oneself one must ceaselessly test and cultivate oneself. That requires long study as well as watchful self-monitoring, admonition, and sincere striving to be good. There are two kinds of failure in ceremonial behavior: awkward performance lacking learning or skill, and mechanical performance lacking commitment. Beautiful and effective ceremony requires sincere personal presence fused with long practiced skill.

As the Zhou dynasty declined (Spring and Autumn period), old class divisions began to erode. Agricultural production increased, due in part to innovations centuries ahead of the rest of the world. Population grew, trade expanded, and eventually commoners were receiving education and participating in government, while ancient titled families declined. Kongzi is the scion of such a family. That background did not make him reactionary. On the contrary he leads the attack on the barriers to privilege, especially in the practice of the *li,* which tradition reserved to the ruling elite. He opens participation (in principle) to "everybody" (A 15.39). Rank belongs to merit, not lineage. The word then for members of the ruling class was *ren,* persons,

仁 (인) ren.

in distinction from *min,* the masses. The adjective form, also said *ren,* is initially a descriptive term for genteel decorum. Kongzi makes it a name for the summit of virtue, the virtue that completes all others. This singular semantic charge makes the word difficult to translate into modern English. In later tradition, *ren* becomes a more specific virtue, usually called *benevolence, humanity,* or *human-heartedness.*[8]

Another barrier divides ceremonies and their morality from politics and government. Rulers in his day want to *do* a lot—devise policies, prepare defenses, issue decrees, augment taxes, study war. To Kongzi, all of that is futile. If a king is not virtuous, clever policy cannot compensate, and if a king is virtuous such policies are superfluous. The Confucian ruler's most important contribution to government is moral rectitude, righteousness, highly visible, charismatic virtue (*de*). The way to attain that virtue is through

 德 日 (dé)

rigorous self-cultivation and scrupulous ceremonial practice. Kongzi envisions government conducted as far as possible by ceremony (A 2.3, 4.13). The usual verbs of government (what kings and ministers do) should be replaced by the ceremonial words and deeds of the *li.* Government should be all principle and no pragmatism, high-minded gentlemen working on their goodness and inspiring everyone around them to do the same. If the king does that, so will the ministers; if the ministers do it, so will the officials; if the officials do it, so will the hundred clans.[9]

The Confucian approach to ritual is unfailingly secular. Ceremonies are not practiced to appease spiritual beings, whom we are told to keep at a distance (A 6.22). By Kongzi's time this secular attitude is ubiquitous among the elite, who appreciate ceremonial proprieties as something more practical and reliable than a magical effort to win Heaven's favor. The value of ceremony is to spiritualize life, to make every action, especially every *inter*action, feel meaningful, appropriate, natural, and fair. The virtue of *ren,* humane goodness, requires these ceremonies for expression. The *li* provide commonly understood opportunities to practice goodness. Without them people could not understand each other and cooperate.

What Kongzi teaches is a *way,* a *gongfu,* or spiritual practice. There are no theories, no speculations; only prescriptions on the conduct of life. This "philosophy" is good or bad as a system of instruction, but says nothing true or false. Like Socrates and the Buddha, Kongzi will not speculate about nature (A 5.13). His topic, as that of these other teachers, is humanity. Consider Socrates. He sought knowledge of himself, and identified such knowledge as the highest good and cause of every other. We do bad only from ignorance. Replace ignorance with knowledge and the natural appeal of the good is unobstructed.

In Socrates's time there were other Greek teachers called sophists. For a fee they taught young men how to speak well. To many of his contemporaries Socrates seemed like one of these sophists, even if he charged no fee. In his defense, Plato made much of the difference between a philosopher like Socrates and a sophist. How could we have confused them? What the sophist says is calculated to be effective and persuade others; there is no relation between what he says and who he is. For Socrates, however, there is no other concern. He never tries to impress *others*; he is in search of *himself*. In *Phaedrus,* Plato has Socrates explain how he lost interest in the cosmological speculation about principles and the origin (*arche*) of things. "I have no time for such matters; and the reason, my friend, is this. I am still unable, as the Delphic inscription orders, to know myself; and it really seems to me ridiculous to look into other things before I have understood that."[10]

Sophists promote cleverness and skill. What they teach cannot be truly wise, though, not the *sophia* sought by the philosophical lover of wisdom, because the sophist's art can be used for good or bad alike. Wisdom should be knowledge of the good, a knowledge that can *only* be good, and thus must be completely different from any mere skill or technique, which can always be abused. Here Plato's Socratic conclusion mirrors that of Kongzi and his tradition. The best knowledge, the knowledge of the best, turns of its own accord toward the good (Kongzi calls them neighbors (A 4.1)). Where Plato diverges from his Chinese near contemporary is in his understanding of this good. He envisions a contemplative good, a comprehensive theory. Knowledge of the good requires that we disdain common opinion, forsake shadows for the light, penetrate the appearances, and seek a certainty completely discontinuous from ordinary life and experience.

The prestige of theory in Western thought rests on identifiable assumptions. One is the assumption of Heraclitus, the first to emphasize it. It is that a common *logos* links human beings to the principle of order in the cosmos. What makes us rational and therefore human is the same reason, the same *logos,* the same divine fire that makes the universe a cosmos, an elegant, intelligible system. Grasping that system, apprehending it in thought, seeing all the parts cohere in one intricate, finished cosmos is the only thought Aristotle can imagine for a god. The activity of the god is the contemplation (*theoria*) of truth, and this same divine contemplation is our happiness too, which Aristotle says "extends just so far as contemplation does, and those to whom contemplation more fully belongs are more truly happy, not as a mere concomitant but in virtue of the contemplation; for this is in itself precious."[11]

Why is pure theory so good? In these epistemic acts we actualize the best part of ourselves, the part that connects us to the source of ultimate value. It seems to follow that the more we know about what is logical or *logos* in ourselves (mind, reason, language), the better we can know the truth of nature. Epistemology is considered a preoccupation of modern philosophy, and of course it is. But modern philosophy could be obsessive about epistemology only because of what was established in ancient thought, which is the idea that knowing more about the *logos* within us would greatly improve scientific knowledge (*episteme*) of truth.

The difference between a commoner and a Confucian perfected person (*junzi*) is the latter's diligently cultivated self-knowledge, which makes him adept at completing things, meaning handling them as they should be, in the right, ritually appropriate way. He makes spontaneous, effortlessly benevolent use of whatever comes to hand. So generous an art is alien to the attainment of the Greek philosopher, for whom knowledge of use is the second-class know-how of artisans and mechanics, and too banal to detain a lover of truth. Kongzi shares Plato's conviction of a vital difference between sophistical cleverness—which can be called "knowledge" in Greek or Chinese—and wisdom, meaning the best knowledge, the bright intelligence of the sage. No amount of cleverness or technical skill adds up to wisdom (A 4.1, 12.22, 15.33). He also shares the elite Greek condescension for technical arts (A 8.9, 8.18, 9.2). Despite having trained in a craft as a boy, Kongzi makes it clear that he does not involve himself in the mechanics of anything, not even statecraft. Such work is narrow and takes a narrow mind. He compares intellectual specialization to the manufacture of a highly specialized ritual vessel. A perfected person is not a vessel (A 2.12). "Specialized" is another word for unbalanced. The *junzi* is the one whose long-cultivated balance balances everyone else.

How then does the knowledge of the Confucian perfected person, an art both wise and practical, capable of completing things with benevolent usage, differ from mechanical skill or technique? To find our answer we must follow the Master's thoughts in two related contexts. One is the connection between sage knowledge and book learning or the value of scholarship, where he distinguishes knowledge from cleverness, technical skill, and contrived speech. The other is his explanation of how knowledge contributes to goodness and what he says on the problem of what makes knowledge wise.

Knowledge and Learning

"The Master said, 'How great was [sage king] Yao as a ruler! So majestic! It is heaven that is great, and it was Yao who modeled himself upon it. So vast! Among the common people there were none who were able to find words to describe him'" (A 8.19). The charismatic virtue of the sage is irresistibly potent, and transforms those with whom he interacts so inconspicuously that nobody notices what he does, which seems spontaneous, natural (*ziran*), not anyone's doing. As Mengzi puts it later, "Anywhere a perfected person passes through is transformed. . . . He flows with heaven above and earth below."[12]

Such people are not divine or superhuman. At some level they are just like everyone else. Anyone can be a sage. There is a way. It is a process of self-cultivation, a carefully calibrated transformation that Confucian teachers have down to an art. They know the books to study, the order in which to study them, and how to combine study with exacting ritual practice. Work on that for several decades and anybody can become a *junzi*, a perfected person, ultimately even a sage.

In the *Great Learning*, a Confucian text of the third century BCE (possibly from Kongzi's own school), it is said, "From the son of Heaven down to commoners, all without exception should regard self-cultivation (*xiushen*) as the root." First transform yourself, then transform everything around you. According to the *Book of Rites*, a good ruler has three worries: that there are important things he should know but has never heard of, that he has not properly appreciated that which he has heard of, and that he lacks the competence to put what he has learned into practice. The answer to all three is unceasing self-cultivation. The goal is to become truly at home with goodness and ceremonies.[13]

Ritual propriety eventually becomes second nature. Your spontaneous heart's desire then beautifully accords with the requirements of ceremony for the circumstance at hand. Every gesture, every response is ritually impeccable and joyous to perform. It may take a lifetime to reach that point but it can be done. Kongzi tells us that by the time he was seventy he could follow his heart's desire without overstepping the bounds of propriety (A 2.4).

That is the summit of knowledge. This wise knowledge, combining learning, reflection, and perfected ritual practice, is inherently moral, a power for good, and unlike specialized skill or mechanical art it is never devious or expedient.

What you learn in the Confucian program is the wisdom of the past. Such study is the privileged way to train the mind—the heart and intellect—and renew and extend that wisdom in contemporary practice. The point of the learning is not just to have the knowledge, but to be changed by it, and eventually to love it. "Love of learning" (*hao xue*) is mentioned eight times in *Analects,* and it is in these terms that Kongzi identifies himself to us. "There is no one who matches my love for learning" (A 5.28). To love *knowledge* is to love the goal. To love *learning* is to love the process, the study, inquiry, and practice. "The Master said: I have never been able to do anything for a person who is not himself constantly asking, 'What should I do? What should I do?'" (A 15.16).[14]

Learning means memorizing the classics. It also means sincere self-examination and exacting ritual practice. However, it is never a matter of merely repeating a formula. You also have to learn how to ask good questions. "Zixia said, 'Learning broadly and firmly retaining what one has learned, be incisive in one's questioning and able to reflect upon what is near at hand—goodness is to be found in this'" (A 19.6). You must not be ashamed to admit that you do not know, and even to seek knowledge from inferiors (A 5.15). Loving learning means knowing what you do not know, knowing the limit of your knowledge. "Zixia said, 'Being aware every day of what he still lacks, and after a month's time not forgetting what he is already capable of—a person like this can be said to love learning'" (A 19.5). Above all, one who loves learning knows how to learn from himself, and therefore never makes the same mistake twice. "Duke Ai asked, 'Who among your disciples might be said to love learning?' Confucius answered, 'There was one named Yan Hui who loved learning. He never misdirected his anger and never made the same mistake twice'" (A 6.3).

Confucian *hao xue* may, as Roger Ames suggests, mean "the unrelenting resolve to become consummate in one's conduct as a person." But study remains the context of that, and whatever else love of learning is, it is a kind of success in study. To love learning is not merely to like it a lot, nor to longingly lack it, as Socrates longingly lacks wisdom. To *love* learning, to love the process, is also to *succeed* in learning, to do it superbly, reaping the benefit of effectiveness and mastery in life. Even when Kongzi allows a place for "thinking" or "reflection" (*si*), *what* one reflects on will have something to do with a text under study (A 2.15).[15]

The wisdom one seeks from learning is wise conduct—really the only sort of wisdom Confucians see. Sagacious application is not a detour or derivation from pure knowledge; it is proof that you attained it. To get to the point of wise knowledge requires submission to the insights of other people and the cultural heritage. "The Master said, 'I transmit rather than innovate. I trust in and love the ancient ways'" (A 7.1). The element of trust, confidence in the relevance of what is learned, distinguishes this love of learning from pedantic antiquarianism: "The Master said, 'Both keeping past teachings alive and understanding the present—someone able to do this is worthy of becoming a teacher'" (A 2.11).

In *Symposium,* Socrates proves to his interlocutors' satisfaction that one can love only what one lacks. Confucian *hao* cannot be analyzed in these terms. One cannot longingly lack learning. To love learning one has to live learning, to weave it into the fabric of life. To love learning is be good at learning, successful in it, and joyous at the prospect of more. This love of learning reminds me less of Socrates than Nietzsche and *fröliche Wissenschaft,* gay science, "the idea that life could be an experiment of the seeker for knowledge." For Nietzsche, as for Kongzi, acquiring and perfecting knowledge is a joyous process, not a yearned-for end. It consists of living a certain type of life, and is not a separable goal to which learning is a means. Life and learning, goodness and knowledge, are one becoming, one evolution, one *dao,* or form of life.[16]

Plato holds knowledge and life apart, as he does knowledge and learning. On his account learning is strictly speaking impossible. It is a misnomer for remembering knowledge that cannot be learned because it is eternal and not subject to becoming. Platonic knowledge is discontinuous with the immanent plane of life, and requires submission to something unconditional and quasi-divine. The truth of such knowledge is not measured by its value for life (*our* life). It is measured by being. That this ontological truth is also good for us, that it alone offers lasting happiness—that was a *promise,* an assumption, but never anything the philosophers *knew.*

Knowledge and Goodness

Sages are not stuffed with learning. They do not know everything. They cannot explain the origin of the universe or why people have different destinies. According to the *Book of Rites*, "There are things that even a sage does not know . . . things that even a sage cannot do." The knowledge of a sage is defined by ceremonies broadly understood. A sage knows the ceremonially appropriate way to handle any circumstance, reacting with spontaneous, felicitous propriety. Undistracted by disinterested curiosity, a sage mind does not wander. There is no wisdom outside the rites and classics, and no point to knowledge that does not translate into more "truthful" (sincere, authentic) ceremonial practice. These ceremonies define the value of humanity, and humanity defines the value of everything else. Asked about the meaning of *ren* (humanity, benevolence), Kongzi says it is a matter of "restraining yourself and returning to the rites." Asked to elaborate, he says, "Do not look unless it is in accordance with ritual; do not listen unless it is in accordance with ritual; do not speak unless it is in accordance with ritual; do not move unless it is in accordance with ritual" (A 12.1).[17]

The admonition to confine oneself to the rites precludes such things as disinterested inquiry or practicing difficult techniques (apart from rites, which include, for instance, archery). All of that must be checked by ceremonies and their decorum. Knowledge is valuable only when subordinated to humanity, meaning subordinated to ceremonial practice. When knowledge becomes merely curious, or when its use is calculated and intentional, we lose balance and stray from the path of goodness. "The Master said, 'If your wisdom reaches it [the *dao*], but your goodness cannot protect it, then even though you may have attained it, you are sure to eventually lose it. If your wisdom reaches it, and your goodness is able to protect it, but you cannot manifest it with dignity, then the common people will not be respectful. If your wisdom reaches it, your goodness is able to protect it, and you can manifest it with dignity, but you do not use ritual to put it into motion, it will never be truly excellent'" (A 15.33).

Ritual puts knowledge into practice, where it proves its wisdom in faultless action. Kongzi must therefore denigrate experiments. The self-cultivation necessary to become a perfected person is a program with few electives. You must work on yourself, not investigate things. You must transform yourself, but according to a traditional formula. It would be monstrous to try to become something new and different. Nor is inquiry encouraged into things other than books. The only rationale for the pursuit of knowledge is enhanced ceremony. Learning must not stray from this service. There is nothing better to know than the wisdom required for goodness. If something is irrelevant to ceremony, how can it be "wise" to try to know about it? "The

Master said, 'I once engaged in thought for an entire day without eating and an entire night without sleeping, but it did no good. It would have been better for me to have spent the time in learning'" (A 15.31).[18]

Plato
learning v. thinking
→ more practical.
close to everyday life

Knowledge and Nonaction 無為 (무위) wu wei
비인위적인 자연성. ↔인위.작위.

Even constrained by ritual, knowledge remains wonderfully effective. The Confucian ideal of knowledge, what gives knowledge its point and value, is ceremonial virtuosity, knowing how to conduct life in a way at once spontaneous and completely in accord with Heaven's norm, tranquil amid turmoil, maintaining perfect balance. The Chinese name for effortlessly effective conduct is *wu wei,* or nonaction. In its philosophical sense, *wu wei* means not stasis or immobility but rather doing so little so easily, so artfully, that one seems to do nothing at all. To have this quality, action must flow spontaneously (*ziran*); there is no deliberation, calculation, or indecision. But spontaneity is not all there is to *wu wei,* at least not for Confucians. What you do effortlessly must also be ceremonially impeccable and righteously effective, neglecting no requisite to a balanced, harmonious response.[19]

The interpretation of *wu wei* as effortless action is controversial and I return to it in Chapter 2. The *wu wei* ideal is typically associated with thinkers we classify as Daoists, although an early occurrence of the expression is in the Confucian *Analects* (A 15.5). It seems to me that rather than being the preoccupation of one as against another "school" of Chinese thought, the value of *wu wei* action, and the value of knowledge as conducive to such action, is common ground among Confucians, Daoists, the military philosophers, and many later Neoconfucians. The differences among them lie in their understanding of what *wu wei* presupposes as background conditions (especially what sort of training), and why effortless accomplishment is esteemed. Allow me therefore to suspend this chapter's concentration on Confucians and draw from a wider range of texts to illustrate this association, crucial to my thesis in this book, of knowledge with *wu wei* effectiveness.

maybe because of chinese culture of perceiving nature / Natural rules as crucial thing in daily life.

The *Huainanzi* or *Book of the Huainan Masters* is a Daoist-leaning work presented to Emperor Wu by his uncle Liu An, King of Huainan, in 139 BCE. It is an encyclopedia of Chinese thought collaboratively written by the finest masters of the early Han. The first chapter, entitled *Originating in the Dao,* offers this comment on *wu wei:* "Sages . . . take no deliberate action (*wu wei*), yet there is nothing left undone (*wu bu wei*). In tranquility they do not try to govern (*wu zhi*), but nothing is left ungoverned (*wu bu zhi*). What we call 'no deliberate action' is not to anticipate the activity of things. What we call 'nothing left undone' means to adapt to what things have [already] done. What we call 'not governing' means to not change how things are naturally so. What we call 'nothing left ungoverned' means to adapt to how things are mutually so."[20] When the text explains "no deliberate action" as not anticipating, it alludes to the importance of timeliness and knowing when. One who does not anticipate does nothing premeditated, does not calculate what is coming in order to act preemptively. Instead one waits and responds to things as they arise. When the text explains "nothing left undone" as adapting to what is already done, it refers to how art can make contingently co-occurring things function harmoniously together. When it explains "not governing" as not changing how things are naturally so, relying on what happens spontaneously, it implies that *wu wei* action is inconspicuous in its beginnings and irresistible in its tendency, seeming inevitable and impersonal rather than a willful purpose. As the work says elsewhere, "Non-action does not mean [that the ruler] froze and was inert but that nothing any longer emanated from the ruler personally." Under the best government, people are not aware of government at all, and say, "I do this simply because it is my nature!" Finally, when the text explains "nothing left ungoverned" as adapting each thing to the others, or (an alternate translation) "making use of the mutual causation that obtains among things," it is, I think, referring to action that moves in alliance with the *ziran* evolution of circumstances and does not rely on external energy or force.[21]

Wu wei effectiveness requires an aptitude for the subtle signs of incipience, the beginning or becoming of things, discerning points where development remains pliable and can be inconspicuously diverted. Such an understanding could be called foresight or foreknowledge provided there is no connotation of divination. It is not prognostication, which merely utters future fact and may be right or wrong but not wise. The knowledge active in *wu wei* effectiveness knows how to improvise on the future, discerning and responding synergistically to its incipience. We had an example in the introduction, when a sage servant "effortlessly" foiled Duke Huan's plan for war. Here is another example:

> [In 574 BCE,] when the feudal lords were convened at Zhou, Duke Dan Xiang, observing that Duke Li of Jin looked out far and stepped high, advised the Duke of Lu, "Jin will soon suffer from rebellion." The Duke of

Lu inquired, "Dare I ask if it will be an act of Heaven or because of men?" He replied: "I am not a court astrologer, so how would I know the *dao* of Heaven? I deduced from the Duke of Jin's manner that he would shortly suffer misfortune. Now in the perfected man the eyes determine the intent and the feet follow the eyes. Therefore, when you observe his manner, you can know his mind. When the eyes dwell in what is proper, the feet will appropriately pace it off. However, at this moment the Duke of Jin looks out far and his steps are high, so his eyes are not upon his body and his steps are not in accord with his eyes. His mind definitely has something unusual in it. When the eyes and the body are not in accord, how can something long persist?"[22]

Clearly this foreknowledge is not prognostication. The idea is not to possess future facts and calculate. It is to master the future in its becoming by knowing where its tendencies are birthing and pliant. Such knowledge requires a kind of penetration not from appearance to reality but from the manifest to the latent, from the obvious to the subtle, from the actual present to the virtual and tending. Let me survey some Chinese comment on this subtle, penetrating perception. Passages from the Han Commentary on the *Zhouyi*, the oldest core of the *Book of Changes* (*Yijing, I Ching*), introduce the theme:

The sage uses the *dao* of the changes to study the subtle, activating forces, and therefore he is able to know the subtle, activating forces of all affairs.

Does not the one who knows the incipient (*ji*) possess spiritual power? The superior man, in his relationship with the high, is without flattery, and, in his relationship with the low, is not rude. Does not this show he knows *ji?* The *ji* is the subtlety of movement and the earliest omen of good fortune.

The incipient is a hint of movement from which one can see in advance impending fortune. Exemplary persons having seen the incipient are aroused to action without waiting to see what happens. . . . No one has yet to figure out how to go beyond this, because making the most of spirituality (*shen*) and understanding (*zhi*) the process of transformation is the fullness of excellence (*de*).[23]

A line from the Confucian "Five Modes of Proper Conduct" (*Wuxingpian*, circa 300 BCE) reads: "Knowing it by observing its inchoate beginnings is

Heaven" (*ji er zhi zhi tian ye*). In the Confucian *Maintaining Perfect Balance* (*Zhongyong*) it is said: "The way of perfect truthfulness (*cheng*) is being able to foreknow (*qian zhi*). When a country is about to flourish there are surely some fortunate omens; where it is about to perish, there are surely some omens of weird and monstrous things . . . Whether the calamity or blessing is imminent, the good and bad can be foreknown (*xian zhi*). Therefore perfect truthfulness is like a spiritual power."[24]

According to *Guanzi*, a collection of Warring-States period treatises, the distinction of sages is their knowledge of the subtle beginning of things. They are good at "reacting to things when they come into being. Thus, when something new comes, they will recognize it according to the knowledge they accumulated." "Heaven and earth show symptoms at first and sages can follow them to achieve success. . . . If they act according to these symptoms fully, they will succeed in obtaining the whole world." The argument recurs in *The Spring and Autumn of Lü Buwei* (circa 240 BCE):

> At the beginning the indications of order, disorder, survival, and perdition are as subtle and invisible as the new dawn.

> The reason why sages are more outstanding than ordinary people is that they can foresee the development of things.

> Without thinking or talking about anything, they just wait patiently for the right time. . . . The correct way to react to external things is to remain quiet, let things take their own course, and be upright and disinterested.

> The importance of wisdom is to foresee the development of things before these changes ever take place.[25]

In the *Huainanzi*, sages see the small and know the big, see the near and know the far, see the visible and know the hidden, see the beginning and know the end. "The collapse of the wall begins with a crack; if the sword breaks, there was definitely a nick. The sage sees them early, thus none of the myriad things can do him harm." Dong Zhongshu, the leading Confucian of the early Han, writes: "What is called knowledge (*zhi*)? It is to predict accurately. . . . His actions are successful and his name is illustrious. His person is therefore benefitted and free of harm. . . . One who has *zhi* can see calamity and fortune a long way off, and early anticipates benefit and injury. Phenomena move and he anticipates their transformation; affairs arise and he anticipates their outcome. He sees beginnings and anticipates the end. When he says something, none dare dispute it; when he sets up something, it cannot be disregarded; when he takes up something it cannot be put aside."[26]

In *Huainanzi* again, "Foreknowledge and foresightedness, vision reaching to a thousand *li* away, are the zenith of human talent." That is the genius of Zou Yan, whom Joseph Needham calls China's first man of science. According to Sima Qian, the historian of the early Han, Zou Yan "examined deeply into the phenomena of the increase and decrease of the *yin* and the *yang*," and wrote essays about their strange permutations. "His sayings were vast and far-reaching, and not in accord with the accepted beliefs of the classics." His wisdom was "to examine small objects, and from these [draw] conclusions about large ones, until he reached what was without limit." The *Pheasant Cap Master,* a work of the latter third century BCE, remarks, "He who sees sun and moon is not considered keen-sighted. He who hears thunder peals is not considered of sharp-hearing. . . . In all questions the important thing is to desire from the close at hand the knowledge to be far seeing, from one to know myriads." "The invisible and visible's inseparability is the divine sage's teaching."[27]

The military philosophy knows this idea, which runs throughout the art of war literature (though not in *Sunzi*), for instance in the *Six Secret Teachings:* "When the sage sees the beginning, he knows the end"; "When things are not manifest but he discerns them, he is enlightened." Again in the *Methods of the Sima:* "They know the end, they know the beginning, thereby making clear their wisdom"; and *Wuzi:* "From the visible I can fathom the concealed; from the past I can discern the future."[28]

Sagacity in seeing little things is essential to the Chinese physician's diagnostic finesse, as Go Hong explains in the third century CE *Baopuzi:* "He who understands the way to cure illness obstructs the disease before it appears. He who comprehends thoroughly the key to bringing order out of chaos prevents future calamities before they arrive." The physician must be good at seeing surfaces and knowing depths, reading the inside on the outside. For this purpose physicians attend to the *se,* sometimes translated as color or hue. In classical usage this word apparently goes beyond coloration to the sense of mien, the look, the expression on the countenance, especially the forehead. The Han *Shuowen* defines *se* as "the *qi* that appears in the forehead." The servant in the *Guanzi* tale from my introduction, who divined the secret plan for war, observed the *se* of Guan Zhong's face.[29]

To discern these delicate differences of mien is not commonplace perception. It is difficult, rare, even sagacious to see such little things and know all they betoken. According to the *Yellow Emperor's Inner Classic,* the definitive later Han work on Chinese medicine, "The illness can first be seen in the face (*se*), even though it may not appear in the body. It seems to be there, but not there; it seems to exist, yet not exist; it seems to be visible, and yet invisible. No one can describe it." To gaze and know things (*wang er zhi zhi*), knowing what is not yet present by what is, is "the pinnacle of medical acumen." "By concentrating the mind in this way, one can know [changes] past and present."[30]

The most celebrated name in Chinese medicine is Bian Que. The brilliance of his skill is entirely visual, seeing surfaces and knowing depths. His acumen is vividly portrayed in the story of his encounter with Duke Huan of Qi. When first received he warns the Duke of a disease festering in his pores. Untreated, it will sink deeper. The Duke dismisses the warning, saying he feels fine. Five days later Bian Que warns the Duke that the disease has sunk into the blood vessels. He is dismissed again. After five more days he tells the Duke the disease has sunk into the intestines and stomach. Finally after five more days he sees the Duke from afar and flees. The Duke sends after him and the messenger is told that the disease is now in the bones and marrow and cannot be treated. Five days later the Duke was dead.[31]

Xu Gan, in his late Han *Balanced Discourses,* says, "Our forebears had a saying, 'The obvious comes from the obscure, and the manifest is born of the subtle.'" Ji Kang, a scholar of the Three Kingdoms period, writes, "When knowledge (*zhī*) operates, foreknowledge (*qian shí*) is established. When foreknowledge is established, intelligence (*zhì*) is opened and things are pursued." His third-century contemporary, Zhi Yu, says, "Formerly the sages observed the traces [of things] in the world and determined their appearances." To be able to discern the incipient tendency of circumstances is an accomplishment of knowledge—indeed the paramount one, emblematic of the sage. Sima Chengzhen, founder of the Tang dynasty Twofold Mystery school of Daoism, says that "perfect observation is the foremost mirror of the knight of wisdom, the quality examination of the people of ability. Probing good and bad fortune which chances to come, divining the blessings and calamities inherent in activity and stillness, he succeeds in seeing ahead of life's motions and arranges his acts accordingly." The medieval Daoist *Book of Balance and Harmony (Zhong He Ji)* calls it "deep knowledge": "Deep knowledge of principles knows without seeing, strong practice of the *dao* accomplishes without striving. Deep knowledge is to 'know without going out the door, see the way of heaven without looking out the window' [DDJ 47]. Strong action is to 'grow ever stronger, adapting to all

situations.' . . . Deep knowledge is to be aware of disturbance before disturbance, to be aware of danger before danger, to be aware of destruction before destruction, to be aware of calamity before calamity. . . . By deep knowledge of principle one can change disturbance into order, change danger into
safety, change destruction into survival, change calamity into fortune."[32]

Even the martial arts masters join this celebration of subtle perception.
According to the "Yang Family Forty Chapters," a nineteenth-century taiji
classic, taiji practice is a way to "extend our knowledge and investigate the
world." Referring to the taiji pushing hands exercise, the author says, "If
you want to gain the ability to break and reconnect, you must be able to
observe the hidden and disclose the subtle." Finally, from the terminal point
of my study, the Ming dynasty Neoconfucian Wang Yangming writes, "The
sage does not value foreknowledge (*qian zhi*). When blessings and calamities come, even a sage cannot avoid them. He only knows the incipient activating force of things and handles it in accordance with the circumstance."
The observation of a scholar living shortly after occidental contact sums up
this whole long line of thought, in which he acutely glimpses a difference
between China and the West: "The Western learning is skilled in measuring
palpable objects, but clumsy in penetrating to the incipient impulses that
make things so."[33]

The accomplishment of the sage is, first, to be capable of such penetration; secondly, to translate that perception into sagacious action, by which
Chinese tradition tends to mean action that inconspicuously, effortlessly
overcomes incipient disorder. Here then is my thesis: wise knowledge, the
knowledge of sages, stands out from other things that might be called knowledge, as the best and most worth having, by the capacity it conveys for inconspicuously elegant, effortlessly effective *wu wei* action. This deft touch
derives from the sage's canny capacity to see the little things and to know
how to translate the perception into action effectively addressing inchoate,
looming, still virtual disorder.

Little in this claim distinguishes Confucians from Daoists or Neoconfucians, or most other currents in Chinese thought (apart, perhaps, from
the Mohists and Wang Yangming, qualifications that I discuss in their place).
These lines among so-called schools are easily overdrawn, and the whole
idea of a "school" of philosophy is an obvious Western construction of little
use with Chinese sources. Such differences as these sources show us among
Confucians, Daoists, and so on tend to be ethical differences about how to
acquire the sort of knowledge I have described and how to train it for wisdom.

Rectifying Names

Chinese tradition tends to view language as a way of relating to other people first of all, rather than the primarily semantic relation of a thing and its name, as Western theory prefers. To use words is to be skillful in drawing distinctions that would not exist without language; for instance between good and bad, right and wrong, uncle and neighbor, and so on. Skill with language makes you persuasive, meaning that others like how you divide and arrange things. The value of this agreement is to be effective in making allies, ideally getting others to come around to your point of view as if it had always been their own. A well-made distinction can also soften differences of social rank and class, but only when there is no slippage between the use of names and people's behavior. Those called "king" really have to be kings, "ministers" ministers, and so on down the line.

The distinction is subtle between norms for things and norms for names. Norms for the use of words are in a sense the master norms; for if we did not share a language, we could agree on nothing else. How people use names and what they can justify doing or not doing are, of course, connected. Norms for the use of words inform norms of behavior via the controlling function of normative words. Take for example the word "father." Modern Western society has largely disconnected this word from ritual practice. Its principal meaning is genetic. Suppose you could persuade people to refrain from this promiscuous use, to restrict the word "father" to men who conspicuously fulfill traditional moral and ceremonial expectations. Under those conditions it would be a solecism to call an obviously unfilial man a father. Such men would have a different name, a word connoting opprobrium, and it seems likely there would be fewer such men. "Fathers" would be motivated to be fathers and "sons" sons. Generalize this reasoning across the whole language and you see that a thoroughgoing rectification of names would work a great transformation. The question, of course, is how to do it, how to reform a living language.

At one place in the *Analects* we catch Kongzi fantasizing about such power. The disciple Zilu asks him, "If the Duke of Wei were to employ you to serve in the government of his state, what would be your first priority?" A fascinating question! Suppose Kongzi got the power he always said he wanted; what is the first thing he would do? "The Master answered, 'It would, of course, be the rectification of names'" (*zheng ming*). His first priority is not agriculture, military, commerce, or relations with other states. It is the use of language. Is it really so important, Zilu wonders. "Why worry about rectifying names?" He receives a sharp rebuke. "How boorish you are, Zilu! When it comes to matters that he does not understand, the gentleman should remain silent. If names are not rectified, speech will not accord with reality; when speech does not accord with reality, things will not be successfully accomplished" (A 13.3).

To name a thing well is to deem it well, using a name that connotes the proper formalities for interacting with it. To use a name properly is not to put the right label on a thing. Chinese names (*ming*) are not passive labels but social and political catalysts. Names have a performative quality; they are formative, forming their relation to reality and supporting its emergent actuality. *Ming* (name) can establish *shi* (actuality). That is especially true when we remember that the names Kongzi primarily alludes to in this Analect are terms of rank and class distinction. *Rectification* means making right, making straight, aligning, correcting. A program of language rectification implies that correct usage is known and has been departed from, rectifying usages that deviate from known norms. The proper use of a word like "father" is in accord with ancient rite, though the point of rectification is not simply to use names as the ancients did; it is to reconnect with the ancient norm, making it active again, a norm for now. One uses names as the ancients did only if, in a context unanticipated by ancient usage, one still manages to speak well, judged by the ancient norm, which thus regains its former efficacy.[34]

The rectification of names is more like calendar reform than like the decision to adopt a measuring system (for example, metric), which is more profoundly arbitrary. Reforming a calendar means bringing the names of the months back in line with seasonal expectations, so that December, say, is a winter month and July a summer one. To do that requires tracking the drifting dates of the equinoxes and solstices. A Confucian rectification of names must track social conditions and adjust them where they fall out of line with ceremonial norms. It is a reconstruction of former use, and it is with that former use, preserved in the classics and the rites, that contemporary practice should establish continuity.[35]

Could such a thing be done? One might start with all documents flowing in and out of the palace, insisting that anyone with paperwork for the emperor abide by the new (old) usage. Eventually anyone who interacts with officials at any level anywhere in the empire would be exposed to the new usage, and would have to conform in order to placate administrators. It would take generations before illiterate peasants spontaneously complied, but perhaps in time they would.

It is interesting to compare the Confucian rectification of names with the Western idea of a planned language (like Esperanto) and the "logical reconstruction" of language envisioned by the positivists. Rudolf Carnap, a positivist and Esperantist, believed that a properly normed language would make metaphysical statements grammatically impossible. That is a desirable result because Carnap thinks metaphysics is worthless compared to the demonstrable knowledge of science. The issue is not merely philosophical. Language is too important for governments to lack a policy on, which is why governments should heed the positivists.[36]

You may recall the planned language Newspeak George Orwell describes in *Nineteen Eighty-Four*. "In Newspeak it was seldom possible to follow a heretical thought further than the perception that it *was* heretical: beyond that point the necessary words were nonexistent. . . . It would have been possible, for example, to say *Big Brother is ungood*. But this statement, which to an orthodox ear merely conveyed a self-evident absurdity, could not have been sustained by reasoned argument, because the necessary words were not available." Right-thinking Ingsoc party members were as put out as Carnap by the unruliness of language. It is a scandal that language allows such flagrant pseudostatements as "It is the right of the people to alter or abolish Government" or "*Das Nichts nichtet.*" Language as it is makes no objection to such formulations and that, to Carnap, is a defect.[37]

He does not say much about why language reform is a good thing. He seems to assume that positivists know something about order from their close association with the exact sciences, and have a mandate to reconstruct society, beginning (as would Kongzi) with its language. In the Confucian rectification of names, the rites of the Zhou take the place of mathematical logic. If people are gently manipulated into using the rectified language, then their lives will slowly but surely be transformed. As they become insensibly habituated to ancient usage they will tend to speak and behave as the rites prescribe. It is a project for reconstructing the whole of society by reconstructing the norms of language. More than that, it is a stratagem to make the result seem to have happened by itself, without anyone proposing or directing it.

That makes the rectification of names an example of the effectiveness Chinese thought associates with wise knowledge. It is farsighted, modifying a situation well in advance of crisis, while things are still fluid and evolving.

Such knowledge enables the wise to work effects that seem to come about by themselves without anybody deliberately doing them. For instance, we begin with the relatively inconspicuous command to ministers to issue and receive documents using only the revised vocabulary. Enforce this usage scrupulously and let it sink in, from the ministers to the officials, from the officials to the hundred clans. In time the moral transformation is complete. As Mengzi says, "Wear the clothes of Yao [a sage king], recite the words of Yao, behave as Yao behaved: this is all it takes to be a Yao" (6B2). The ritual proprieties of the Zhou would live again and no one would even be aware of the change. That sort of effectiveness, whether we call it moral or political, is the summit of Confucian wisdom.

A difference between Kongzi's rectification and Carnap's reconstruction is their understanding of how knowledge is effective. Carnap, like his friend and colleague Otto Neurath, believed in planning and its authority. "Neurath and I have criticized the existing order of society as unreasonable and have demanded that it should be reformed on the basis of scientific insights and careful planning." Positivists from Auguste Comte to Carnap concur in their optimism about planning and scientifically supervised progress in the satisfaction of needs. Their thinking is in step with modern rationalism, devoted to standardizing, rendering human relations in a legible, administratively convenient format. It is characteristic of their rationalism to want as much as possible to be made explicit and discursively reasoned out. There should be nothing subtle, nothing allusive. The light of reason shines with equal brightness everywhere. The proof of reason is analysis, making things explicit. Indirection and allusion seem like flaws and impediments, where language cries out for improvement.[38]

It seems fitting that Carnap was an Esperantist. What is good about Esperanto is the promised boon in communication when everybody uses the same words the same way. So much more rational! Never mind that it would take coercion (well meant, of course) to achieve that result and coercion to maintain it. Unfortunately for the positivists, enhanced rationality has proved an inadequate incentive to those who control the instruments of coercion, so we are left with a beautiful idea, good in theory and useless in practice. The Confucian rectification is more realistic and comes with a diagram for its realization. The rectification of names is not one step in an ingenious plan, all analyzed and worked out in Kongzi's sage mind. It is the decisive move in a game, an effective stratagem that unnoticeably sways the evolution of circumstances to realize the normative order it idealizes.

Maintaining Perfect Balance

Zhongyong 中庸 is a Confucian classic whose title used to be rendered *Doctrine of the Mean,* though the Chinese is closer to "Maintaining the Middle" or "Maintaining Balance." Ezra Pound proposed two translations: "Standing Fast in the Middle" and "The Unwobbling Pivot." I follow Gardner, *Maintaining Perfect Balance.* Tradition attributes the work to Zisi, a grandson of Kongzi. Qing dynasty philology dates it to the later Warring States period or possibly early Han. It is in any case a profoundly Confucian work of (near) classical times. Zhu Xi, a Neoconfucian scholar of the twelfth century, began the practice of collecting this work in a Confucian primer called *The Four Books,* which became the core of Confucian (and therefore Chinese) education down to the twentieth century.[39]

We should not understand "balance" or "mean" in the sense of equilibrium. The lesson of the work is the opposite: the value of maintaining constancy under conditions far from equilibrium. The work uses the idea of "completing things" (*cheng wu*) to elucidate the value of knowledge (or wisdom, the best, sagacious knowledge). "Completion of the self is benevolence; completion of things is wisdom." As I understand it, completing oneself means extending benevolence in all directions, including toward nonhuman things, which we *complete* by appropriate handling, or right use. Completing things means handling them well, using them with propriety, finding their best fit in the collective economy of humans and nonhumans. We use things well, human or nonhuman, when we make a viable collective in which things have their name and function, and receive a sapient response that acknowledges their membership in a common world. Doing that, spontaneously and elegantly, as only a sage master of rites can, is completing things, and is this work's Confucian take on the accomplishment of wise knowledge.[40]

Western thinking tends to be discomfited without a clear distinction between nature and society, and more hypocritical about its anthropocentrism. Western ancestors considered clarity on the distinction between nature and convention to be the beginning of enlightenment. Things do not require our use to be "complete." They do very well without us. A Western "thing" is a substance, a substantial being, a thing-in-itself, formed, finished, fully present, identical with itself. In China, by contrast, nothing is finally one thing and not another. Opposites merge into each other; everything eventually becomes something else. It is just a question of time. A thing—what we name or call a thing—is not a substance but a rhythm, a flow within flows. There is no universe in itself with a mechanics of its own, indifferent to human usages, or if there is these Confucians do not see it. "Things do not have independently established principles. Unless a thing, in revealing itself, resembles or differs from something else, contracts or expands, or ends or begins, then even though it may appear to be a thing, it is not a thing" (Zhang Zai).[41]

The ritual proprieties of human interaction give things a normality and appropriateness modern Western nature withholds. Lacking understanding, nonhuman things require human companions. The art of the sage joins with the *dao* of Heaven to assist in the process of transformation. The difference vanishes between the work of our hands and the work of nature. Success in life is a special case of nature's productiveness. Use that completes is not any use but the best one, the wise one, the most appropriate, humane, benevolent use. We complete things by turning them into black boxes, with which we can interact without forcing, permitting humans and nonhumans to vanish into each other prosthetically, each augmenting the other. Once such usages are established, anyone can employ them, but it is the part of wise knowledge to create and sustain them where they are not yet established. Things are completed when people interact *wu wei* with them. Wise knowledge creates, discovers, devises, and establishes the *dao* or way of such interaction.

Zhongyong says that through *truthfulness (cheng)* the profound person acquires the responsibility and authority as well as the knowledge and power to complete things. Older translations speak not of truthfulness but sincerity, being true to oneself, being what you seem and as you say. Authority to know the good use of things belongs to those who are truthful with themselves. In knowing themselves they know the good of knowledge; in knowing knowledge they know how to handle things well. Or if they do *not* know, they know *that*, know what they do not know and how to inquire, what questions to ask and of whom.

Obviously this truthfulness has nothing in common with ontological truth. It is not a logical representation of reality. It is the normative form of a relationship among humans and nonhumans. *Zhongyong* says that truthfulness "is the beginning and end of things; without truthfulness there is nothing." Nothing, because the patterns and processes that complete things remain merely virtual, without complete or perfected presence. *Zhongyong* deduces this conclusion in an elegant sorites: "Only he who is most perfectly truthful is able to give full realization to his human nature; able to give full realization to his human nature, he is then able to give full realization to the human nature of others; able to give full realization to the human nature of others, he is then able to give full realization to the nature of other creatures; able to give full realization to the nature of other creatures, he can then assist in the transformative and nourishing processes of heaven and earth." The conclusion is confirmed ten chapters later: "Only he who is most perfectly truthful is able to put in order the world's great invariable human relations, to establish the world's great foundation, and to know the transformative and nourishing processes of heaven and earth."[42]

The Song dynasty Neoconfucian Cheng Yi explains truthfulness as the absence of falsity. That means more than merely refraining from deception, which implies effort and purposiveness whereas truthfulness is spontaneous and ingenuous. This truthfulness is what Jürgen Habermas would call dramaturgical action. To be truthful is to be so for oneself and for others; at once to *be* and be *seen to be* sincere. The necessary and sufficient condition of this truthfulness is the absence of selfish desire, proving a disinterested motive to do the right thing. You do not have to rid yourself of desire, which is probably impossible. Just the selfish, narrowly self-regarding desires should go. Truthfulness comes down to impartiality (*gong*), an interpersonally acknowledged, dramaturgically authenticated freedom from self-serving interest.[43]

Western moral theory carefully distinguishes truth from sincerity. It is the difference between reason or logic and emotion. Truth concerns the relation between statement and fact; correspondence is the norm. Sincerity concerns the relation between motive and speech; honesty is the norm. You can be sincere, intending to tell the truth, but mistaken, wrong about the facts; and you can be truthful but insincere, for instance by telling the truth in a way intended to mislead. This sincerity is purely subjective, a matter of the will, while truth implies objectivity. There is philosophical disagreement over how to understand this objectivity. Does it mean correspondence with reality, or merely that a statement holds up, withstands refutation? There is also skepticism, beginning with Nietzsche, concerning the value of this whole idea of truth, but Confucian truthfulness is untouched by these doubts. It idealizes speakers known for impartiality. They both are, and are known to be, disinterested. Such people set the standard for the use of things. Whatever they do with things comes from the nature in them, and the nature in them is Heaven's nature, the *dao*, the nature in everything. Hence they respond with a use that completes the patterns of things, unforced despite being artificial or invented, a difference that tends to vanish.

[handwritten margin note: ① link btw cheng and zhongyong]

Western tradition assumes we are truthful when we accord with things as they are in themselves. For Confucian tradition knowing the truth of things is not a problem of correspondence; it is a problem of use. We misuse and abuse things without a truthful person to establish norms. This "doctrine of the mean" seems to have little in common with Aristotle's idea. He defines the virtues as middle states between usually vicious extremes. While this mean is not calculated or arithmetical, it is a ratio that has to be judged and made a reason for action. Confucians envision something more circumstantial. Zhu Xi says in a comment on *Zhongyong*, "There is no fixed shape to the preservation of perfect balance; it depends on the circumstances of the moment." Also, *zhong* (middle, balance) is not a norm peculiar to humanity, as Aristotle's virtuous mean is. This balance is that of a person, a community, an environment, "all under Heaven." Lastly, for Aristotle, keeping the mean, a life of virtue, is most of *eudaimonia, happiness*. Happiness is not something *Zhongyong* addresses. Its concern seems to be harmony, including good relations with nonhumans (Heaven, earth, the ten thousand things). Inasmuch as no man is an island, this global flourishing may be a presupposition of personal happiness, though the Chinese make this point only indirectly, by not making it.[44]

Comparing Greek and Chinese ideas, historian of science G. E. R. Lloyd says that the "key distinguishing feature" between Warring States China and classical Greece "relates to the importance of the Chinese conception that the classics are the repository of ancient wisdom." Not even Homer has that stature for the Greeks, "nor in general do they express much sense that there *was ancient wisdom* there to be preserved or to be recovered." When the Greeks picture a Golden Age it is discontinuous with the present, populated by heroes of a distinct creation before present-day people. Time even flows differently, with old age proceeding youth. Like Socrates, Kongzi reveres a wisdom he admits he does not have. Socrates pursues this wisdom in himself, Plato pursues it in another world, and Confucians pursue it in the past, or more exactly in translating the past into the present by reading the present in the light of the past.[45]

To do that well (truthfully) goes beyond book learning, though it takes book learning to get to that point. Confucian wisdom thinks in oceans, encompassing opposite points of view without dialectical reconciliation. "Taking a single fixed position disregards a hundred others," Mengzi says

(7A26). The proof of knowledge is always circumstantial. There is no de-contextualized argument you can read in a book, understand on your own, and benefit from privately. It all comes down to what you do, how you live, effectiveness, success in life, in whatever way that may be understood. The contrary of Confucian knowledge is not the false but the partial. Wisdom has no terminus; its value is to keep a way open, to avoid accumulating obstructions, to sustain viability. The value of wise knowledge is not a way *to* the highest end, as a place you might finally reach; it is rather a way to stay on course amid transformation, never halting, never stuck, maintaining perfect balance.

Four lines of thought intersect in this emerging profile of sage knowledge:

1. The knowledge is circumstantial, a kind of foresight into the evolution of a situation.
2. The knowledge is not merely correct prediction but appreciates the latent tendency of things in their first form, recognizing opportunities for effective yet (nearly) effortless intervention, improvising an emerging future by discerning and responding to those little things, incipient and tending, where multiple futures compete to be born.
3. Such knowledge is expressed rather than represented. The knowledge is not a quality of belief, proposition, or theory, but of action, eloquent action that is at once easy and irresistibly effective. This expectation of expression, making a difference to practice, distinguishes Chinese thinking about the value of knowledge from Western philosophy, which tends to emphasize the intrinsic value of theory and truth.
4. Finally, the use of this effectiveness, or what knowledge offers to practice, is to handle well anything that instigates a response. Whatever the circumstance, knowledge handles it with finesse, not doing too much but omitting no requisite to a humane, benevolent, sagacious response to disorder or its antecedents. Confucians understand "handle well" in terms of ritual propriety; later we will see Daoists take a different view. Knowing how to handle things requires truthfulness, sincerity, an impartiality born of vigilant self-cultivation. That is what makes knowledge wise. Confucian wisdom is knowing how to live poised in the middle, never one-sided, never off-balance. Such knowledge makes one good at centering, Pound's unwobbling pivot, despite incipient chaos.

Anti-Confucian Interlude: Mòzǐ and Yang Zhu

Most Western readers will have heard of Confucius or the *Daodejing.* Fewer know about Mozi. In his day, though, Mozi, an acknowledged master of fortifications, was a force to reckon with, having organized his followers into a private militia, lending their force to victims of siege in accordance with their master's teaching against military aggression. Perhaps the school was a bit too militaristic for the first emperor's liking, because it was around the time (213 BCE) when the emperor carried out a burning of books and (according to legend) a holocaust of scholars that Mohism disappears from history, forgotten even in China until modern times.[46]

The Mohists were the first in Chinese tradition to recognize a need as scholars to respond to the objections of critics with a defense of their ideas based on principles. Especially unusual was their effort to clarify the logic of their arguments, something no other current of traditional Chinese thought had done or will do again. This impetus to make things as explicit as possible goes against the grain of Chinese thought then and later. The innovations in logic were in service of the Mohist program of moral reform, which includes an egalitarian norm of impartial care and the right of the people to render judgment against officials at every level.

The founder, Mozi, was about one year old when Kongzi died. He is thought to have spent time in Confucian studies but has the distinction of being the first thinker of influence to reject Confucian principles categorically. There is no subtlety in the critique. He calls the Confucians "vile and hypocritical." Their benevolence is inhumane, their ceremonies unrighteous, their commitment to learning treacherous. The decisive difference from the Confucians is the Mohist egalitarianism of impartial care (*jian'ai*). Each should care for all the others as we care for our parents or children. Of course Confucians approve of impartiality and want people to care for others too, but they think care should be graded and discerning, and hold family relationships above all others. It is this graded, discerning care that Mozi criticizes. He wants all our loving, all our caring, to be impartial and equitable, based on need.[47]

We should train ourselves to feel no distinction between our children and those of a stranger in a city we may never visit. "There [must be] no difference between loving others and loving oneself. . . . If deserting one's personal love can bring benefits to the people in the world, one must desert one's personal love" (44). It is no loss really; such love is superficial precisely because it is personal. "Profound love is established on the basis of righteousness, and not on the basis of intimacy" (44). Good order must elude us until we have remade humanity in a more readily governed form. "We must get rid of pleasure, anger, joy, sorrow, love, and hate, and replace them with righteousness" (47). The demand for an emotional reform, a reform of the heart, confirms that impartial care is not spontaneous. It may sound impossibly difficult. It seems to require that we put aside self-interest, yet it does not. It is a strategy for being really good at self-interest. Once we see how well impartial caring serves self-interest we will want to practice it despite having no natural predisposition toward it.

One thing Mozi and Kongzi agree on is how far we have fallen from the magnificent time of the early Zhou dynasty. Kongzi does not have an explanation for *why* the sons of Zhou have fallen so low. It does not matter why, the question is what to do about it. But Mozi thinks the right solution requires the correct analysis of the disorder. The trouble is that we have fallen into partiality, which for him means irrationally graded care. There is no overcoming the troubles of the times until we restore impartiality in all things. Forget about *ren*, Confucian goodness. What we need are not good men but consistent standards (*fa*).

法 법 (*fa*)

Mozi praises artisans for having such standards, as well as for the usefulness of their work. Scholars and councilors should be like that—more workmanlike, consistent, and useful. References to skill (*qiao*) are for Kongzi apparently always negative. The connotations range from deception, trickery, and narrow specialization to vulgar self-interest. Mohists restore the value of skill and artifice to the positive column. "Achievement that is beneficial to people (*li ren*) is said to be skillful (*qiao*), and anything that is not beneficial is said to be clumsy" (49). This is one of Mozi's criticisms of the Confucians. They discredit skillful knowledge, whether that of humble artisans or the masters of statecraft. The same prejudice makes them denigrate experiments and resist innovation.

The Mohists pioneer an epistemology with Chinese characteristics. For them the critical question is not, How do we know that we know—that we know the truth? They ask instead how to establish the best claims, those that are righteous to make and wise to entertain. Impartiality is crucial. One must rely on consistent standards, not the opinions of men. "When one advances claims, one must first establish a standard of assessment. To make claims in the absence of such a standard is like trying to establish on the surface of a spinning potter's wheel where the sun will rise and set. Without a fixed standard one cannot clearly ascertain what is right and wrong or what is beneficial and harmful" (35). Standards are rules for performing norm-governed activities. For instance, "We should select the lesser harm out of all the harms. . . . We need not select the bigger benefit out of all the benefits, but we must select the lesser harm out of all the harms" (44).

Statements, too, or what people say, their claims, require a standard. To arrive at this standard, the Mohist argument begins by making explicit what the point of discourse is: "The purpose of disputation (*bian*) is to distinguish clearly between right and wrong, inquire into the principles of order and misrule, clarify the points of sameness and difference, discern the patterns of names and objects, judge the benefits and harms, and resolve confusions and doubts" (45).

In furtherance of their program Mohists make unprecedented efforts at logical analysis and explicit definition. For example:

Inferring (*tui*) is using what is the same in that which he refuses to accept and that which he does accept in order to propose the former. (45)

The negation of something may proceed from the negation of something similar to it, because only the things of the same category can have common grounds. (41)

When one says that something is an ox and the other says that something is a nonox, they are offering contending arguments (*zheng bi*). It is impossible for both of them to win. As it is impossible for both of them to win, one of them will certainly lose. (42)

And explicit norms for disputation:

If someone gives a statement to say that it is like this, you should refute him by a negative statement. (42)

Things of different categories are not comparable, for the measuring standards are different. (41)

The value these principles express is not logical validity or necessary truth, but rather something like pragmatic verification. A well-made statement is verifiable in the sense that it is assessable, having a content that can be made explicit and tested. This is not a test of truth, though, but of application and benefit. The standard for a serious statement is Mozi's Three Gauges (35):

1. Has the statement a basis in the words and acts of the ancient authorities?
2. Is it verified by experience and observation?
3. Is there an application; can you act on it to advance important goals?

Application sounds fine, but wickedness can be as skillfully executed as the good. What determines an "important goal"? For that Mozi has another standard. Goodness of application is determined by four supreme goals:

1. Enrich the poor.
2. Increase the population.
3. Remove dangers such as war.
4. Enhance social harmony.

The Three Gauges and Four Goals establish the standard to which Mozi holds his own and any other claim to knowledge, and it is by appeal to this standard that he proves the imperative of impartial care, which he demonstrates to have basis and verification and to serve the primary goals. That makes impartial care more than just a good idea. Mohists call it the will of Heaven. How do they know the will of Heaven? The Mohist answer seems to equate the heavenly with what can be demonstrated to be supremely reasonable and benevolent. To show how heavenly, how divinely sanctioned impartial caring is, Mozi shows how benevolent it is for the people. How could something so beneficial not be right, or something so right not be divine?[48]

Some may recognize in Mozi a profile of Western rationalism: the preoccupation with analytical explication, the demand for consistent standards, the optimistic expectation that reason rules. There is always a reason: "If something is so, there must be reasons (*suo yi*) why it is so" (45); "proper reasoning (*lü*) will dispel any doubt" (41); "those who are not in the right will comply with those who are in the right, those who lack knowledge will comply with those who have knowledge; lacking valid arguments (*wu ci*), they will acknowledge defeat" (39). However, this is not our rationalism. Reason is not something Mozi has a theory of (in contrast, say, to Heraclitus on the *logos*), and unlike Socrates he does not stake his optimism on knowledge of truth. What seems to give him confidence is not belief in reason but in the heart, a presumption of benevolence, the goodness of contending parties. If they are not good, they cannot be expected to behave reasonably. "If both parties are benevolent by nature, they will have no reason to become enemies. . . . Seeing anything good they will be won by it" (39). Not because they are so rational, but because they are good enough to respond impartially to impartial benefit.

The work we have under the title *Mozi* includes texts that entered the corpus sometime after the founder. These later treatises, referred to as the *Mohist Canons,* are the pinnacle of traditional Chinese logical thought. For the first time in Chinese literature we have demonstrations applying explicit definitions and standards of proof, as well as the first (sometimes the last) Chinese contributions to mechanics, optics, and epistemology before occidental contact. While these *Canons* seem dedicated to the value of making everything clear, the texts themselves are anything but. They are among the most obscure and confusing of China's literary remains. Our understanding of them is largely the result of the brilliant insights of translators and philosophical interpreters, above all Angus Graham.[49]

Ideas about knowledge in the *Canons* are infinitely more explicit and theoretical than anything in other authors. These texts associate knowledge and wisdom with capability (*cai*), clear vision (*ming*), thought (*lü*), planning (*mou, ji*), and skill (*qiao*). They distinguish four capacities that must collaborate in the completion of knowledge:

1. Intelligence (*zhī*), explained as the means or faculty of knowledge;
2. Thinking (*lü*), explained as seeking by means of intelligence but not necessarily finding;
3. Knowing (*zhī*), explained as being able to relate things to other things and to describe them;
4. Wisdom (*zhi*), explained as a discourse that is clear and illuminating. We have this explanation of the difference between knowledge and wisdom: "With human intelligence one uses his perceptual ability to seek knowledge of an object and to describe it. It is just like seeing the object with one's eyes. Wisdom is a better understanding of the object under study through human intelligence, which will be improved at the same time. It is like clear eyesight, with which one sees clearly."[50]

The *Canons* additionally distinguish three differences in the just-distinguished sense of knowing as describing and relating things:

1. Different sources for knowing things, including reports, explanations, and experience.

Explanation (*shuo*) is explained as making a matter clear (*ming*). An example of knowledge by explanation is knowing that a cube will not roll. Perception is explicitly excluded as a source of such knowledge. Perception is a source of data but there is no knowledge without the involvement of thought and language. "Knowing is different from having a pictorial idea. . . . When one knows, it is not by means of the five senses." It takes intelligence, a power of the heart, to make something of what the senses provide. This is among the Mohists' most influential ideas, silently appropriated on all sides in later thinking about the senses.[51]

2. Different branches of descriptive-relational knowledge, including knowledge of names, of objects, of relations between names and objects, and of how to act.
3. Different capacities on which knowing things draw, including:
    3.1 A capacity to sort and grade with names;
    3.2. A capacity to investigate things;
    3.3. Skill at dialectics, articulating distinctions and relations;
    3.4. Ability to apply dialectical knowledge to action, which requires the mastery of names, the understanding of standards, and knowledge of the relation between names and objects.

Everything in the analysis is new. Scholars had never seen their language used with such regimentation and a tenacious will to make things explicit. The Chinese undertook this experiment exactly once, and when Mozi's school disappeared no one wanted to do it again.

For Confucians, moral life is a condition on knowledge. It is impossible for an immoral man to be wise, to master the best knowledge. If he mastered it, he would be good. For Mohists knowledge is the source of morals. Knowledge, in perfecting itself, comes consistently under the rule of impartial care, and must perfect morality too, which is a special case of knowledge (impartial knowledge of what benefits the people). Morality is therefore a problem of knowledge, of intelligence in policies, making their consequences explicit, and setting them in motion. To be a good king you have to *know* something, many things, a whole art of rulership.

Confucians shudder at that. They reject technique and calculation. The most important thing about a ruler is charismatic virtue. That includes wisdom, and wisdom is a kind of knowledge, but it is not the technical, managerial, calculating knowledge of merchants, artisans, or military commanders. All of that Kongzi discredits when he tells his disciples not to be vessels (A 2.12). Above all a king must not be a vessel, a specialist, a technician. He must work on self-cultivation, and not lose himself in arguments about the advantages of policy. If the ruler is not balanced in himself, no clever policy can balance the state.

We have no text known to be written by Yang Zhu, but his ideas were notorious in antiquity, as we know from the report of usually hostile critics. Yang seems to have provoked the Confucians to think about human nature. Before him, for instance in Kongzi and Mozi, there is no reflection on this notion, while after him there are several competing theories. China's oldest idea of human nature is that we naturally pursue our own pleasure and longevity, indifferent to the general good. Yang Zhu turns this idea against the Confucians. He may even have taken up his brush and publicized his views to oppose them, and he would have felt no better about the Mohists. Both make the same mistake. They call for self-sacrifice. That must deform our nature, a nature heaven-sent; to deform it must be a mistake.

According to our sources Yang taught three ideas:

1. Keep your nature (*xing*) intact, where "nature" means a heaven-sent capacity to live out one's term of life.
2. Protect your spontaneous genuineness (*zhen*) from corruption.
3. Do not let your body be captured by things.

To explain that last point, in a notorious text Yang supposedly says, "The men of antiquity, if by injuring a single hair they could have profited the world, would not have done it. Had the world been offered to them as their exclusive possession, they would not have taken it. If everybody would refuse to pluck out even a single hair, and everybody would refuse to take the world as a gain, then the world would be in perfect order." That is what Yang is mostly remembered for, the apparently uninhibited selfishness of slogans like "Everyone is for himself" and "Accord priority to self." As Mengzi will put it, Mozi has no father (care for everyone impartially) and Yang has no ruler (place self above all).[52]

The term translated as (human) nature is *xing*. Scholars say this word can be translated as direction, path, norm, or potential, the connoted theme being how something changes when not interfered with. We may wonder how to distinguish interference from normal interaction, but the idea seems to be that human nature, or what is heaven-sent about us, is a package of developmental potentials we all start life with. This nature develops from birth without training or effort. The thought is not exactly our idea of innateness or instinct. The Chinese are more consistently developmental, something increasingly favored in biology too. They are interested in natural tendencies, how things develop when they are not obstructed. They are especially interested in ecological tendencies, expressed in interaction with other things; how a thing gets along with others in the common world. In the explanation of Tang Junyi, "In saying that [something] has a *xing* what is important is not saying what the nature and characteristic of this entity is, but saying what the direction of its life's existence is."[53]

Yang's thought seems to be that if we avoid artificial interference (like a Confucian education), people develop in a preferable way. The Confucian regime must therefore be contrary to Heaven and should not be practiced. Confucians must hate this argument but they cannot ignore it because they cannot tolerate what Yang teaches about human nature, and require a counterteaching. I mentioned that Kongzi deliberately avoids the topic of nature. His followers were therefore on their own to develop a response that makes sense in terms of their philosophy and overturns Yang. That is what Mengzi did, and it made him the second name in Confucianism.

Mengzi

Chinese tradition remembers Mengzi for his thought that human nature is good. We will want to ask what that means, but on the supposition that we are naturally good it seems to follow that knowledge, which is laborious and artificial, cannot be vital to a harmonious society. What *is* vital is sound development, nurturing the seeds of goodness a heaven-sent nature plants in us. Acquiring knowledge is part of that development, but we do not need reasoning or scholarly learning to be good. Our intuitions and inclinations, appropriately cultivated, are enough. Goodness is less a problem of knowledge (knowing the right thing to do) than of motivation, attention, commitment, or will (*zhi*). The need for commitment explains how despite being good by nature some turn out badly. It is not the nature in people that goes bad, or has any bad in it. Badness begins in how we use the nature we are given, how we apply ourselves, our determination, commitment, effort, will.

It is Mengzi who, in his explanation of commitment and its power, introduces the concept of *qi*, vital breath or energy, into Chinese ethical

气 qi (기)

literature. "Your will (*zhi*) is the commander of the *qi*. *Qi* fills the body. When your will is fixed somewhere, the *qi* sets up camp there. Hence, it is said, 'Maintain your will, do not injure the *qi*'" (2A2). *Qi* is a word for any gaseous substance—steam, clouds, smoke, the air, and breath itself. It is the modern Chinese word for weather. *Qi* has extension and is material, provided that matter is understood dynamically, as interchangeable with energy and never at rest. This *qi* is in constant transformation independently of awareness, being the original material of all things, penetrating all things and making them flow. It has always been associated with the dynamics of *yin* and *yang*, as the stuff of which they are phases or the material of their continuum; for instance, in the earliest recorded pairing of the words: "This *qi* of heaven and earth does not lose its order. If it goes beyond the order, the people are in confusion. *Yang* bends over and cannot go out; *yin* rushes and cannot distill away, so there is an earthquake." *Qi* fills the body more dramatically than the animal spirits of Descartes. Where Cartesian animal spirits, being matter (however volatile), are inert and move solely by impulse, *qi* is undulating, vibratory, and never stops moving. It is the very substance, or rather energetic configuration, of natural bodies. A scholar of Chinese medicine offers a bracingly unqualified statement concerning this concept: "Whatever the context and absolutely without exception [*qi*] always implies a qualitative determination of energy." Not a quantum, or not only a quantum, but a *quality*, at once a configuring energy (Spinoza's *natura naturans*), and an energetic configuration (Spinoza's *natura naturata*).[54]

Mengzi's thought is that deliberate choice and commitment can command the corporeal *qi* and must do so if one is to realize the good one has (developmentally) by nature. The image of a commanding will should not be understood dualistically, as mind directing body. There is no Cartesian firewall between body and soul. If will can command the *qi*, the *qi* can fortify the will. "When your will is unified, it moves the *qi*. When the *qi* is unified, it moves your will" (2A2). When invited to describe himself, Mengzi says he is "good at cultivating my floodlike *qi*" (2A2). *Qi* accumulates with cultivation. Care for it and it becomes concentrated, stronger, and more beneficial to you and everyone around you. Nourishing *qi* is like throwing a dam over a rivulet. From day to day there is little change but after a season a great force accumulates. That is Mengzi's floodlike *qi*, born of cumulative righteousness. Trying to speed its growth is as bad as starving it. Our nature is developmental, and must be left to unfold without interference, even though interaction with people and training with artifacts belong to our natural conditions of existence, much as domesticated grain requires weeding and irrigation.

Mengzi cites the *Book of Songs*: "If there is a thing, there is a norm (*fa*)," and comments, "Kongzi said, 'The one who composed this ode understood the *dao!*' Hence, if there is a thing, there must be a norm" (6A6). Why *must* there be a norm? The conclusion is an astute eco-logical inference from original becoming. What a thing "is" has no substantial, intrinsic determination or identity. Instead, what a thing is depends on what other things it relates to, in ramifying networks and processes without end. Nothing happens without resonance elsewhere. Every change is simultaneously a polyvalent incitation and a multiplex response. Resonance implies reticulation and concatenated energetic exchange, an immanent economy of real, original multiplicity. There is no dualism, in part because we do not know how many kinds of thing there are in the world. You cannot guess such a thing, you have to investigate. And partly because opposites include and transform into each other, and nothing is beyond transformation through interaction with anything else.

An implication of this eco-logic is the existence of an optimal way for things to coexist, a condition of mutual adaptation under which things avoid provoking a destructive response. That does not make them indestructible. Instead, it gives things their time, bestowing a natural duration whose power to absorb disturbance contributes to the ecological stability of an entire economy. In the words of *Maintaining Perfect Balance:* "produced and developed without injuring one another . . . the courses of the seasons, the sun, and moon are pursued without conflict."[55]

What a thing *is* (the difference it makes to an environment), and what it *ought* to do or how it *ought* to be handled, belong together, grow from the same conditions, and are not so indifferent to each other as modern logic assumes. We cannot understand what a thing is without understanding how it ought to behave in relation to others upon whose existence it depends, the norm of its interaction. This reading seems confirmed by later commentators. Zhu Xi, a Confucian author of the Song dynasty, says, "The blue sky is called heaven; it revolves continuously and spreads out in all directions. It is sometimes said that there is up there a person who judges all evil actions; this assuredly is wrong. But to say there is no ordering principle would be equally wrong." Another commentator, another five hundred later, says, "Nature and obligation are not two things. If one considers the nature of something, then the clearer one makes it without straying from it in the slightest is what it necessarily ought to be."[56]

Mengzi does not say a lot about knowledge. One thing he does say is this: "To fully fathom one's heart is to know (*zhi*) one's nature. To know one's nature is to know Heaven. To preserve one's heart and nourish one's nature is the way to serve Heaven. To not become conflicted over the length of one's life but to cultivate oneself and await one's fate is the way to take one's stand on fate" (7A1). I think the first part of this remark—that in fathoming our heart we know our nature—means that the way to the most important knowledge is through the commitment to be good (the word for commitment, as for knowledge, is also *zhi,* though with a different tone and graph). Only those who constantly work on their goodness really know themselves, know what they can do, and the difference they make to the world. The knowledge most worth having therefore passes through this phase of ethical life. You cannot achieve the best knowledge apart from ethical accomplishment in self-cultivation.

Mengzi goes on to say that the knowledge we have of our nature is a knowledge of Heaven (*tian*), meaning, I think, knowledge of the cycles and patterns in cosmic and terrestrial nature, which join everything under the sky like veins coursing through a piece of jade. Knowing Heaven is knowing the pattern, and knowing the pattern is knowing how to translate it into wise, timely, effective interactions. To know Heaven is to know the heavenly use of things. We recognize the argument of *Maintaining Perfect Balance.* Mengzi's idea in the passage is that the knowledge required to complete things, to dispose of things according to their norm, comes from the truthfulness, meaning sincerity and impartiality, that self-cultivation fosters.

The heart, heaven-sent—actuated by the same *qi* that energizes the ten thousand things—is capable of knowing the right response to anything that affects us. This is the epistemological implication of our good nature. The spontaneous response of the heart is good, and moves us to do the right thing, meaning the ceremonially correct thing. The value of knowledge is knowing how to find that ecological norm and handle things without conflict, as the ancient sages did so masterfully in establishing the *li* rites. Mengzi is saying that we find those norms within, we discover them by discovering ourselves, or what is nature in us. What you learn about yourself through committed self-cultivation leads to knowledge of the right way to handle anything in the world. "The ten thousand things are all brought to completion by us" (7A4)—by use, right use, the knowing of which is genuine knowledge, distinguished from mere cleverness, of which Mengzi is contemptuous. "Those who are crafty in their contrivances and schemes have no use for shame" (7A7).

Craft is shameless because while it may be clever and effective it is also meretricious, serving bad as well as good. To this treacherous technical knowledge Mengzi opposes an intuitive natural spontaneity, the unlearned, innately developing knowledge of the heart. He calls it *liang zhi*, pure knowing, or in an older translation, innate knowledge. "That which people are capable of without learning is their genuine capability (*liang neng*). That which they know without pondering is their genuine knowledge (*liang zhi*)" (7A15). This pure or innate knowing plays a leading role in the thought of Wang Yangming some fifteen hundred years later, and we shall return to it. In Mengzi the idea seems to be that what we know and do spontaneously, before we even begin to scheme, plan, desire, or try, grows from heaven-sent sprouts that have only to ripen.

Confucian self-cultivation is not so unnatural as Yang supposed, no more so than weeding and watering sprouts of grain. On the one hand, then, knowledge is not especially important; on the other, the best knowledge (knowing the right thing to do) is innate, tacit, and not readily reduced to a verbal formula. What makes the knowledge best is not because it knows everything, but because it knows the best thing, which is how to maintain balance, responding to all things in season, completing things with ceremonial propriety. To follow Yang in selfishness is to lack a ruler, to follow Mozi in indiscriminate love is to lack a father (3B9). Both courses are depraved and unworthy of a human being. Only the Confucian way is balanced and humane. It takes diligent self-cultivation to hold this middle, but doing so is more like improvising music than matching a fixed standard.

Xunzi

Xunzi writes about 250 years after Kongzi. In his day there is still a Mohist school, as well as a thriving (albeit clandestine) art of war literature and a well-endowed Daoist literature (although the word *daojia*, Daoist or Daoism, is not yet in use) that includes *Zhuangzi* and the *Daodejing*. These Daoist authors agree with the Confucians that to withdraw from the world and live as a recluse is unbalanced. One remains attached, in a way Chan Buddhism will later analyze, to detachment. Zhuangzi envisions a sage of engaged detachment, attending to the world, working productively; for instance, as a wheelwright or cook. This sage has overcome the preoccupation with enlightenment. He no longer knows whether he is enlightened or not, and is unremarkable in every way, except perhaps for performing flawlessly without apparent effort, never tiring, and never seeming to grow old.

As Xunzi reads them, the Daoists wrongly devalue the world of culture, convention, and artifice, which they present as an obstacle to natural spontaneity. These Daoist authors agree that a sage cannot be sage without the human world, which cannot fail to include artifice and convention. So how can artificiality be an objection to taking something into your life? It must be wrong to devalue ritual and convention, as these Daoist authors seem to do, in favor of a supposedly more natural existence, since for us artifice *is* nature. In drawing this conclusion against the Daoists Xunzi reminds me of Nietzsche against the Stoics, who also wanted to live according to Nature: "'According to Nature' you want to *live*? O you noble Stoics, what deceptive words these are! Imagine a being like Nature, wasteful beyond measure, indifferent beyond measure, without purpose and consideration, without mercy and justice, fertile and desolate and uncertain at the same time; imagine indifference itself as a power—how *could* you live according to this indifference?"[57]

For Xunzi, as for Nietzsche, art is a power we have from nature to make what we are by nature into something polished and perfected. The human world of convention, language, art, and technics is third in a triad with Heaven and Earth. This artificial world, regulated by ceremonies, deserves the admiration and reverence Daoists reserve for the *dao*. "If you cast aside the concerns proper to humanity in order to speculate about what belongs to Heaven, you will miss the essential nature of the myriad things" (17.13). What people can do depends on their knowledge. Xunzi says that we have the capacity for knowledge from *xing*, our heaven-sent nature, while the knowableness of things comes from their place in the natural order. The means of knowing is awareness, and knowledge is awareness tallying with fact, like matching portions of a tally stick. "Knowing" (*zhī*) is explained as understanding (*ming*) the connection of phenomena, and assigning things to categories, like placing bamboo with the grasses (3.6). The completion or perfection of knowledge is knowledge of right and wrong: "To recognize as right what is right and as wrong what is wrong is called wisdom (*zhī*)" (2.3).[58]

Xunzi sees a seldom-noticed connection between knowing and sharing knowledge. Knowing anything includes knowing how to pass it on. You do not really know something until you know who can best use the knowledge and how to communicate it at the right time. "Speaking when it is appropriate to do so is knowledge; remaining silent when it is appropriate is also knowledge. Hence knowing when to remain silent is as important as knowing when to speak" (6.11). Not knowing how to pass on knowledge devalues it, because knowing proves itself, realizes or completes itself, in right action. Without the action, without its rightness, there is no proof of knowledge. "Not having heard something is not as good as having heard it; having heard it is not as good as having seen it; having seen it is not as good as knowing it; knowing it is not as good as putting it into practice (*xing*). Learning (*xue*) reaches its terminus when it is fully put into practice" (8.19). Xunzi clearly appreciates the unity of knowledge and action (*zhi xing he yi*) that becomes thematic with the Neoconfucians, especially Wang Yangming (Chapter 5).

Perceiving Perception

There is not a lot of disagreement in Chinese thought about sense perception or its relation to knowledge, and Xunzi's treatment of the topic may be the best. Western theories of knowledge invariably discuss the senses. Whether sense is inimical to knowledge (Plato, Descartes), or merely the beginning of knowledge (Aristotle, Spinoza), or even its principal source and verification (Epicurus, Locke), no Western theory of knowledge omits critical reflection on the senses. The senses do not perplex Warring States thinkers, however, who do not feel the problem that the senses raise for Western thought. Can we imagine Xunzi's bewilderment at the words of his near-contemporary Plato: "Everywhere in our investigations the body is present and makes for confusion and fear, so that it prevents us from seeing the truth. . . . It is impossible to attain any pure knowledge with the body"? Indifference to this problem is not China's epistemological optimism again. Ontological truth is not the essence of knowledge, and the senses are not expected to do the heavy lifting Western epistemologies require when truth is at stake.[59]

All authors distinguish the same five senses and agree that sense discrimination is an important discipline. There is no disdain for the senses, no suggestion that they should not be trusted, or that they cannot penetrate to the most important objects of the best or wise knowledge. The different senses have their strengths and weaknesses, but what the senses discriminate are differences as real and potentially valuable as any we know. There is nothing contemplative about sense consciousness. Sensations are not atomistic data with intrinsic qualities. Sensation is contextual, occurring as a phase of life, in a context of action, which tinges sensation with futurity and memory. Sense perception is discrimination, responding selectively to a multiplicity of sensible differences. "Forms, colors, and designs are differentiated by the eye. Pitch and timbre, bass and treble, modal keys and rhythms, and odd noises are differentiated by the ear. Sweet and bitter, salty and bland, pungent and sour, and distinctive tastes are differentiated by the mouth" (22.5).

Sensations come to us on the air, borne by the wind. Hence the power of music. The energy of the music flows into the ears of the audience and harmonizes everyone's *qi*. The discipline of ceremonies is the best way to regulate the senses. When they are not artificially harmonized, the senses instigate their own desires (the eyes love colors) and tend to excess. Xunzi says the eyes not only desire colors; they desire the most extreme differences of color, as the other senses crave their extremes (11.11). By themselves the senses are helpless to control these appetites. That is why the heart-mind (*xin*) is integral to the sagacious instrumentality of the senses. "The heart-mind that dwells within the central cavity is used to control the five faculties—it is called the lord provided by nature" (17.4).

As we see in this passage, Chinese thought localizes thinking and feeling in the heart rather than the brain. This heart is conscious and intelligent; it understands and feels, and whatever knowledge there is from the senses depends on its judgment, which combines and modulates the senses somewhat like the "common sense" of Aristotlean psychology. Xunzi silently follows the Mohists. It takes synthesis in the heart to make sensation knowing or wise. He says the heart thinks (*lü*) and chooses, that thinking is seeking, and knowing is finding, which again recalls the Mohists, who define thinking (*lü*) as seeking with intelligence but not necessarily finding.[60]

Western ideas about the contribution of the senses to knowledge tend to focus on the problem of getting past a subjective sensation to an objective reality. Do things in themselves cause sensations, or are sensations self-caused, as in dreams? Even if sensations are caused by realities, must they resemble their causes, so that we can know the truth of things by contemplating sensations? Chinese thought is uninterested in mimetic fealty, but values the efficacy of an impartial response. The concern is not with correspondence between consciousness and object, but rather with irreproachable spontaneity in a response, assisted (as it may be) by delicate discernment. This response is not a private event in consciousness, because insofar as it is potential knowledge, the response tends toward appropriate action. Knowledge is not isolated from the will, and not complete until put into practice. To look is to see, to see is to know, to know is to know what to do, *and do it.*

Another usual topic in Western theories is the relation between perception and words or names. Confucians conceive the relation of names (*ming*) and things (*shi*) as it were ceremonially. The right word to use on any occasion (what Western philosophy calls "truth") is the normatively traditional one, the one wise ancestors used. The relation of name to named is conventional, or so these thinkers agree, but *conventional* does not mean *arbitrary*. The relation is not merely conventional; it is also inherited, a legacy. In using words we should keep faith not just with contemporary coconveners; conventional as words are, they are also a sacred covenant with sage ancestors, and use should respect that.

As for the things names name, the name of the named in Chinese is *shi*. There has been a tendency to heavy-handed translation: "reality," "substance," "essence," "actuality." These are unfortunate choices because each word draws from the Latinate vocabulary of metaphysics and is burdened with irrelevant connotations. The idea behind Western talk about essences, substances, and realities is to indicate something that does not change, what is most veritably in being, fully present, identical to itself. What the Chinese see when they see a thing is not a finished form like that, but a fruit, a fruition, the maturity of a process. The *shi* graph shows a roof sheltering goods below, a full house. Xu Gan, writing in the second century CE, glosses *shi* as *fu*, rich, wealth; and glosses *fu* as *bei*, to be provided for, endowed with. These connotations somewhat resemble the etymology of the Greek *ousia*, which meant real estate and household wealth before metaphysics made it a name for substance, essence, and being. But the *shi* names name is not a finished, fully present form (which is what "actuality" means). It is rather an endowed potency that can be expected to develop in a particular way.[61]

If we have to use a metaphysical word for *shi* we might better say *conatus* than *actuality*. "Actual" metaphysically implies form, fullness; potential lies in matter, not form. But the wealth, the development, the potency of the *shi* is a *conatus,* the energetic endeavor by which things become what they are. The opposite of *shi* is *xü*, empty. Form is never more than a phase in evolution. The name should fit the evolution, not the passing form. Things are well named not simply because of what they are (now), but because of what they are becoming. The nonactual future matters as much as the present, which can be a misleading indication of the future, or of what name best fits a passing thing. The ancient sages understood the hazard, of course, and named things in accordance with their developmental norms. To rectify names is not to adjust names to intrinsic realities or timeless forms of being. It is to overcome deviation and return to the regular.

What Do Sages Know?

Xunzi proposes an elaborate analogy to distinguish levels of people's engagement with knowledge (8.18). Beginning at the bottom, those who know nothing are like people who neither see nor hear. The knowledge of scholars is like that of people limited to seeing and hearing: "what their hearing and seeing has not reached, their knowledge cannot classify." The superior knowledge of spiritual people is a heightened seeing and hearing still subject to their limitations, while the best knowledge goes beyond what one has actually seen and heard. For masters of such knowledge, "regarding what they have not heard or that which they have not seen—if one corner is suddenly held up, they can pick out the whole classification and respond to it" (8.18) These are the sages (*shengren*). They are wise because of their knowledge. What do they know?

Knowledge of things is always going to be specialized, knowing a lot about some part of a greater whole. Such knowledge has value, but it cannot be the wisdom of a sage. Knowledge of things measures one thing against another; for instance, a carpenter's knowledge in comparing lumber and selecting the best pieces. The specialized training required for this or any *techne*-art is useless for measuring many things together, which requires the *dao* as a standard. The Confucian *junzi* is a virtuoso on that arcane instrument. Not a specialist, mind, but trained to a metaexpertise that makes him good at orchestrating many things together. A sage "is the artisan and manager (*zhi*) of the *dao*" (22.8).

Wise knowledge makes a sage good at composition, orchestration, putting things together and making them harmonize. One knows how to handle the multiplicity of things, to elicit their latent concord, and avert conflicts, maintaining balance, not privately but throughout the collective of humans and nonhumans. This sage "lays out all the myriad things and causes himself to exactly match how each settles on the suspended balance" (21.6). Wilfrid Sellars says philosophy is the investigation of how things, in the broadest sense, hang together in the broadest sense. Xunzi might say, how things in the broadest sense should be handled—the norms of interaction. Sellars is something of a Platonist: Things hang together; there is an order to be known; as Parmenides said, "Being is." We belong to this order and can understand it, but it does not ultimately depend on or involve us more than it does anything else. For Xunzi, however, things, in the broadest sense, have their ends in the economy of our means.[62]

The perfected person is skilled and knowledgeable in the ways of the *dao*. Xunzi says such knowledge requires a prepared and disciplined heart (*xin*). That means a heart made empty (*xü*), unified (*yi*), and still (*jing*) (21.8). Emptiness is an idea from the *Daodejing*, and we meet it again in Chapter 2. Xunzi seems to learn from this work while deflating its nebulous prose, explaining an empty mind as one that does not allow the past to bias the present. He explains a unified mind as one that does not allow the perception of one thing to confuse the perception of another. A still mind is undisturbed by dreams and fantasies, another source of bias. Clearly for him the obstacle to wise knowledge is obtuse prepossession, obsessions, and one-sided views. "It is the common flaw of men to be blinded by some small point of the truth and to shut their minds to the great ordering principle (*da li*)" (21.1). Perfected people know not to do that.

Xunzi's most insistent theme is his penetrating insistence that cooperation and harmonious social life are not given by nature; on the contrary, what is given by nature is inimical to concord. Therefore conventions, artifice, artifacts, their norms, and knowledge are indispensable to human existence. The best of this artifice was invented by the ancient sages, but their nature is the same as ours today. Among their most important works are ceremonies, which should be studied and practiced religiously because it is through them that we connect with the wisdom of sages and their magisterial art of using things. I think this is among Xunzi's most interesting thoughts, so let me follow it a step further. He writes: "Inborn nature is the root and beginning, the raw material and original constitution. Conscious activity (*wei*) is the form and principle of order, the development and completion. If there were no inborn nature, there would be nothing for conscious exertion to improve; if there were no conscious exertion, then inborn nature could not refine itself. Only after inborn nature and conscious exertion have been conjoined is the concept of the sage perfected, and the merit of uniting the world brought to fulfillment" (19.15).

Humanity is a thorough artifact—all the more so the perfected person: "A piece of wood straight as a plumb line can, by steaming, be made pliable enough to be bent into the shape of a wheel rim, so its curvature will conform to the compass. Yet, even though it is then allowed to dry out completely in the sun, it will not return to its former straightness because the process of steaming has effected this change in it. So, too, wood that has been marked with the plumb line will be straight and metal that has been put to the whetstone will be sharp. In broadening his learning, the perfected person each day examines himself so that his awareness will be discerning and his actions without excess" (1.1).

A perfected person is a work of art, a sage all the more so, and their most important function is artifice, using things artfully, judged from a ceremonial perspective. "He is responsive to every transformation, modifying as necessary to obtain for each thing its proper place" (6.19). He is a natural administrator, making things happen, and a natural diplomat, responding impartially to anything. "He bends and unbends as the occasion demands . . . flexible and tractable like rushes and reeds. . . . His use of his sense of what is morally right to change in response to every situation is because of knowledge (*zhi*) that is precisely fitting for every occasion" (3.5). He "responds to things as they arrive, discriminates matters as they occur" (21.6), being "limitlessly responsive to every transformation" (31.2). "In his responses to evolving phenomena, he is quick and alert, prompt and agile, but is not deluded" (12.3). "He responds appropriately to every change of circumstance as easily as counting one, two" (8.11).

Anyone can become a sage (23.14). All it requires is a clear mind and a settled heart capable of an unobstructed response. That is not easy, not natural, but it can be accomplished. What obstructs response is partiality. The problem is not desire but desire out of place and imbalanced. Xunzi's perfected person has not overcome desire, as if it were a taint or culpability. Instead, desire becomes so aligned with the changes that nothing disappoints him. "The sage follows his desires and embraces all his dispositions, and the things dependent on these simply turn out well ordered" (21.12).[63]

Xunzi says that sages observe nature but do not try to understand it (17.3). I think he means that they do not investigate it with detached curiosity. He is averse to inquiry into ultimate origins and abstract truth. "Discriminations and theories, illustrations and examples, though clever and sufficient, convenient and profitable, that do not follow the requirements of ritual and moral principles are termed 'dissolute theories'" (6.11). A profound person is "indifferent to the real nature of truth and falsity and the true nature of what is the case and what is not"; his superiority lies elsewhere, in "causing each affair and changed circumstance to obtain its proper response" (8.5). "In response to the myriad things of Heaven and Earth, he does not devote his attention to theorizing about how they came to be as they are, but rather tries to make the most perfect use of their potentialities" (12.3). "How can brooding over the origins of things be better than assisting what perfects them?" (17.13).

Xunzi takes up an idea we met in *Zhongyong*, that the value of wise knowledge is the completion of things. To complete things is to give them an appropriate place in the collective economy. That is what perfected people do, the accomplishment of their knowledge: "For putting the myriad transformations in good order, controlling and completing the myriad objects, rearing and nurturing the myriad common people, and universally regulating the whole world, no one excels the humane man (*ren ren*). Hence, his knowledge (*zhi*) and thought (*lü*) are adequate to put the people in good order" (10.6). The best knowledge is artistic or technical in a philosophical sense, a ceremonially appropriate synthesis.

The most important thing to complete—the one that completes all the rest—is our own nature. Heaven produces a minimum of humanity—a body, life, emotions, senses, mind. Everything else depends on deliberate acts and the use of artifacts. The best of these, the ones that make the most well-turned-out individuals, are the ancient ceremonies. These embody elementary norms of social existence, discovered and refined by sages in something like the way potters form their clay:

> Ritual principles and moral duty are born of the acquired nature of the sage and are not the product of anything inherent in man's inborn nature. Thus, when the potter shapes the clay to create the vessel, this is the creation of the acquired nature of the potter and not the product of anything inherent in his inborn nature. When an artisan carves a vessel out of a piece of wood, it is the creation of his acquired nature and not the product of his inborn nature. The sage accumulates his thoughts and ideas. He masters through practice the skills of his acquired nature and the principles involved therein in order to produce ritual principles and moral duty and

to develop laws and standards. This being the case, ritual principles and moral duty, laws and standards, are the creations of the acquired nature of the sage and not the products of anything inherent in his inborn nature. (23.7)

The first sages were in the unique position of being able to teach people to be good without having been taught themselves, because they invent the rites that teach people to love goodness. They are like Freud in relation to psychoanalysis. It is a condition on practicing orthodox psychoanalysis that one undergo a training analysis. Yet Freud invented psychoanalysis and taught all of the first generation of psychoanalysts, even though he was never analyzed. (It is said he analyzed himself, which is absurd and technically impossible; whatever he did by himself cannot have been psychoanalysis because the other person is required for transference and is therefore not optional.) The first sages had to create rituals where there were none, and create artifacts from nothing artificial.

This has seemed to raise a problem for Xunzi. On the one hand life is impossible without the ceremonies sages invent. On the other hand sages are just like anyone in what they begin with. If they are just like us and do not need ceremonies, why do we? If we do need them, how can sages lack them and be just like us? In the words of one critic, "The model given by the sages informs cultural life without being part of culture; strictly speaking, it is prior to it and stands apart from it. . . . The sages' unprecedented invention of ritual is the pattern and necessary precondition of every other kind of artifice," which supposedly makes culture "inexplicable in the natural course of things, a deus ex machina solution to a legitimate sociological question."[64] The question is where standards come from. Its legitimacy remains to be seen.

Consider the position of the first sages. They are human beings, the same by nature as anyone today. They appear at a time before artifice, before convention, before art and knowledge, and by their deeds these qualities first come into the world. What did the sages use, if they did not have artifacts? The answer seems to be that they used Heaven/Nature (*tian*). Use it how? As a source of patterns for analogical extension. The first artifacts, the first art, were analogies, ritual patterns analogically extending natural processes. An example may help us to understand. The following words are ascribed to Zi Chan, the man responsible for China's first promulgated law, which he had inscribed on a bronze vessel in 543 BCE. In a text on rites, he says:

> Rites are created for rectification. . . . The distinction between king and subjects and that between the inferior and the superior are used to follow the righteousness of the earth. The relationship between husband and wife and between outer and inner is established to regulate the opposites (*yin yang*). The relationship between father and son, that between elder and younger, and that between uncle and nephew, as well as the rites of marriage, are set to imitate the brightness of heaven. Endeavor in government is devoted to modeling oneself after the four seasons. Punishments and jails, which make people fearful of illegal actions, are employed in imitating thunder and lightning, which kill things. Benevolence and harmony are cultivated in emulating heaven in creating things and nurturing them to grow.[65]

The eight trigrams (*bagua*), the foundation of the *Yijing* or *Book of Changes,* have a similar origin. The sage Fu Xi "observed the patterns on birds and beasts and what things were suitable for the land. . . . He thereupon made the eight trigrams in order to become thoroughly conversant with the virtues inherent in the numinous and the bright and to classify the myriad things in terms of their true, innate natures." The Han commentary says, "Heaven creates spiritual things, and the sage follows them. Heaven and earth transform and the sage imitates them."[66]

All that the first sages did is make analogies, but they did it superlatively well, finding exactly the right correspondence for synergy among human and nonhuman things. The art of the sage is to analogize nature into this collective. The more closely ceremonies imitate natural analogies, the more harmonious the economy of human and nonhuman things. That is the assumption. Natural order provides no more than hints about how to integrate humanity into its flows. Unknown generations of sages experimented until ritual order reached its acme under the early Zhou kings. The first sages construct their analogies as anyone might, and they institute them as any charismatic leader inspires people to obedience. Anyone could do it, as anyone could have written *Hamlet.* Writing the play is a completely natural act in the sense that there is no anomalous causation; on the other hand it is rare and artful invention. In both respects that is like what sages do.[67]

So who did it for the first sages? In a condition of no arts and no rites, how could these brilliant innovators survive long enough to endow posterity with their inventions? Mengzi says sage king Shun when he was young "differed only slightly from the wild people of the deep mountains. But as soon as he heard one good saying or saw one good deed, it was like a river overflowing its banks, torrential, so that nothing could stop it" (7A16). Xunzi might think there is something wrong with the question of first sages. The dramatic polarity we imagine between culture and nature, with sages apparently responsible for bootstrapping humanity over the line, is overwrought. There could be first sages only if there were first people, and therefore a time before humanity—which assumes that nature has some determination in itself apart from humanity, whereas Xunzi tells us that humanity forms a triad with Heaven and earth. If we take that thought seriously, then there is no origin of norms and culture from out of an independently constituted nature. There is no specifically sociological genesis of norms, and culture is not an order of "purely sociological" relations. This purity is overwrought. The only nature we know already includes sages, normative conventions, and works of art.

I mentioned Xunzi's scorn for speculation on ultimate origins; he explicitly abjures debate about the origin of ritual (19.16). I do not see that as evading a legitimate problem. Instead it circumvents a pseudoproblem that cannot be resolved and does not matter to practice. Whether there have always been sages and people have always needed what sages do, or there was a time when people, profoundly uncivilized and barely recognizable as human, were without sages, cannot be determined and does not matter. We know what sages do, which is to invent and charismatically institute ceremonial analogies, and we know the value of their work, which is to compose a viable, enduring collective of human and nonhuman beings. There is no fallacy, and despite Xunzi's ardent defense of artifice, it is not a deus ex machina solution to the origin of culture. It is a pragmatic, genealogical, historicist rejection of speculation on ultimate origins, which can never not be a mythopoeia inimical to righteousness in thought and practice.

Human Nature and Morality

If the modern critic's dichotomy between culture and nature is overwrought, so may be Xunzi's own insistent distinction between deliberate effort and natural spontaneity, which would deflate his trenchant dispute with Mengzi about human nature. "Human nature is good (*shan*)," says Mengzi (3A1). No, says Xunzi, "human nature is bad (*e*)" (23.1). As I understand it, Xunzi's criticism is that Mengzi makes morality seem natural and easy, failing to appreciate the laborious training goodness requires in the wholly artificial framework of ceremonies. It is as if Xunzi agreed with Yang Zhu that Confucian discipline is unnatural, that it goes against our heaven-sent nature. Mengzi says Yang's conclusion is a mistake; moral development is perfectly natural. Xunzi seemingly agrees with Yang, but thinks there is nothing wrong with "violating" our nature because sagacious artifice does not *violate* nature, it *completes* it. Our heaven-sent natural endowment is not enough, or not the right sort of thing, for harmonious collective existence. By submitting to ethical cultivation we do not lose something we had as a free gift of nature; we gain immeasurable artificial powers that supplement and complete what Heaven only started.

I think "Human nature is bad" means we are not developmentally calibrated for life with others. Our heaven-sent nature leaves us unprepared for social existence. Goodness, being completely social, is completely artificial and our greatest work of art. Before there is any goodness, any morality, any standard, you have to step into the collective economy. Once you do, you step into a ceremonial world of convention and artifice. I see Xunzi as siding with thinkers like Hobbes, Spinoza, Nietzsche, T. H. Huxley, and Freud, for whom instinctual life is selfish and social life requires a renunciation of instincts. Our nature, meaning what we are by evolution—what Huxley calls our "ape and tiger promptings"—is at odds with morality and civilization; everything that makes us survivors is incompatible with cooperation and impartiality. Like these Western thinkers, Xunzi supposes that what nature (development, evolution) provides falls short of what harmonious social existence requires. We are not made by nature for life in society; only society can socialize.[68]

That is a difficult conclusion for anyone who takes Darwin seriously. How can our natural endowment (our evolution) fail to be compatible with a social existence that is an obvious condition on human survival? The greatest threat to infant survival is an adult. The greatest threat to group survival is another group. How is it possible that *all* the natural selection, *all* the adaptive instincts, every endowment of nature favors *obstacles* to social existence? From a Darwinian point of view it makes no sense. Nietzsche, Huxley, and Freud were not following but ignoring Darwin, for whom it is a mistake to think evolution makes us selfishly antisocial, or that social harmony requires an unnatural repression of the instincts. From the necessity of social life Darwin infers adaptation for it, and assembles copious evidence for social instincts. His conclusion is not that we are naturally good, but rather that social adaptations make us good enough for functional social life, disposed to sympathy and remorse, though not always or without resistance, creating opportunities for callous selfishness and the growth of evil.[69]

That does not seem so different from Mengzi's thought. Xunzi reads Mengzi as saying that our innate capacity for goodness will manifest itself as an ability to do the right thing. Xunzi does not deny the innate capacity but argues that merely having it does not guarantee the developed ability. An artificial structure of ceremonies, with their duties and expectations, has to be in place before this ability can function. To reply on behalf of Mengzi let us ask why ceremonies (moral culture) are supposed to be *entirely* a matter of *wei*, deliberate effort, and not in the least degree *ziran*, or spontaneously emergent. Xunzi is in something like the position of a modern-day creationist. There are phenomena he thinks can originate only through deliberate effort (design), never by a blind and purposeless natural mechanism. His reason is that what comes about by nature is unlearned, spontaneous, and effortlessly exercised. No one has to teach the eyes to see, and eyes cannot depart from seeing; for example, through the acquisition of bad habits. Yet people can depart from goodness by acquiring bad habits. If goodness were as natural to our hearts as vision is to our eyes such departures would be impossible. Hence, goodness must not be the work of mere nature.

That conclusion is probably not one Mengzi would disagree with. Those sprouts of good he postulates (2A6) are universally given in human nature, but they do not unfailingly develop into full-blown goodness. It takes teachers, cultural reinforcement, and, Mengzi insists, commitment, will (*zhi*). That is his answer to King Xuan of Qi (1A7). The king asks Mengzi, what is a genuine king? The sage replies that a genuine king is one who cares for the people. Can I do that? he asks. Mengzi assures him that he can, and recounts an anecdote he heard, according to which the king was so affected by the terrified bellowing of an ox as it was led to sacrifice that he had it released. That fleeting tenderness indicates that Xuan has all he needs to be a true king. He must cultivate it, but were the seed not there, all the cultivation in the world would not compensate, or make him a true king. He needs to extend what he felt for the ox until it reaches the whole people. To have been able to make this kind of extension was the genius of the ancient sage kings. Eventually, however, further discussion reveals King Xuan's real problem, which is not that he is unable to care for the people; it is that he does not want to try. His heart is not in it. There is no resolution, no commitment, no will.

Xunzi says nature is not enough for goodness; art and deliberate effort have to supplement what nature provides. Mengzi says nature provides the material that sets each one on the path of goodness, but that without personal commitment and guidance from others, individuals may stray and their moral nature fail to develop. Without commitment, Mengzi's sprouts of good wither; without sage art and deliberate effort, what Xunzi grants as a heavenly endowment is insufficient for goodness. How different are these positions? Xunzi seem to think our heavenly endowment has to be supplemented by something that is in a strong sense human rather than heavenly, some art that does not arise through the operation of nature alone and takes, as it were, a special creation by the sages. The nature of the sage is the same as the nature of the wicked man. Sages transform their nature by their own deliberate effort, just as a potter transforms clay by a deliberate effort to produce a beautiful or useful vessel. We have to ask, however, why some accomplish the transformation and become sages, and not others. The difference seems to indicate individual variation in natural endowment, despite Xunzi's reluctance to acknowledge such variations, as if what we have from Heaven must be the same in all and develop the same way, as we all have eyes that see and ears that hear.

Is our natural endowment really so monotonous? If sages did not feel something at the start, before they were accomplished sages, some prompting, some urge to benevolence, how would they initiate the course to their eventual achievements? Not all grains of rice are the same. Spontaneous, natural variations occur, which people seize upon and amplify through art. That is the origin of every domestication, which evolves an organism whose conditions of existence include artifice. Mengzi says goodness is like that. Given that we need what only sages can provide, natural selection predicts some tendency to endow it or its preconditions; and if not everyone is an accomplished sage, there must be individual differences, natural variations. We do not need everyone to be a spontaneous natural sage. We only need a few with a natural disposition to stay the course, and they can teach the rest, just as we need only a few grains of rice suitable for domestication and can with time and effort achieve the rest for ourselves. But if natural variation did not prepare the material, all our art would be unavailing. Such an account requires a conception of nature less monotonous than Xunzi seems to allow, but it is a complication for which there is independent evidence in the natural variation that enables domestication, and it explains something that Xunzi leaves mysterious, which is why sages are rare.

Confucians want to extend ceremonial appropriateness to everything we handle. The epitome of Confucian self-cultivation is a person who responds to anything that happens in a way that is not calculated, inferred, or consciously recollected, but comes from the heart *ziran,* of itself, and perfectly suits the circumstances, as judged by ritual proprieties and precedents. This sagacious response requires both sincerity and knowledge. As sincere, it is impartial and selfless, more nature acting through us than intentional purposiveness. But spontaneity is not enough. The response must also concretize the conditions of harmony latent in the situation, completing things, inconspicuously but artfully *making* the situation harmonious, orchestrating a rapport that is aesthetic no less than moral.

To become good at this orchestration, managing the changes and togetherness of things, requires that discipline take the place of spontaneity until spontaneity spontaneously returns in the transformed character of a perfected person. What you learn in the Confucian curriculum are the circumstances of sage action in the past. Such study is the privileged way to train for goodness. Through a long discipline of memorization, recitation, and exacting ceremony, the heart becomes at home with the wisdom of the past and capable of extending it in the present. The difference between an accomplished Confucian and anyone else is self-knowledge. This hard-won self-knowledge makes one profound, and profound people are good at using things, completing them, responding to them with impeccable ceremony, and settling their proper place in the economy of human and nonhuman things.

There is more to say about ideas of knowledge in the Confucian tradition, but the more comes after a hiatus of a thousand years. The prestige of Confucian education rises with the Han dynasty, though philosophical innovations become sparse. With the establishment of state examinations for the civil service concentrating on Confucian learning, Confucian education becomes a career path. It is not until the so-called Neoconfucian renaissance of the Song dynasty that important fresh contributions appear.

— 2 —

Daoists

> Neverbegan said, "Ignorance is profound, knowing it is superficial. Not knowing it is inward, knowing it is outward." Translucence looked upward and sighed. "Is it by not knowing it that you know it? Is it that if you do know you are ignorant? Who knows the knowing which is ignorance?"
>
> —ZHUANGZI

The coherence of language, ethics, and wise knowledge is a given for Confucians. The terms of praise and condemnation in language make morally valuable distinctions, as wise knowledge confirms. With the Daoists this continuity is thrown into doubt. These thinkers criticize the Confucians' expectations for language and knowledge, and regard ordinary moral distinctions as an obstacle to sagacious virtue. There is more to knowledge than words can say, and the best knowledge does without words at all.

The *Daodejing*

I begin with the *Daodejing,* the Classic of the *Dao* and Its Power (also known as the *Laozi,* after its legendary author), not because I assume it is the oldest work in this tradition (a disputed question I take no view on), but because one has to start somewhere, and I have more to say about the *Zhuangzi,* for which some discussion of the *Daodejing* is a good introduction.[1]

I take exception to a presumed priority for the political in this work, the assumption that it is written for rulers, offering sage advice to a king. It does some of that, to be sure, but I do not find rulership to be more than one of many layers in what seems to be the work of multiple hands and perhaps multiple agendas. Taking it to address a ruler seems like a Confucian misprision of the sage in the person of a king. The important thing in the *Daodejing* teaching, it seems to me, is not that the ruler is wise or advised by sages. What is important is that sages are among the people, where they

66

are an inconspicuous source of harmony. The primary effect of mastery in the art of the *dao* is on the sage's own body, then on the local environment, and only indirectly on the body politic.[2]

Such a sage is not a dramatic personality, not a Solomon or Faust, lacking even the charisma of the Confucian *junzi*. This sage is unremarkable, inattentive, vapid, muddled, like a child who has not yet learned to smile. All the same, it is impossible to oppose this sage, to attack him, or be an enemy to him, because he has emptied himself of the desires that fuel dissent, and enjoys the maximal advantage of noncontention (*bu zheng*). You cannot strike him, nothing connects. He is not struck because he is not *stuck,* never in one place to the exclusion of another. Not contending, unobstructed, flowing like water:

> Water is good at benefitting the myriad creatures, while not contending with them. . . . Only by avoiding contention can one avoid blame. (DDJ 8)

> Because sages do not contend, no one in the world can contend with them. (DDJ 22)

> It is the *dao* of heaven not to contend but nonetheless to conquer. (DDJ 73)

> The *dao* of the sage is to act but not contend. (DDJ 81)

Images of sage efficacy in this work include flowing water (DDJ 8, 78), a mirror (DDJ 10), and a woman (DDJ 28, 61). Water benefits without contention; women overcome by softness; mirrors reflect anything without discrimination, and become serenely empty the instant things pass. This emptiness is not a deficiency. It is an awesome resource, a virtual potency without form, like an infant (DDJ 10, 20, 55), or an uncarved block of wood (DDJ 15, 28, 32, 37); potentially any form, actually (rigidly) very little at all. Growing up means growing rigid, losing potential, becoming fixed and settled, frittering away *qi* in futile contention.

The *Daodejing* makes a new connection between *wu wei* effectiveness and the condition it calls *xü*, tenuous, empty. The oldest meaning of *xü* is "a big hill," and by extension anything vast and expansive, which implies (a kind of) emptiness, not filled up. That is also the emptiness of the sky, or of clouds and steam, virtual vapors that can coagulate into any form. This emptiness is not nonbeing, but unformed, uncommitted, not rigid, or fully present. The virtual, which is my philosophical gloss on this emptiness, *is,* is in being, real, existing; it is the opposite of actual, not of existing, being, or reality.

The empty is not the null and void, not sheer nonbeing (we meet *that* emptiness in Buddhism). Empty is empty of commitment, of presence, or finished form; its model is the potent virtuality of an infant or the plasticity of an uncarved block.[3]

Images of *wu wei* in this work are images of efficacious emptiness, like the potent void at the center of a wheel, the hollow of a jar, or the space between walls. Effortless *wu wei* effectiveness requires that we cultivate this emptiness, empty ourselves of desire, forget about words. Then the response to circumstances becomes spontaneous, natural, so-of-itself (*ziran*), and in that sense effortless. A line of the *Daodejing* reads, "Attain extreme tenuousness; preserve quiet integrity" (DDJ 16). Making ourselves tenuous we make ourselves integral and in that sense maintain our integrity, never being indecisive, unresponsive, or conflicted; hence steady, constant, reliable. Tenuousness requires emptiness where desire used to be; only then can you change daily with the course of things. Otherwise some interest, some clinging attachment makes you fear change, lose impartiality, and get stuck in a position. Until we get over that attachment to forms we are incapable of constancy and without integrity.

To be constant is not to be changeless but to respond to circumstances spontaneously, *ziran*. This is a thought that Chinese tradition will never forget. It recurs in the *Zhuangzi*: "To be transformed day by day with other things is to be untransformed once and for all."[4] Xunzi draws the idea into Confucianism, as does the *Zhongyong*. By the Song dynasty the thinking is orthodox. "Being long lasting does not mean being in a fixed and definite state. Being fixed and definite, a thing cannot last long. The way to be constant is to change according to circumstance" (Cheng Yi).[5]

The opposite of *wu wei* is *wei*, purposive, deliberate doing and its results or artifacts. The *Daodejing* seems to say that such artifice is futile, which is the argument Xunzi found so wrong-headed. All our artifice, our planning and purposiveness, all the aggressive, knowing intentionality with which we set upon things to "complete" them, merely entrench the hold of custom and language on consciousness and thus on action and especially on desire, which they arouse when the challenge is to subdue it. *Wu wei* is not sheer nonactivity; it is doing without help, minimal artifice, an art of appearing artless, *doing* "not doing," *wei wu wei* (DDJ 63). Such action meshes with unfolding circumstances to a result that seems natural, inevitable, not anyone's deliberate purpose. The action is effortless in the sense that it produces its effectiveness by an inconspicuous expenditure, as Duke Huan's attendant started a rumor and stopped a war.

Wu wei action is more than merely efficient, for more is measured than cost and benefit. The idea, as I understand it, is to maximize the *difference* between effectiveness and intervention, with "doing nothing" and "nothing left undone" as the ideal limiting case. It takes art to eschew instrumentality without sacrificing effectiveness. A sage has a knack for getting the world to do the heavy lifting, for being in the right place at the right time, for being lucky. Of course, it is not luck; it only looks like luck to one who would not know what to do with those little things even supposing he could see them. The art of the *dao*, of viably changing with changes, is a technics of exquisite minima. "Looked for but not seen, its name is 'minute' (*yi*). Listened for but not heard, its name is 'rarified' (*xi*). Grabbed for but not gotten, its name is 'subtle' (*wei*). . . . The ability to know the ancient beginnings, this is called the thread of the *dao*" (DDJ 14).

The opening verse of the *Daodejing* reads in part:

Always eliminate desires in order to observe its mysteries;
Always have desires in order to observe its manifestations. (DDJ 1)

The implied, unspecified reference of "it" is *dao*, which for this work if not more generally I gloss as *becoming*. To observe *dao*'s mystery bracket your desires. To observe its manifestations indulge them. If you have desires, the forms things acquire or leave behind will be conspicuous, and their changes alternately distressing or joyful. As you eliminate desires, and become less distracted by craving, you experience the mystery of unity, the indifference of change. All things become phases of one movement, one flow, one spontaneous arising, which is the One, the Ancestor, the Becoming from which beings are born. When driven by desire, perception is avaricious and partial. Passion imposes its ardent grid. We see only what we want or fear; the rest is background noise, which our grasping heart filters out.

Constant and inconstant seem like opposites, as do desire and satisfaction, or agitation and quiescence, but they are not. They share an enigmatic unity—all arise from one source. When we align with this source, blend with it, we flow without turbulence and vanish into the becoming of things. Eliminating desire we can penetrate the *dao*'s silent transformations. Think of planting a tree. You begin with a seedling. Year by year you see the change but you never see the changing, the invisible minutiae that add up to obvious change. These smallest beginnings are hard to discern not merely due to underground darkness, but from a different kind of obscurity, an ordinary insensitivity to what George Eliot calls "that roar which lies on the other side of silence." The beat of tree-becoming is not synchronous with our own. We cannot resonate with it except at the most common scale. To achieve penetrating perception, to discern and potentially respond to such little things, you have to overcome confinement in selfish desire, shed craven attachments, forget about likes and dislikes. The more fondness fades, the more impartial you become to becoming, and the more prescient your perception of the incipient and birthing.[6]

There is a pattern of seeming hostility to knowledge, a repudiation of its supposed value, in the *Daodejing* (DDJ 3, 10, 18, 19), and we shall see something comparable in *Zhuangzi*. On inspection, the animosity seems to touch only what certain scholars *call* knowledge, a ponderous pedantry of ceremonies and ancient texts combined with the naive belief of the literati in the value of language. The criticism allows for something better suited to the name of knowledge. It takes subtle eyes to see unostentatious opportunities imperceptible to others, to discern the germ of future things, and know how to modify evolving circumstances when they are pliable and easy to change. "What has yet to begin is easy to plan for"; "Work at things before they come to be"; "Sages . . . study what is not studied and return to what the multitude pass by" (DDJ 64). This artful knowledge does not require theory, science, or ontological truth. It may not even require language. Zhuangzi says you need to learn to breathe from your heels (Z 84), which suggests taiji and the knowledge of a martial artist, knowing how to respond to the smallest change with an effectiveness impossible to contend with.[7]

I have suggested that Chinese tradition associates wise or sagacious knowledge with the effortless *wu wei* effectiveness such knowledge funds. The thesis is not peculiar to the *Daodejing*, though it is, I think, found there. A question I noted in Chapter 1 is whether *wu wei* action, truly effortless efficacy, is seriously possible. Critics have dismissed it as a philosophical fantasy. "The ancient Chinese conception of *wu wei* is based on a fundamental misconception of action," says one. Multiple misconceptions, it seems. The first is to think action might be nonintentional, forming no part of an intentional pattern of behavior, without goal, purpose, or motive. It is certainly possible for people to do things without deliberation or calculation, and in fact all action is like that at some level. That is how we walk, operate vehicles, use tools, and so on. But such uncalculated action occurs only as part of a larger pattern that is intentional and motivated. "The tennis champion may return service automatically, without a single conscious thought. But first she must intentionally set out to play the game."[8]

Hence a second mistake, which is to think that the *wu wei* quality of habitual or skilled action could be abstracted from a specific context of practice and generalized, as if *life* could be a matter of unconscious skill. Daoists are supposed to have "thought they could isolate the phenomenon of *wu-wei*-like skilled or habitual activities and detach it from the context of an intentional flow of action and the desires, values, education, and social norms typically incorporated into any such context." That assumption supposedly encourages the expectation that one might suspend self and agency and ground action purely in the *dao* and its normative authority, which is another mistake. We should not have to choose between acting on desires and vanishing into the *dao*. Nothing people do is innocent of education, training, habit, or convention. The capacities that would enable *wu wei* action (for instance, being able to walk or speak) are not innate, and have to be acquired by practice that is anything but effortless.[9]

Xunzi makes this argument, and it is correct as far as it goes. But the emptiness to which the *Daodejing* alludes does not exclude habit or training. What it excludes is being stuck in them. The point of cultivating emptiness, it seems to me, is not to transcend habit and convention; it is to get over what makes them obstacles instead of resources. The best lessons on this point are from Zhuangzi; for instance the finesse of Cook Ding, so effective that his knife needs no sharpening after nineteen years of carving oxen. He is beyond skill: "I have left skill behind me. When I first began to carve oxen, I saw nothing but oxen wherever I looked. Three years more and I never saw an ox as a whole. Nowadays I am in touch through the daemonic in me, and do not look with the eye. With the senses I know where to stop, the daemonic I desire to run its course. I rely on Heaven's structuring (*tian li*), cleave along the main seams, let myself be guided by the main cavities, go by what is inherently so. A ligament or tendon I never touch, not to mention solid bone" (Z 63–64).[10]

To me this passage says that the development process was required. Cook Ding had to pass though the less accomplished condition to bring his body to the point where it performs effortlessly. To empty oneself of training and habit is to empty oneself of what is limited and ineffectual about them; it is not to revert to the pretrained body, which is surely impossible. The idea is not to forget what one knows, but not to allow knowledge to forget what it does not know. We do not leave one plane of being for another. We remain where we have always been and learn to move like a pivot in any direction. The ideal unbiased response is a limiting case only. In other words, *wu wei* is an intensive quality, a matter of degree, and not something either fully present or simply absent.

The same reasoning refutes the criticism that *wu wei* presupposes an implausible absence of desire, will, or motive. To think that *wu wei* action must be unconditioned by desire is, as it were, a Buddhist reading that misprisions the *Daodejing* in idealized absence. It seems to me that when this work says "get rid of desire," it means a certain sort of desire, selfish desire, and not desire per se. I admit there is language suggesting otherwise. "Nameless unhewn wood is but freedom from desire (*yu*). Without desire and still, the world will settle of itself" (DDJ 37). But many of this work's references seem to qualify desire; for instance, "The worst calamity is the desire to acquire (*yu de*)" (DDJ 46); and "Those who preserve this *dao* do not desire fullness (*yu ying*)" (DDJ 15). A person can work on reducing desires without anticipating a pure, unearthly state. The idea is to dampen desire, to cultivate a minimal form, not to eliminate or transcend it. We act from desire and with motivation, but the desires do not have to be selfish, and can be artfully minimized so that desire tends to diminish rather than dominate.[11]

When it is said that sages desire to be without desire I take that to mean they have the second-order desire to be without first-order desires of a particular kind, such as for precious goods. "Sages desire to be without desires (*yu bu yu*) and show no regard for precious goods" (DDJ 64). One still has desires, for instance the second-order desire not to not have selfish, private, material desires. Of course this argument raises the question of what makes desire selfish; is there really another kind? Selfish desires are not those that flow from a thing called "self," a reification the Chinese avoid. A selfish desire is, I think, an excessive desire—unbalanced, rigid, resisting change, reactive, premised on fear. It is *that* desire that is to be overcome, not simply anything psychological analysis might identify as a conative vector of action. To use my earlier example, the sagacious servant who penetrated Duke Huan's secret plan had the desire to spare the people a war and acted on it, though he did very little, perhaps no more than start a rumor, idle chat in a teahouse, with an unseen efficacy out of all proportion to the apparent expenditure of force.[12]

Critics have also objected to glossing *wu wei* as "effortless action." One critic says that even if *wu wei* activity "may sometimes be effortless," there is "little reason to think this is its distinguishing feature." Taking the expression quite literally, he says, "*wu wei* is the absence of *wei*," that is, the absence of "action undertaken intentionally, for some motive of the agent," which seems to mean that *wu wei* "requires that the agent be motivated by no reasons at all." Yet that is as good as to say there is no *action* at all; it just happened, a fortuitous accident. What seems right about this argument is that nonintentional action is a misconception. Why call something "action" if there is no intentionality, if it just happens? Intentional means *intentional under a description*. Any action falls under many descriptions. It may be intentional under one, not intentional under another, an accident under one, deliberate under another, and so on. But if what happens is indeed action, there must be a description under which it falls intentionally. There need be no prior intention, as in a plan, or even consciousness of purpose for an event to qualify as intentional. The action can be immediate, spontaneous, and without conscious intention, as in the tennis example. The tennis player performs intentionally; the play, the serve, the return are all intentional, despite there being no specific, conscious intention to do anything in particular.[13]

These points of action theory would raise a problem for effortless efficacy only if doing *wu wei* were supposed to require the radical nonpresence (or ideal absence) of intentionality. We do not have to make that assumption. I think a better understanding is in terms of intensive, qualitative effortlessness. *Wu wei* action is intentional in the sense that it is an ethically optimal response to a situation. That sort of thing does not just happen. It confirms the inaction as intentional, indeed artful, even sagacious, and not a happy accident of inanition. *Wu wei* effectiveness always has its *wei,* a doing, whose invisibility is relative to an observer's knowledge. The idea is not that *nothing* be done (an always virtual limiting case), but that little if anything *seem to be* done, which may not really be easy, though art can make it look that way, and which is not literally not acting, though it may seem so to one who does not appreciate the artfulness and cannot see the little things.

A prominent proponent of the "effortless action" interpretation says that *wu wei* "properly refers not to what is actually happening (or not happening) in the realm of observable action but rather to . . . the phenomenological [inner mental] state of the doer," which is primarily distinguished by an absence of self-consciousness. I agree that a characteristic phenomenological state is involved, though the intentionality seems mainly negative, distinguished by what it lacks (representation, calculation, selfishness). But beyond the private inner mental state, there is always some real doing, however slight, and it is intentional, even if there is no deliberation, calculation, or causation by a representation (Kant's definition of purpose). "Even if the doing becomes minimal, so discreet as to be hardly discernable," writes François Jullien, "*allowing* things to happen constitutes active involvement." As this active, intelligent response to circumstances, *wu wei* must be intentional; however, that does not exclude effortlessness, which is an intensive quality of intentionality, a matter of degree, and does not require a paradoxical intending not to intend or trying not to try. Action can be qualitatively relatively effortless and still intentional. In fact, it can be effortlessly intentional, and effortlessly intentional without being intentionally effortless.[14]

Wu wei effectiveness is always intentional under some circumstantially sagacious description, and effortless only in the sense that it produces its effect by an inconspicuous expenditure, an appearance that is relative to an observer's acuity. Effort and intention are not simply absent but vanishing, diminishing, coming less and less to dominate action. Such action is the outcome of long discipline and attentive self-cultivation, ideally in a mountain cave. With practice, the need for instrumental adjuncts like obvious effort, deliberate intention, or purposive calculation diminishes as a consequence of enhanced efficacy and disciplined desire. Yet a sage is a natural being, however daimonic. Even his inaction is intentional; what he does, no less than what he does not do, or merely allows to happen, is to some degree desired and motivated. The point of Daoist discipline is not to attain Buddhist will-lessness but to practice a vanishing will. Not no intention at all, but vanishing intention. Not no effort at all, but vanishing effort, cultivating the uncomplicated ease that canny perception of the little things enables, and which supports a life of enhanced harmony with the *dao*, the way of changes, when purpose vanishes into the spontaneous becoming of things.

It has been suggested that the basic conception of knowledge in early Chinese tradition is a practical ability to distinguish and name things. Chinese thinkers supposedly consider the fundamental cognitive operation to be what they call *bian*, distinguishing similar from dissimilar, typically by comparison with a standard or model. Knowledge is the right, correct, or indisputable discrimination of similar and different. What for European logic is evaluating the truth of an assertion is in Chinese construed as an act of distinguishing, with respect to some contextually specific term, whether its application in a given case would be *shi* or *fei*, meaning at once "so" or "not so," and "good" or "bad." To say *F is G* is to say that *F* and *G* are the same or similar in some understood way, while to evaluate the truth of that statement is to judge the implied sameness *shi* or *fei,* so or not, good or not.[15]

This interpretation captures what might be called China's majoritarian conception of knowledge, to use a term from Gilles Deleuze. It describes major knowledge, official, royal knowledge, suitable for the court. It also silently disqualifies minor, nomadic knowledge, knowledge for action, expressed in perspicacious choice more fraught than a court debate or memo to the minister. The major interpretation misses qualities that matter most to those with most to lose by not knowing well, like military commanders, physicians, or those whose resources are limited to sagacity or cunning. What the major interpretation identifies as knowledge *is* knowledge (is correct, right, indisputable), but it is not all that knowledge is because it overlooks what makes knowledge sagacious. By overlooking the difference that makes knowledge great, major knowledge of *shi* and *fei* proves to be no more than what Zhuangzi calls petty knowledge (*xiao zhi*).[16]

Suppose I recognize a pattern. Fine, but the value of that recognition depends on *when* I do so, and what I *do* with my recognition. It is timeliness and application that distinguish the cognition of a sage. Discrimination is perhaps the first part of knowledge, but does not account for what makes it sagacious, which lies in the qualitative dimension of sapient exploitation, or what Confucians euphemistically call "completing things." Wise discrimination detects those latent little things lesser discernment disregards, upon which the unfolding future pivots; nor does it stop at recognizing a pattern, but enrolls it in prescient action, well before the development becomes obvious and anybody can see it or agree with words that define it.

Not all traditional Chinese thinkers emphasize these intensive qualities of knowledge. Mozi does not and neither does Xunzi, unlike other Confucians, the military thinkers, or the Daoists. To base an interpretation of Chinese knowledge on the analyses of Mozi and Xunzi therefore silently dismisses those who understand only a sagaciously effective discrimination to be knowledge in the best or philosophical sense. The emphasis on subtlety correlates with the expectation of *wu wei* action. Thinkers who expect discrimination to be subtle and not merely correct do so because they expect knowledge to ripen into *wu wei* action. The philosophers who do not esteem such action—preeminently Mozi and Xunzi—do not emphasize the subtlety of sagacious discrimination. To build an interpretation of knowledge on Mozi and Xunzi, then, peremptorily writes *wu wei* out of the account.

The art of the *dao,* sagaciously changing with changes, is in part an art of knowing what is not known and what not to do. To remain fluid and capable of seizing opportunities when they are easy is in part knowing how to evade the need to act at all. A negative kind of knowing, a knowing-not (on the model of knowing-how and knowing-that)—knowing not to act, not to decide, not to continue—seems indispensable to sage action, as the *Daodejing* confirms:

> To know when to stop is how to stay out of danger. (DDJ 32)
> Know when to stop and avoid danger. (DDJ 44)
> There is no greater calamity than not knowing what is enough. (DDJ 46)

How do you know when to stop? You need to know what you do not know:

> To know what one does not know is best. Not to know but to believe that one knows is a disease. (DDJ 71)

A Confucian might agree. An Analect explains wisdom as recognizing what you know and what you do not know (A 2.17). Where the *Daodejing* seems to break new ground is when it says:

> Those who know are not full of knowledge.
> Those full of knowledge do not know. (DDJ 81)

With this passage the work introduces the interesting idea of a difference between sage knowledge and something only called knowledge by those who do not know better. For the first time, there can be a philosophical mistake about knowledge, and the suggestion is that Confucians and Mohists ("those who are full of knowledge") make it. The different knowing of those who are not full of knowledge is in part that negative knowing-not, knowingly refraining from action without compromising what has to be done. This knowing-not is not nescience or brute ignorance. It is a kind of knowing as *wu wei* is a kind of doing. Deleuze makes an inadvertently apropos comment: "This non-knowledge is no longer a negative or an insufficiency but . . . something *to be learnt* which corresponds to a fundamental dimension of the object"—"object" here meaning not a *thing* but a *problem,* whose objectivity consists in better and worse responses.[17]

This knowing-not is a theme in the philosophy of Spinoza, as Deleuze emphasizes. Spinoza distinguishes two aspects of inadequate ideas: they involve privation in the knowledge of their cause, yet still involve that unknown cause in some way and are therefore not entirely privative. There is something positive, something true, in even the falsest, most inadequate idea, and this kernel of truth can be grasped clearly. As finite minds we must assume that none of our ideas are finally adequate. The problem of knowledge is therefore not that of knowing what we know; it is knowing what we do not know, knowing the inadequacy of our ideas. For us, therefore, as Isabelle Stengers observes, "To approach the non-knowing at the heart of all knowledge is an undertaking that is meticulous, grave, and always to be taken up again."[18]

Resistance to knowing-not runs deep in Western tradition. Parmenides warned philosophers about this *not*. "Say and think only this: being is." If reality is knowable, it must be what is without qualification: it cannot *not* be in any respect. That is how Plato understands Parmenides. "How should something that *is not* be known? . . . What *is* completely is completely knowable, and what *is* in no way is in *every* way unknowable." However, the *Daodejing* does not operate with a dualism between being and not-being. What "is not" is not actual, not finished, not fully present, through it may well be latent, virtual, potential, or tending. Knowing-not means, in part, knowing the tension of tendencies and the potency of propensities not yet actual. It means knowing what is not settled, where there is room to maneuver and improvise with the future. It does not mean knowing *that which* is not known, something surely impossible. I do not have to see over the horizon to see that the horizon is a horizon and know there is more than I see. Rather than transcendental knowledge of a priori limits to knowledge, knowing-not is an astute knowledge of the limits of what passes for knowledge.[19]

Knowing how to recognize limits as limits and ignorance as ignorance is a veritable *ars nesciendi,* bringing savvy sapience to the problem of how to remain unimpeded by what you do not know. Shrewd skepticism prevents one getting stuck in knowledge. The more you think you know, the less you know what you do not know, and the more stuck you are in knowledge. The better you are at knowing-not, the more you know what is not known, and the less stuck you are, remaining flexible and undogmatic, hence more spontaneously responsive, therefore more effective. Obstacles to sapient action arise not from what we do not know, but from *not knowing* what we do not know. Only by knowing that can we know the good questions and what would be worth knowing but is not.

Knowing-not grows with foreknowledge, which is another kind of knowing the nonpresent. Part of knowing not to act is not needing to react to developments because they have been foreseen and responded to at an earlier, easier stage. "Plan for what is difficult while it is easy," says the *Daodejing*. "Work at what is great while it is small. The difficult undertakings in the world all start with what is easy. The great undertakings in the world all begin with what is small. That is why sages never work at great things and are able to achieve greatness" (DDJ 63). One can plan for what is difficult when it is easy only if one foresees the snags. Such foresight is not prediction, more a penetrating insight into the potential evolution of circumstances. Of course if you penetratingly see into the development of things you can make predictions. But the important thing is to counter-act, or respond effectively to the incipient development.

That is how I understand the line, "The ability to predict what is to come (*qian shi*) is an embellishment of the *dao*, and the beginning of ignorance (*yu*)" (DDJ 38). A prediction is valuable only as part of a plan, and a plan is a plan (not a spontaneous response) because it is worked out, discursively articulated, with the prediction playing a role in the reasoning that makes the scheme seem feasible. That is the beginning of ignorance because it is the beginning of reliance on what we know, slighting what is not known for the sake of acting decisively, even if it means becoming mired in knowledge. Perhaps that is why Zhuangzi says the perfection of knowledge is knowing not-knowing (*zhi bu zhi*). "To know what is Heaven's doing and what is man's is the utmost in knowledge. Whoever knows what Heaven does lives the life generated by Heaven. Whoever knows what man does uses his knowledge of the known to nurture his knowledge of the unknown against premature death. That is the perfection of knowledge" (Z 84).

Zhuangzi

I divide my look at the *Zhuangzi* into several parts, first considering only texts modern scholars agree in attributing to Zhuang Zhou (mid–fourth century BCE). These are traditionally referred to as the Inner Chapters, and comprise the first seven of thirty-three chapters in the received redaction. The remainder, the so-called Outer and Mixed Chapters, make up more than two-thirds of the traditional text, and are a mixed bag in every way—

authorship, date, style, and philosophical invention. So it seems appropriate to divide my look at this extraordinary work accordingly. The Inner Chapters are too rich in ideas for me to comment in detail, but I stick to my theme of knowledge. Knowledge is first to be experienced as a disappointment, then as an obstacle, then as foolishness. This disenchantment has to be worked through before we can attain a balanced view of the value of knowledge.[20]

Zhuangzi Inner Chapters

A reader habituated to the format of Western philosophy may be disconcerted to find this masterpiece of Oriental thought begin with a fish story. Once upon a time there was a fish named Kun (minnow), so big nobody knows how many thousand *li* around it is. Kun lives in the North Ocean, and has a wonderful capacity for transformation. Simple as that, this fish leaves the sea, turns to the sky, and becomes a bird named Peng, also enormous. When Peng puffs out its chest and departs for the South Ocean its wings are like clouds hanging from the sky.

The text relates these changes without any suggestion of the extraordinary. They are no more marvelous than any transformation. The word Chinese thinkers use for spontaneous transformation is *ziran,* happening so of itself. The changes are, of course, effects of earlier causes, and not spontaneous in the Western sense of an unconditioned cause. Plotless, purposeless, the transformations from fish to bird, north to south, sea to sky just happen to happen, with no cause other than a totality of circumstances.

A cicada and a dove watch as Peng rises. Cicada wonders, "What's the big deal? Way up there the sky still looks blue. A bird way up there still needs the wind. What's so great about Peng's greatness?" At this point the author breaks in for the first time. "What do these two creatures know?" Literally little. They know the little. "Little knowledge (*xiao zhi*) does not measure up to big knowledge (*da zhi*)" (Z 44). He repeats this interesting distinction in verse in the next chapter:

Great knowledge is effortless,
Petty knowledge picks holes.
Great speech is flavorless,
Petty speech strings words. (Z 50)

Great knowledge knows the art of transforming spontaneously, *ziran,* in response to any circumstance. Words of great knowledge lack flavor. They are not passionate, committed, decisive, or precise. To be any of those re-quires little knowledge. Little knowledge is good with language, knowing how to do things with words. It is the knowledge that gets you through school. Great knowledge gets you through life, being the art of nourishing life, a counteraction to happenstance that fortifies rather than etiolates. It is not-knowing, knowing how to avoid contention, how to accomplish without needing (or seeming) to act, how *not* to act (but leave nothing un-done). The promise of such knowledge is not ontological truth (the leading incentive of Western theory), but something more realistic: to prolong your vitality to the limit of human capacity.

Following the fish story we read, "It is said that perfect people have no self (*wu ji*), spiritual people have no accomplishment (*wu gong*), and sagely people have no name" (*wu ming*) (Z 45). What is this "self" perfected people lack? Not a Platonic, Cartesian, or Hindu *atman* self. Zhuangzi does not work up a theory of the self as Plato, Descartes, or the Indians do, as the substance of the person, or personal reality. The closest in his thinking to such a self is simply the living body (*shen*), and he is not suggesting we get rid of *that*. It is precisely what we should care for, though only in the right way. The "self" to get over is selfish desire, meaning desire driven by the fond belief that you are different from others, that you have your own likes and dislikes, that some changes are preferable to others, that there are things you would rather die than go along with. To overcome this self is to blend with others, abandon right and wrong, commingle anywhere, meld with anything, swing like a pivot, flavorless in speech, vanishing into things.[21]

Selfish desires are self-defeating. They leave us exhausted with conten-tion and confirm that we do not know how to take care of ourselves. To nourish our vitality we should work on our capacity to evolve. The great mistake in life is to get stuck, anywhere; immobilized in a position, cap-tured by cupidity, limited to a perspective. Then, as François Jullien observes, life "ceases to feed itself because it loses its virtuality, bogs down, becomes stalemated, and no longer initiates anything new." Desire is susceptible to anxious clinging, while life is unremitting change. The problem is not the changing but the clinging. To be constant one has to change without clinging. To reach that point we have to extinguish desires that make us hate change. That is the *gongfu*, the spiritual exercise, the adept's paradoxically decon-structive work on the self.[22]

Zhuangzi's first chapter introduces the difference between big and little knowledge. Epistemology is accustomed to apparently similar distinctions that are really quite different. Since before Plato, Western theory has distinguished between knowledge and mere opinion or *doxa*, knowledge and belief, knowledge and error. The distinction Zhuangzi introduces is different from any of these. Small knowledge is knowledge, not error. It is certain, not merely believed or opined. What it lacks is not truth or justification (qualities it may have in abundance) but sagacity, as Zhuangzi's next chapter—a skeptical, relativistic, even nihilistic critique of little knowledge—shows.

The traditional title of the second chapter is *Qiwulun,* an expression ambiguously wavering between Discourse on Equalizing Things and Equalizing Discourse on Things. One line of argument emphasizes the relativity of linguistic distinctions. Is Mount Tai "big" or "small"? Choose your perspective, and either statement is true. Apparently the same would go for any use of language, and so for any expression of (little) knowledge. Whether a person "knows" or not depends on where one is and who evaluates. What people call knowledge is ignorance or foolishness from another perspective. It is in this context that Gaptooth asks Wang Ni what he knows about knowledge. Wang Ni tries to evade answering, but tenacious Gaptooth will not let go. Finally Wang Ni says this: "Let me try to say it—'How do I know that what I call knowing is not ignorance? How do I know that what I call ignorance is not knowing?' Moreover, let me try a question on you. When people sleep in the damp, their backs hurt and they get stiff in the joints; is that so of an eel? If they sit in trees they shiver and shake; is that so of the ape? . . . In my judgment the sprouts of benevolence and righteousness and the pathways of right and wrong are inextricably confused: how could I know how to discriminate between them?" (Z 58, modified after Kjellberg).

We expect knowledge to be universally valid. It should not depend on perspective, not if it really is knowledge. That is what Zhuangzi questions. There is no universal validity for little knowledge, for knowledge of linguistic distinctions, common-sense knowledge, and a scholar's so-called facts. Such knowledge is condemned to relativism. Affirmation and negation, right and wrong, being and not being—these are linguistic perspectives that confine quotidian cognition and make it petty. Endorsing them generates the opposites that contradict them. "What is It is also Other, what is Other is also It. There they say 'That's it, that's not' from one point of view, here we say 'That's it, that's not' from another point of view. Are there really It and Other? Or really no It or Other?" (Z 53). Nothing is exclusively, intrinsically *this* and not *that*. There is no universally valid truth, and no unequivocally present being. Everything is always becoming something else, even this very statement. Punctuation is mere practicality. "If the 'it' is really it, there would be no longer a disputable difference from what is not it; if the 'so' is really so, there would no longer be a disputable difference from what is not so" (Z 60, modified after Kjellberg). Yet such contention is interminable, confirming the contrived pretense of the alternatives and the pettiness of "knowledge" confined to their terms.

Being, nonbeing, right, wrong, same, different—there is little knowledge in these distinctions. "To discriminate between alternatives is to fail to see something" (Z 57). The distinctions have their origin in language, but the constant words of lessons and books are ill-suited to a world of original becoming. "The *dao* has never had borders, saying has never had norms" (Z 57). There is no right or wrong except for someone poised on the brink of transformation, a circumstance for which there are no rules. Anything one decides will be right in one way, wrong in another. The idea of ceremonial propriety, of handling things righteously, as they *ought* to be handled, is nonsense. "It seems that there is something genuinely in command, and that the only trouble is we cannot find a sign of it" (Z 51). Received value distinctions *seem* to be about something real, but that is the effect of perspective on the naive, who do not think about perspective, especially their own. For them *the sky* is blue, *the fire* is hot. But of course the blue, like the hot, is an interaction, an appearance, a perspectival, perceptual response. So too are apparently more robust distinctions like being and not being. "A way comes about as we walk it; as for a thing, call it something and that's so" (Z 53).

That may sound like "linguistic idealism," as if talking *makes* things so, the form of speech determining reality; however I do not think Zhuangzi's point is ontological. The concern in responding to things should not be righteousness (and "truth" is a kind of righteousness); it should be vitality. We are no good dead. To expend vitality contending over which of an opposite pair of names (or which ceremony) would be righteous is much too serious about words. People ruled by words are like the monkeys in Zhuangzi's tale "Three in the Morning." "A monkey keeper handing out nuts said, 'Three every morning and four every evening.' The monkeys were in a rage. 'All right then,' he said, 'four every evening and three every morning.' The monkeys were all delighted" (Z 54).

A second line of argument in this chapter develops implications from the complementarity of opposites. In Plato opposites exclude each other. In Hegel they overcome each other in a higher synthesis. In Zhuangzi (as in the *Da-*

odejing) opposites interpenetrate and generate each other. Approval engenders disapproval, right engenders wrong, birth engenders death. These oppositions are not what Western thought calls "mere appearance," though they are phenomena, effects of language, of people's clinging to language like those monkeys. The trick to living well is not to be wearied by oppositions or let them confuse you. Put all such distinctions on one level: "It is inherent in a thing that from somewhere that's so of it, from somewhere that's allowable of it; of no thing is it not so, of no thing is it unallowable. Therefore when a 'That's it' which deems picks out a stalk from a pillar, a hag from beautiful Xi Shi, things however peculiar or incongruous, the *dao* interchanges them and deems them one. Their dividing is formation, their formation is dissolution; all things whether forming or dissolving in reverting interchange and are deemed to be one." (Z 53)

The point of this passage is not that "all is one," an inane proposition that, as Graham observes, "immediately distinguishes itself from the world which is other than it." I take the point to be that there are no "things," not if that means a being, a thing that is definitely *this* and not also the opposite. That is Plato's idea of a thing. "It is clear that things have some fixed being or essence (*ousia*) of their own. They are not in relation to us and are not made to fluctuate by how they appear to us. They are by themselves, in relation to their own being or essence, which is theirs by nature." That seems to me exactly what Zhuangzi is disclaiming.[23]

Contending thinkers do not really disagree; they divide changes from different standpoints. We are enjoined to waste nothing on disputation. When someone clings to assertions despite changing circumstances, or insists on unconditional validity despite conflicting judgments, he is guilty of contrived affirmation (*wei shi*). If he changes judgments with circumstances and refrains from disputation, he practices adaptive affirmation (*yin shi*). Guo Xiang explains the difference in his early commentary. "If one takes a temporary abode in a thing and then moves on, he will silently understand. If, however, one stops and is confined to one place, he will develop prejudices. Prejudices will result in hypocrisy and hypocrisy will result in many reproaches."[24]

Instead of taking oppositions seriously, we should emulate the *dao,* which is like a pivot, turning freely in all directions. The pivot in its socket achieves effectiveness through what it is not, which is stuck, fixed, rigid. Its capacity to turn freely allows it to respond to incitement from any angle. The pivot is beyond perspective not because it has transcended space and time, but because it can turn in any way and adapt to anything. "Where neither It nor Other finds its opposite is called the pivot (*shu*) of the *dao*. When once the pivot finds its socket it can respond endlessly. What's right is endless. What's wrong is endless too" (Z 53, modified after Kjellberg).

A third line of argument in Zhuangzi's chapter bears some resemblance to Western skepticism. The words *skeptic* and *skepticism* enter Western languages from a Greek word (*skeptikos*) that first meant simply one who inquires. It was later used for the followers of Pyrrho of Elis (circa 360–270 BCE). Pyrrho is supposed to have traveled to India with Alexander, then returned to Elis where he was honored as a philosopher but apparently had no school and left no writings. About a century later, a group around Aenesidemus called themselves *skeptikos* (inquirer) and *ephektikos* (one who suspends judgment), and said they were following Pyrrho, though again we have only the report and no writings. Nearly all we know about ancient skepticism comes from a much later source, Sextus Empiricus (circa 200 CE). He explains the goal and method of skeptical philosophy with a famous parable:

> The Skeptic had the same experience that is related in the story about Apelles the artist. They say that when Apelles was painting a horse, he wished to represent the horse's foam in the painting. His attempt was so unsuccessful that he gave it up and at the same time flung at the picture the sponge with which he wiped the paint off his brush. As it struck the picture, the sponge produced an image of horse's foam. So it was with the Skeptics. They were in hopes of attaining mental tranquility (*ataraxia*), thinking that they could do this by arriving at some rational judgment that would dispel the inconsistencies involved in both appearances and thoughts. When they found this impossible, they withheld judgment. While they were in this state, they made a chance discovery. They found that they were attended by mental tranquility as surely as a body by its shadow.[25]

Ataraxia means indifference, an impassive tranquility these Skeptics consider divine. Other schools of ancient philosophy esteem this tranquility too, and identify *ataraxia* with wisdom. The Skeptics are different in their understanding of what training for *ataraxia* requires. They have given up on philosophy and are ironical about enlightenment. The only "enlightenment" is to realize that there is no enlightened knowledge—that knowledge is empty, a Buddhist might say. Once resigned to ignorance, Skeptics discover the peace of mind they *thought* required wise knowledge. A thoroughgoing Skeptic ceases to trust the world. Outwardly he goes along with whatever is said on anything, while privately suspending judgment on everything.

These Skeptics use a number of arguments to undermine the philosophical idea of knowledge. One is the problem of the criterion. Knowledge requires a criterion; there must be a way to distinguish it from nonknowledge. But to function, the criterion has to be something we *know*; we have to *know* that, say, conditions *a* and *b* are adequate for knowledge. So before we can know, we have to know what knowing is, which shows what a hopeless contradiction the whole idea of knowledge is. Sextus formulates the argument like this:

> If a person prefers one sense-impression to another and one circumstance to another, he does so either without judging and without proof or by judging and offering proof. But he cannot do so without judgment and proof, for then he will be discredited. Nor can he do so even with judgment and proof, for if he judges the impressions, he must at all events use a criterion in judging them. . . . We shall ask for a proof of this criterion, and for this proof another criterion. For the proof always needs a criterion to confirm it, and the criterion needs a proof to show that it is true. . . . And so both the criterion and the proof fall into circular argument, in which both are found to be untrustworthy. . . . It is impossible, then, for a person to give the preference to one sense-impression over another.[26]

Here is a comparable argument in *Zhuangzi*:

> You and I having been made to argue over alternatives, if it is you not I that wins, is it really you who are on to it, I who am not? . . . Whom shall we call in to decide it? If I get someone of your party to decide it, being already of your party how can he decide it? If I get someone of my party to decide it, being already of my party how can he decide it? If I get someone of a party different from either of us to decide it, being already of a different party how can he decide it? If I get someone of the same party as both of us to decide it, being already of the same party as both of us how can he decide it? Consequently you and I and he are all unable to know where we stand, and shall we find someone else to depend on? (Z 60)

Others who compare this chapter of *Zhuangzi* with the Skepticism of Western antiquity find the Chinese arguments to perform much the same function, which is to induce uncertainty but not to disprove knowledge.

Zhuangzi and the Skeptic are said to share the assumption "that people need only be uncertain whether something is good or bad, rather than certain that it is neither, in order to remain unmoved." It seems right that Zhuangzi and the Western Skeptic aim to induce uncertainty, the kind that leaves one reluctant to trust those who claim to know. And it seems right that this collapse of trust is not the same as a dogmatic thesis on the impossibility of knowledge. However, I think these are not ultimately comparable arguments.[27]

Sextus is serious about so-called knowledge in a way Zhuangzi is not. The Skeptic defines knowledge as Plato and the Stoics did. Knowledge is knowing the truth of beings. Plato did not doubt the possibility of such knowledge, though by the time of Sextus it has become doubtful. But the problem the Skeptic raises rests on assumptions about knowledge and truth that it is unlikely Zhuangzi would share. Skeptical arguments like the Criterion or the Ten Modes prove the difficulty of holding two assumptions together: the idea of things-in-themselves, and the idea of truth as vicegerent adequacy or mimetic fealty. The argument of Sextus is that we cannot know whether any supposed knowledge really is knowledge (that is, truly adequate to things in themselves). Assume that knowledge is the truth of the thing (*its* truth), and knowledge becomes unascribable. The Skeptic gets impressive effects and seems to undermine knowledge only when these assumptions are not made explicit and problematic, as they rarely are.

The arguments of Sextus are supposed to impart a consciousness of profound ignorance concerning whether anything is good or bad, right or wrong, so or not. Zhuangzi has a more insidious aim, and is less a skeptic than a nihilist. His arguments leave us uncertain not whether knowledge *exists* but whether it *matters*, whether it is worth contending for. Does knowledge, so-called, count for as much as scholars suppose? Such "knowledge" is not enough, not even the right sort of thing, to make us good at living well. That is not the argument of Western Skeptics, neither Sextus, Descartes, nor Hume. We did not have such a skeptic until Nietzsche, whom Zhuangzi, at this moment and elsewhere, must remind us of. Yet their concurrence is denied. For Nietzsche, as P. J. Ivanhoe observes, "facts are precisely what there is not," whereas he thinks Zhuangzi affirms "the world as it really is." Zhuangzi's sage "not only sees the world as it really is and provides a standard for determining what is and what is not the case, but in 'reflecting' the world, the sage responds to each situation in a highly effective and efficient manner."[28]

I doubt that there a common understanding between Nietzsche and Zhuangzi about exactly what we say when we say "the world as it really is." Presumably it would not occur to Zhuangzi that this "really is" is an essence, a true being with an identity of its own, a finished form to which knowledge must correspond. But that is exactly the metaphysical and epistemological context of the remark Ivanhoe alludes to from Nietzsche: "Against positivism, which halts at phenomena—'There are only *facts*'—I would say: No, facts is precisely what there is not, only interpretations. We cannot establish any fact 'in itself': perhaps it is folly to want to do such a thing." In a separate note from about the same time Nietzsche writes, "Everything of which we become conscious is arranged, simplified, schematized, interpreted through and through. . . . The apparent *inner* world is governed by just the same forms and procedures as the 'outer' world. We never encounter 'facts.'"[29]

"Fact" here seems to mean something nonperspectival, a simple presence, a finished form, an Idea, Platonic or Cartesian. Nietzsche expresses implacable skepticism regarding such things, and it is difficult, at least for me, to imagine Zhuangzi wanting to disagree and stand up for "what really is." In another remark from the same notebook Nietzsche says, "Insofar as the word 'knowledge' has any meaning, the world is knowable; but it is *interpretable* otherwise, it has no meaning behind it, but countless meanings.— 'Perspectivism.'" What Nietzsche here calls "knowledge" Zhuangzi calls "little knowledge" and Plato "opinion." Nietzsche's point—that whatever is "known" (in this perspectival way) might be interpreted otherwise—seems also to be Zhuangzi's point, that what is called "knowledge" in one place may be called "foolishness" or "ignorance" somewhere else. Great knowledge is not a special, sagacious perspective; any perspective becomes petty when one settles into it. Great knowledge is an art of evading capture by perspectives altogether.[30]

The famous butterfly dream passage in this chapter is partly a contribution to these arguments and partly a step beyond them. As this is probably the most famous passage of Chinese philosophy in the West, it is worth a closer look. To understand the butterfly dream we have to begin a page earlier, when Qu Que, a (fanciful) disciple of Kongzi, tells Chang Wuzi what he heard about sages and tried to tell his Master. What he heard is that, "In saying nothing [the sage] says something and in saying something says nothing, and roams beyond the dust and grime." When he repeated this to Kongzi the Master dismissed it as a flight of fancy, but Qu Que thinks there is something to it.

Chang Wuzi is unsurprised by Kongzi's reaction. Expecting him to understand is like expecting eggs from a rooster. Then they begin to discuss dreams. Chang Wuzi first argues that in a dream you do not know you are dreaming. We do not *know* anything when we are dreaming, not even that we are dreaming. He adds that a dream may include its own interpretation, which is, of course, no less a dream, and no less not knowledge. However, there may come a day, perhaps after ten thousand generations, when a great sage arrives and the people undergo an awakening. At that time we would realize that all this "history," which seems so real to us, has been one long dream. This very conversation we are having and this philosophizing may be no more than a dream interpreting a dream. Of course stupid people dismiss the possibility. They know when they are awake. Such people are like the cicada mocking great bird Peng, however. They think they know it all, but have no idea what they do not know.

Shortly after this passage we are back to the subject of dreams, this time Zhuangzi's butterfly dream. Here is what we are told. Zhuang Zhou dreams he is a butterfly. While he dreams, he has no awareness of himself, and does not know that he dreams. Then he wakes up. Now he knows he is awake and is a man, not a butterfly. However, he starts to think. Does he know this supposed knowledge is not nonknowledge? Could it be little knowledge, ordinary, worthless common sense? Might this supposed waking that he "knows" be a dream? What if he wakes from *that* dream? Perhaps after *that* awakening there would be no Zhou, as after his recent waking there is no butterfly. He could be something entirely different (a butterfly, say) dreaming he is a man. People think they know when they are awake and not dreaming, but what if that is just little knowledge, no better than a dream interpreting a dream? What if we *dream* that we "know we are awake" when we *dream* that we wake up? Then we do not *know* we are awake because we are *not* awake, and merely dream that we are not dreaming. Perhaps when we *really* awaken we will know it, but then we might be butterflies.

Zhuangzi's butterfly dream will remind some of the famous passage on dreams and knowledge in Descartes's *Meditations*. At the beginning of his argument Descartes raises the question of the difference between dreams and waking, but only on the last page of the last *Meditation* does he finally explain the difference. His idea is that the evidence of continuity—spatial continuity, when we see where things come from and where they go, and temporal continuity, where everything has a before and after—demonstrates wakefulness. In waking experience these continuities rule, in dreams they fly apart, and that is how we tell the difference.

Descartes never seriously argues that we cannot know this difference. His argument is that we cannot know it by sense perception. We are not guided in distinguishing dreams from waking by the look and feel of things, which is supposedly just as realistic in dreams. Instead, knowing that we are awake and not dreaming is for Descartes a judgment of reason. We distinguish dreams with geometrical judgments about space and continuity. Without reason to judge, the senses are mere survival mechanisms, as they are for animals, and useless for scientific knowledge.

Descartes's skepticism is entirely heuristic; it is false, he knows it is false, but it has a pedagogic utility, or so he thinks. It is a useful fiction, eventually to be replaced by knowledge, which Descartes never seriously doubts he has attained. Zhuangzi is more consistently skeptical. The argument about dreams contributes to the theme of untenable individuation. Every difference blurs into others, even that between waking and dreaming. Taking into account how little knowledge is, the distinctions seem continuous, transformations of each other, without a dramatic difference among them. It is fine to speak of spatiotemporal continuity. But what if we merely dream that this continuity distinguishes dreams? Or what if we *dream* the continuity? Zhuangzi seems to leave such questions interminably open. All our individuation and scrupulous attention to distinctions is a dream, or might as well be for all we know.

Descartes is not the only modern philosopher to raise a question about the difference between dreams and waking. Schopenhauer thought that "the dream-like character of the entire world is really the basis of the entire Kantian philosophy, is its soul and its very greatest achievement." Unlike Descartes, he does not think there is a metaphysical difference between dreaming and waking. Probably encouraged by Leibniz, Schopenhauer flatly denies the assumption that dreams inevitably violate the Cartesian continuities. Dream experience can be just as continuous. "Life and dream are pages of one and the same book," he concludes, and "one is forced to concede to the poets that life is one long dream." Nietzsche concurs, although for him it is not a reluctant concession to disreputable poets but a new idea for philosophy liberated from its obsessive polemic against poetry: "I suddenly woke up in the middle of this dream, but only to the consciousness that I am dreaming and that I *must* go on dreaming lest I perish . . . that among all these dreamers even I, the 'knower,' am dancing my dance; that the one who comes to know is a means of prolonging the earthly dance and thus is one of the masters of ceremony of existence, and that the sublime consistency and interrelatedness of all knowledge may be and will be the highest means to *sustain* the universality of dreaming, the mutual comprehension of all dreamers, and thereby also *the duration of the dream*."[31]

Schopenhauer and Nietzsche seem closer to Zhuangzi than to Descartes in being seriously skeptical not just of the theoretical possibility of distinguishing dreams and waking but of the value or urgency of doing so. There may be differences between what people call waking and dreaming, but they do not add up to a dramatic metaphysical difference like that between Appearance and Reality or Phenomena and Noumena. We have experience of continuity and experience of discontinuity. Why say that one is "true" and the other not? Why like one and dislike the other? Nietzsche subversively suggests we concentrate on how dreams and waking experience are *similar,* to embrace the dreamlike quality of existence, its poetic plasticity, and turn it to an ethical, existential, self- and culture-cultivating purpose.

As for Zhuangzi, by raising the problem whether everyday waking might be a dream, and questioning the common sense that knows it can distinguish dreams from waking, the butterfly dream contributes to the skepticism of the *Qiwulun* chapter. But there is more to it. The text continues with the reflection that there must be some difference between Zhou waking from a dream, when he "knows" he is Zhou and has been dreaming of butterflies, and the great awakening Chang Wuzi alluded to, on the other side of the dream we call history. And of course there is. It is the difference between little knowledge and great knowledge. As we can awaken from a dream, so might we awaken from little knowledge to a more competent awareness as different from petty knowledge as a man from a butterfly.

Knowledge is always limited, whereas the unknown is not. That poses a problem. There is no end to knowledge, always more to know, but there is an end to life. How can pursuing the boundless nourish the bounded? Zhuangzi's third chapter begins with a seriously playful admonition to the lover of knowledge. "Life flows between confines, but knowledge has no confines. If we use the confined to follow after the unconfined, there is danger that the flow will cease; and when it ceases, to exercise knowledge is purest danger" (Z 62). Because at that point we forget what we do not know.

To follow knowledge, to wait upon it, to make knowledge the principle of your practice is dangerous because if you do not know what you do not know you may wear yourself out and come no closer to your goal than when you started. The keenest foresight has horizons. There are places you cannot see even standing on Mount Tai. Knowledge grows from the obscure into clarity, but clarity never penetrates so far as to overcome the obscurity of its birth. We reach again a conclusion of Zhuangzi's second chapter, that what the world calls knowledge is futile, an insight that may itself fairly be called an accomplishment of knowledge of a different order.

Little knowledge thrives in scholarship. Any dispute, any contention, is ipso facto little knowledge. Great knowledge lives among the artisans, not as an equal but a paramount. What seems to impress Zhuangzi about skilled artifice is its responsiveness to change. The artisan's perception is unencumbered by conventional thinking or scholarly baggage. Both Zhuangzi and the *Daodejing* suggest that life can be lived like that. There is an art of response, an art of replies, of resonance, a *dao*-art of viably changing with changes. A sage response is active and knowing, not fearful or resentful reaction, the response focused on the specificity of the stimulus, responding precisely to the event and its changes, and not to what we fear, presume, or overlook (Deleuze calls such a response "counter-actualization," and identifies it with the Stoic sage).[32]

I mentioned the passage from Zhuangzi's third chapter that relates a conversation between Cook Ding and Lord Wenhui. This cook has a way of carving meat that is beyond technique. He has not had to sharpen his knife in nineteen years. When he works he does not use his eyes, only his spirit. He follows the heavenly patterns (*tian li*) in the flesh. The space between bones and ligaments becomes ample and easily negotiated. Meat falls off his knife like clods from a spade. Having listened to his explanation Wenhui comments, "I have heard the words of a cook and learned how to care for life!" What has he learned? The way of optimal effectiveness, the importance of nurturing vitality, the need to care for himself before trying to govern others.

Zhuangzi's cook is an image of mastery for the Chinese martial arts, although they are a much later development. That cook responds to the obstacle before him as the martial artist (*xiashi*) does an opponent. He does not use his eyes but his *qi*. What seems fast to others is to him slow and clumsy. There is so much time, and the adversary's moves are so obvious that an effortless evasion can evolve into a devastating response. A Qing dynasty martial arts author writes: "The book [*Zhuangzi*] says: 'strike in the big hollows, guide the knife through the big openings.' Why does it say so? Because when Cook Ding cut up oxen 'he no longer saw the whole ox.' I say it is the same with hand combat. Why? Because I am looking for my opponent's soft points, acupuncture points, and those forbidden to strike as I engrave them in my mind's eye. For this reason, the moment I lift my hand, I am able to target my opponent's empty points, and strike at his acupuncture points, 'no longer seeing the whole person.'" Another martial arts author, in a Preface (1784) to the *Hand Combat Classic,* also looks to Zhuangzi for images of his art: "The subtlety of the method's application depends entirely on internal strength (*nei li*). It cannot be exhausted by words. Like an old hunchback who catches cicadas. [*Zhuangzi,* chap. 19] . . . When one's resolution is not distracted, when his spirit is concentrated, he will begin to acquire the agility of 'mind conceiving, hands responding.' At this point there is sure to be no straining of muscles nor exposure of bones."[33]

A connection between Daoism and the Chinese martial arts is not as ancient as legend suggests, but there is something to it, as we can see where they have common ground, for instance in the so-called *daoyin* exercises, which *Zhuangzi* explicitly mentions. *Daoyin* means "guided stretching," and is explained as the art of making joints flexible. Gentler than gymnastics and involving more than mere stretching, not least training in breathing, no one modern English word conveys exactly what these exercises are. Yoga is one comparison, as is taiji, though taiji is a much later development. *Daoyin* exercises are illustrated on Han tombs where an important early *Daodejing* was also found. However, the "*dao*" in *daoyin* is not the *dao* of Daoism; it is a different word, a different pronunciation, and, in modern Chinese, written with a different character. Nevertheless it seems likely that the author of the *Zhuangzi* Inner Chapters followed this or other inner cultivation practices, and *daoyin* practice is explicitly alluded to in chapter 15: "To huff and puff, exhale and inhale, blow out the old and draw in the new, do the 'bear-hang' and the 'bird stretch,' interested only in a long life—such are the tastes of the practitioners of the *daoyin* exercises, the nurturers of the body, Peng Zu's ripe-old-agers" (Z 265).[34]

There are additional references to breath and posture discipline in the *Inward Training* (*Nei ye*), a proto-Daoist text of the fourth century BCE:

> Be not joyous, be not angry,
> just let a balanced and aligned breathing fill your chest.

When your body is not aligned,
the inner power will not come.

. . .

Align your body, assist the inner power,
then it will gradually come on its own.

When the four limbs are aligned
and the blood and vital breath are tranquil,
unify your awareness, concentrate your mind,
and then your eyes and ears will not be overstimulated,
and the far-off will seem to be close at hand.

A modern Chinese editor of this work comments, "Inward training means inner achievement. It refers to the practice (*gongfu*) by which one cultivates and nourishes the inner mind and preserves vital essence and vital energy. . . . While the author of this text points out the importance of proper drinking, eating, and physical movement, the most basic and emphatic point of this practice lies completely within the inner mind. Therefore it is called *Inward Training*." Like the *daoyin* exercises, these are techniques for health and spiritual enhancement with no connection to martial arts. But the theory and practice of so-called inner boxing (*yiquan*) are a development of this Daoist inner training, a spiritualization of supremely effective martial practice. We shall revisit the intersection of martial arts and Chinese philosophy in Chapter 4, when Zen discovers its affinity with the martial arts.[35]

References to artisans or masters of notable skill occur many times in the later parts of *Zhuangzi*. Chapter 19 mentions no fewer than five such figures. Kongzi interviews a hunchback who is enormously skilled at catching cicadas. How does he do it? He practices concentration. The Master draws the moral: "Intent sustained undivided will verge on the daemonic" (Z 138). Artisan Chui draws perfect circles without a compass. He attributes his skill to his power to forget. While traveling, Kongzi sees a man in dangerous waters above a fall, and tries to save him. Turns out he swims at ease in the treacherous current. How? He accommodates to the water and does not make the water accommodate him. The extraordinary works of Carpenter Qing are the fruit of concentration, dispelling thoughts of the outer world, becoming imperceptible, closing the gap between nature in him and nature in the material. Horseman Dongye does the opposite in driving his horses, and they all die. In chapter 22, a buckle-maker's skill is said to come from negligence. In chapter 31, a sage fisherman tells Kongzi that his teaching merely augments the disorder it is supposed to abate. He is like a man who fears his shadow, so runs, or despises his footprints, so walks faster. The solution is to rest in the shade. Give more care to yourself, learn to nourish your vitality, and forget about benevolence and ceremonies.

These examples allude to a knowledge of the sage that resembles skill or art more than scholarship. This sagacious knowledge does not take one beyond nature. It is an intensification of our physical being in the world, of our *qi* and its resonant ecology. François Jullien suggests that for Zhuangzi wisdom is a matter of freeing oneself "from all internal obstructions and focalizations in order to recover the communicative [that is, resonant] aptitude of the *qi*." This aptitude must be kept alert, unencumbered, free to respond, inventive, evolving, unobstructed. To be constantly flowing (as in the movements of taiji), never stymied or forestalled, is the way to remain sharp and effective, swimming at ease in treacherous currents.[36]

Is it not an art to find the unimpeded path? The art of the *dao*, artfully changing with changes, is not a technique on par with spinning silk or carpentry. Those arts are obviously limited, feeding one side of life only. Zhuangzi dreams the ultimate art, an art of the unobstructed path, which reaches perfection when one greets change with gratitude, responding gracefully and adequately without having to do much at all.

In chapters 5 and 6 we encounter examples of extraordinary detachment. For instance, these words from a man so hideous that he frightens people: "Wonderful! how the maker of things is turning me into this crumpled thing. He hunches me and sticks out my back, the five pipes to the spine run up above my head, my chin hides down in my navel, my shoulders are higher than my crown, the knobbly bone in my neck points up in the sky. The energies of *yin* and *yang* are all awry." A companion asks if he hates it. "No, why should I hate it? Little by little he [the maker of things] will borrow my left arm to transform it into a cock, and it will be why I am listening to a cock-crow at dawn. Little by little he'll borrow my right arm to transform it into a crossbow, and it will be why I am waiting for a roasted owl for my dinner. Little by little he'll borrow and transform my buttocks into wheels, my spirit into a horse, and they'll be there for me to ride, I'll never have to harness a team again! Besides, to get life is to be on time and to lose it is to be on course; be content with the time and settled on the course, and sadness and joy cannot find a way in. This is what of old was called 'loosening the bonds'; and whoever cannot loosen himself other things bind still tighter" (Z 88).

The detached attitude bears some resemblance to the ancient Stoics; for instance, Epictetus, "Never say about anything, 'I have lost it,' but only 'I have given it back.' Is your child dead? It has been given back." Stoics were great believers in the rationality of the universe, convinced, with Heraclitus, of a divine fire penetrating everything, a fiery *logos* that orders all things for the best. All things happen under the dispensation of this divine rationality. The universe is an organism and every part makes a purposeful contribution. A Stoic therefore accepts events gladly, firm in the knowledge that whatever happens is ultimately reasonable and good. Stoic theory defines *virtue* as a "consistently rational disposition," even identifying it with "reason itself, consistent, firm, and unwavering." In an argument Kant reprises in the eighteenth century, Stoics say that only virtue is good without qualification; nothing else is of any value except in collaboration with virtue. This virtuous rationality is a kind of art, combining practical wisdom, justice, moderation, and courage. They define all of these virtues in terms of their master virtue of knowledge; for instance, courage is "knowledge of things that should be endured." The summit (*telos*) of the sagacious life is "to live in the continuous use of exact knowledge of those things that happen naturally."[37]

A Stoic vests nothing in the outer world, and nothing external can harm him. All that he cares for is inside and inviolable. What is truly up to us, determined solely by choice and will, is our *prohairesis,* the volition or willing we put into all we do. Everything else, being external, is liable to compulsion, but the freedom of volition is unlimited. "My leg you will fetter, but my volition not even Zeus himself has power to overcome." The reason is because nothing can affect volition except another volition, and my volition is most essentially me, untouchable by another will. Stoics develop Socrates's thought that the cause of evil is mistaken judgment. The mother of all mistakes is to take something external to be of value. Everything external is worthless. Learning to really live that knowledge liberates one from the irrationality and unpredictability of circumstance and fate. One is untouchable, attaining the tranquility Stoics identify with happiness. "Wherever you may be," Epictetus promises, "whatever you may be doing, you will feel no pain, no anger, no compulsion, no hindrance, but you will pass your life in tranquility and in freedom from every disturbance."[38]

A Stoic need not be indifferent to the suffering of others, yet he cannot but regard their unhappiness as the price people pay for the mistake of investing in external things, and he should not let their suffering make him suffer too. Epictetus encourages one to remember the transitory nature of everything external. Do not allow the enjoyment of a thing to become a serenity-destroying attachment. Preserve your *ataraxia,* your divine indifference. "Purify your judgments, for fear lest something that is not your own may be fastened to them, or grown together with them, and may give you pain when it is torn loose."[39]

This Stoicism somewhat resembles the detachment Zhuangzi depicts. Both esteem flexibility, being able to adapt to anything. Both teach against becoming invested in things, reluctant to let them slip away. Stoics say we should detach from everything that is not up to us, which is to say everything external. Stoic detachment withdraws from anything risky, uncertain, or beyond the control of reason. But this detachment is one-sided. From another perspective Stoicism intensifies attachment. Perhaps the Stoic is not attached to externals, but his attachment to himself is overwhelming. Attachment to your will is fine on their account. That is your true self, your rational substance. Zhuangzi expects detachment to go further. It must include that will, that self, and its *prohairesis.* Forget about what is up to you. Deliberation and calculation are not the best, most effective ways to govern life. In fact, they seem shot through with futility. It is not attachment to externals that is the problem; it is attachment plain and simple, including especially fondness for a "true self," something substantial that sets you apart from everyone else.[40]

Detachment itself can become an attachment. One may acquire a name for oneself as a paragon of detachment, "a real Stoic." Detachment from self and selfish desire is then dangerously incomplete. In chapter 6 Kongzi and his favorite disciple Yan Hui discuss the behavior of Meng Sun at his mother's funeral. He cried without tears, showed mourning without feeling anything. His body can be afflicted but not his mind. He has become indifferent to change, and even does not know whether he changes or remains the same. Kongzi says Meng Sun is really awake, while he and Yan are asleep and dreaming. Yet there is a problem. Meng Sun is attached to his detachment. He does not mind people seeing detachment in his countenance. Arranging the funeral and seeming to mourn reveals Meng Sun still attaching significance to change. He can bear the death of a parent but he cannot bear to avoid the ceremony others expect. He could not just forget about the funeral, fail to show up, or show up playing gay music. So he is stuck there, attached to his detachment.[41]

This problem arises only for a spiritual *junzi*, a virtuoso self-cultivator and lover of enlightened knowledge. The problem is introduced at the beginning of *Zhuangzi*, in a passage from chapter 1 about the magician Liezi, who has learned to ride the wind. "Though he manages to avoid walking he still relies on something. If he could chariot the norms of heaven and earth and ride the changes in the six mists to wander the inexhaustible, then what would there be to rely on?" (Z 44, Kjellberg). Liezi is not entangled in affairs, not stuck in one place, yet still he depends on something, the invisible, formless wind. He is stuck, as Meng Sun is stuck, on his way to enlightenment.

This problem of getting stuck comes up again in chapter 4, where we meet a cheerful hunchback named Zhili Shu. He knows his deformity makes him ugly, and the ugliness keeps him impoverished and unmarried, but it also makes him useless for the army and corvée labor. So his life is a lesson in the usefulness of the useless. It is impressive that Zhili Shu can sustain this attitude and enjoy life despite his deformity, but he still depends on something—that virtue, that inner power of his, which he is proud of. He is admonished: "If you make a cripple of the power in you, you can do better still" (Z 74). He is a virtuoso, but he would go further if he could forget about virtuosity, and forget his cheerfulness, which may be merely another face of egoism. Forget all that and let wisdom return to foolishness, brilliance to dimness, and the adept to the origin, "vanishing into things and leaving no trace." Failing that, Zhili Shu is one more obstructed spiritual *junzi* like Meng Sun and Liezi, stuck in success on the way to enlightenment.[42]

We see the necessity of a double detachment—detachment from others, not being stuck, fixed, or unyielding; and detachment from detachment, overcoming a preoccupation with enlightenment, getting over what you know, learning to live knowing what is not known and what not to do. Cultivate indifference to your long-cultivated indifference, so that especially not *that* becomes an obstacle. Detachment means stopping. Meng Sun stopped feeling grief for a parent, Liezi stopped relying on his feet, Zhili Shu stopped caring about his hideous appearance. But stopping comes to nothing without the step that completes the transformation, which is to stop stopping: "You have heard of using wings to fly. You have not yet heard of flying by being wingless; you have heard of using knowledge to know, not of using no knowledge to know. . . . The blessed stop stopping. Not stopping means galloping while you sit. . . . This is the transformation of ten thousand things, the secret of the ancient sages" (Z 69, modified after Kjellberg). Elaborating in his influential commentary, Guo Xiang says: "Having no deliberate mind . . . [means] not only to discard right and wrong, but also to discard this discarding. They are discarded and again discarded, until no-discarding is reached; only then do we have nothing discarded and nothing not-discarded, and right and wrong vanish of themselves."[43]

This double detachment is the "twofold" referred to in the Tang dynasty Daoist cult of the Twofold Mystery. The founder, Cheng Xuanying, says, "Adepts must first discard all desires, then proceed to discard the level of no-desires. Only then can they truly accomplish twofold discarding of the two sides and wondrously merge with the *dao* of Middle Oneness. Beings and ego looked upon in equalized fashion, mental states and wisdom both forgotten—when someone makes such a state his principle of government, then everything will be well ordered." Sima Chengzhen, a later teacher of this school, admonishes those who would practice the Daoist technique of sitting in oblivion: "Guard stillness without getting attached to emptiness."[44]

The Inner Chapters end as they began, with a tall tale. The Emperor of the North Sea and the Emperor of the South Sea are friendly with the Emperor of the Central Sea, whose name is Chaos (*huntun*). They pity their friend because unlike them, he has no apertures, no openings. So they decide to help him. Every day they make a hole, and on the seventh day Chaos died. Why did he die? With apertures come differentiation; with differentiation comes fixed form, specialization, the expectation of certainty, and all the accomplishments, such as they are, of little knowledge. Chaos lost his chaos, the virtual source of his virtue. He lost his chaotic capacity for limitless change, and therefore the changes killed him.

A Know-Nothing Polemic?

The Marquis de Sade exploits a paradox of Western rationalism when he challenges his enlightened readers to explain how it is possible for the depravities he depicts not to be natural. How can anything that happens not be natural, especially if you are an atheist and materialist? I was reminded of that paradox (if it is one) when I began to read Daoist works. How can anyone *fail* to follow the *dao*? Why is such accord so difficult for us and so easy for everything else?[45]

There is the hint of an answer in the second chapter of the *Zhuangzi,* where the lighting up of *is* and *is not* is said to be the reason why the *dao* is flawed (Z 54). The reason seems, then, to have something to do with language, which is impossible without a wider fabric of norms and conventions. The argument is developed in chapter 11, where Laozi makes a fanciful appearance. We learn that our difficulty in being natural arises from habits ingrained with language and morality, although that begs the question why those are not as natural as anything else. A deeper cause seems to be the heart-mind itself, its singular virtuosity. The human heart is more akin to the *dao* than any of the ten thousand things. Like the *dao* this heart is profound, remote, and mysterious. "Be very careful not to meddle with man's heart (*renxin*). . . . When hot it is a scorching flame, when cold it is congealed ice, it is so swift that between a glance up and a glance down it has twice gone right around the four seas. At rest it is still from the depths, in motion it takes to the air on the course laid down by Heaven. Is there anything as eager and proud and impossible to tie down as the heart of man?" (Z 212).

Chapter 32 reprises the argument, which it puts in Kongzi's mouth. "The human heart (*renxin*) is more dangerous than steep cliffs and more difficult to know than heaven." He goes on to speak of the problem raised for our knowledge of others. The argument also appears in the Inner Chapters, where this fluency in changes is singled out as the specifically human distinction. "As a human, you can change ten thousand times without ever reaching the limit" (Z 86, Kjellberg). We are in the world but do not have to be quite as helplessly of the world as everything else, tied to a form, limited by an essence. Our essence is to be without essence, which is mysterious, and makes us daimonic, virtually as virtual as the *dao*.[46]

A Ming dynasty comment explains that while human beings "are no more than one among the ten thousand things," they are "the most miraculous, sensitive, and efficacious (*ling*) among them, for they receive the entirety of the great *dao* as their human nature, which controls their bodies. . . . To know how the human and heavenly virtuosities merge into one is the ultimate knowledge." In our time, Tang Junyi observes how "the discussion of human nature (*renxing*) in Chinese thought has had as its one common feature a reference to this capacity for boundless change as wherein the special nature of the human lies. This is the human's spiritual nature (*lingxing*) that differs from the fixity and lack of spirituality in the nature of other things." The problem with the human heart is not its agile motility though, which is in fact a resource, and makes wisdom possible. The problem is stubbornness, clinging attachment, the perverse desire to be an obstacle to change, the heart's tendency, in Benjamin Schwartz's words, "to arrogate to itself the attributes of a fully closed off, fully individuated entity." A Platonic thing. Zhuangzi calls such a heart *chengxin,* fixed mind, prejudiced mind, the socially constructed self, and source of all error.[47]

That ambivalent potency of the heart helps to understand Zhuangzi's advice (put again in Kongzi's mouth) that we abandon plans and fast the mind (Z 68). What separates us from the rest of nature also points the way back. Because of our heart we can recklessly deviate from the *dao,* yet because this heart is tenuous and can be stilled and made empty, the recovery of authentic personhood is also possible. The later *Huainanzi* offers a variation on the argument. Nonhuman things are "separate and not interconnected, differentiated as the myriad things." As such, none can "return to their Ancestor," "the Great One" (*tai yi*). People are different. "In antiquity, at the Great Beginning, human beings came to life in Non-being and acquired a physical form in Being. Having a physical form, [they] came under the control of things. But those who can return to that from which they were born, as if they had not yet acquired a physical form, are called Genuine. The Genuine are those who have not yet begun to differentiate from the Great One." That potential distinguishes humans from nonhumans; its actuality distinguishes sages from ordinary people.[48]

Zhuangzi discusses the character of the sage in chapter 5. A sage has great potency or virtue (*de*), which makes him indifferent to form, an indifference Zhuangzi calls true forgetfulness. Such forgetfulness means changes cease to trouble him. He looks at forms but does not see something complete, finished, fully present; he sees phases and evolution. You are given a body by Heaven; if it is human, accept a human form. But you do not have to have a human essence (*qing*). That is a chain around your neck, obstructing transformation. Zhuangzi's sidekick and straight man, the incredulous Huizi, asks how people can fail to have their essence; if they are human, must they not have human essence? Zhuangzi explains: "Judging 'That is, that's not' is what I mean by 'the essence of man.' What I mean by being without essence is that the man does not inwardly wound the person by likes and dislikes, that he constantly goes by the spontaneous and does not add anything to the process of life." Huizi remains perplexed. How can one refrain from helping life along? "Do not inwardly wound yourself by likes and dislikes," is the reply (Z 82). "Likes and dislikes are failings of the heart" (Z 266).

If you are human be human and flock with others, but do not let their right and wrong get to you. To regard something as right or wrong is to be stuck in a perspective and not see that something else is no less right or wrong. *Huainanzi* again seems to make the *Zhuangzi*'s conclusion explicit. "If you take the sage as a standard . . . there can never be a 'right' and a 'wrong.'" That is because of what the sage knows. There is no difference between right and wrong for anyone who knows how to use well, or respond appropriately, to anything. "There is no [distinction] of noble and base among things. If one values things in accordance with what ennobles them, there is nothing that is not noble." Key to this art of ennobling response is mastery of nonaction. The sage becomes one body with everything under heaven. When he is still, it is the stillness of *yin;* when he is active it is the activity of *yang,* a spontaneous response to changes without self-serving intentionality (Z 265).[49]

This potent potential is a fruit of wise knowledge, the great knowledge earlier alluded to. Some of the Outer and Mixed chapters seem to say that a sage is beyond knowledge altogether, but that only means beyond somebody's so-called knowledge. Zhuangzi's sage is sage in his knowledge. Counterstatements that may be cited to this valuation of knowledge are likely to come from a know-nothing polemic mostly confined to chapters 8 through 13. Chapter 8 declares that what is long by nature should not be shortened nor the short lengthened. Tools and their skill, which exist to alter things, should be forbidden. The argument resembles that of Yang Zhu against Confucian education. In chapter 9 the work of those who train horses, turn pots, and carve timber is declared aberrant. The polish, the finesse, the perfection of their work is perverse. Horse trainers make horses sly.[50]

Apparently no one hungered for knowledge till so-called sages showed up, nor were there thieves or usurpers to confuse people. Sages brought on all of that with their so-called knowledge. So successful were these sages in duping people that today no king rules without them. Chapter 10 then attacks those rulers who crave knowledge and neglect the *dao.* Knowledge produces confusion; the more people know the more confused everything becomes. What is supposed to be a source of order (namely, knowledge) becomes a source of disorder and neglects the true source, which is presumably beyond knowledge. In chapter 12 the Yellow Emperor has lost his mysterious pearl. He sends Knowledge to find it, without success. Then he sends Nothing, who brings it home.

It is not entirely clear what the target of criticism is. It is said there should be no boats or bridges. Artisans are criticized for carving ritual vessels. Yet we are also told that people of uniform integrity (*tong de*) weave cloth and till land. Why this distinction between textiles and nautics? Is a loom not an ingenious machine? No cunning required to entice silk from a worm? The rant against art and knowledge is over by chapter 16, when something more recognizable from the Inner Chapters appears. Knowledge is firmly linked to *dao* and *de*, and sagehood identified as its accomplishment. Sages do not make a display of knowledge, like a scholar. They take no pains to ornament their knowledge with eloquence. But they definitely know something big. Plainly it is not what Confucians teach, but how to characterize it is less clear. The problem is not that the knowledge is ineffable, but that it is circumstantial and not theoretical or formulaic, redoubling the usual difficulty of linguistic description for the arts.

In chapter 22, Knowledge wanders north to ask Nonaction about the *dao*. He gets no answer, Nonaction knows nothing about it. Next Knowledge asks Wild Witless, who says he used to know all about the *dao* but has forgotten everything. Finally Knowledge asks the Yellow Emperor, who tells him that to know the *dao* one must not think, to comply with the *dao* one must do nothing, and to obtain the *dao* one must go nowhere. This is, of course, a superficial explanation. In an ironic gesture of self-disqualification the Emperor paraphrases *Daodejing* 56: Those who say do not know, those who know do not say; which he follows with a paraphrase of *Daodejing* 48: Pursue knowledge and you enlarge daily; pursue *dao* and you diminish daily. No knowledge (*bu zhi*) is said to be more profound than knowledge. Are we back to the know-nothing Primitivist? I would say we have returned to the thinking of the Inner Chapters, and the distinction between big and little knowledge. There is a sagacious knowledge worth mastering, but it is an unconventional knowing the knowledge of knowing-not (*zhi bu zhi zhi zhi*).

In chapter 25 knowledge and language are said to be confined to worldly things and declared incompetent when it comes to the ultimate source. That a cock crows, that a dog barks—these things can be known; they belong to what Zhuangzi's first chapter calls petty knowledge. But words and discursive knowledge cannot penetrate ultimate things, like infinitude, origins, and fate. The patterns of transformation are regular but endless, and must defeat the most careful analysis. "If we examine something for the root from which it grew, its past is limitless; if we search for its offshoots, their future never stops" (Z 153). Zhuangzi wonders why "people value what their knowledge can reach, but do not know how to rely on what they do not know to get to know what is beyond the reach of their knowledge." A sage does not have this limitation. He knows how to use what he knows is not known to avoid getting stuck in what little knowledge knows.[51]

Vanishing into Things

I do not know what to say about the know-nothing polemic except that it is attributed to a so-called Primitivist among the later "school of Zhuangzi," and seems discordant with the more nuanced view of the Inner Chapters and elsewhere in the later chapters. This way of evading the problem was not available to traditional readers, who did not take the modern view that *Zhuangzi* is a work of many hands. They felt obliged to explain how such seemingly antagonistic evaluations of knowledge were part of one sage teaching. Perhaps the most notable result is Guo Xiang's Jin dynasty *Zhuangzi* commentary, the earliest one we have. The hermeneutical problems he encountered in explaining this work led him to create one of the most re-markable products of Chinese speculation. One hesitates to use the word "metaphysics," but there are in Guo ideas strongly reminiscent of Plotinus, Leibniz, and Hegel. Let us take a look at some implications for the idea of knowledge.[52]

A principle for Guo is that there is no causation, no determination, no conditioning of one being by another. Nothing is made to be as it is by some-thing else; everything is spontaneously self-so, from itself, its activity un-folding without external determination, like monads in Leibniz. "Ultimately there is no thing that makes things what they are"; "there is nothing that generates things . . . all things simply generate themselves." He thinks through the implications of this idea with impressive rigor. One result is a new understanding of *dao*. All things are self-so. There is simply *nothing required* to make things as they are. And that's what the *dao* is: nothing. "The *dao* has no power. When the text [*Zhuangzi*] says, 'They attained it from the *dao*,' this is merely to show that they spontaneously attained it." Another result is this thesis on creativity: "Only after you understand that the forms form themselves can you understand what is meant by creation. . . . All agency vanishes. Thus, creation is without any lord or master and each being creates itself."[53]

Human beings are no less *causa sui* than anything else, except we have a tendency to dampen spontaneous *ziran* responses and react instead to the traces (*ji*) of *ziran* activity in other things, acting not from ourselves but in reaction to traces of another's activity. Like slaves in Plato's cave, who deem it knowledge to react to shadows, we think we have knowledge when we know these traces. This attachment to traces is not a cognitive error. It is cognition itself *as* error, a view we also find in Nietzsche. There is no superior cognition that rises above our aberrant nature and finally gets things right. Knowledge at its best cannot penetrate *ziran* process, which will not stop long enough to constitute an "object." Every "object" is a phase in a network that has already transformed by the time we react to its traces. Nothing endures; all that is left are these traces. It is these that language names. Cognition is recognizing what names name. But those names are artifacts of perspective, conveying an empty image of what has come and gone.[54]

The alternative to such futile cognition is to vanish into things. Brook Ziporyn translates Guo's use of the character *ming* as "to vanish into." In a more prosaic context this *ming* might mean dark, obscure, distant, or hard to see. In Guo it is a transitive verb ("to darken" something), but used with reference not to the darkness endured by a luminous agent but to agency in eclipse, the moon vanishing into the luminous sun. To vanish into things is to interact with them without obstructive, forceful desires, or "self." To achieve this trackless mind is to overcome the mind, to reach no-mind (*wu xin*). The heart is not extinguished, only become imperceptible. Knowing, cognition, consciousness—these appear when vanishing stumbles. Awareness means something does not fit. No one is aware of comfortable shoes. "Cognition is born out of a loss of proper match, but it is destroyed in vanishing into the ultimate limits. Vanishing into the ultimate limits means to allow one's utmost determinacy to run its course while adding not the slightest fraction of an ounce to it. . . . This is the secret of nourishing life."[55]

It is also the secret of *wu wei,* though we can no longer say *wu wei effectiveness,* since for Guo efficacy is precisely what does not exist. We do *wu wei* when we respond *ziran*. Nonaction means not reacting to traces. Sagacious nonactivity fits and forgets, flowing from self-rightness ("to do as one does") and ignoring traces. "To do as one does is the true activity; to do this true activity is nonactivity." The way to do nothing is to refrain from reaction. *Wu wei* intentionality is creative, not representational; inventive action that does not merely react to the action of another (Nietzsche again, and Spinoza). This nonaction is disengaged from efficacy, though it retains what we thought we wanted efficacy *for,* namely, well-being and harmony.

"Only he who vanishes into things and follows their vast transformations is able to be unconditioned and always unobstructed. . . . Having no right and wrong, blending them into oneness, we can ride on the transformations and allow the changes to proceed, encountering all things without fear."[56]

Such fearlessness is not, as in Stoicism, a result of scrupulous cognition. It is not the experience of standing before a thing and knowing what it is in itself. We have to overcome the limitations that make us think in terms of *is* and *is not,* or in terms of boundaries and forms rather than relations and evolution. Instead of *knowing* things (knowing their names and how to talk about them) we become resonant and spontaneously change with them, assimilating to their economy, losing fear of loss and inheriting joy:

> The sage has no self. . . . Thus he penetrates all things, ribald and shady and grotesque and strange as they are, and makes them one; he lets all their differences each rest in what it rests in, and all the different people not lose what they affirm. Thus he does not use his self on things, but lets all the ten thousand things use their own uses on themselves. When all things use their own uses, which is right and which is wrong? Thus even the perversions of dissipation, the strange and twisted differences of things are curvingly followed along with and given over to their own uses. Hence although there are ten thousand differences among their uses, each illuminates itself in perfect distinctiveness.[57]

We may wonder whether knowledge is destined to reaction and confined to traces. Is not knowledge as self-so as anything else? What is knowledge when it is self-so, and not merely reacting to traces? Guo says, "The eye's ability to see does not come from its knowing how to see; we see without knowing how to see, we know without knowing how to know, and this is what makes it self-so." Knowledge *ziran* sees through traces and vanishes into things. Guo explains what Zhuangzi calls the "mind bent on knowledge" (Z 62) as that of a person motivated by love of fame or victory striving to satisfy wishes. The knowledge of such a mind is petty and calculating, and Guo says it "can be extinguished by vanishing into one's own limits." Not finding a special, privileged perspective but overcoming perspectives, which are precisely what generate the misleading appearance of cause and effect, right and wrong, essence and accident.[58]

Zhuangzi's great knowledge is knowledge self-so, and is, as Guo explains, a kind of knowing-not. "Knowing does not know by someone 'doing' knowing. Knowing is spontaneously knowing; it is self-so. As self-so knowing, knowing is not a result of knowing, is unknown, is itself a kind of non-knowing." One knows what not to deem, what not to value, what not to individuate or distinguish, also what is not settled, and not known. But the knowledge is not merely negative, since it seeks the network, the relationships, to adjust and vanish into things instead of trying to stand aloof and represent them. What knowledge seems to know when it is self-so is how to overcome the self, see through boundaries, elude perspectives, and not get stuck in names, which is, as I have suggested, most of Zhuangzi's distinction between big and little knowledge. Little knowledge is everyday trace-cognition, settled in perspective. Big knowledge ceases to react to traces and vanishes into things, of which we have the following account from *Zhuangzi*, chapter 33:

> Within yourself, no fixed positions:
> Things as they take shape disclose themselves.
> Moving, be like water,
> Still, be like a mirror,
> Respond like an echo.
> Blank! as though absent:
> Quiescent! as though transparent.
> Be assimilated to them and you harmonize,
> Take hold of any of them and you lose. (Z 281)

Song dynasty poet Su Dongpo also writes of this vanishing and its productivity:

> When Wen Tong painted bamboo
> He saw bamboo and not himself.
> Not simply unconscious of himself,
> Trance-like, he left his body behind.
> His body was transferred into bamboo,
> Creating inexhaustible freshness.
> Zhuangzi is no longer in this world,
> So who can understand such concentration?[59]

Haiming Wen renders Guo's *ming* as "oblique unification." Deleuze and Guattari write of *becoming imperceptible,* and sound almost Chinese: "One has suppressed in oneself everything that prevents us from slipping between things and growing in the midst of things." John Dewey gives a similar account when he describes "the uniquely distinguishing feature of aesthetic experience," as having "no distinction of self and object." Experience is aesthetic "in the degree in which organism and environment cooperate to institute an experience in which the two are so fully integrated that each disappears." Like Guo, Nietzsche regarded consciousness and quotidian knowledge as a secondary reaction to things, one that tells more about our own body (its health or sickness) than the thing we think we know. Consciousness, memory, habit, nutrition—these are all corporeal reactions to environmental traces. They may promote survival but are useless for knowledge. There is virtue in the negligent capacity to forget about traces. Such negligence is a sign of health. You metabolize your experience and have done with it. You do not ponder the past, linger on defeats, nurse grudges, or cultivate bitter weeds of resentment. This forgetting is not repression but overcoming, working through experience, which does not cling or clamor for deferred reaction. The joy Guo associates with vanishing is the joyful wisdom of Nietzsche's "gay science," joy in the becoming of knowledge, not in a finished result.[60]

In selecting Ziporyn's rendition of *ming* as the title of this book I do not mean to refer specifically to Guo or even to Daoism at the expense of other traditions. It seems to me that Guo is not singular in his thought on this point—that "vanishing into things" epitomizes the accomplishment of sage knowledge as understood in most of the Chinese thought I discuss. The kernel idea is the loss of "self," which is understood not substantively, as an entity, but in terms of desire and the folly of individuation. Whether we think of overcoming desire, or acquiring an appropriate discipline of desire, the point is to lose stultifying confinement to a perspective. Wise knowledge is inconspicuous, a self-eclipse, deftly vanishing into things. A sage is not renowned for prodigies. He acts imperceptibly, before things take visible shape, and his influence is unknown. So too the greatest generals. They are not heroes of conspicuous glory. They are so good at the art of war that they seldom have to fight. We shall examine the *wu wei* logic of that argument in Chapter 3.

Physicians also have this unseen efficacy, or at least the best of them do. The Warring States period *Pheasant Cap Master* (*Heguanzi*) tells of a celebrated physician who, as it turns out, comes from a whole family of physicians, and he, the one everybody has heard of, is least talented of all: "My oldest brother, with a disease, watches the spirits and dispels them before they take shape. Therefore his name does not go beyond the family. When my second brother cures a disease, he attends to the fine hair on the skin.

Therefore his name does not go beyond the neighborhood. Someone like [me] acupunctures people's veins, prescribes them drugs and herbs, and cuts skin and flesh . . . and his name is heard among the feudal lords." The moral *Pheasant Cap Master* draws is that if those who would rule others use them as the older brothers do, people are not even aware that they are being used, and collaborate believing they are doing what they spontaneously want to do. Thus do the wise "rule [people] without name, order them without shape. The completion of the utmost success those below him call *ziran*."[61]

Engineering Spontaneity—Technics and the *Dao*

Joseph Needham observes that probably no country in the world has so many legends about heroic engineers as China. The usual word for technical artifice is *gong*. This usage is medieval. The oldest word is *jiang*, attested in the oracle bones (the oldest source for Chinese writing), where the character shows a man holding a carpenter's square. Under the empire the greater part of artisans were employed or supervised by authorities of the central government. Imperial workshops were apparently never staffed by slaves. Scholars tend to disdain artisans, slighting them for lack of eloquence in speaking of their art, though some rebuke the indolent literati, like this third century CE author: "To discredit extraordinary ability in other people with light words is like someone who would impose his wisdom on the affairs of the universe instead of handling the endless difficulties in accord with the *dao*. This is the path to destruction. . . . Wise rulers pay no attention to [eloquence] and base their judgment on tests." That peremptory practicality may always have been the opinion of the people, as popular interest in technical knowledge attests when print made it available to anyone who could read. Compendia on farming, sericulture, and crafts were the mainstay of China's (and the world's) first commercial printing, from the tenth century.[62]

The *Huainanzi* reminds readers that Shen Nong, legendary sage inventor of agriculture and medicine, thoroughly investigated the suitability of land for cultivation, trying and tasting plants, streams, and springs, to teach people what to use and what to reject. "He suffered poisoning as much as seventy times a day." *Zhuangzi* dramatically reverses scholarly values, making the impossibility of verbal description evidence of superior knowledge. In chapter 13 a duke is reading "the words of a sage." A wheelwright working nearby makes bold to ask what the duke is reading, and when told declares such writings rubbish. The duke demands an explanation, and the wheelwright says this: "I see it in terms of my own work. If I chip at a wheel too slowly, the chisel slides and does not grip; if too fast, it jams and catches in the wood. Not too slow, not too fast; I feel it in the hand and respond from the heart, the mouth cannot put it into words, there is a knack in it somewhere which I cannot convey to my son and which my son cannot learn from me. This is how through my seventy years I have grown old chipping at wheels. The men of old and their untransmittable message are dead. Then what my lord is reading is the dregs of the men of old, isn't it?" (Z 140).[63]

The Warring States period *Book of Artisans* (*Kao Gong Ji*) says, "All that is done by the hundred artisans was originally the work of sages. Metal melted to make swords, clay hardened to make vessels, chariots for going on land and boats for crossing water—all these arts were the work of sages." Presumably the thinking is to make arts respectable by tracing them to the ancient sages. If sages invented these arts, they cannot be contemptible and must instead participate in the sage's wisdom and goodness. The point would not need making, however, if contempt were not the default position of the literati, who nevertheless accepted the genealogy, which flatters artisans with sage ancestors the literati invented. Thus, for instance, Xu Gan, an elegant author of the early third century: "The sages relied on wisdom to create the arts, and they relied on arts to establish affairs properly.... The arts are the means to highlight wisdom, to establish ability, to bring affairs under control, and to steer the masses.... These two things [the arts and virtue] do not function separately and are not independent of one another."[64]

Some practitioners took exception to the legend of sage origins. Artisanal accomplishment is learned not from sages, they said, but from the things themselves. A fourth century CE author says, "As regards the people who protect and manage the dikes and channels of the nine rivers and the four lakes, they are the same in all ages; they did not learn their business from Yu the Great, they learnt it from the waters." An eighth-century author writes, "Those who know how to manage ships learnt from boats and not from Wu the Shipman. Those who can think learnt from themselves, and not from the sages." These words recall the *Huainanzi,* which combines and reconciles both positions. Arts of weaving, carpentry, agricultural implements, boats, shoes, wheels and carts, metallurgy, and weapons are all attributed to ancient sages, but what these sages did is very little. They learned from the things themselves. "When Yu drained the flood, he followed the water as his master. When the Divine Farmer [Shen Nong] sowed grain, he followed the seedlings as his teacher."[65]

Others say the age of sages is not over. What the ancient sages did adepts might do today, perhaps even more. The emergence of a new cosmology of *qi* in the fourth century BCE challenged the demarcation between humans and spirits (*shen*). Since everything in the world, the human body not excepted, is made of *qi*, learning to control one's *qi*, which is the promise of the inner cultivation manuals new at this time (teaching, for example, the art of *daoyin* and the five animal stretches), enables the adept to participate in the daimonic powers of the spiritual world. Needham suggests that operations like smelting and steelmaking, in which Chinese were early masters, persuaded some that they could imitate natural processes and even improve them; they can "stand in the place of nature," and "bring about natural changes at a rate immensely faster than nature's own time." According to a Song dynasty alchemical work, sages appropriate "the mechanisms of the shaping forces of nature (*zao hua zhe*) and [make] them work for human benefit." "The sage can rival the skill of the shaping forces."[66]

Those attracted by such thoughts would probably fit a stereotype of "Daoist." Yet scholars also see hostility to technics in Daoist thought, where Needham finds an "anti-technology complex," including "an ambivalent attitude to those techniques which the society of force and dominance could use for its own ends." For instance, the *Huainanzi* has a detailed account of the rise of technics, arts of all kinds—metallurgy, agriculture, carpentry, fortifications, architecture—all presented as evidence of decline. What is deplorable about these arts is the desire that drives their invention and use. It is not the desire of the people but "desires of the rulers of men." The misadvised effort to improve life through technology leaves the people impoverished and their rulers wallowing in excess.[67]

The reproach against technology is that it does not work, and exacerbates the disorder it is introduced to dispel. Machines teach people that they can *make* things happen and need not wait for things. The more machines do for us, therefore, the more dissatisfied we are with what happens naturally. We are better advised to forgo trying to make things happen, and instead become adept at letting things happen and flowing with the changes. The problem with machines begins with the disequilibrium they introduce, their rigid *yang* energy, which destroys people's balance with the environment. Mechanism always comes too late, when things are in a solid, resisting phase, requiring willful force to change them. A greater art would be more inconspicuous, lodging its effects further upstream, where things are still fluid, flexible, easily altered, provided you know how. The better people are at that, the less use they have for mechanical contrivances. They work with the spontaneous self-organization of nature, not in defiance or ignorance of it, and so, the *Daodejing* avers, "all obstacles can be overcome" (DDJ 59).

We have to balance evidence of an antitechnical animus with the profusion of references in Daoist classics to artisans (like the wheelwright and cook in *Zhuangzi*), and images drawn from the use of tools and what tools make (urn, window, pivot, wheel, compass, balance, mirror, hinge, lock, trigger, bellows). Examination of these references confirms that these artisans and their tools are images of *wu wei* effectiveness. A tool is indifferent to social distinctions. A scale or measuring stick settles disagreements with indisputable impartiality. They are detached, unbiased, and precisely responsive, the model of sage action. *Huainanzi* says such instruments "act through non-action." The scale "is impartial but not resented. It bestows but is not benevolent. It condoles but does not rebuke." The carpenter's square "is majestic and not contrary. It is hard and unbroken. It seizes but does not provoke resentment, [penetrates] within but does no injury. It is stern and severe but not coercive."[68]

These remarks may seem limited to a special type of tool, a measuring instrument, and recall the six standards—beam, plumb line, carpenter's square, marking cord, level, and compass—associated with the legendary Fu Xi and Nü Wa at the origin of civilization. Later, though, there is mention of a pillar supporting a roof and a bolt securing a door, and elsewhere the forged bronze trigger of a crossbow, unleashing a force out of all proportion to its small, easy movement. The peculiarity of these mechanisms is that their effectiveness has nothing to do with size. "How can this small amount of material be sufficient for the task? The position they occupy is the important thing." "What makes a cart able to travel a thousand miles is in three inches of axle." A bolt, lock, hinge, trigger, or axle is a machine that works by remaining inconspicuous and still, letting things move around it. That is the point of the *Daodejing*'s image of the empty center of a wheel (DDJ 11). Without its motionless void, the rigid mechanism would tear itself apart.[69]

Antitechnology is therefore an unsatisfying attribution. *Ambivalence* is no better, implying indecision on the part of these thinkers, as if they were unable to find their way to a coherent understanding of this vital dimension of their civilization. It may seem helpful to distinguish between tools and machines. If there can be a *dao* of fishing, butchery, or carpentry, if the practice of these arts is an image of *wu wei* effectiveness, then perhaps there is an important difference between tools we work with our hands and machines that go on their own. The stroke of a knife or the draw of a plane can be spontaneous and highly effective. That seems impossible for a water-driven saw, for instance, where the price of efficiency is the exclusion of spontaneity. How could something be at once spontaneous and mechanical, effortless and engineered? Hence the shame in using machines, which is to confess that something more subtle is beyond you. The distinction between tools and machines is difficult, however, and historians of machinery find they have to give it up; it does not mark a coherent technical difference in the field of mechanical devices. There is no technical distinction between a tool or how it works and a machine. Mechanically speaking, tools *are* machines.[70]

The shame of using machines is the theme of a tale in *Zhuangzi* about an encounter between Kongzi's disciple Zigong and an old man irrigating vegetables. Zigong is traveling in the countryside when he encounters the man laboriously drawing water for his crops. He interrupts his journey to tell the old man about a machine, the well sweep, that can irrigate a hundred fields in the time it takes him to do one. The old man begins to grimace as he listens to the pedantic harangue. Finally, he tells Zigong that he knows all about this machine and would be ashamed to use it. He says ingenious machines (*ji xie*) require ingenious minds (*ji xin*), which cannot be pure and simple (*chun bai*); they are restless, and no restless mind (*shen sheng bu ding*) moves with the *dao*. He dismisses Zigong with a curse and returns to work.

Disciples accompanying Zigong were an audience to the encounter, so he interprets it for their benefit. He tells them the old man is wiser than Kongzi. Kongzi taught him to be sympathetic and humane, but the old man is indifferent to success and has forgotten about tricks and schemes. He is of sound virtue while he, Zigong, has an unsettled mind—presumably because he was bothered enough by the old man's "inefficiency" to stop his travel and initiate their exchange. He evidently thinks the world is not all right just the way it is, which is to have an unsettled mind. Isn't anyone who uses a machine obviously afraid that what happens *ziran* is not enough? The point of a machine is to substitute reliable artifice for what simply happens of itself. To bring a machine into the world reveals no understanding of the true source of efficacy. Technology is never more than a consolation.

To need a tool, to rely on a machine, is to confess that the art of the *dao* is beyond you.

Is this an objection to *any* machine, however, or only some? Is *every* machine proof of purposiveness gone awry and intentionality out of kilter, or only some uses of some machines? Could the old man be objecting to the *kind* of machine Zigong describes? He is evidently able to obtain the water he needs without the sweep. If he had it he could irrigate a hundred times more crops, but why should he want to? Only if he is no longer working for himself perhaps, if he is working for somebody else, probably the one who installed the machine and enlarged the fields a hundredfold. Perhaps the old man is not objecting to machines per se but to mechanization from above, machines forced on the people by hypocritical benefactors like Zigong.

What we know of Zigong confirms this reading. He is a Confucian disciple mentioned many times in *Analects,* where he is depicted as a paragon of *zhong,* conscientiousness, but deficient in *shu,* sympathetic understanding (A 5.12). On one occasion he has the brass to ask Kongzi, "What do you think of me?" The Master replies that he is a *vessel* (*qi*), meaning a ritual implement. "What kind of vessel?" "A *hu* or *lian* vessel," he is told (A 5.4). The reply is usually understood to refer to highly specialized and archaic ritual implements, and taken to be a criticism of Zigong's inflexible, unsympathetic, mechanical approach to rites and ceremonies, a major failing in a Confucian ("The perfected person is not a vessel" (A 2.12)). *Analects* also tells us Zigong is good with money (A 11.19), which is not praise if it implies that he is overly committed to external things, contrary to his Master's teaching (A 4.9). In later life Zigong acquired a reputation for deception, and became a notorious spy (*jian*) who profited from his machinations. The Han historian Sima Qian depicts him as duplicitous in serving his state of Lu, cleverly subverting enemy states while exploiting internal dissension to personal advantage. Assuming some or all of this reputation was known to the author of the *Zhuangzi* chapter, the choice of Zigong to confront the old man becomes significant. The reference to machinery may concern not the technology of the machine but the political economy for which it is a metaphor, an economy in which technics serves the advantage of the few.[71]

The old man attributes ingenious machines to ingenious minds, a quality he turns against them. How should we understand "ingenious machines" (*ji xie*)? The phrase *ji xie* has something of the sense of "mechanical machines" or "machinish machines," the two words *ji* and *xie* both meaning "machine" when used alone (as they are and are so translated elsewhere in this passage). The old man does not say all machines are the work of impure hearts, only the really machinish ones. I think that means machines lacking subtlety, being obviously contrived to force what would not otherwise happen. Not all machines are like that, and there is nothing notably ingenious about the ones that are. A different machine could be more ingenious, more subtle, more artful *dao*-engineering, which I do not take the *Zhuangzi* author to preclude. On the contrary, if there were no other sort of machine, the old man need not qualify his curse against "ingenious" ones. What offends him about the well sweep may be that it is not ingenious enough. It is too crude, obvious, and rigid. It is artless. Bad engineering.

A well sweep is a fairly primitive machine; simple, not without elegance, and obviously more efficient than drawing water by hand, though we have seen reason to question the value of efficiency. Why should people want to be more efficient in this or any task? And more efficient for whom, themselves or others? Still we may think that farmers' lives would be agreeably less onerous if they did not have to draw water by hand. We might imagine that having acquired such a device they would be happy to have it, other things being equal. In chapter 14 the same device has a quite different value as an image of inconspicuous effectiveness. Music Master Shijin speaks with Yan Hui: "Haven't you ever seen a well-sweep? When you pull on one end, the other end will fall; if you let go, the other end will rise. Because it is pulled by men and does not pull men, it will not offend anyone (*de zui*) whether it falls or rises."[72]

The old man would be right to deem the sweep's installation bad engineering if it were truly superfluous, or if there were a more elegant, subtle, artful way to obtain a comparable effect. He seems to favor the argument of superfluity. Whether or not we agree, machines as such are not condemned. Superfluous ones are, implying that a more artful design would not be offensive. The old man seems repelled more by the ingenious minds (*ji xin*) of those who devise such machines than by their works. Again though, we have to ask whether "ingenious" is the right word and how to understand it. Ingenious has a positive sense, meaning elegant, intelligent, artful, or well designed. Or it can be understood negatively to mean clever, facile, or contrived. I suggest that when the old man condemns *ji* machines, it is the clever, facile, and contrived that displease him. *Those* machines do not evince notable engineering or inventive minds. We might say the old man condemns *mechanical* minds, *facile* minds, minds whose *techne* is merely clever and superficially fixed on an unproblematic "efficiency," as Zigong seems to be.

Chapter 10 confirms that the problem is not machines but the people who use them, or more exactly their knowledge: "If there is too much knowledge of bows, crossbows, bird-snares, stringed bows, triggered traps, the birds are disordered in the sky. If there is too much knowledge of hooks, baits, nets, and basket-traps, the fish are disordered in the water. When there is too much knowledge of pitfalls, springs, snares, traps, gins, the animals are disordered in the woodlands. When we have too much of the vagaries of cunning and deception, of wrenching apart 'the hard and the white' and jumbling together 'the same and the different,' the vulgar are perplexed by disputation. Therefore, if the world is benighted in utter confusion, the blame rests on the lusters after knowledge" (Z 209). In chapter 11 we learn that the disorder goes back to the time of the Yellow Emperor, when "the whole world lusted after knowledge and the hundred clans were in turmoil. From that time on we have hatcheted and sawed to get things in shape, inked the carpenter's line to trim them, hammered and chiseled to sunder them, and the world has been jumbled in utter chaos. The fault was in meddling with men's hearts" (Z 213).

The passage from chapter 10 goes on to say that the problems it identifies are the fault of a *knowledge that is not knowing enough*: "Everyone in the world has enough sense to inquire into what he does not know, yet we do not have the sense to inquire into what we already do know. Everyone knows how to condemn what he judges to be bad, yet we do not know how to condemn what we have already judged to be good. This is why we are in utter disorder" (Z 210). It is not knowledge that causes confusion and disorder; it is confused, disordered knowledge—inadequate, artless, compromised, petty. That suggests not all technical invention is the same. Some inventions may be coercive and unbalanced, others generous and sagelike. The implication is not that we should get rid of machines or would be better off without them, but that we can be more artful and less selfish (more Daoist) in technical knowledge. The problem is not the machines but the ethics of the engineers. The argument does not devalue technics but aspires to liberate engineering from despotic ideas of efficiency and profit.

It is equally possible to find antitechnics in the *Daodejing;* for instance, "The more cunning craftsmen there are, the more pernicious contrivances will be invented" (DDJ 57). In a well-ruled kingdom there are hundreds of devices (*qiao*) but none are used (DDJ 80). People do not need them. They do all that needs doing without *doing* (contriving, planning, engineering) anything. Once again, however, a more artful engineering seems prefigured:

> Push far enough toward the void,
> Hold fast enough to quietness,
> And of the ten thousand things none but can be worked on by you. (DDJ 16)
> Sometimes diminishing a thing adds to it. (DDJ 42)

> The most supple things in the world ride roughshod over the most rigid.
> That which is not there can enter even where there is no space.
> This is how I know the advantage of nonaction. (DDJ 43)

These are, or could be, principles of Daoist engineering, dedicated to maximum effect with minimum intervention. Such a reading was discovered relatively early in the Daoist tradition. Consider this explanation from the *Huainanzi* of the *wei* in *wu wei* action: "If you use fire to dry out a well or use the Huai [River] to irrigate a mountain, these are cases of using personal effort in contradiction of the natural course. Thus I would call [them] 'taking deliberate action' (*you wei*). But if on the water you use a boat, in the sand you use a [sledge], in the mud you use a [sleigh], in the mountain you use a [litter], in the summer you dig [ditches], in the winter you pile up [dikes], in accordance with a high place you make a mound, and following a low one you dig a pond, these are not what I would call 'deliberate action'" (*wei*).[73]

The *Huainanzi* author seems to envision a distinction between those who use artifice in a sagelike way, following the veins of nature, and those whose machines impose on or distort nature. Instead of forcing a choice between technology and nature, the passage offers the prospect of a *dao*-technics, a *poiesis* of artificial, artifactual, engineered *ziran* effectiveness.

The idea recurs, somewhat unexpectedly, in Mengzi. "What I dislike about 'wise' people is that they force things. If 'wise' people were like Yu in guiding the waters, then there would be nothing to dislike about their wisdom. Yu, in guiding the waters, guided them where no effort was required. If 'wise' people also guided things where no effort was required, their wisdom would also be great" (4B26). Again in a later chapter: "In water management, King Yu followed the way of water. For this reason, King Yu had the Four Seas as his reservoir" (6B11).

The *Book of Artisans* also alludes to this *dao*-engineering: "Every canal should be made so as to take account of the characteristic forces of water;

every dike should take account of the characteristic forces of the earth. A good canal is scoured by its own water; a good dike is consolidated by the sediment brought against it." According to Needham, by the Tang dynasty Daoist authors envision a thorough mastery of natural forces. "There [is] no force in nature which man could not, if he knew the right techniques, control." Such is the conviction that spawned the search for an elixir of immortality. According to a tenth-century author, "Utilizing the divine power of the myriad things, [a sage] can get the highest rewards from nature and from man, and can ride on the glory of the horses of the wind."[74]

Needham suggests that the whole idea of *wu wei* in Daoist authors is the Chinese version of empiricism. I think he means that extolling *wu wei* is a call to diminish or overcome subjective interference and see things with greater detachment and ecological insight. The knowledge required for *wu wei* effectiveness is not ceremonial knowledge of ritual. It is empirical, experimental knowledge of what happens (and can be made to happen) *ziran*. Needham suggests that the *wei* these authors deplore is "forcing things in the interests of gain, without reference to their intrinsic principles." Presumably the expectation of gain is the motive for the forcing, though it is the forcing that is the mistake, greed only compounding the error. Thus Guo Xiang: "*Wu wei* does not mean doing nothing and keeping silent. Let everything be allowed to do what it naturally does, so that its nature will be satisfied." That is also the idea in the *Huainanzi* text I cited, which begins by explaining that *wu wei* means "not allowing private ambitions to interfere with the public *dao*, not allowing lustful desires to distort upright techniques. [It means] complying with the inherent patterns (*li*) of things when initiating undertakings, according with the natural endowments of things when establishing accomplishments, and advancing the natural propensities of things so that misguided precedents are not able to dominate." A similar understanding already appears a century earlier in *The Spring and Autumn of Lü Buwei*: "The intention of letting things take their own course is to dominate the development of everything and to succeed in every field."[75]

Letting things do what they naturally do suggests leaving things alone, letting them be, not using them, or caring what they might be used for. Such an ascetic repression of resourcefulness is perhaps a Heideggerian reading. But we can also understand the passage to exalt the technics that discover merely potential *ziran* effectiveness, and create machines that use what we make happen spontaneously. That may sound unlikely, but in fact it happens all the time. For instance, some materials only work together with a lot of extraneous force. Others readily blend in a synergy more potent than the components alone. A good (though not Chinese) example is reinforced concrete. This material consists of cement and aggregate laced with steel, either as rods or wire mesh. The advantage of the combination is that like stone, concrete is strong in compression but weak in tension, while metals like steel are the opposite. Key to their use together is the happy accident that stuff so disparate expands and contracts at nearly the same rate, which prevents thermal stress from tearing the combined material apart. Instead, the strength of each compensates the weakness of the other. Combining them creates the most nearly perfect material ever devised: an artificial stone that can be molded to any shape and does something no stone can do, resist force in tension.[76]

Reinforced concrete is an example of what might be called an intensive material, one that combines heterogeneous compounds while preserving (rather than homogenizing) their differences. The difference between stone and steel is maintained and expressed, because reinforced concrete is strong in tension, as no stone is, and strong in compression, as no metal is. Engineering with such materials is, as Deleuze and Guattari say, "no longer a question of imposing a form upon a matter but of elaborating an increasingly rich and consistent material the better to tap increasingly intense forces. What makes a material increasingly rich is the same as what holds heterogeneities together without their ceasing to be heterogeneous." The result is a *ziran* effectiveness that would not exist apart from human intervention (our *poiesis,* to use the Greek word for productive efficacy). Other materials, and many structures and machines, exploit comparable potentials for self-organization. These potentials are entirely natural; what is unnatural, what would not happen *ziran,* or without art, is their assemblage. Yet once they are assembled, the synergy, the artificially amplified effectiveness, is a *ziran* outcome of a *dao* we engineer.[77]

The principle that design works best when it does not appear to work at all is attested in many different technical cultures. A machine does not appear to be working (laboring, forcing) when it seems to work like nature despite obvious artifice. In other words it has become a black box. The best-designed artifacts seldom look like nature. Everyone sees they are artificial. In neither art nor technology are we like the birds who tried to eat Zeuxis's painted grapes. The consummate work of *techne*—an ancient Greek word alive to the since-fragmented unity of art, knowledge, and technics—is not a mimesis of form but of effectiveness, creatively imitating not nature's shapes but its creativity, its fecundity in forms. The best design, in fine art as in engineering, does not *look* like nature; rather, it *works* like nature, having an efficacy that imitates nature's. It operates *ziran* despite being obviously artificial.

Effortless efficacy is neither an esoteric mystery nor a philosopher's fantasy. The pragmatic meaning of *wu wei* is creative (rather than reproductive) artifice to an effect out of all proportion to visible, calculated intentionality. *Wu wei* effectiveness, while known under this name only in China, is a design quality of innumerable works of art and technology all over the world: Brooklyn Bridge, Hagia Sophia, the violins of Stradivarius, paintings by Leonardo or Kandinsky, to mention arbitrary examples. Of course there are abundant examples from China. In mentioning a few my point is not that the inventions appear in China centuries before they arrive in the West, which is true but irrelevant. The point is to illustrate a particular art of engineering. A good case to begin with is the double-action bellows, from the fourth century BCE. The *Daodejing* praises this device, and it seems clear that the double-action bellows is specifically referred to, something translators do not always appreciate:

Heaven and Earth and all that lies between
Is like a bellows with its nozzle;
Although it is empty it does not collapse (*qü*).
And the more it is worked, the more it gives forth.[78]

It is a technical peculiarity of the double-action bellows that it does not collapse. It blows with each stroke, expelling a blast with the same stroke as draws in air for a new one. Single-action bellows were known in the West since antiquity, but these blow on one stroke only, requiring a second stroke to reinflate their chamber; the double-action bellows did not reach Europe until the sixteenth century, presumably arriving from China. This bellows is praised for its efficacious use of the void it encloses, which collaborates with what is full and solid about the mechanism to realize an efficacy fullness without void cannot achieve.

Another example of design with the efficacious void is Great Stone Bridge, crossing the river Jiao Shui (Shansi Province). Designed by Li Chun and completed in 610, Great Stone Bridge is the world's first segmental arch bridge. Li evidently realized that an arch need not be semicircular; in fact, a smaller segment of the circle uses less material and provides greater strength than semicircular arches. This is already a case of doing more with less, gaining strength by eliminating material. The effect is heightened by the addition of two smaller so-called spandrel arches on each side of the principal arch, in the triangular space between the deck, the embankment, and the rise of the arch. These diminish the dead weight of the bridge, save a lot of material, and being normally above the water line permit the safe passage of floods. The structure is an example of effectiveness amplified not by adding force but eliminating it. It does more by doing less, being less, effacing its difference from the water and the sky.[79]

The principle that allowed Li to puncture the sides of Great Stone Bridge and make it at once stronger and lighter appears earlier in the invention of the fenestrated rudder. The rudder itself is a Chinese invention, from the first century CE, unattested in Europe before the twelfth century. A fenestrated rudder is punctured by a pattern of holes, which reduces its resistance to the water, making control easier without diminishing the steering function. Removing material, creating voids, makes a more precise, responsive, effective machine. It moves better in the water, functioning more effortlessly, with less rigid opposition to the flow. The more the wood vanishes into the water, the less obstacle between the way of the water and the way of the wood, which we guide.[80]

Deliberately putting things together is not *ziran*. But things that have been deliberately combined may themselves operate *ziran*. We engineer the spontaneity, as we engineer the spontaneous strength of reinforced concrete. Through inquiry we can learn how to combine materials that actualize otherwise merely virtual potentials, engineering *ziran* effectiveness. A lesson of *Zhuangzi*'s Inner Chapters is that not all knowledge is the same. Little knowledge is futile; great knowledge nourishes life. A lesson of the Outer Chapters is that not all machines are the same. What makes machines convivial also makes knowledge great. What is great about great knowledge is its effectiveness, maximizing the difference between inputs and outputs, especially by finding and exploiting potential *ziran* effects. Sagacious knowledge is at once poetic and technical. Sages are artist-engineers of *ziran* effectiveness, poet-technicians of the *dao*.

— 3 —

The Art of War

Know the enemy, know yourself, and your victory will never
be endangered. Know the ground, know the weather, and your
victory will be complete.

—SUNZI

The greatest work of China's military philosophy is also the oldest we know
of, perhaps even the first, the famous *Art of War* (or *Military Methods, Bingfa*)
attributed to Sunzi. The insights of this work have never been surpassed,
and stand unchallenged after more than two thousand years of study in
China and abroad. For a long time, scholars believed this work to date from
the late Spring and Autumn period in the sixth century, which would make
it roughly contemporary with Kongzi and perhaps a century before the first
Daoist classics, whose ideas it would anticipate. If, as many now think, assigning the work to the Spring and Autumn period is untenable, then it may
date from the latter fourth century BCE, which would make it approximately
contemporary with the *Daodejing* and *Zhuangzi's* Inner Chapters. In any
case, establishment of the *Sunzi Bingfa* as a written text opened the way for
additional works on strategy attributed to other semilegendary military figures, including Taigong and Wuzi, and contributions by historically attested
postclassical figures like Zhuge Liang and Tang emperor Taizong.[1]

If *Sunzi* is correctly placed in the fourth century, its language is deliberately archaic, using a court language of the Spring and Autumn period. The
language puts the work in an ideal past, and its arguments are presented as
the wisdom of a sage "Master" (*zi*) no less venerable than Kongzi. This ar-
chaism may have seemed attractive to advocates of the philosophy the work
espouses. The text emerges at a time of transformation in China's military
culture. The face of war is changing, from the seasonal ritual combat of
chariot-borne aristocrats to mass infantry bureaucratically organized, with
iron weapons and plentiful horsepower. With a new kind of war, whose

emergence marks the transition to a "Warring States" period, comes an urgent need to reappraise military methods. That is the context in which *Sunzi Bingfa* is born.

It has been suggested that this work revalues the term *jiang* (commander) much as Kongzi did the term *junzi* (gentleman). In earlier military practice, command was no great task, noble birth the adequate qualification. The *jiang* commander *Sunzi* theorizes is by contrast an extraordinary individual possessed of specific knowledge and skill. The art of command requires someone who is intelligent and not heroic, armed with carefully investigated knowledge of the adversary and terrain. This reliance on intelligence and investigation is new, and so is the premium placed on the commander's knowledge, presenting the new approach to command its advocates deemed necessary to realize the potential of the new military technology. War in the Warring States period becomes a problem of knowledge, with solutions sought in an art or *techne* that can be epitomized and taught.[2]

The essential discovery in the art of war is that there can be an *art* (a *dao* and *techne*) of war. "Victory is something that you can craft and bring into being" (SZ 6). War is therefore not condemned to brutality; it becomes instead a problem of art and knowledge. The *art* of war lies not in victory but victory achieved in an artful, perhaps even sagacious way. The challenge (to art and knowledge) is not merely to triumph, or cover oneself in glory, but to win the most with minimal exposure, doing very little, ideally nothing at all. "To prove victorious in every battle is not the best possible outcome," says Sunzi. "The best possible outcome is to subdue the enemy's troops without fighting (*bu zhan*)" (SZ 3). There is no glory in war. Only barbarians praise bravery. "One who fights and attains victory in front of naked blades is not a good general," says Taigong, legendary strategist of the dynastic Zhou conquest.[3]

According to *Sunzi*, "the victories of those good at waging war do not bring them fame for sagacity or merit for courage" (SZ 4). Yet neither are they flukes. These commanders win because they position themselves where they are sure to win, prevailing over those who have already lost. That is the art, the knowledge, the *techne* of strategy. Since the decisive actions are inconspicuous and practically invisible, there is nothing glorious in the victories. They look easy, though it is a case of "easy once you see it." If you do not see it and it traps you, you are defeated. It is not a fluke. It is a work of art, *techne*, superlatively effective knowledge.

War as a Problem of Knowledge

The opening chapter of the *Sunzi* states, "The *dao* of war is deception (*gui*)" (SZ 1). Deception is not merely one weapon in the armory; it is the very *dao* of war and victory. "Deception" means more than lies and ruses. It means anything contrary to the norm. The term *gui* is sometimes glossed with *qi*, unorthodox, extraordinary, another important term for the military philosophy. The ascendancy of deception or unorthodoxy is consistent with how this tradition tends to frame strategic problems. The immemorial victory of Chinese tradition—the Zhou conquest of the Shang—is the military philosophy's paradigm problem of strategy. The forces in that war were almost cosmically asymmetrical. The Shang army may have been larger than the entire population of the Zhou territory. Yet the much smaller Zhou army (supposedly led by the sage strategist Taigong) decisively defeated the Shang, killed their wicked king, and established the great dynasty of classical antiquity.[4]

China's military philosophy never forgets this origin, working out its idea of strategy from the perspective of the disadvantaged party. Here is an example from *Wuzi*: "Marquis Wu asked: 'Their forces are extremely numerous, martial, and courageous. Behind them are ravines and dangerous passes; on their right, mountains; on the left a river. They have deep moats and high ramparts and are defending their positions with strong crossbowmen. Their withdrawal is like a mountain moving, their advance like a tempest. As their foodstocks are also plentiful, it will be difficult to defend against them for very long. What should be done?' Wuzi replied: 'A great problem indeed! This is not a problem of the strength of chariots and cavalry but of having the plans of a sage.'" Earlier, in *Sun Bin Bingfa* (Sun Bin may be the historical Master Sun):

> Suppose one army encounters the enemy and both establish encampments. Our chariots and cavalry are numerous but our men and weapons few. If the enemy's men are ten times ours, how should we attack them?

> To attack them, carefully avoid ravines and narrows. Break out and lead them, coercing them toward easy terrain. Even though the enemy is ten times [more numerous], [easy terrain] will be conducive to our chariots and cavalry and our Three Armies will be able to attack.[5]

Luck aside, there is only one way that a weaker force can overcome a stronger, and that is by reversing the strategic situation (*shi*). The disadvantaged opponent is sure to prevail if precisely the strength of the stronger becomes a liability. The weak are only weak when they lack resources; if they can make the adversary's resources a liability, then they cannot be defeated. The problem is how to do it, and the answer is deception—fight the mind. Deception is effective without being *seen* to do anything at all (until it is too late). That makes it the only reliable method for accomplishing the most decisive victory possible with the least exposure of your weakness. When by art and knowledge you "effortlessly" manipulate where enemies *think* their strength lies, and lure them to attack emptiness, they wear themselves out lunging at shadows. Pick a time and harvest your victory. War is so much more about strategy than violence that violence can be eliminated or at least abated with no loss of efficacy. No fighting (*bu zhan*) is not a moral principle of nonviolence; rather, nonviolence (or abated, minimal violence) is a byproduct of artful strategy.

The acme of deception is the unorthodox strategy. "In general," writes Sunzi, "one engages with the orthodox and gains victory through the unorthodox. Thus one who excels at sending forth the unorthodox is as inexhaustible as Heaven" (SZ 5). The word "unorthodox" translates *qi*, which also describes the marvelous, strange, and extraordinary. Military usage emphasizes the unexpected and uncanny. Unorthodox strategy is fathomless and inexhaustible. "The changes of the unorthodox and the orthodox can never be completely exhausted. The unorthodox and orthodox mutually produce each other, just like an endless cycle. Who can exhaust them?" (SZ 5) According to the *Six Secret Teachings* (*Liu Tao*), "In employing the army nothing is more important than obscurity and silence. In movement nothing is more important than the unexpected. In planning nothing is more important than not being knowable." It falls to knowledge to appear not to know, as it falls to art to look artless. A commander should be as unfathomable as his plans, and not just to the enemy but to his own troops. According to a Ming dynasty military commentary, "Only when there is no constancy can the mysterious be preserved in the mind. Therefore it is called subtle." The appropriately obscure Ghost Valley Master (*Gui Gu Zi*) says, "The best strategy is to adapt: transformations follow one upon another without interruption every time there is a particular configuration with a particular potential. You determine whether to go one way or another, depending on the situation."[6]

Unorthodox strategies are born in the obscurity of the tenuous and virtual. One must appreciate not the being but the becoming of the situation, its multiplicity and nascent transformation, which requires knowledge not limited to truth or the representation of what is. The art of war literature frequently remarks on this deeper knowledge. According to the *Six Secret Teachings*, "The wise follow the time and do not lose an advantage"; "When things are not manifest but [the commander] discerns them, he is enlightened." A Song commentary on the military classics says, "Those who innovate strategic plans for decisive victory esteem bringing about minute, subtle opportunities. . . . There are subtle moments of appropriateness for all tactical measures, moments when minute changes allow penetration. The unorthodox and orthodox are techniques, their employment is a matter of a subtle moment." There is no rule for unorthodoxy. That is another reason strategy requires a subtle mind. In the Sun Bin *Art of War* it is said, "Whoever has form can be defined, and whoever can be defined can be overcome." Therefore "employing one form of conquest to conquer the myriad forms is not possible. That by which one controls the form is singular; that by which one conquers cannot be single. Thus when those who excel at warfare discern an enemy's strength, they know where he has a shortcoming. When they discern an enemy's insufficiency, they know where he has a surplus."[7]

A famous example of unorthodox strategy is attributed to Tian Dan, a commander of the fourth century BCE. The city of Jimo had been under siege for five years. Modern scholarship estimates a besieging force of a hundred thousand troops. Tian Dan's mission was to break the siege. He got himself and a small force inside the fortified city, producing a textbook example of the asymmetry unorthodox strategy exploits. Tian Dan concealed his able-bodied troops while ensuring that spies saw only the weak and wounded. He ordered that food offered in sacrifice be left in the courtyards, where it attracted flocks of birds, creating omens to puzzle and unnerve the besieging soldiers. Using double agents he spread word among the enemy that the graves outside the city wall contained fabulous riches. The resulting desecrations enraged the defending population and steeled their loyalty and courage. These preparations accomplished, Tian Dan assembled a herd of cattle, draped them in red silk with multicolored dragon-vein patterns, strapped naked blades to their horns, and bound their tails with greased reeds. In the early morning hours the cattle, tails ablaze, were sent stampeding toward the sleeping enemy camp. Behind them Tian Dan led an orthodox deployment of his troops. Everyone with whom the enraged cattle collided was wounded or killed and the following force destroyed the army.[8]

Another famous unorthodox strategy is the empty city ploy of Zhuge Liang, China's most storied strategist, immortalized in the *Romance of the*

Three Kingdoms, a Ming dynasty novel. Zhuge Liang is left in Hanzhong with a small force while the rest of his army redeploys. Suddenly an unexpected diversion of some hundred and fifty thousand enemy troops under Sima Yi appears on the horizon. Spies have already informed him that Zhuge's soldiers are few and weak. Since Sima Yi thinks Zhuge is weak, Zhuge reinforces the assumption by withdrawing his battle flags, silencing the drums, and commanding the inhabitants to remain indoors. The apparently deserted city falls eerily silent. At this point, he has the city gates thrown open and the ground before them ostentatiously swept and sprinkled. Then Zhuge took up his famous fan of crane feathers and his silk scarf and ascended the wall, followed by two boys carrying his *qin*-zither. Reclining on a watchtower parapet, he burned incense and played music. The city is Sima Yi's for the taking. It really is. Fearing ambush, however, he moved on. Zhuge does practically nothing and is victorious against a vastly superior force without firing a shot. His trick is a masterpiece of misdirection. The trick is to make his opponent think there is a trick. The trick is there's no trick.[9]

Successful deception is a form of *wu wei* effectiveness, doing something highly effective while not being seen to do anything at all, and it depends on the canny discernment we have seen major Chinese traditions extol. This approach to combat coincides with the discovery of new problems of knowledge and directions for inquiry. Li Jing, the preeminent commander of the Tang dynasty, summed up the military philosophy in terms of the inquiries it mandates: "The measures for achieving decisive victory lie in investigating the opposing general's talent and abilities; analyzing the enemy's strengths and weaknesses; determining the configuration and strategic advantages of terrain; observing the advantages of the appropriate moment; and first being victorious, only thereafter engaging in combat and defending positions without losing them. This is termed the *dao* for certain victory."[10]

Sunzi begins with an appeal to inquiry. "War is a major affair of state, the ground of life or death, the way of preservation or oblivion. One cannot fail to investigate and study it. And so, manage it according to five concerns, and carry out a comparative assessment between yourself and the enemy, in order to investigate and study how things really stand" (SZ 1). According to the Warring States *Strategies of Huang-shih Kung,* "The key to using the army is to first investigate the enemy's situation. Look into their granaries and armories, estimate their food stocks, divine their strengths and weaknesses, search out their natural advantages, and seek out their vacuities and fissures." Rulers contemplating war are enjoined to withdraw to the ancestral temple for a planning exercise, where they study maps and three-dimensional models of terrain, and quantify variables material to success, assigning points to different factors and using some kind of tally board. "Terrain gives rise to measurement," says *Sunzi*. "Measurement gives rise to weighing. Weighing gives rise to calculation. Calculation gives rise to balancing. Balancing gives rise to gauging the likelihood of victory" (SZ 4).[11]

Sunzi's praise for these investigations is almost immodest. "Those who understand them are victorious; those who fail to understand them are not. . . . By assessing these concerns I know who will win and who will lose" (SZ 1). Rulers and their generals cannot know enough about the variables material to victory: the strategic position, tactical options, military capability, the enemy, the terrain, and weather. The value of such investigation is to discern and exploit opportunities latent in circumstances. Terrain gives birth to measurement when considered from the point of view of its affordances, seeking the *ji* pivots, with their potential *ziran* effectiveness. This is knowledge of terrain in virtual depth—not how it is in itself (Greek essence), but how it is becoming and might change. To know the situation in virtual depth is to know the tensions of its tendencies and how to channel them. Such knowledge always leads to something new and different, because the strategic situation is different every time. A general who repeats himself is doomed. "I never repeat the ways in which I achieve victory; I respond to the infinite variety of ways in which forces can be disposed" (SZ 6).

There is a value in strategy for what may be called foreknowledge. The more you know about what is coming, the more artfully you can control the time of battle. If you control that, you join the battle even before you begin to march. "What enables the enlightened ruler or worthy general to conquer others whenever they deploy their forces, and realize achievements that far surpass the common run of men, is that they know things beforehand (*xian zhi*)" (SZ 13). "If one can foreknow the place of battle and can foreknow the time of battle, one can join in a battle even though it be a thousand leagues away" (SZ 6). *Sunzi* carefully stipulates that divination plays no role in military foreknowledge, which "cannot be obtained from ghosts or spirits, it is not prefigured in situations or events, nor can one determine it though [astrological] calculation." On the other hand, spies, well used, are inestimable. Reliable foreknowledge "must be gained from people who know the enemy's situation and condition" (SZ 13). The argument is impressively reprised in a Song dynasty commentary: "Enlightened rulers and wise generals esteem advance knowledge. . . . One who has advance knowledge knows the subtle and shadows, knows preservation and extinction. Someone who is enlightened about things that have not yet materialized, who knows the minuscule and makes decisions, employing them before things have rushed forward and sunk, can thus arise in an instant, the interstice of a thread."[12]

Another new problem of knowledge, never faced by the old Zhou nobility in their ritualistic combat, is the value of tactical investigations in the field. *Sunzi* twice recommends testing enemies to discover where they are vulnerable. First in chapter 6: "Analyze the enemy in order to understand their strengths and weaknesses. Provoke the enemy in order to discover their principles of operation. Ascertain the enemy's disposition of forces in order to know the shape of the field of battle. Provoke the enemy in order to know where their strength is deficient or abundant." Then again in chapter 10: "Being able to assess the enemy in order to ensure victory and accounting for the danger, difficulty, and distance of terrain is the *dao* of the superior general. Those who understand this and engage in battle are sure to be victorious. Those who fail to understand this and engage in battle are sure to be defeated."

A sagacious commander must be good at knowing people (*ren zhi*). The advantages of testing the enemy carry over to the problem of knowing how to select the right men for offices—good commanders, good officers, good archers and infantry, good diplomats and spies. It is a technical problem, and also one with the aspect of a game, to compel others to reveal what they want to hide. The *Secret Teachings* devotes six chapters to it. The difficulty goes beyond the obvious one of detecting liars and knowing who to believe. There are further problems of fame, whether to trust a reputation; of inferring motives from behavior (a thief ran west to escape, his pursuers ran west to capture him); and of misjudgment. To use others well one must recognize the worth of people who may have been obliged to live obscurely, or may have something to hide that is irrelevant to their capacity for an office.

A wise strategist foresees changes when they are small and manipulates them to advantage when they are pliable. He is good at changing, good at waiting, and really sees the little things. He knows how to meet fullness with emptiness, how to make the circuitous straight, how to leave last and arrive first. All of these ideas for strategic effectiveness exploit opportunities to make war a problem of knowledge, where knowledge is understood as I have suggested it typically is in Chinese tradition from the Warring States period on, as a perspicacious insight into the becoming of things, confirmed by the *wu wei* effectiveness it funds.

Most of the philosophical differences among Confucians, Daoists, art-of-war thinkers, and others concerning the value of knowledge are at the ethical level of the use of knowledge so defined. What is it to handle things well? What sort of things *can* be handled well, and "well" according to what standard? For example, does a sage concern himself with military formations? Kongzi implies not (A 15.1). But battles can be handled well or poorly no less than a family or an office, and the art or *techne* of this military finesse is the sagacious knowledge *wu wei* effectiveness proves.

Sunzi and the Western Way of War

Our Western "classic of war" is *Vom Krieg,* by the Prussian general Carl von Clausewitz, unfinished at the author's death and published posthumously in 1832. Unlike *Sunzi,* this is not the first work of its kind or in its tradition, being more a summit than a source, and like Newton, Clausewitz stands on the shoulders of giants, including Julius Caesar and Machiavelli. War, he says, is "composed of primordial violence, hatred and enmity, which are to be regarded as a blind natural force; of the play of chance and probability within which the creative spirit is free to roam; and of its element of subordination as an instrument of policy, which alone makes it subject to reason." He directs his entire discussion of strategy against the idea that an art of war could make tactical confrontation superfluous, or that a general might have alternatives to hard fighting. He disparages deception and scorns unorthodox strategies, which he calls stratagems. "He believes in combat rather than show of force," writes Raymond Aron, "in soundness of judgment and energy rather than stratagem."[13]

In dismissing the deception *Sunzi* esteems, Clausewitz is not criticizing the Chinese. His target is closer to home. It was seriously argued in Prussian military circles that skillful tactics might eliminate the need for battle. The heresy was not limited to Prussia, as an eighteenth-century British militarist attests: "Whoever understands these things [topography, supply lines, and so on] is in a position to initiate military operations with mathematical precision and to keep on waging war without ever being under the necessity of striking a blow." For Clausewitz, Napoleonic warfare exposed such ideas as dangerous folly. A military maneuver is pointless unless it is designed to culminate in a decisive battle. "Direct annihilation of the enemy's forces must always be the *dominant consideration*. We simply want to establish this dominance of the destructive principle."[14]

Clausewitz has qualified appreciation for ruses, but he does not believe in strategic surprise and derides the value of deception. These are trifles out of place in a scientific treatment of war. "However much we feel a desire to see the actors in war outdo each other in hidden activity, readiness, and stratagem, still we must admit that these qualities show themselves but little in history." He means, of course, European history. The problem with stratagems is that "the pieces on the strategic chess-board lack that mobility which is the element of stratagem and subtlety." The modern, industrialized military mass is too inertial, as if already dead, and not easily deflected by the pure conceptuality of a ruse. It is like throwing eggs at a rolling boulder.[15]

Sunzi seems to anticipate this criticism, and replies with confidence. The troops of a commander adept in the art of war are like the snake of Mount Heng. When struck on the head, its tail attacks; when struck on the tail, its head attacks; when struck in the center, both head and tail attack. An interlocutor asks, "Can an army be made to respond as [that snake] does?" "Yes," comes the ready reply. The secret lies in the commander's ability to manipulate his own troops no less than his enemy. "One who is good at deploying troops gets them to join hands and work together as one by leaving them no other choice but to do so" (SZ 11).

This confidence expresses a very *Sunzi*-like and non-Clausewitzian belief in war as a problem of knowledge. For Clausewitz, the successful commander is not one who wins at a game of strategy. He is one who through genius imposes his rule on the opponent. The uncertainty and hazard that make war unpredictable and uncontrollable are for him not barriers to be eliminated but opportunities to grasp and exploit. But notice that his answer to the uncertainty of war is not better knowledge. It is courage and self-confidence in lieu of knowledge. The commander's most important quality is serene assurance against temptations to second-guess himself. A Clausewitz protégé says, "military qualities are rooted in character rather than in knowledge," a remark that has been called "a perfect Clausewitzean formulation, and one which professional military men have loudly echoed ever since"—for instance, military historian John Keegan, who says that in none of history's famous and decisive battles (this in a book without any reference to China), "did thought play much of a part in bringing victory; courage and unconsidered self-sacrifice did."[16]

The reason Clausewitz dismisses the strategic value of knowledge is his celebrated concept of the fog of war. "War is the province of uncertainty: three-fourths of those things upon which action in war must be calculated are hidden more or less in the clouds of great uncertainty." A commander cannot wait upon certainty, and like a Cartesian, Clausewitz assumes that certainty is the essence of knowledge. The commander must act decisively despite the fog, which takes a special sort of mind. Clausewitz calls it "searching rather than inventive," a "fine and penetrating mind . . . to search out the truth." Fine and penetrating, yet strong rather than brilliant, "an intellect which, even in the midst of this intense obscurity [the fog of war], is not without some traces of inner light, which lead to the truth." "Truth" here means military victory. The commander must possess the courage to follow his inner light toward that truth. The language is baffling. What Clausewitz praises as courage for the truth (the courage of the liberated slave in Plato's cave, struggling toward the light) is in fact implacable tenacity (the commander's inner light) in place of knowledge forsaken to the fog of war.[17]

Clausewitz understands knowledge in the most classical sense, made modern by Descartes. To know a thing is to have a clear and distinct apprehension. Clausewitz thinks that whatever can be known in this way is necessarily highly abstract and general. The only things a person clearly and distinctly *knows* are portentous abstractions like Newton's laws of motion. These gems of pure theory are the crown jewels of science, but that explains why there cannot really be a science of war. Nothing as synoptic and speculative as knowledge has to be is useful to a commander in the field. "When the discernment is clear and deep [that is, science], none but general principles and views of action from a high standpoint can be the result." Such results are unfortunately useless in war. It is too uncertain how to derive useful deductions from theoretic laws. With knowledge defined in these Cartesian terms it becomes perversely reasonable for the prudent commander to refuse to be detained by what may or may not be known. He must instead revert to tested habit. "Between the particular case and the principle, there is often a wide space which cannot always be traversed on a visible chain of conclusions, and where a certain faith in self is necessary and a certain amount of scepticism is serviceable."[18]

Clausewitz sounds serious about the cognitive demands of warfare. "Everywhere intellect appears as an essential cooperative force; and thus we can understand how the work of war, although so plain and simple in its effects, can never be conducted with distinguished success by people without distinguished powers of the understanding." But what really distinguishes such people? Not skill in devising deceptions or unorthodox strategies; not the artful ability to achieve much by exposing little, even to the extent of defeating an enemy without raising a battle; nor comprehensive empirical knowledge of the strategic situation. To Clausewitz, the fog of war makes mockery of all such cognitive resources. Do not prepare your calculations. Prepare your battalions. It is force, not knowledge that wins wars.[19]

The contribution of intellect to Clausewitzian strategy is to provide "a sense of unity, and a judgment raised to such a compass as to give the mind an extraordinary faculty of vision." What is extraordinary about this vision is not what it sees, but what it does *not* see, does not *need* to see, does not get stuck trying, hopelessly, to see despite the fog. This mind "sets aside a thousand dim notions which an ordinary understanding could only bring to light with great effort, and over which it would exhaust itself." The most important quality of intellect for this commander is what he does not waste time trying to know, what he can ignore with serenity, concentrating on the decisive point, at which he throws everything he's got, unwavering, not dissuaded by grim reports from the foggy field.[20]

Clausewitz believes victory by stratagem must be a fluke. The outcome of modern warfare is determined by wearing down forces before the coup de grâce. The largest force necessarily takes the battle. Clausewitz would therefore not accept that deception is the *dao* of warfare, though he is apparently unacquainted with the Chinese art of war, which he never mentions. He dismisses what for the Chinese is the pinnacle of military accomplishment. "Let us not hear of generals who conquer without bloodshed." Courage, tenacity, boldness, and backbone are more important qualities in a commander than knowledge. War is a moral problem and finds its solution in the moral qualities of the commander, "moral" meaning "not cognitive," qualities of character in lieu of knowledge. Clausewitz "saw his main problem as the moral one; the capacity of the commander to maintain his determination, in spite of all temptations to the contrary, to concentrate his forces against that decisive point."[21]

Chinese thinking is, of course, very different. The *Secret Teachings* of the Taigong says, "'Know them and know yourself' is the great essence of the military strategists." In the twentieth century, Mao Zedong still regards the strategic value of knowledge as a "scientific truth" (*kexue de zhen li*). A Chinese commander is the intelligence that makes the army's *qi*, its potent intensity, artful, technical, and victorious. This commander is like a dance master, tamping out the rhythm and choreographing corporeal flows. A Han dictionary explains: "Martiality (*wu*) means 'to dance' (*wu*); the movements of an assault are like the drumming out of a dance." *Wuzi* calls the commander "the pivot (*ji*) of *qi*," meaning the army's *qi*, its intensive force, fighting spirit, or morale. Without the art of command this *qi* devolves into barbaric bellicosity and reckless heroics. Joined to a commander's strategic intelligence, however, and supplemented with carefully researched knowledge, the army performs with the *wu wei* potency of a sage.[22]

Sunzi also refutes the supremacy of force which for Clausewitz ultimately decides every conflict. As his French disciple, Marshal Foch, explains, "To fall on, but to fall on *in numbers,* in masses: therein lies salvation. For numbers, provided we know how to use them, will allow us, by means of the physical superiority placed at our disposal, to get the better of the violent enemy fire." To which *Sunzi* replies, "In my view, although Yue has many troops, what benefit is this to determining victory or defeat?" (SZ 6). Troops and weapons decide nothing because "in war, numerical superiority alone affords no clear advantage. If you avoid attacks that rely on military power alone, unify your forces, and properly assess the enemy, you will be able to take them. If you do not think things through ... you will surely end up being captured" (SZ 9). Because war is a problem of knowledge, not courage and numbers.[23]

Modern scholarship notes with some exasperation how the literature on Chinese military culture "is soaked with the notion that in Chinese strategic thought war was a 'last resort.'" Traditional Chinese culture had a collective perception of itself as fundamentally at odds with military as opposed to civil and literary values. Sunzi's "no fighting" (*bu zhan*) principle is taken to mean that the best victories are bloodless. Violence is a last resort against implacable enemies. That is how the Confucian masters of literate *wen* culture depict sanctioned violence when they write the histories. However, the *Military Classics* (of which *Sunzi* is the first) and their commentary tradition acknowledge that conflict and war are relatively constant features of interstate affairs. Violence inheres in social existence, and its use is requisite to self-preservation. Western tradition has a saying, *Si pacem parabellum,* If you want peace, prepare for war. The Chinese knew it too; for instance, in the *Zuo Zhang Commentary:* "When residing in peace, think of danger." War is inauspicious not absolutely but relatively; some uses of war are more righteous than others. Against an unrighteous adversary one should respond with righteous force to restore the order of things, as this Song dynasty *Military Classics* commentator explains: "Using perfect benevolence to punitively attack those who are not benevolent, and using perfect righteousness to punitively attack the unrighteous, this is 'cultivating the *dao.*' "[24]

These texts urge strategists to exercise patience, constantly weigh the changing nature of conflict, and at the opportune moment strike violently and decisively at the enemy's exposed weakness. "Not fighting" does not mean not fighting *at all.* It means not having to fight a lot, for a long time, with hard losses—not fighting as Clausewitz fights and thinks one *has* to fight to prevail. The stratagems that make "not fighting" effective are seldom decisive on their own. They merely expose the enemy's weakness, which is then attacked in a more or less orthodox way. Stratagem in Sunzi is not a bloodless alternative to violence; it is a way to enhance the effectiveness of violence, so that a little goes a long way. The *Military Classics* agree that the commander must have the right balance of orthodox and unorthodox deployments. Unorthodox misdirection sets up the violence of an orthodox strike to follow the opening that stratagem creates.

One may wonder who is right. Is strategic art and a cunning commander really as important as Chinese tradition thinks, or as irrelevant as Clausewitz implies? One of Clausewitz's harshest critics makes just the argument we might imagine coming from the pages of the *Sunzi.* The criticism is motivated by the responsibility Clausewitz is thought to bear for unprecedented slaughter in the First World War, where his ideas reigned supreme, and not only among the Germans. Observing that for Clausewitz, "the road to success was through the unlimited application of force," military historian B. H. Liddell Hart says that the outcome of this teaching "was to incite generals to seek battles at the *first* opportunity, instead of creating an *advantageous* opportunity. Thereby the art of war was reduced in 1914–18 to a process of mass slaughter." In the next war, Hitler dramatically departed from Prussian orthodoxy, to the consternation of his generals, with strategies redolent of China's military thought. "Our strategy," Hitler explains, "is to destroy the enemy from within, to conquer him through himself."[25]

Hart accuses Clausewitz of nothing less than "a *revolution in reverse*— back towards *tribal* warfare." The prestige of his theories and the willingness of commanders to apply them "has gone far to wreck civilization." Hart's idea of more civilized warfare reproduces distinctive features of Chinese strategy, despite his silence about a military philosophy he is clearly aware of. An epigraph to his book *Strategy: The Indirect Approach* reproduces nearly the whole first chapter of *Sunzi,* including the definition of deception as the *dao* of war. Yet thereafter, not one word about the bearing of Chinese thinking on his argument. At many points, however, Hart's ideas have parallels in Chinese thought, the most obvious being the very idea of strategy as an *indirect approach.*[26]

The direct clash of force against force to which Clausewitz reduces war is for Hart obvious folly. "To move directly on an opponent consolidates his balance, physical and psychological, and by consolidating it increases his resisting power." In recommending indirection Hart sounds almost Chinese: "In strategy, the longest way round is often the shortest way home." In Sunzi's formulation, "What is difficult about the clash of arms is to make the indirect route the most direct and turn misfortune to your advantage." Difficult, but crucial. Those who understand indirection "can set off after [the enemy] departs but arrive before them. This is to understand the strategy of making the indirect route the most direct." (SZ 7).[27]

Hart's indirect approach is, in effect, Sunzi's teaching on deception as the *dao* of war. Indirect strategy is deceptive strategy; you are not seen to be doing what you nevertheless make happen. Hart acknowledges that strategy "is largely concerned with the art of deception." His reason is the same as Sunzi's. Mislead enemies about where their strength and your weakness lie, and their strength becomes yours, while they inherit your disadvantages. Such deception, as I mentioned, means fighting the mind, and Hart agrees. "The true aim in war is the mind of the hostile rulers, not the bodies of their troops. . . . The balance between victory and defeat turns on mental impressions and only indirectly on physical blows." Whatever *form* a strategy may take, "the *effect* to be sought is the dislocation of the opponent's mind and dispositions—such an effect is the true gauge of an indirect approach."[28]

That pinnacle of Chinese strategy, subjugating the enemy's army without fighting, is not peculiar to the *Sunzi,* appearing in most of the texts of its tradition as the epitome of the new Warring States art of command, a tradition Hart witlessly rediscovers. Strategy, he says, "has for its purpose the reduction of fighting to the slenderest possible proportions." Its logical perfection would therefore be "to produce a decision without any serious fighting." Clausewitz mocked this idea, which earns him Hart's rebuke. Decisive near-bloodless victories have occurred in Western military history. Hart's examples include Caesar's Ilerda campaign, Cromwell's Preston campaign, Napoleon's Ulm campaign, Moltke's encirclement of MacMahon's army at Sedan, and Allenby's encirclement of the Turks at Samaria. "While such bloodless victories have been exceptional, their rarity enhances rather than detracts from their value—as an indication of the latent potentialities in strategy."[29]

Hart has a very Chinese appreciation of the quality Sunzi explains in terms of fluidity and formlessness: "The ultimate disposition of forces is for them to have no discernable shape or form" (SZ 6). "To be practical," Hart says, "any plan must take account of the enemy's power to frustrate it; the best chance of overcoming such obstruction is to have a plan that can be easily varied to fit the circumstances met; to keep such adaptability, while still keeping the initiative, the best way is to cooperate along a line which offers alternative objectives." "Fluidity of force," he adds, "may succeed where concentration of force merely entails a perilous rigidity." "The unexpected cannot guarantee success. But it guarantees the best chance of success."[30]

Sunzi and the art of war tradition also praise the quality of flexibility. Unforeseen circumstances cannot inconvenience one who remains uncommitted, when precisely the unforeseen becomes an advantage. Strategic flexibility is epitomized in the expression *quan bian*, weighing changes, which a *Military Classics* commentary explains as "weighing changes in the interactive relationship with the enemy." To be good at weighing changes means fighting when conditions are optimal, so that gains are maximized and losses minimized. Strategies originate in what the opponent gives, not in a predetermined plan. Like later Chinese "martial arts," the military art of war is an art of response, departing second, but arriving first. The adversary makes the first move and the strategy captures him. A Ming dynasty minister of war says, "The methods of employing the military instrument are hard to perceive, just like *yin* and *yang;* and hard to comprehend, just like ghosts and spirits. Thus one should stress responding to change at any particular moment. It is difficult to seek [victory] on the basis of a fixed [plan]."[31]

What to Clausewitz is fog, a barrier to knowledge, is a resource for one who can really see the little things. Flexibility flows from all kinds of emptiness, which impart a fluidity to the deployment of forces that never stops, a restless potency that never "is" (fully committed to) one form to the exclusion of another. "The strategic potential of an army has no fixed course or expression; just as water has no fixed disposition or form. Those who are able to achieve victory by changing and transforming in response to the dispositions of their enemies are called 'spirit-like' (*shen*)." Sunzi's praise invokes the awesome and numinous. "Subtle! So subtle! They are without form (*xing*). Spirit-like! So spirit-like! They make no sound. And so the enemy's fate lies in their hands" (SZ 6). Such commanders act like a force of nature, and like nature silently transform to bring forth effects unanticipated by those who are not good at seeing little things. What is spiritlike about their action is precisely its subtlety. The best explanation I have seen of the Chinese idea of "spirit" (*shen*) is in the medical tradition, which glosses it as righteous *qi* (*zhengqi*). A commentator on the *Yellow Emperor's Classic of Medicine* (*Huangdi Neijing*) explains, "The spirit is the integrity of the mind, i.e., the ability to react to changes in the environment. . . . Righteous *qi* is the capacity of the body to adapt to a changing environment with corresponding changes of the internal environment." Substitute the commander and army for the body and internal environment, and you have the military philosophy's understanding of strategic potency.[32]

If Clausewitz sees no place in war for knowledge, why did he write a book? There are of course things a commander should know in order to be successful. He should, for example, know how to accurately calculate a day's march for his columns. However, inquiry into enemy deployments or the personal details of enemy commanders is immaterial to victory. Clausewitz thinks this argument needs making because some well meaning but wrong-headed experts treat war as if it were a problem of knowledge. That is a dangerous folly. Wars are not won by knowledge. They are not won by stratagems or cunning intelligence. They are won by superior forces under the unwavering command of generals habituated to the conditions of war. The most important thing that a general should know about knowledge is not to expect or trust it.[33]

There is no better confirmation of the disesteem in which Clausewitz holds knowledge than what he says in a chapter on information in warfare. He explains that by "information" he means "all the knowledge which we have of the enemy and his country; therefore, in fact, the foundation of all our ideas and actions." However, this "foundation" turns out to be shifting sand, as everything Clausewitz says undermines information's value. War is a resistant medium to cognition. The greater part of intelligence garnered on the battlefield proves to be contradictory, false, or doubtful, "and the timidity of men acts as a multiplier of lies and untruths."[34]

He concedes that some kinds of information, including books about the enemy land or a leader's character and the reports of spies and reconnaissance, may have value, but their utility is easily exaggerated. "If we are not so near the enemy as to have him completely under our eye . . . then all that we know of his position must always be imperfect, as it is obtained by re-connaissances, patrols, information from prisoners, and spies, sources on which no firm reliance can be placed because intelligence thus obtained is always more or less of an old date, and the position of the enemy may have been altered in the meantime." More valuable than any information is "a talent for forming an ideal picture of a country quickly and distinctly." Only this talent, a matter of intuitive genius rather than knowledge, combined with the experience that habituates a commander to the conditions of war, "saves him from a certain mental helplessness, and makes him less depen-dent on others." Undaunted by the contradictory influx of reports from the field, "firm in reliance on his own better convictions," the Clausewitzian commander "must stand like a rock against which the sea breaks its fury in vain."[35]

There may be no blunter contrast with the Chinese esteem for strategic knowledge than in Sunzi's analysis of espionage, a topic Clausewitz disdains even to discuss. His single use of the word "spies" (or cognates, including espionage) is to deny their usefulness. For Sunzi, however, to remain igno-rant of the enemy's condition through inability or unwillingness to deploy spies is "the height of inhumanity. Such people are not fit to serve as gen-erals; they are not true counsellors, nor are they masters of victory" (SZ 13). A commander cannot know enough about the family and personal names of the enemy leaders, their closest associates, messengers, gatekeepers, and attendants. Also crucial is to discover who the enemy has spying on you, so that you can turn or manipulate them. The work distinguishes five vari-eties of spies: local, meaning the inhabitants of a district; inner, meaning the enemy's own officials; double, meaning enemy spies who have been turned; dead, meaning one's own spies who are unwittingly given misleading information and then sacrificed; and live, meaning spies in the usual sense, who observe the enemy's encampment and detect his plans and survive to report back to their masters.[36]

It is not easy to weave all these sources into a coherent fabric of strategic knowledge. One has the impression that the *Sunzi* author(s) would acknowl-edge the difficulties Clausewitz enumerates for the use of information on the battlefield. But the Chinese expect a commander to rise above these ob-stacles through subtle strategic intelligence, so that knowledge, especially the information gained by espionage, becomes a resource rather than the dangerous impediment it remains for Clausewitz. "If one is not sagely and wise, one cannot use spies. If one is not benevolent and righteous, one cannot deploy spies. If one is not subtle and sensitive, one cannot get the truth out of spies. How subtle! How subtle! Spies can be used everywhere!" (SZ 13).

Whatever we now believe about the strategic value of intelligence, espionage, and deception comes from looking to the Chinese for something systematically undervalued in Western theory. This singular estimation of knowledge emerges with the Chinese art of war in an early development of ideas that define the Chinese contribution to the philosophy of knowledge. A war machine on Sunzi's principles would be difficult for alert men of any class or rank to ignore. They do not have to *like* it, and Confucians scorn the military philosophy. The point is, how could they ignore it, or consider it mistaken in what it teaches about the effectiveness of knowledge?[37]

There may be better ways to demonstrate wisdom than military victory, but civilian thinkers tend to want the effectiveness the military lauds without the martial function. Art-of-war thinkers differ from Confucians and Daoists in how they direct the effectiveness they expect from sage knowledge, but that is a difference amidst agreement about what such knowledge is and why it is valuable. The value of the best knowledge, what makes it canny and sagacious, is its specific productivity, an inconspicuous yet unsurmountable *wu wei* effectiveness.

— 4 —

Chan Buddhism

In understanding, nothing is attained; where we obtain it, we cannot say we "know." When I teach you this matter, can you withstand it?

—CHAN MASTER HUANGBO

Buddhism seems premised on knowledge in a way other religions are not. The salvation it promises is a kind of cognitive breakthrough, an accomplishment of knowledge. Ordinary life is cloaked in illusion, being no more than a dream. People do not understand that, so they form attachments to these apparitions, and consequently suffer. If knowledge were perfect, there would be no attachments and no suffering. That is not how we (inheritors of monotheism) usually think of religious faith. Faith is not knowledge. Its certainty is not the certainty of knowledge, its difficulty not the difficulty of knowledge. The difficulty of knowledge is achieving it; the difficulty of faith is sustaining it. Faith, being a mystery, can disappear as mysteriously as it came, but achieved knowledge can no more be lost than yesterday can become tomorrow.

I do not mean to deny a place for faith in Buddhism. Practitioners must have faith that their effort will bear fruit, faith in the teachers who oversee their practice, and faith in the Buddha's merit. A peculiarity of Buddhism, however, is its thought that the origin of suffering is ignorance, entrenched but not unreachable. With appropriate effort a follower can internalize a set of Buddhist categories sufficient to overcome the ignorance that dooms us to suffering and rebirth. We suffer because we act on volitions formed in ignorance of the facts about existence. Born into a body, we experience sensory objects, whose pleasures and pain fuel desire. Ignorance brings suffering and suffering reinforces ignorance, as we tenaciously cling to the delusion of personal existence. Once we are enlightened, and perceive things as they really are, the root of suffering is removed and salvation attained.[1]

Enlightenment, liberation, nirvana—these are salvific accomplishments of Buddhist knowledge. To find your way to such knowledge you need a method, a teacher, and some provisional doctrine. Those requirements seem to epitomize the way Buddhism was taught in India at the time of the Mahayana rift, in the first century BCE, about a century before Buddhism arrived in China. Indian teachers had reduced salvation to a problem of knowledge. The Mahayana movement is an internal dissent among these teachers, who resist, from within knowledge, the liberating value of knowledge. Mahayana Buddhism is known for its idea of emptiness (*sunyata*, Chinese *kong*). The idea breaks sharply with their tradition, by subverting the Buddha's sutras' stature as ultimate truth. This Mahayana legacy emerges with inventive tenacity in Chinese Buddhism and especially Chan (Zen), which would grow to become the most influential sect in China for a time, controlling some 90 percent of the temples.[2]

We see the characteristic Mahayana swerve from earlier tradition in a sequence of passages from the *Lankavatara Sutra*, a classic Mahayana statement. First it is said that "the disciple must get into the habit of looking at things truthfully. He must recognize the fact that the world has no self-nature, that it is unborn, that it is like a passing cloud, like an imaginary wheel made by a revolving firebrand." With that insight attained, "these discriminations come to be seen as mutually conditioning, as empty of self-substance, as unborn, and thus come to be seen as they truly are, that is, as manifestations of the mind itself—this is right knowledge." The salvific *paramita*, the perfections of the Bodhisattva, "are grounded in right knowledge." To achieve that knowledge is Buddhist insight, Buddhist wisdom, but not yet nirvana. There is one more step. "The disciple should then abandon the understanding of mind which he has gained by right knowledge." The last step steps out of the system to embrace the empty sky.[3]

We have taken the measure of Chinese concurrence on the value of knowledge. Chan, a descendent of India's Mahayana tradition, reverses this value. Knowledge is part of the problem Buddhism addresses—the problem of suffering. Yet if that idea is true, or if it works, is it not wise to know? How could anything except knowledge point knowledge beyond knowledge? Of course Buddhist enlightenment is not theoretical knowledge. Its difficulty is not that of mathematics. It is the corporeal difficulty of meditation for an unruly body, combined with the challenge of internalizing a paradoxical orientation in everyday life. It requires knowledge not of objects but of the mind, and not knowledge of its nature but disenchanted knowledge that mind is not an entity, that it has no nature, indeed that it is empty, nothing at all. Knowledge takes one that far. The next step is to realize that knowledge is as empty as the mind that knows no knowing.

That sounds sort of Daoist. It can be made to sound even more Daoist, and Chan authors sometimes labor to make their message appeal to Daoists. Some scholars think Chan *is* Daoist, a Buddhist Daoism, or Daoist Buddhism. One calls Chan "typically Chinese, practical, concrete, and above all Daoist. Chan thought, at odds with the scholasticism of the Buddhism of the Great Vehicle, borrowed from Daoist mysticism its shattering of concepts, its teaching without words, and its spontaneity." Borrowed, he is saying, from the *Daodejing, Zhuangzi,* and later Daoist thought, rather than from Indian sources, such as Nagarjuna and the Mahayana tradition, or Yogacara or Tathatagarbha Buddhism.[4]

There is something to this interpretation. Daoist monasteries provided the model for Buddhists in China, where monks are temple based, a Daoist practice not usual in India. The first Buddhist books selected for translation into Chinese respond to Daoist preoccupations with medicine, breathing, and meditation. Buddhists and Daoists were from an early point also sharing sacred mountains, notably Songshan, which had been a holy place for Daoists since the first century CE. Buddhist monasteries appear there in the third century. Legend tells of a Chan monk defeating the local deity of Songshan, and converting it to Buddhism. The monk confronts the Songshan spirit, who threatens to kill him. "Since I am unborn, how could you kill me? My body is empty and I see myself as no different from you: how could you destroy emptiness, or destroy yourself?" Songshan's famous Shaolin Temple (founded 497) becomes a center of Chan teaching in the eighth century. It is probably then that the link is made between Bodhidharma, Chan's first patriarch, and Shaolin (its reputation for martial arts, however, is still in the future).[5]

Daoism is in its splendor during the Six Dynasties period, from the fourth to sixth centuries CE. Inner cultivation, breath control, *daoyin* moving meditation, and alchemy take center stage. Life and death come to be seen not as fates to endure but technical challenges to superior, esoteric knowledge. Longevity, even a kind of immortality, can be obtained by careful management, nourishing the *qi* with diet, stretching, and respiratory and sexual exercises calibrated to counteract decrepitude. Among these Daoists, Buddhism had the reputation of a new method for the immortality that fascinated them. It was supposed to be an especially pure, moral, balanced practice, one that avoided alchemy and emphasized meditation. That early reputation "gave it a luster," writes Henri Maspero, "which the small number of its adherents and its foreign character would otherwise not have allowed it to hope for." Chan reciprocates this prestigious interest by presenting its masters as Laozi look-alikes. The Chan legend of the death of Bodhidharma, which tellingly imitates a Laozi legend and is new in the eighth century, is an example.[6]

Nevertheless, I think similarities between Daoism and Chan are easily exaggerated and often largely verbal, a skillful means for Chan authors to make missionary use of vocabulary and concepts that are Daoist only to a point, before they depart in a predictable way. What makes the departure predictable is a completely different idea of *emptiness* in Chan and Daoism and a no less different understanding of the value of knowledge.

Emptiness and Nonduality

The first record of Buddhists in China is from 65 CE, referring to a community in Suzhou under the protection of a Han prince. It is not until the late second and third century that Buddhist belief and practice take hold at all levels of society. I want to clarify that my concern is specifically with the Chan school of Chinese Buddhism, whose teaching became known throughout the world under the Japanese name Zen. Chan is many things. It has roots in Mahayana Buddhism and the ideas of Nagarjuna; it appropriates from the Daoist classics, as well as from earlier developments in Chinese Buddhism; and it is a Sinitic critique of Indocentrism, impatient with a Buddhism of translated sutras, imported relics, and foreign traditions.[7]

Complicating the genealogy of Chan is an internal history that proves to be a fond fable. For instance, according to the internal account, Chan goes back to Bodhidharma, and has been in China since his arrival (at Shaolin) from India in the fifth century. But scholars cannot see any Chan at all until the eighth century, when it first becomes an established identity with a corps of monks and temples, and that happens not at Shaolin but elsewhere, among a community unaware of descent from Bodhidharma known as the Dongshan or East Mountain school. As for Bodhidharma, he seems to be a historical individual and not entirely legendary; a native of south India, a Brahmin, Mahayanist, and meditation instructor, who arrived in south China around 479, and moved north to the Loyang (Songshan) area, where he died around 530. More than that is hard to say on the evidence, legends excepted. Perhaps evidence is thin because he was not as extraordinary in life as in latter lore. He may be less important as a historically effective influence than as a fabled founder constructed centuries later, when he becomes Chan's first Laozi look-alike.[8]

The Dongshan school eventually established a master at the Shaolin Temple on Mount Song, which had already become a site of Buddhist-Daoist interaction. It is apparently at this time that the name of Bodhidharma is connected to the Dongshan teaching that will eventually be called Chan, and to Shaolin Temple, which becomes a staging center for its expansion into the nearby capitals of Chang-an and Loyang. Around 730 the Dongshan school is very publically attacked in the capital by a monk named Shenhui, whose philippics create a crisis within the local Buddhist community, and the beginning of the myth of a Northern and Southern School of Chan, supposedly at odds over important points of Buddhist theory and practice. In the aftermath of the horrific An Lushan rebellion (755), possibly the most violent insurrection in world history, Chan orthodoxy passes to Mazu's school in Hongzhou (well away from the capital), and his disciples establish monastic centers throughout the empire and abroad. They were superseded by the Linji (Japanese, *Rinzai*) school, whose founder is a third-generation disciple of Mazu. This school went on to define Chan orthodoxy throughout East Asia.[9]

I want to look at one of Chan's many sources, the Indian Mahayanist Nagarjuna, and especially his teaching on emptiness. I select this moment of Chan genealogy not because of the legend that Bodhidharma followed Nagarjuna's Madhyamaka Buddhist sect, but because Nagarjuna's ideas help us appreciate what is philosophically at stake in Chan thought on emptiness (*kong*) and especially the emptiness of knowledge. Emptiness in Nagarjuna means absence or nonpresence. What is not present, what Nagarjuna says the world is empty of, is *svabhava,* a Sanskrit word meaning "self-nature," "inherent existence," or "own being." Something is *svabhava* when it has a characteristic property that individuates it and renders it namable and knowable. Chandrakirti, in the classical commentary on Nagarjuna, says, "This is the definition of it: *Svabhava* is not artificially created and not dependent on anything else." To use a Platonic expression, *svabhava* is *auto kath auto,* itself from itself, self-identical, enjoying intrinsic, nonrelational identity and existence. The comparison seems legitimate. One scholar sees in the term *svabhava* "the same overall meaning as *substance* in Western metaphysics—it is the 'really existent' substratum that underlies contingent 'accidents' and phenomenal change."[10]

Nagarjuna's teaching on emptiness corrects the mistaken belief in *svabhava*. The emptiness he reveals is the radical absence of *svabhava* being. *Svabhava* is a miscognition, an inextricable fallacy built right into concepts and their use. We spontaneously conceive of objects as enduring rather than unrelated momentary arising and ceasing, and think that enduring things exist apart from their perception. The conviction that something somewhere, at some level, enjoys *svabhava* being is an ontological error and a faulty cognition, a misconception we unwittingly project on phenomena, which besides being completely false commits us to suffering and rebirth.

Nagarjuna presents emptiness as a deduction from dependent origination, the Buddhist theory of the reciprocal causal dependence of all things upon each other. "It is dependent co-arising that we term emptiness," he says. "The cessation of ignorance occurs through right understanding. Through the cessation of this and that, this and that will not come about. The entire mass of suffering thereby completely ceases." According to Chandrakirti's commentary, "the one who sees dependent origination correctly does not perceive a substance even in subtle things." Another commentary asks, "What knowledge (*jnana*) does one cultivate to cut off ignorance?" and replies with Nagarjuna that it is "the knowledge that cognizes dependent co-arising, that knowledge of emptiness that denies that all the entities have their own-being, that understands persons and dharmas to be ... without self."[11]

There is nothing to the appearance of things, no substantial, true identity or being. Neither have things a nature, latency, or virtuality; there is nothing to them that is not already actual in their causes, their causes' causes, and so on. Everything is what it is conditioned to be, and that leaves everything altogether empty of substantial being. Emptiness reigns everywhere we think being is. That may seem to make "emptiness" a new name for being, but the subtle Nagarjuna evades this objection. Critics were eager to fault his irrealism. Are Nagarjuna's assertions empty? If so, then he has nothing to say and says nothing. If he communicates at all, then it cannot be true that everything is empty, because his assertion is not empty, not if it truly is an assertion. Nagarjuna agrees with this argument but says it does not refute him. "If I had a proposition, this defect would attach to me. But I have no proposition. Therefore I am not at fault."[12]

Another work elaborates this gnomic refutation with another reference to dependent co-arising. "Just as such things as chariots, clothes, and pots, although they are empty of substance by virtue of being dependently co-arisen, function in their respective tasks—i.e., transporting wood, hay, or soil, containing honey, water, or milk, protecting from the cold or wind or heat, etc.—just so, this statement of mine ['all things lack substance'], although it lacks substance on account of being dependently co-arisen, functions in establishing the inexistence of substance." All concepts, all terms, no less that of *sunyata* (empty) itself, are incomplete symbols composed of provisional names. It is not assumed that they stand for entities or even make sense, whatever that means. But they do function, they have effects. "Emptiness" is not a metaphysical concept or ontological reality; it is not the ultimate truth of the world, and not a name for being. It does not say: nothing exists, nothing is real; instead, it directs us to eliminate substantializing thought and especially the delusional apprehension we fondly call "self." That requires an endless work of negation: nothingness, the nothingness of nothingness, the nothingness of nothingness's nothingness; an endlessly annihilating movement of pure negation, until delusion is burnt to ashes and personal existence is extinguishing.[13]

Emptiness is not an ontological reality, like the void of Democritus. "Empty" is not a first-order term supposedly referring to a feature of the world; rather, it is a sign in a second-order system for describing first-order systems. Of course, pieces of language are entities too. One can imagine an infinite series of metalanguages: languages describing languages describing languages. Nagarjuna cuts the series short with his thought that the symbols of language are empty of object-content. It is languages describing languages from the beginning and all the way down. Verbal discourse is imaginary, its expression only metaphorical, words for words. There is no such thing as a literal statement. Nothing is simply true. Nagarjuna develops a dialectic of suspended reference known as the Double Truth, meaning conventional truth and ultimate truth. This is not exactly a dichotomy, and not Plato's distinction between *doxa* (opinion) and *episteme* (science). Nagarjuna distinguishes "ultimate truth" only to say that it is empty. That does not mean emptiness is the ultimate truth. It means that "ultimate truth" is an empty predicate. The higher truth is that there is no higher truth. "No truth has been taught by a Buddha for anyone, anywhere," says the Buddhist teacher. It is conventional passing-for-true all the way down.[14]

The idea of emptiness is not for the philosophically flatfooted, as Nagarjuna knows. "Emptiness wrongly seen destroys the slow-witted, like a serpent wrongly grasped or magic wrongly performed." Is the thought true? No, not in the sense of adequacy to the self-nature of an ultimate reality. There is no self-nature, only emptiness of self-nature, therefore no ultimate truth, only a provisional passing-for-true, of which this teaching on emptiness may be an example. Conventional truth is like paper money. A banknote has currency if it passes, that is, by usage, not through relation to anything intrinsically valuable. So too what passes for true. What is important (to pragmatic functionality) is that others accept it, not that it is "really true," in the sense of adequacy to a pristine *Ding an sich*. Nagarjuna could not be more clear: "*It is empty* is not to be said, nor that something could be non-empty, nor both, nor either."[15]

How does this famous tetralemma (*catuskoti*) manage to exclude all those possibilities (*all* the possibilities)? It is because "*empty* is said only in the sense of 'conceptual fiction.'" We think, *Either p or not-p*. It has to be one or the other. Unless p depends on an assumption. If *not-p* depends on the same assumption, then anyone who denies the assumption must deny both *p* and *not-p*, which is what Nagarjuna does. Either cold or not cold. But to be cold is to be a body; if something were not a body it would be neither cold nor not cold. *Either empty or not empty* implies that *something* enjoys *svabhava* being, *something* "is." Nagarjuna denies the assumption. Any *is* presupposes a *not*. To think *x* (*x is*) is to think that something is *x*, which is to think of something *x* is not, from which it is differentiated. So *X is empty* is not empty. Emptiness simply cannot be said. That sounds like Parmenides (nonbeing cannot be thought or said), except it is Parmenides in a looking glass. Instead of forbidding thinkers recourse to the *not*, Nagarjuna suspends thought's presumption of being. The Eleatic thinker has the lover of truth "say and think only this, being is." After Nagarjuna the apothegm must become more ambiguous. "Do not say or think this, nothing is."[16]

Parmenides says we must suspend the *not*, say and think only *being*. Adhere to that stricture and we are promised access to ultimate reality. For Nagarjuna, the emptiness of *not being* does not imply the ultimate reality of *being*. Instead, the distinction of being and not being is found defective. The difference from Parmenides is that for the Eleatic, nondifferentiation (thinking only "Being is") is true, the ultimate truth, disclosing the monadic essence of being. Nagarjuna never says emptiness is the truth. In fact, he says that nothing is true in the sense Parmenides wants. It is because he believes in ultimate truth that Parmenides thinks we face a momentous decision, that we have to choose between two ways, two paths, those of Being and Not Being, which Plato will gloss as Reality and Appearance, and interpret in terms of Mind and Body. To insist on these distinctions, to say we *must* make them, must make them *clear*, might look to alert Buddhist eyes like clinging, an expression of suffering, suffering from the delusion of being and truth.

Another word for emptiness is nonduality. The usual opposite of dualism is monism; for instance, against the dualism of Plato and Descartes range materialist theories of nature from Democritus to Diderot. However, monism is not the same as nonduality; indeed, monism is dualistic through and through, since it discriminates and opposes dualism. The most consistent nondualism is not monism but emptiness. First you overcome all the distinctions, then you overcome your overcoming, overcome thinking of having overcome something, of having realized something others do not.

Duality seems inextricable from thought. What would we think if we made no distinctions? However, nondualistic thought is not *thinking* "emptiness" (as a paradoxical object). It empties thinking of objects, empties consciousness of objectivity, forgets about distinctions, even the distinction between *is* and *is not*. The effect is not merely to render thought void of objects; one ceases to care about objectivity or lack of it, becoming indifferent to whether things are the same or different, better or worse, right or wrong, and so on. The cessation of ignorance comes not with the truth of emptiness but the emptiness of truth.

Chan's approach to enlightenment seems to translate Nagarjuna's teaching on emptiness into their new Buddhist practice. The cultivated absurdity of Zen *koan* and the fugitive rationality of statements like "If you meet the Buddha, kill him" seem like practical inferences for practicing emptiness. Chan teaching is emphatic that enlightenment cannot be understood in words. Even to say that words point to something beyond words is too many words, introducing a dualism between *words* and *beyond words*, and suggesting that we have to make a choice and cling to one or the other. Doctrinal formulations are fatal. You cannot say the most important thing. Instead, Dharma mastery transmits directly from one mind to another, going all the way back to the Buddha, and passing from India to China in the lineage descending from Bodhidharma, Chan's first patriarch.

That understanding of tradition (which might also be called its nullification) places teachers in a new position. Their teaching cannot be a doctrinal exposition, so how should they interact with students? Almost everything we know about classical Chan masters derives from the record of their unprecedented repartee, which confirms Chan's reputation for being strange even to other Buddhists. Confucians spoke of *kuang chan,* mad zen. It is this "madness" that Chan's greatest writers cultivate.[17]

Chan calls for a return to immediate experience, that is, meditation, hence the name (*chan,* meditation). Yet reading and writing are never eliminated, and Chan masters are notably literate. That should not surprise us. We should not expect to have to choose between reading or not reading. Both are wrong in isolation and as a dualism they represent objects of clinging. The problem is *how* to read. The solution Chan finds is a mode of reading that does not venerate and reify a text as an object of knowledge, but instead puts the text into practice as a skillful means of enlightenment. There is a need to write emptiness, to reach emptiness through a practice of reading and writing, of which the *gong'an* (Japanese, *koan*) are the fruit.

Chan *gong'an,* with their intense vernacular language and inexplicable iconoclasm, begin to appear in the eleventh century. To remind you or quickly introduce you to the genre here are three classic *gong'an* from the Record of Master Yunmen:

> Someone asked, "What is the pure immaculate Dharma body?" Master Yunmen replied, "That peony hedge!" The monk asked, "Is it all right if I understand it in this way?" The Master said, "A golden-haired lion!"

> Someone asked: "Life and death is here; how am I to cope with it?" The Master said, "Where is it?"

> Someone asked Master Yunmen, "What is the absolute concentration which comprehends every single particle of dust?" The Master replied, "Water in the bucket, food in the bowl."[18]

What is one to do with these? In a passage modeled on Nagarjuna's tetralemma, the great Chan master Huangbo says this about *gong'an:* "You should not start reasoning from these perceptions, nor allow them to give rise to conceptual thought; yet nor should you seek the One Mind apart from them or abandon them in your pursuit of the Dharma. Do not keep them nor abandon them nor dwell in them nor cleave to them." Perhaps we should expect that only a paradox can explain a paradox. Another teacher recounts his instruction for *gong'an* meditation in training a nun: "I cited Mazu's [*gong'an*] 'It is not mind, it is not Buddha, it is not a thing' and instructed her to look at it. Moreover, I gave her an explanation: 'You must not take it as a statement of truth. You must not take it to be something you do not need to do anything about. Do not take it as a flint-struck spark or a lightning flash. Do not try to divine the meaning of it. Do not try to figure it out from the context in which I brought it up. "It is not the mind, it is not the Buddha, it is not a thing; after all, what is it?"'" This teacher, Dahui Zonggao, was the most prominent Chan master of the Song dynasty. His use of *gong'an* emphasizes what he calls "observing the key phrase" (*huatou*). An example he favored is Zhaozhou's reply to a monk's question whether a dog has the Buddha nature. Zhaozhou answered, "No" (*wu*). Dahui writes:

> When you observe it [this *huatou*, this *wu*], do not ponder it widely, do not try to understand every word, do not try to analyze it, do not consider it to be at the place where you open your mouth, do not reason that it is at the place [in your mind] where you hold it up, do not fall into a vacuous state, do not hold on to "mind" and await enlightenment, do not try to experience it through the words of your teacher, and do not get stuck in a shell of unconcern. Just at all times, whether walking or standing, sitting or lying, hold on to this "*wu*." "Does a dog actually have the Buddha nature or not?" If you hold on to this *wu* to a point where it becomes ripe, when no discussion or consideration can reach it and it is as if you were caught in a space of one square inch; and when it has no flavor, as if you were chewing on a raw iron cudgel, and you get so close to it you cannot pull back—when you are able to be like this, then that is really good news.[19]

It is sometimes said that meditation on the *gong'an* can take one beyond dualistic thinking. For Dahui it is no less important to overcome doubt. Doubt on the way to enlightenment is inevitable. What treatment avails? Dahui's answer is to concentrate on the immense doubt a Chan *huatou* produces. Let it swell. Eventually, he says, it will shatter like a bubble and doubt will disappear. Perhaps that is why he favors Zhaozhou's "*wu*." Denying the Buddha nature of a dog seems an obvious contradiction of the Chan teaching that all sentient beings have the original Buddha nature. Thus Zhaozhou's *wu* must inspire doubt. How could a great Chan teacher say that, mean that? What should one do with it? At least stop pondering it—the masters agree that is futile—and start pondering your own pondering. Think about what presupposition makes the *huatou* absurd. It often seems to come down to the assumption that there is a self-nature, an ultimate truth, *svabhava* some-where. That empty assumption spins the trap you are stuck in. It is the trap of knowledge, the expectation that it is not empty, that on the contrary it can make sense of things, and lead to liberation. It cannot. Knowledge be-longs to the problem of life, not its solution.

No Mind

Chan is a monk's Buddhism, a Buddhism for spiritual virtuosi. First you eliminate views—emptiness—then you eliminate the elimination and find—emptiness. You are left not with a knowledge of emptiness, but the empti-ness of knowledge. Among the attachments you shed is the need to make sense. That an enlightened one would speak with someone still in fetters is a pure act of compassion for the other's unknowing suffering. The expecta-tion of communication is delusional, and there is no ultimate truth at stake between opposed views whatever they may be. Making sense is a kind of clinging, a compulsion to be understood that gives others power over you and submits you to their delusion. To expect a serious answer from a Chan master to a serious question is a serious misunderstanding from the start, like offering a bribe in open court. "Take me seriously—share my delusion!" No wonder the masters resorted to blows. The Chan *Platform Sutra* says, "Don't try to see the true (*zhen*) in any way. If you try to see the true, your seeing will be in no way true."[20]

Chan is not a metaphysical idealism; it does not teach that objects be-long to consciousness or are constructions of the mind. It is not an ontology, and does not lay claim to the ultimate truth about reality. If we must have a Western term, Chan seems like a nonintentional phenomenology, which is a paradox inasmuch as phenomenology is the science of consciousness, and consciousness is defined by intentionality, or reference to an object. If there must be an object, Chan is a phenomenology of the vanishing object, the seen-through, senseless, unfulfilled, void, and vacant.

For an example of its analyses I turn to the *Platform Sutra,* attributed to Huineng, sixth of the Chan patriarchs going back to Bodhidharma. The main points of its argument seem to be these:

1. The identity of wisdom and meditation. Meditation is the expression of wisdom, the functioning of wisdom's substance. Meditation is the lamp and wisdom the light.

2. Radical detachment, including detachment from detachment.
3. The Buddha nature of all sentient beings. To recover this nature is to regain the original mind. The function of meditation is that recovery, though we do not know in advance what it is to meditate. Anything (cutting bamboo, carrying water, perhaps even practicing martial arts) might be meditative and a way to enlightenment.
4. The idea of no-thought (*wu nian*), which this work identifies as its principal teaching.

As *wu wei* does not mean no action but rather a special kind of action with a peculiar intentionality, so "no thought" does not mean no thinking but rather thought of a peculiar quality. "No-thought is not to think even when involved in thought." The idea is to eliminate attachment, clinging in thought. Western theory calls this clinging "reference" or "intentional relation to an object." The Buddhist claim is that this relation is a kind of clinging, a kind of suffering, and a delusional, empty non-relation to nothing at all. No-thought is not no thinking. It is thinking without clinging. "The Dharma of no-thought means: even though you see all things, you do not attach to them." You see things, or what the world calls "things," but they are not endorsed as reidentifiable referents of egocentric attitudes, because they have not become objects to which thought clings. They are whirling embers, a rainbow over a waterfall. Same, different, why want to know?[21]

Someone versed in Western psychology might say such consciousness is impossible. Consciousness is defined by intentionality, which means aboutness or reference to an object. Thus Brentano writes, "Every mental phenomenon is characterized by . . . immanent objectivity. Every mental phenomenon includes something as object within itself." For Husserl, "In every wakeful *cogito*, a 'glancing ray' from the pure Ego is directed upon the 'object' of the correlate consciousness for the time being." Such conviction in these expressions of the creed! However, it is the unintentional contribution of Chan to reveal this intentionality thesis as optional and burdened with baggage Buddhists won't bear. They think the delusion of objects is a karmic effect of clinging and selfishness. Can it be the foregone conclusion of "transcendental logic" that consciousness is condemned to this suffering, and Buddhism futile?[22]

Referring to "the reckless fabrications of worldly discourse," the eighth-century *Surangama Sutra*, a defining work for Chan, says that "the establishment of perceived objects such that they exist separately within your

awareness is the foundation of ignorance." Objects and intentional reference are not just transcendental presuppositions of thought; they are selfishness and ignorance in their most entrenched form. "Because you have
lost touch with your mind's true nature by identifying yourself with the objects you perceive, you keep on being bound to the cycle of death and rebirth." Those who have mastered meditation "are able to redirect the attention of their faculties inward to the faculties' source . . . [and] no longer pay
attention to objects of perception."[23]

Do not stop thinking, stop clinging, stop stopping. "If one instant of
thought clings, then successive thoughts cling; this is known as being fettered. If in all things successive thoughts do not cling, then you are unfettered." Invoking the trope of "the other shore," a figure for the quiescence
of nirvana, the *Sutra* says, " 'The other shore' means ever separating from
all objects so there is no arising-and-perishing, like water constantly flowing
everywhere without obstruction." In Huangbo's later words, "Your sole concern should be, as thought succeeds thought, to avoid clinging to any of
them." Intentional thought is fettered. Thinking *of* some object—an object
of knowledge, description, desire, or purpose—is a form of clinging to a moment, the delusion of presence, a reidentifiable object with a nature of its
own. Successive thoughts that do not cling are unburdened by objects. You
are thinking, there are thoughts; but you are not clinging, they are not your
objects, you do not know whether they are "the same" again or different.
No object is posited, thought is without thesis; it is mind alone, edging on
emptiness.[24]

Which is not catatonic. The awakened are not incapable of ordinary
(seeming) action—eating, doing chores, and so on. The Chan *Blue Cliff Record* depicts an awakened being as "like the sun and moon moving though
the sky without ever stopping. . . . In the midst of no activity, he carries out
his activities, accepting all unavoidable and favorable circumstances with
a compassionate heart." According to the *Lankavatara Sutra*, liberation is
"not the cessation of perceiving functions, but the cessation of discriminating
and naming activities." "The old body continues to function and the old
mind serves the needs of the old body." A novice may stumble here. "Disciples may not appreciate that the mind system, because of its accumulated habit-energy, goes on functioning, more or less unconsciously, as
long as they live. . . . The goal of tranquilization is to be reached not by
suppressing all mind activity but by getting rid of discriminations and
attachments."[25]

The point continues to be made in later tradition; for instance, Zen master Bankei Yotaku: "You have no difficulty telling what is hot and what is cold, without having to give rise to a thought to make such a distinction. . . . The Buddha-mind with its illuminating wisdom is capable of discriminating things with a miraculous efficiency. It is anything but indifferent. How could any human being, who is able to think, be indifferent?" Differences register, the mind is sensate, just there is no attachment. For Korean master So Sahn, "A true man of the Way who has nothing left to accomplish . . . is completely unfettered and from moment to moment does not make anything: when hungry, he eats; when tired, he sleeps. He wanders freely among the clear streams and blue mountains. He mingles easily and without hindrance in the busy ports and alehouses."[26]

The masters agree, however, that plans and purposes are counterproductive. The enlightened are "constantly thinking, yet nothing is pursued." For Linji (of "if you meet the Buddha, kill him" fame), "When a man *tries* to practice the *dao,* the *dao* does not function. If you engage in any seeking it will all be pain. Much better do nothing." He responds to a stock question put to Chan masters: "Someone asked: 'What was the purpose of the Patriarch's coming from the West?' The Master said: 'If he had a purpose he couldn't have saved even himself.'" This proposed purposelessness is not an unconscious, unthinking, mechanical reaction to uncomprehended causes. It is consciousness of vanishing intentionality, vanishing reference, consciousness vanishing into the emptiness of things.[27]

With the empty consciousness of unfettered thinking we recover the original condition of the mind, which is called the Buddha nature. This original mind makes each of us already a Buddha, fully enlightened, only we fail to realize it. When you start thinking from the original mind rather than fettered consciousness, with its incessant demand for an object, then, returning to the *Platform Sutra,* "although you see, hear, perceive, and know, you are not stained by the manifold environments, and are always free." The result is not to know something; it is to realize the emptiness of knowledge, which is still an accomplishment of knowledge, vanishing knowledge.[28]

"Ignorant, a Buddha is a sentient being; with wisdom, a sentient being is a Buddha." "Wisdom" here is *zhihui,* translating Sanskrit *prajna.* This wisdom is said to be "like the sun, knowledge is like the moon"—clear per se and reliable, but when our mind "clings to external environments" we bring on the cloud of false thoughts (that is, fettered, objective thoughts), losing the light and losing our way. The false or delusional is not the inaccurate, inadequate, or noncorresponding. It is the objective. Falsehood is being stuck in objects. The absence of delusion is emptiness, but we should not despise appearances. The enlightened see through them, but all they see vanishes into the emptiness on the other side, so it is not as if they have access to something truer and more substantial. There is nothing more real if you do not like appearances, nothing truer to believe if you do not like passing-for-true. Buddhist wisdom is not knowledge attained, it is knowledge vanishing into the emptiness of things.[29]

There do not seem to be large differences between Huineng's no-thought and Huangbo's later no-mind teaching. "No mind is the absence of all kinds of discriminating mind," that is, all kind of referential consciousness. "Mind is Buddha; no-mind is the *dao*. Simply do not give rise to conceptual thoughts, thinking in terms of existence and nothingness, long and short, others and self, subject and object." Mazu's "ordinary mind" (*ping chang xin*) is another version of Chan no-thought. "What do I mean by 'ordinary mind'? It is a mind that is devoid of contrived activity and is without notions of right and wrong, grasping and rejecting, terminable and permanent, worldly and holy." Mazu's Chan emphasizes the Mahayana insight that opposing nirvana to samsara (appearance) is just another futile dualism. "There is no specifiable difference whatever between nirvana and samsara," Chandrakirti says, expounding Nagarjuna. "There is not even the subtlest difference between the two." Enlightenment is not a goal (that is, an object). We are already there, nirvana is here, now. Therefore stop aspiring, stop searching, stop stopping, and return to the ordinary, except without the dualism of ordinary and enlightened. "If you would only rid yourself of the concepts of ordinary and enlightened," Huangbo says, "you would find that there is no other Buddha than the Buddha in your mind."[30]

Chan wisdom is not knowledge. It is, if anything, vanishing knowledge, vanishing into its emptiness. In the words again of the *Surangama Sutra*, "This is a teaching that must be left behind, and the leaving behind, too, must be left behind. That may be called the Dharma that transcends idle speculation." A monk who thinks he knows something others do not is lost in idle speculation. In the *Record of Baizhang*, from Mazu's school, we read: "If one uses one's mind to engage broadly in intellectual study, seeking merit and wisdom, then all of that is just birth and death, and it does not serve any purpose as far as reality is concerned. Blown by the wind of knowledge, such a person is drowned in the ocean of birth and death.... [Monks] should be taught to leave all things, whether existent or nonexistent, to forsake cultivation and attainment, and let go of the very notion of forsaking."[31]

According to a sermon attributed to Bodhidharma, "Erudition and knowledge are not only useless but also cloud your awareness." A passage worthy of Zhuangzi reads: "If you use your mind to study reality, you won't understand either your mind or reality. If you study reality without using your mind, you'll understand both. Those who don't understand, don't understand understanding. And those who understand, understand not understanding. . . . True understanding isn't just understanding understanding. It's also understanding not understanding. If you understand anything, you don't understand. Only when you understand nothing is it true understanding."[32]

I take "True understanding is understanding not understanding" as the cognitive complement of the thought that enlightened detachment requires detachment from detachment. You have to throw away detachment, with its dualism of the detached and the clinging, and vanish into careless consciousness. That comes from understanding, but what is understood is what is not understood; what is understood is our condition of not understanding. How could anyone "understand" emptiness? There is no understanding, understand? It comes with wisdom. "The appearance of appearance as no appearance can't be seen visually but can only be known by means of wisdom." To look at appearance and see no appearance is to entertain appearance with no thesis aforethought, without positing an object, or presuming the presence of what Nagarjuna called *svabhava*. Everything looks as it always did, except you do not think that some appearances are better than others, that some ought to be and others not.[33]

In another sermon Bodhidharma says perfect knowledge means "being always aware (*ming*) and nowhere obstructed (*ai*)." The *Heart Sutra* calls these obstructions "attainments," and they are to be avoided. "Because there is no attainment in the mind of the Bodhisattva who dwells in *prajna paramita* [enlightened wisdom], there are no obstacles and therefore no fear or delusion." This freedom from obstruction sustains the affinity between Chan/Zen and the martial arts. The association is improbable given that violence is against Buddhist law, and weapons and fighting forbidden to monks. The principle of *ahimsa*, nonviolence, is among the most important precepts in all Buddhist traditions. Buddhists, and especially monks, should have no association with the military, no involvement in war, no violence, no fights, no killing. However, that Shaolin was a Buddhist monastery where martial arts were taught and practiced for centuries is not a myth. A Buddhist practice of martial arts may not go back to Bodhidharma, but at Shaolin and probably elsewhere Chan monks were also highly trained martial artists.[34]

Martial arts are unmentioned in Chinese Buddhism's doctrinal corpus, which is unsurprising given the illegality; however, secular sources confirm that Shaolin monks were prosecuted for rebellion during the Northern Wei dynasty (386–534). By the early Tang dynasty evidence of Shaolin military monks abounds. Their first fame was for staff fighting (*gun fa*), not hand combat, which did not become a Shaolin specialty until the sixteenth century. A *Treatise on Military Affairs* (circa 1560) says, "the Buddha is an expert magician, master of many techniques, [and] Shaolin hand combat in the entire world is hardly equaled." The *Exposition of the Original Shaolin Staff Method* (1610) calls their fighting technique "unsurpassed Buddhist wisdom." The author claims that Shaolin monks consider martial training a technique for "reaching the other shore," and describes his own mastery of their martial arts as a "sudden enlightenment."[35]

Takuan Soho, a seventeenth-century prelate of the Zen Rinzai sect, uses the no-thought teaching to develop the comparison between Zen and martial arts. His "Mysterious Record of Immovable Wisdom" is addressed to a martial master. He says people's ignorance is the obstacle to their enlightenment, an entrenched ignorance that arises from and feeds delusion. Delusion does not mean untrue representation, or appearance instead of reality. It means stopping. To be deluded is to have a mind that stops, and every stopping point is a delusion. To allow his mind to get stuck on his adversary is fatal to the martial artist. So too in Buddhism. "In Buddhism we abhor this stopping and remaining with one thing or another. We call this stopping *affliction*. It is like a ball riding a swift-moving current: we respect the mind that flows on like this and does not stop for an instant in any place." Be like water, even in your mind, especially in your mind. "In not remaining in one place, the Right Mind is like water."[36]

It is not a question, in martial arts, of being fast. It is more important simply that the timing is right. The belief that speed is important is an insidious liability, as the Zen master understands. "When the mind stops, it will be grasped by the opponent. On the other hand, if the mind contemplates being fast and goes into quick action, it will be captured by its own contemplation." One must stop stopping. "While hands, feet, and body may move, the mind does not stop any place at all, and one does not know where it is." A mind that stops stopping is a mind in ceaseless flow. Such a mind is unmovable precisely because it never stops. Moving implies stopping, moving from one stop to another. What never stops is thus unmovable, and the wise never stop. The effortless efficacy cultivated in the martial arts therefore finds its ultimate realization in Buddhist enlightenment.[37]

Skillful Means

The problem in Buddhism is never with views, whether they are right or wrong. The problem is with people's attachment to views. It is attachment that makes knowledge a liability. Consequently nothing in Buddhism must be allowed to become an attachment. For instance, speaking of dependent origination (the idea that everything depends on everything else), a key concept of Buddhism if there is one at all, the Buddha says, "Even this view, which is so pure and so clear, if you cling to it, fondle it, if you treasure it, if you are attached to it, then you do not understand that the teaching is similar to a raft which is for crossing over, and not for getting hold of." Dependent origination, foundation of so much Buddhist analysis, is not an ultimate truth, is in fact no more than an expedient to get people to a place where they no longer need it. Strictly, dependent origination is not a *concept,* which posits an object and implies truth value. It is an expedient, a therapy, a "skillful means."[38]

"Skillful means" translates a Sanskrit expression, *upaya kausalya.* The Chinese translation is *fang bian,* an ordinary expression for method or convenience. In Buddhism "skillful means" is a philosophical term that defines a Buddhist teaching as contrived in accordance with the disposition of those who are to hear it. The skill in skillful means is a teacher's knowledge of others, knowing how to penetrate the selfish heart. The skill is not logical or rhetorical, not skill in judging or expressing truth; it is soteriological skill, skill in saving people despite selfish resistance to their own liberation.

Buddhism is not a theory or conceptual construction, implying a worldview and an ontological truth. It is a toolbox, a collection of expedient means. This understanding of Buddhism seems to trace back to the *Lotus Sutra,* a Sanskrit work of the second century CE, with a Chinese translation by Kumarajiva. The second chapter is entitled "Skillful Means." The *Perfection of Insight* sutras, also translated by Kumarajiva, repeat the message: "Skillful means is to see that there are ultimately no dharmas and no living beings, while saving living beings." "The Buddhas have the power of countless skillful means, and the dharmas are indeterminate in nature; so to bring nearer all the living beings, the Buddhas sometimes declare the reality of all things and sometimes their irreality, sometimes that things are both real and unreal, and sometimes that they are neither real nor unreal."[39]

Any skillful means is utterly provisional and must be left behind to be fully effective. While there is a certain art to skillful means, there is no cunning. They are the devices of a perfected Bodhisattva. Elements may be less than true without being fraudulent when they are indispensable to salvation (Augustine and Jerome debated this too, Jerome siding with the Buddhists). Skillful means are the Buddhist alternative to concepts, with their clamorous objectivity and pretension to truth. Perhaps there is nothing in Buddhism that is *not* skillful means, which would make everything we think of as "Buddhist religion" an expendable expedient and not a precious tradition, an implication the *Lotus Sutra* is not reluctant to draw: "Apart from the skillful means of the Buddha, there is no other vehicle to be found."[40]

The whole idea of the Buddha, his life, enlightenment, and nirvana is a skillful means, no more. The idea of nirvana as a heavenly state unlike ordinary existence is only necessary to help those who do not understand that existence is nirvana to begin with and they are already Buddhas. There is no truth in Buddhism, which is indifferent to the dualism of true and false, as Mazu's school expressly teaches: "True words cure sickness. If the cure manages to bring about healing, then all are true words. If they cannot effectively cure sickness, all are false words. True words are false words insofar as they give rise to views. False words are true words insofar as they cut off the delusions of sentient beings."[41]

We see a Chan author using Daoist ideas about knowledge as skillful means to enhance the appeal of Buddhism in a work entitled *Illuminating Essential Doctrine (Xian Zong Ji)*, attributed to Shenhui, a disciple of Huineng, and possibly the real author of the *Platform Sutra,* the work that establishes Huineng's patriarchy. *Illuminating Essential Doctrine* makes an unexpectedly strong case (in Chan) for the value of knowledge. This knowledge may not be what the world calls knowledge (not learning or craft), but it is a subtle, enlightened, esoteric knowledge that turns out to resemble nothing so much as the knowledge Daoists want to do *wu wei* (which is how Chinese Buddhists translate "nirvana"). "Acting through non-action reaches the Other Shore." This *Dao*-ish knowledge is identified with the Buddhist *prajna,* a wise knowledge described as "the highest of the high." "*Prajna* is the cause of nirvana (*wu wei*); nirvana (*wu wei*) is the result of *prajna.*" Later, this wise knowledge is outright identified with enlightened *wu wei*: "Nirvana and *prajna* differ in name, yet in actuality they are the same."[42]

The wisdom of this knowledge, its function, is to act despite being empty— "it is empty yet it always acts." Such knowledge "is not knowledge"—is "knowledge which is no knowledge" (*hui wu hui*), the substance whose function is *wu wei* efficacy, "action that is free from action." This wise knowledge is said to be secretly transmitted from the Buddha through the Chan patriarchs, using a Chan lineage legend Shenhui himself may have invented to make Buddhist enlightenment appeal to the esoteric quality Daoists cherish in genuine knowledge. Buddhist wisdom is like an alchemical stone, "the crown jewel of a king which [must] never be given to the wrong person."[43]

Like the Daoist authors, Shenhui neutralizes the value of what the world calls knowledge, while reserving a place for the greater knowledge of the enlightened. But then comes the predictable swerve. Enlightened knowledge is vanishing knowledge that does not know or act. It is not effortlessly effective. It is empty. The last thing to know is the emptiness of knowledge. That puts you beyond the functioning of knowledge, a consummation of knowledge with which one passes over to the other shore. "I have not acquired even the least thing from the consummation of incomparable enlightenment," says the Buddha in the *Diamond Sutra*, "and that is called the consummation of incomparable enlightenment."[44]

The Virtual and the Vacant

One question knowledge poses for Confucians is how to distinguish the wise knowledge of the perfected person from mere cleverness. They seek their answer in terms of sincerity, truthfulness, and humanity, all of which are ultimately understood in terms of ceremony. Knowledge has to function with these virtues to be the wise knowledge of the good. If a man is conspicuously clever, he must care more about being clever than about being good. He is therefore unbalanced and has lost the way.

Another question concerns the difference between the knowledge of the perfected person and that of an artisan. The perfected person is not a vessel, not an instrument, not a technician for hire. Confucians confront a problem Plato would recognize. Is the wisdom a philosopher seeks the technical knowledge of a special art or skill? Plato decides it is not. An art or *techne* is a morally neutral instrument. It can be used for good or bad. Like Confucians, Plato assumes that the best knowledge, the knowledge sought by a

Socratic lover of wisdom, aligns with the good and cannot be used badly. Since art can always be abused by bad people, the best knowledge, the wise knowledge philosophers esteem, must not be any art or *techne*. The philosopher too is not a vessel.

Confucians find a different way to a comparable conclusion. The wise knowledge of the perfected person is neither normal know-how nor Platonic truth. It is a unique kind of technical knowledge, an art unimaginable to Plato, who knew nothing of the *li,* or China's ceremonial traditions. The art of the perfected person turns any occasion into a ceremony, artfully handling circumstances with faultless propriety, as defined by the prescriptions of the early Zhou court such as we understand them. Under Confucian custodianship, the *li* enable a kind of art Plato never thought of, an art that has sincerity and truthfulness as conditions of technical success—an art, therefore, that cannot be used badly.[45]

The Socratic philosopher is not a vessel because he is devoted to a knowledge that is beyond *techne,* that is not good *for* anything, being the achievement of the good itself. This knowledge exists on an entirely different plane from *techne*-knowledge. It has different objects and different subjects—the thing in itself, known by the soul by itself. The Confucian *junzi* is also not a vessel, of course, but for another reason. This perfected person possesses an art that is beyond specialization, a training that makes him uniquely responsive to the *dao* not in the use of this or that, but the "political" use that collects many things, human and nonhuman, into a functional harmony.

Plato and Kongzi are both lovers of wisdom but what they value as wisdom is incommensurable. The wisdom Plato seeks has never been known. We began in the cave and are there still, struggling toward the light. No one has found a way out yet, at least none who have returned. The way out, the Way of Truth, belongs to the future. Wisdom lies not in a past continuous with the present, but on a transcendent level of reality discontinuous with the immanent order of time. Confucians make an opposite assumption, that there is a legacy of wisdom, the wise works of the ancient sages, the *li* and the classics. We can reconnect with this past provided we approach its relics in the right way.

Such a past is unthinkable for Plato no less than for modern philosophers. Starting with Socrates, European philosophers tend to arrogate to themselves the right to devalue conventional values, to ignore everything merely contingent, and interpellate, or formally question the putatively noncontingent, to expose its contingency, and liberate themselves from error. The

Socratic may not be a vessel, but he also does not have a father. He will question and challenge anything, almost. Sustaining this "philosophical" attitude toward authority or tradition (*muthus, doxa*) is the anticipation of a relation to something beyond the contingency of what actually happens and passes for true. When this fond expectation comes into question (as it does with Nietzsche and the pragmatists), philosophers for the first time confront doubt about the "truth" in whose name they cast so many idols down.

Daoists make problems for the problems Confucians find in knowledge. They continue the Mohist critique, which also says Confucians are wrong about a raft of important questions, including the value of knowledge. For Mohists the value of wise knowledge is not limited to the perfection of ceremonies. Wisdom should be an instrument in the cause of impartial care. Mohist worthies are proud vessels, eager instruments in a divine cause. The Daoist critique of Mohism seems to be that its adherents try to perfect the world before they have perfected themselves. Daoists and Confucians have a commitment to self-cultivation Mohists do not share. To the Confucians, Mozi has no father (that is, no filial piety). To the Daoists he chases the limitless with the limited and must therefore exhaust himself, leaving as much undone as before he started. Is that not pathetic?

Daoists do not say Confucians are wrong about knowledge, but that they are superficial. They are stuck in a limited view. What they call knowledge is little knowledge. Confucians say the best life is a strenuous effort to be good. To Daoists it is a mistake to depend on language, ceremonies, and classics. The problem with these artifacts is not their artificiality, however, as is often thought. It is that depending on them keeps us focused on other people, trying to be humane and sympathetic, and fixed on what has already been done, its traces or refuse. The genuine person turns inward to nourish unseen powers, learning to listen with the *qi*, to breathe from the heels, to make words flavorless. Daoists look to wise knowledge to nourish life. They do not want to rely on artifacts as Confucians rely on the classics and the *li*. They want instead to create forms, to participate in the *ziran* productivity of nature.

Daoist emptiness is actually empty and virtually replete. Knowledge of this emptiness is knowledge of the world in virtual depth instead of actual configuration. It does not know beings, or the truth of beings. It knows tendings, not actual beings but potent becomings, many and different, contending for the future. When we see things we do not merely see their geometry. We see not lines or shapes but stabilities and instabilities, obstacles and tendencies, actual forms and virtual shadows. All vision is like that to an extent; the sage is simply better at it than the rest of us. Penetrating to this tacit dimension discloses the virtual and potential of what is extended and present. Such perspicacious perception (really seeing the little things) can be trained, enhanced, made skillful, even sagacious. The knowledge is apophatic, achieved through emptying, overcoming obstacles that confine knowledge to a perspective. The knowledge is a kind of emptiness, empty of actuality, actual form, hence not equivalent to a formula or representation. It is an improvisatory knowledge, does not reiterate, and functions in the fog of incipience, Eliot's roar on the other side of silence, where forms vanish into their becoming and passing away. Such knowledge continues to function with enlightenment. Indeed, the point of pursuing enlightenment is to master a knowledge that continues to function and enhance one's efficacy.

Daoists want to overcome attachment to little knowledge and get to the good stuff, knowledge that feeds life and does not exhaust it, realizing the singular efficacy with which the sage vanishes into things. Buddhists do not want to vanish into things. Things too must vanish. Their emptiness (*kong*) is unconditional, without dynamism or potential. It is as if Buddhists say to Daoists, "You are right to think the Confucians are superficial, right that they are stuck in their knowledge, right that there is a better knowledge, one that reaches what their little knowledge does not know. But a 'genuine person' must break through the delusion that still haunts you Daoists too—the dualism of knowledge great and small."

Buddhist wisdom realizes the emptiness even of the virtual, of past and future, and the radical emptiness of knowledge in all forms great and small. Knowledge vanishes in this Buddhist wisdom, which exhausts life and does not nourish it. The wisest knowledge overcomes itself and ceases to function, doing nothing, *wu wei*, nirvana, extinction. Despite the skillful appropriation of the lexicon, this Buddhist thinking is alien to Daoist traditions early and late. Chan claims a transcendence that reveals the virtual plane of immanence to be empty. The tenuous *xü*-emptiness Daoists extol is *kong*-empty—a resourceless vacancy, and just more *samsara*, more delusion, more suffering. This nullification of Daoist emptiness is an implication of the Buddhist teaching on dependent origination. No unactualized potential, no latent, merely virtual tendency not already actual. In the words of Nagarjuna, "As realness does not occur for existents that lack own-being, 'this being, that becomes' is not a fact either."[46]

Conventional English translation obscures a profound difference between Daoist *xü*-emptiness and Buddhist *kong*-emptiness. Daoist *xü* is a fallow field, Buddhist *kong* is a sterile desert. Zhuangzi must give up giving up and forget about forgetting; the *dao* is emptier than even he imagined. It is an apparition without virtuality, a form without virtue or power, actually dead, and only given the appearance of life by a cozening karma. An eighth-century Daoist writes, "Emptiness means seeing in darkness and hearing in silence, and is not the quietude of Chan." A comment on *Zhuangzi* by a Republican-era thinker epitomizes the difference: "The main principle of Buddhism is emptiness: nothing is wanted; all is to be abandoned. The main principle of Daoism is vastness: everything is wanted; all is to be included." Daoism conveys "the wonder of true emptiness," writes Isabelle Robinet, stressing the idea of "the fullness intertwined within emptiness." Daoists "emphasize, to a larger extent compared to the Buddhists, the reality of the world, which is made even more real by being traversed by emptiness." Eventually even Confucians recognize the difference and side with Daoists against Buddhist *kong*-emptiness. Although the source is somewhat out of place given my concentration on China, the point is nicely expressed by the fourteenth-century Korean Confucian Chong Tojon in his *Criticism of Buddhism*:

> We [Confucians] say "emptiness" and they [Buddhists] say "emptiness." We say "quiescent" and they say "quiescent." But our emptiness is empty yet existent. Their emptiness is empty and non-existent. Our quiescence is quiescent yet responsive. Their quiescence is quiescent and negative. We say "knowledge and action," they say "awakening and cultivation." Our knowledge means to know that the pattern of the myriad things is replete within our own minds. Their awakening is awakening to the fact that the original mind is empty, void of anything whatsoever. Our action means to accord with the pattern of the myriad things and act [in harmony with] it, without any error. Their cultivation means to sever the connection with the myriad things and regard them as unconnected to the mind.[47]

Buddhism is not an ontology of emptiness but the emptiness of ontology. It denounces not delusive objects (e.g., appearances) but the delusion of objects and the presumption of ontology. Daoist emptiness, by contrast, is enthusiastically ontological. The virtual exists, is real but not actual, and is therefore, to Buddhist eyes, not nearly empty enough. That is a difference between Daoist concepts and Chan, despite the avidity with which Chan authors imitate Daoist philosophemes. Daoism remains optimistic about knowledge in a way Chan is not. Daoism envisions conditions under which knowledge enhances life. For Chan even that knowledge is an obstacle. Life cannot be enhanced. Buddhism's First Noble Truth explains that life is suffering through and through and has to be gotten over. The self, the body, the *qi*—all of that is empty—empty of actuality, empty of virtuality, empty of virtue or power, incapable of overcoming the obstacles that keep us stuck in this so-called life.

I mentioned the Confucian epithet "mad Chan" (*kuang chan*). Chan's appeal dismayed Confucians, who were scandalized by its ideas; for instance, the rejection of learning, placing a personal search for enlightenment above filial obligations, and the claim that everyone, indeed every sentient being (every dog!) is already a sage, already a Buddha. Yet *kuang* (mad, cracked) is an ambivalent pejorative for Confucians. According to *Analects,* only such a person is a worthwhile student (A 13.21). For Wang Yangming, "a divine abyss separates *kuang* and sagehood. Truth and error diverge on an infinitesimal point." Perhaps it is not entirely surprising that Chan was attractive to the Neoconfucians of the Song dynasty and later. Most of the leading figures studied sutras and discreetly weighed their ideas. When we turn to their works we find carefully recontextualized traces of Chan skillfully woven into the relentlessly secular fabric of Confucianism.[48]

— 5 —

The Investigation of Things

We must understand the subtle, incipient, activating forces of
order and chaos. . . . This is the investigation of things.

—ZHU XI

From the eleventh century, at the height of the medieval Song dynasty, there
is a revival of philosophy known as Neoconfucianism (or, in China, *lixue,*
study of principle). What is new about it is, first, that it separates study and
reflection on the classics from cramming for the civil service examinations.
Over the last thousand years, the study of Confucian classics had so meshed
with preparation for an administrative career that by the eleventh century
this career was practically the only reason a person took up study. Some of
the teachers began to protest. There is no sincerity in such learning, only
calculation, a travesty of the Confucian ethos. These "new" Confucian
teachers urge the autonomous ethical value of self-cultivation in the new
context of the empire. A second innovation is that these teachers are knowledgeable about Buddhism, especially Chan. Buddhism did not come to
China until some five hundred years after Kongzi. The Neoconfucians of
the Song dynasty live at the height of Buddhism's prestige, which is also the
height of Chan, and they study and respond to Buddhist works. Last, Neoconfucian thought takes on a mixed bag of other intellectual innovations
introduced since classical times; for instance, the *yin-yang* scheme and the
theory of Five Phases. Confucianism is now a philosophy of nature.

Why rehabilitate classical learning? What good is it, and what is the point
of study, if not the office one prepares for? These teachers find their answer
in a Confucian treatise called *The Great Learning* (*Daxue*) and what it says
about the "investigation of things."

166

The *Great Learning*

Conventionally attributed to Kongzi, the *Great Learning* is thought by scholars to be a work of the third century BCE. In the Song dynasty, more than a millennium later, it was assembled with *Analects, Mengzi,* and *Zhongyong* into the so-called Four Books, which became the foundation of Confucian education thereafter. Down to the twentieth century (when the civil service examinations, the principal rationale for Confucian education, was finally abandoned) this concise tractate of some seventeen hundred characters was not merely read but memorized by every educated Chinese. The elegant syntax of two consecutive chapters makes them among the finest passages of Chinese philosophy. The text makes many points, but I am interested in what it calls the *extension of knowledge (zhi zhi)* and the *investigation of things (ge wu)*:

> Those of antiquity who wished that all people throughout the empire would let their inborn luminous virtue shine forth put governing their states well first; wishing to govern their states well, they first established harmony in their households; wishing to establish harmony in their households, they first cultivated themselves; wishing to cultivate themselves, they first set their minds in the right; wishing to set their minds in the right, they first made their intentions true; wishing to make their intentions true, they first extended knowledge to the utmost; the extension of knowledge lies in the investigation of things.
>
> Only after things are investigated does knowledge become complete; knowledge being complete, intentions become true; intentions being true, the mind becomes set in the right; the mind being so set, the person becomes cultivated; the person being cultivated, harmony is established in the household; household harmony established, the state becomes well governed; the state being well governed, the empire becomes tranquil.[1]

The most influential comment on this passage comes from the Neoconfucian scholar Zhu Xi, who first placed the *Great Learning* in his standard-setting edition of the Four Books. In editing the text he came to the conclusion that something had been lost from the end. He was convinced that the work continued with an elucidation of that phrase "the extension of knowledge lies in the investigation of things." He felt able to reconstruct the missing chapter, which he included in his soon-to-be-canonical edition, creating this self-authenticating commentary:

> If we wish to extend our knowledge to the utmost, we must probe thoroughly *the principle* in those things that we encounter. Now every person's intellect is possessed of the capacity for knowing; at the same time everything in the world is possessed of *principle*. To the extent that *principle* is not thoroughly probed a person's knowledge is not fully realized. For this reason the first step of instruction in the *Great Learning* teaches students that, encountering anything at all in the world, they must build on what they already know of *principle* and probe still deeper, until they reach its limit. Exerting themselves in this manner for a long time, they will one day suddenly become all penetrating; this being the case, the manifest and the hidden, the subtle and the obvious qualities of all things will all be known, and the mind, in its whole substance and vast operations, will be completely illuminated. This is what is meant by "the investigation of things." This is what is meant by "the completion of knowledge."[2]

I have italicized the word *principle* (*li*) in this text. It is new and not (yet) orthodox to use this concept to elucidate what the classic calls "investigation," so that to investigate things means to investigate their principle, to probe principle to the end. Zhu's editorial coup canonizes an interpretation of the classic that seems to originate with Cheng Yi, the effective founder of the new Confucianism a century earlier. Cheng reads *ge* (investigation) in *ge wu* as "to arrive at" (it can also mean "to oppose" or, as Wang Yangming insists, "to correct"). He says that to "arrive at things" means to reach their *li*, their principle, an attainment that defines both understanding (the cognitive goal) and integrity (the ethical goal): "To learn *li* from what is outside and grasp them within is called understanding. To grasp them from what is within and connect them with outside things is called integrity. Integrity and understanding are one."[3]

To Western ears, talk of "the investigation of things" sounds like empiricism. It has seemed a paradox that this apparent call for empirical inquiry should come from the heart of the literati, who tend to be snobs about knowledge other than their scholarship and ceremonies. Needham says sinologists "have always had difficulty in believing that the frank charter for the natural sciences implied by the Neoconfucian interpretation could have emanated from a milieu so preoccupied with ethics and self cultivation as that of the early Confucian school." Is it a paradox, though? Empiricism seems implicit in the Confucian lessons on epistemic humility in *Analects,* which teach students not to preclude an encounter, or refuse to learn from events, or be insensitive to circumstances (A 20.3). Kongzi restricts the perfected person's pursuit of knowledge to matters subtending ceremony, yet he also reimagines ceremonies so that little if anything in life is *not* ceremonial. When the idea of knowledge in support of ceremony encounters the idea of ceremony as the perfected human response to environment and circumstance, then what is *not* suitable for ceremonial handling? The value of knowledge becomes the good handling of anything, of everything, which cannot be investigated too closely. What may look from the outside like curiosity preempted is instead an imperative to inquiry.[4]

Such investigation is at once empirical and applied, an investigation not of disinterested truth but the right use of things, seeking a norm of peaceful coexistence. For Angus Graham, the *li* "account not for the properties of a thing but for the task it must perform to occupy its place in the natural order," its "function" (*yong*). Chen Shun, a Zhu Xi student, says, "The men of old, investigating things to the utmost and searching out *li,* wanted to elucidate the nature of the inescapableness of affairs and things; and this simply means that what they were looking for was all the exact places where things precisely fit together. Just that." Fitting together means fitting with us, having a place in the collective economy. Having a place means having a use, a "function," a right, normative, best way of being handled. The investigation of principles (*li*) therefore coincides with the perfection of ceremonies (*li*).[5]

Zhu Xi

Zhu Xi is famous as a Song dynasty editor and commentator. His commentaries on the Confucian classics are classics in their own right. His curriculum became the Confucian standard, defining which books a student must read and in what order. Ironically these are mostly works neither Kongzi nor any pre-Han Confucian could have read:

1. The Four Books, these being the *Great Learning, Analects, Mengzi,* and *Zhongyong.* None of these were read by pre-Han Confucians except possibly *Analects.*
2. The Five Classics, these being the *Book of Songs, Spring and Autumn Annals, Book of Changes (Yijing), Book of History,* and *Book of Rites.*

Only two of these (*Songs* and *Annals*) were studied by pre-Han Confucians.

3. Dynastic histories, all written after the Qin empire.[6]

Zhu's name for his teaching is *daoxue, dao* learning. He offers it as a sane middle way between insincere careerism and a Buddhist retreat from commitment. The accusation Neoconfucians level against Buddhism is first of all selfishness, which is ironic in light of the *anatman* (no self) teaching. For a young man to abandon his family and retire to a monastery for the rest of his life is appalling selfishness, and a vast blasphemy against fifteen hundred years of Confucian teaching on filial piety. Zhu shares this objection, though he more acutely locates the problem with Buddhism in its thought of emptiness. He attacks the idea that the original mind is empty. The opposite is true. As Mengzi explained, the heart comes seeded with germs of morality. These are a heavenly nature in us, and our life's function is to cultivate them. This nature fits us for social life. There is nothing empty about ceremonies, morality, family, or imperial service. That is where our heart is and where it should stay, steadfast against Buddhism's exotic attraction or the anarchy of the Daoists.[7]

I explained the value to Zhu's milieu of the *Great Learning.* The opuscule began as a chapter in the *Book of Rites,* though it had long been treated as an independent work. Its basic ideas, as Zhu reads it, are, first, that there *is* a *greater* learning. The lesser learning teaches the mechanics of goodness and propriety. The greater learning is learning the *li,* the inner principle and coherence of things, "probing coherence, setting the mind in the right, cultivating oneself, and governing others." Virtue and irresistible charisma beam from the countenance of those who achieve this great learning, enabling them to complete the work of renewing the whole world. Furthermore, this appeal to virtue is addressed to anyone, and not only a king. Anyone can achieve this greatness. It is a work of self-cultivation, a work on the self that includes the investigation of things and the extension of knowledge.[8]

On the older reading Zhu revises, investigation becomes fruitful only under a true king, whose charismatic virtue motivates the whole empire to leave no stone unturned searching out useful things. The careful study of heaven and earth is a happy fruit of good rule. For example, in the *Institutions of Emperor Yao,* the sage emperor first unifies the realm and makes prosperity the norm, *then* directs the astronomers to organize the calendar.

Zhu's third innovation is to reverse this priority. We cannot separate self-cultivation from the investigation of things. As Cheng put it, understanding and integrity are one. Finally, in what may look like a bold intrusion of Chan, Zhu reads in the text an idea of two minds, original and human, and the urgency of recovering the original mind.[9]

Is this Buddhism, or was Chan already borrowing from a Confucianism that Zhu renews? He backs up his reading of the two minds with the *Book of History*, which if not as ancient as he thinks, is certainly pre-Buddhist and explicitly distinguishes *renxin* (ordinary mind) and *daoxin* (original *dao*-mind). He explains the difference between these with Mengzi's thought that the heart is innately endowed with a heavenly principle (that is, a normative development). This is the original *dao*-mind. The function of inquiry is to cultivate this heaven-sent seed and make it active in our response to every circumstance. An ordinary human mind is that original *dao*-mind fallen under the domination of selfish desires and appetites.

These are not really two minds, of course, and obviously not two substances; they are two dispositions, two tendencies toward which we lean, one being developmentally earlier than the other—the later-born selfish self. Ordinary mind is the unrefined mind of an ordinary person. *Dao*-mind is the potential of everyone to be a sage. The challenge of self-cultivation is to reverse the preponderance of ordinary mind and recover the original *dao*-mind. That is the value of what Zhu calls the learning of the mind (*xinxue*), epitomized in the apocryphal words of sage king Shun to his successor Yu: "The human mind (*renxin*) is precarious; the mind of the way (*daoxin*) is subtle. Be discriminating and single-minded. Hold fast to the mean."[10]

Zhu's reading of the *Great Learning* makes the investigation of things and the extension of knowledge the principal moments of self-cultivation. What does "investigation" contribute to cultivation, or the learning of the mind? Zhu takes his answer from Cheng Yi, whom he cites: "Someone asked what the first step was in the art of moral cultivation. There is nothing prior to 'setting the mind in the right' and 'making the thoughts true.' Making the thoughts true lies in the extension of knowledge, and 'the extension of knowledge lies in *ge wu*.' *Ge* means *zhi*, 'to arrive,' as in the phrase *zu kao lai ge*, 'the ancestors arrive.' In each thing there is a manifestation of principle; it is necessary to pursue principle to the utmost."[11] That is what Zhu confirms with his reconstructed chapter of the *Great Learning*: You study things to learn about yourself. You seek principle in things as a strategy for finding principle in yourself, which is the original *dao*-mind. Such a reading is scarcely an innovation, though to emphasize it may be. Mengzi had said, "The way of learning and inquiry is no other than to seek for one's lost heart-mind" (6A11).

For Zhu, studying the classics is a privileged form of investigation. The best way to investigate *things* is to study *books:*

> With regard to the way of learning, nothing is more important than a thorough study of principles; and a thorough study of principles must of necessity consist of book-learning. . . . The words and deeds [of the sages] have all become permanent and fundamental exemplars for later generations to emulate. . . . These visible traces and necessary results are all contained in the classics and histories. A person who wishes to have a thorough knowledge in the principles of the world without first seeking for them [in the classics] is one who wishes to go forward but ends up standing right in front of a wall. That is why we say "a thorough study of principles must of necessity consist in book-learning."[12]

There may be several reasons for this view. One is that Zhu believes "every word of the sages is heavenly principle and as it should be"; "the words spoken by the sages and worthies are naturally coherent, each arranged in its proper place." Also, the reading he commends is not private or disengaged from action. "In reading, we cannot seek moral principle solely from the text. We must turn the process around and look for it in ourselves. . . . We have yet to discover for ourselves what the sages previously explained in their texts— only through their words will we find it in ourselves." It is as certain that principle is in books written by sages as that it is in other phenomena. "When we read we investigate principle in the printed word." Reading is a way to investigate things, and we cannot read effectively unless we bring knowledge of the world to the text. "In reading history, we must understand the subtle, incipient, activating forces of the order and chaos shown. . . . This is the investigation of things." Also there is continuity between the mind of the sages who wrote those words and ourselves. "The mind from start to finish has always operated together with heaven and earth." Sounding like a Chan master sermonizing about people's Buddha nature, Zhu Xi says, "What the sages and worthies said is no different from your own mind today."[13]

It is unlikely that Zhu's blurring a distinction between nature and convention or what is in the world and what is in a book struck his contemporaries as a daring novelty, but the idea of using study to perfect oneself

may have. The usual reason a man studies is to prepare for the state examinations. Zhu's message is study to think, to understand, to cultivate yourself. You cannot attain the perfection of self-cultivation without sincerely
investigating things. You will never get back to the original mind unless
you first of all get *out* of the ordinary mind and into things, even if those
things are books.

He emphasizes the need for sincerity in learning against its decline into
a career path, but learning for what? For acting well, for doing and being
right, for a knowledge that completes itself in benevolent action. Knowledge and action are a unity. Knowledge is only complete or completely realized in wise action. It is this relation to action that makes wisdom skill-
like. Wisdom is like being able to shoot a bird at a hundred yards (an analogy
from Mengzi): it takes strength to pull the bow, and skill to hit the target.
Knowledge gives direction to strength, leading to action that is at once right
and effective.[14]

The principle investigation seeks is everywhere. It is in the classics, in the
sage's heart, in nature, and in our original mind. The classics are a peda-
gogically proven point of entry, though what one seeks is not textual per
se, and other ways of investigating cannot be excluded. What makes a text
sagely, or the handling of things appropriate, or the heart's mind original,
is all one; it is what Zhu and his colleagues call principle (*li*). Any knowledge of things, extended and investigated thoroughly, is knowledge of
principle, and any part knowledge of principle is virtual knowledge of the
whole. The wise discern patterns (*li*) in phenomena. This perceptiveness,
combined with perspicacity (*ming*) and skill (*qiao*), enables sages to respond
with spontaneous appropriateness. They deliberately *do* very little, almost
nothing, yet there is nothing they do not handle well. Things are not complete and knowledge not extended until our interaction becomes natural
(*ziran*) and effortless (*wu wei*). To invoke a different vocabulary, we complete things by making them black boxes, the smooth, facilitating interface of human-nonhuman interaction. Once these usages are established
anyone can employ them, but it takes sagacious investigation to find them
when they are unknown.

In early use (for instance the *Book of Songs*), the term *li* (principle) is a
verb meaning to divide, section, or quarter, as in the division of a field or
carving jade. The earliest Chinese dictionary (*Shuo Wen Jie Zi*) defines *li* as
"to treat jade," meaning to cut or carve it for some use. The character does
not occur in *Analects,* and first appears in a classic in the *Book of Rites:* "Man

is changed by things; they destroy heavenly *li* and exhaust him with desires." The character also does not occur in the *Daodejing*, though it is frequent in *Zhuangzi*, where it has the sense of patterns in nature that the wise know how to exploit. We met this *li* in the earliest layer of *Zhuangzi*, with the cook who had not had to sharpen his knife in nineteen years. In butchering oxen he follows the natural patterns (*tian li*) and flesh falls from his blade like clods from a spade. Elsewhere in *Zhuangzi* it is said, "The sage in fathoming the beauty of heaven and earth penetrates the *li* of the myriad things" (Z 148); and "Whoever knows the *dao* is sure of penetrating the *li*" (Z 149).[15]

In the Mohist *Canons*, *li* is a multivalent technical term designating either the semantic organization of words in a sentence, or the pattern or organization of things in nature, or the logical pattern of correlated names and things in accordance with which we accept or reject judgments. Mohist usage is silently appropriated in *The Spring and Autumn of Lü Buwei*: "What in the distinctions of disputation does not coincide with *li* is false, what in the clever man does not coincide with *li* is deceitful. . . . *Li* is the ancestor of judgments of right and wrong." In *Xunzi* and *Hanfeizi*, *li* has the sense of a model or pattern for behavior. One of the earliest clear explanations is this passage from the Warring States period work of administrative philosophy *Hanfeizi*: "The *dao* is that through which the myriad things are so, that in which the myriad patterns run together. A pattern (*li*) is the texture of a thing as a whole, the *dao* is the means by which the myriad things become wholes. Hence it is said, 'The *dao* is what patterns them.' Things having patterns cannot encroach on each other; consequently, the patterning of them is the cutting up of things."[16]

Wang Bi (third century CE) defines *li* as "what is universal yet gathers to one." That language inspired the first Western readers to identify *li* with the Stoic *logos* and Platonic *idea*. This insidious gloss surreptitiously eliminates the word's anthropocentric connotation, which ill fits the absoluteness, transcendence, and contemplative character of Western metaphysics. Brook Ziporyn restores the suppressed allusion in this gloss on *li*: "the discernable guidelines in any object that allow one to take worthwhile action with respect to it, or any guideline that can be discerned, such that action in accordance with it (or dividing it along that particular line) will lead to a valued arrangement of things, that is, to a 'coherence.'" The *li* are patterns, yes, but not an impersonal pattern simply present, a finished form. The unity *li* promise is not actual but virtual and requires actualization, which is where we come in. We understand the principle of a thing when we know how to use it with propriety, how to handle it well, do right by it, domesticate it, make it a smoothly functioning black box with a dignified place in the ceremonial economy of human and nonhuman things.[17]

Take for example a flower or a blade of grass. As with any organism, parts cohere with parts—roots, stem, colors, shapes, seasons. The whole plant also coheres with other plants and animals in the environment, with which it shares an adaptation. This ecology includes the people who bring their goats to feed, or who sell the flowers. These people have families and villages, villages belong to districts, families have relatives, and on it goes, widening circles of relationship, until at some point practically anything anywhere becomes entangled with that flower or blade of grass: correlated, coadapted, coherent.

Knowledge of *li* is an appreciation of the relations we need to know for the harmonious handling of anything that instigates a response. The principles of things repay investigation with enhanced effectiveness. The *li* let you know where to begin, how to integrate, what to put together with what, enabling minimum intervention and maximum effectiveness for all concerned. According to Cheng Yi, "there is a difference between acting after grasping [a principle] and acting after thought. If you have grasped it in yourself, the action will be as simple as using your hand to lift a thing; but if you have to think, it is not yet within yourself, and action is like holding one thing in your hand to take another."[18]

Zhu Xi and others in his tradition assume that the many *li* of the many things are themselves coherent, the many *li* ultimately forming one cosmic Principle. The assumption seems to go back to Cheng Yi, who says that the principle found in any one thing can be extended, analogized, pushed (*tui*), leading to the discovery of all the rest. "In investigating things to exhaust their principles, the idea is not that one must exhaust completely everything in the world. If they are exhausted in only one matter, for the rest one can infer by analogy. . . . There are innumerable paths by which you can get to the capital, and it is enough to find one of them. The reason why they can be exhausted is simply that there is one principle in all the innumerable things, and even a single thing or activity, however small, has this principle."[19]

Li now does what earlier thinkers attributed to *tian* (nature/heaven), transforming a natural order into an intelligible one. "What is called heaven [or nature] is *ziran li*," says Cheng Yi. Clearly *li* is not bare, abstract coherence. Platonic ideas are wonderfully coherent, repeating identically in different individuals and participating in the universal coherence of a system closed under the idea of the Good. Yet for Plato all of that coherence originates beyond the human heart. The order of ideas, the system of the Good, has a place for us, but does not *need* us or await any contribution from us.[20]

Let that be enough about the *li*. The next question is what knowledge can do with them. For Cheng Yi, principle exists in the same sense as material things do, and can be perceived (*jian*) and understood (*ming*). Still, the perception takes more than an ordinary human mind. Zhu follows Cheng in thinking we can detect *li* because our original mind belongs to its order, itself participating in *li*, part of the coherence *li* denotes. "Principle in things and in our mind are essentially one. Neither is deficient in the slightest. What is necessary is that we respond to things, that's all. Things and the mind share the same principle." The mind he refers to is of course the *dao*-mind, the original mind before being bent by selfish desire. Discipline the desire, cultivate impartiality, stifle selfishness, and you can recover this *dao*-mind. With a restored mind you know what is most worth knowing in the world, which is how to use things well, effortlessly responding to anything that happens with impeccable propriety.[21]

This idea of an original mind empty of desire is prominent in Chan, and so too in the Daoists, though we know how Daoist *xü*-emptiness and Chan *kong*-emptiness differ. Cheng Yi (and thereafter Zhu) follows the Daoists: "The mind is at bottom void (*xü*), responding to things without retaining a trace of them. To hold on to it, it is necessary to find standards for it by looking at things." That is what the *li*, or more precisely knowledge of *li*, provide—standards to distinguish good and bad responses. Rather than dwelling on the question of Buddhist influence, then, which may be misleading, let us pursue a Western comparison where influence is out of the question.[22]

Heraclitus envisions a universal *logos* permeating all things with the fire of reason, making nature at once beautiful and intelligible, a cosmos. The soul is no less permeated by this *logos* and assimilated to its order. By their common *logos*, cosmos and psyche are commensurate, which is this hinting thinker's hint about the cognitive essence of wisdom. Aristotle takes up the hint when he says that "the mind is in a sense potentially whatever is thinkable" and "the soul is in a way all beings." There is a receptivity of the soul to the forms of things. It accepts them "effortlessly" and knows them just as they are. In a similar way Zhu seems to say that our original *dao*-mind spontaneously resonates with the changes of things and thus is "in a sense" all patterns, all changes. Except that Aristotle means a mind that takes on the form—the whole, complete, finished form of a thing—and in that way becomes essentially one presence with it. Only fully present form can be taken in all at once, as required for intuitive evidence, the foundation of scientific knowledge.[23]

What Zhu supposes is a mind capable of responding to things with spontaneous sagacity. Spontaneity guarantees (and is the fruit of) impartiality. When mind is partial, calculation intervenes between incitation and response, as one ponders how to use the situation to advantage. A spontaneous response is impartial, the original *dao*-mind doing what it naturally does without selfish desire. As spontaneous, the response is not a "doing," not planned, deliberated, or calculated; and as righteous humanity, there is nothing to object to, nothing unfinished, or badly done. To have knowledge of principle is to respond like that, effortlessly extending or completing knowledge in a sagacious response to incipient or tending disorder.

Aristotle's theory requires an immaterial soul. If there is any matter at all to the soul that thinks and judges, then mental isomorphism, and therefore evidence and science, is impossible. A material soul would already have a form—its matter must have some form, and that must be an inestimable interference to theoretical knowledge. Zhu's assumption is that with careful guidance and discipline the mind can slough off selfish desire. There is something like that idea in Chan, but also and more originally in the *Daodejing*, which seems the deeper source, making Zhu more Daoist than Buddhist. His idea of emptiness is a mind so little bound to a selfish point of view that it is nowhere obstructed and vanishes into things.

For Zhu the extension or completion of knowledge is a wise response to circumstances. For Aristotle the wisest knowledge is purely theoretical, a divine contemplation, perfectly useless and beautifully true. He might accept Zhu's knowledge of principle as a kind of *phronesis*, practical wisdom, good in its way, but not *the* Good, and not the best and highest knowledge (*episteme*) of the truly wise. Of course Confucians have no use for concepts like *episteme* or pure theory and its truth, nor do they need the idea of practical wisdom since they see no other kind. Wise knowledge is realized in humane and righteous action. In a passage I cited earlier from *Zhongyong*, another work Zhu introduced into his canonical Four Books, it is said, "The truthful person does not just complete himself. He also completes things. Completing oneself is benevolence; completing things is [wise] knowledge."[24]

You cannot sensibly give someone the direction to investigate things. You have to indicate what to look for. The instruction to look for patterns or co-herence is no more helpful. Not that one will not find them; one will find too many, with no way to determine which are relevant to what. We have to make investigation relevant, which means related to something else we want to do. That is the value of the *li*. The vague imperative to investigate things becomes an imperative to investigate the *li* of things, which directs attention to appropriate use. How (in the light of everything else) should we handle anything that instigates a response?

A notorious passage from Wang Yangming is an example of the nonsense "investigation of things" devolves into without the thought of appropriate use. He recounts a youthful effort to "investigate" bamboo:

> People merely say that in the investigation of things we must follow Zhu Xi, but when have they carried it out in practice? I have carried it out ear-nestly and definitely. In my earlier years my friend Qian and I discussed the idea that to become a sage or a worthy one must investigate all the things in the world. But how can a person have such tremendous energy? I therefore pointed to the bamboos in front of the pavilion and told him to investigate them and see. Day and night Qian went ahead trying to in-vestigate to the utmost the principles in the bamboos. He exhausted his mind and thoughts and on the third day he was tired out and took sick. At first I said that it was because his energy and strength were insufficient. Therefore I myself went to try to investigate to the utmost. From morning till night, I was unable to find the principles of the bamboos. On the sev-enth day I also became sick because I thought too hard. In consequence we sighed to each other and said that it was impossible to be a sage or a worthy, for we do not have the tremendous energy to investigate things that they have. After I had lived among the barbarians for three years, I understood what all this meant and realized that there is really nothing in the things of the world to investigate, that the effort to investigate things is only to be carried out in and with reference to one's body and mind.[25]

He might have tried thinking about the relationship between qualities of the bamboo and the climate or environing animals and other plants; he might have thought about how people interact with all these nonhuman things, and how the fruit of their interaction reacts on other beings, human and nonhuman. The *Detailed Record of Bamboo* (*Zhu Pu Xiang Lu*), by the Yuan dynasty painter Li Kan is an abundantly illustrated investigation of bamboo especially for painters. The work is a triumph of empiricism. Li provides systematically organized, minutely detailed, carefully illustrated observations on all aspects of bamboo relevant to the painter, including their process of growth; differences in their appearance in light or heavy rain, breeze or heavy wind, in sunshine, with dew, or withering; and the appearance of their clusters, leaves, stems, and branches. He distinguishes seventy-six species as good for painting; other species of abnormal shape, color, or spirit (*shen*); species that look like bamboo but are not; and species that are called bamboo but are not. What he investigates so attentively is not an arbitrary clump of bamboo "thing-in-itself," shaved of all relations. It is a multiplicity of conditioned appearances, their use (to painters), and norms for smooth interaction.[26]

What Zhu Xi ultimately expects from an investigation of principle is the perfection of self-cultivation, of which the wise use of things is a fruit. "All that appears before one's eyes are affairs and things. Just probe them one by one to their limit and gradually the many, of themselves, will become interconnected. The point of convergence is the mind." He means the original *dao*-mind, not the sodden psyche called ordinary mind. As to how we lost that original mind, the reason seems to be selfish desire. "Never do heavenly principle and human desire permeate each other." Why is desire a problem, though? If our heart's mind is so good at the beginning how do we get saddled with desires that debauch our nature? Zhu again takes his answer from Cheng Yi. The original mind arises in life with the maturation of the animal organism. The incessant demands of the organic system precipitate into personality, driving an economy of selfish desires that all but starve the original mind of *qi*-vitality. Wearied by the futility of desire, the *qi* becomes dark and viscous, eclipsing the heart's original mind and ruining knowledge with partiality, the mother of all error.[27]

The explanation of error has been thought to present a difficulty for Zhu. He attributes error to cloudy *qi*, but corporeal *qi*, cloudy or clear, is continuous with *qi* everywhere, the *qi* of all forms and forces in nature. Hence what we rely on to know *li* is equally the source of error. If Zhu seems untroubled by this problem (epistemological optimism?) the reason may lie in his theory and practice of education. Learning restores and nourishes *qi,* makes it clear, bright, and balanced. Zhu's program for the recovery of the original mind partially resembles Chan's program for recovering the Buddha nature. He combines meditative quiet sitting to settle the *qi* with study, that is, investigating things, probing principle to the utmost, extending knowledge. Zhu describes quiet sitting as inner mental attentiveness. "It's simply to collect your own mental energy and concentrate it on a certain spot." Doing that supposedly assists in cultivating what Mengzi called his floodlike *qi*.[28]

The difference from Chan meditation is obvious. Zhu directs students to concentrate on specific objects, problems urgently requiring solution, while Chan meditation relaxes concentration and launches out beyond intentional objects. Also, Zhu says his meditation is not arduous, an unlikely claim for Chan. The closer one gets to mastery, he says, the easier concentration becomes, to the point of eventual effortlessness. "If a person is able to remain mentally attentive, his mind will be perfectly clear and heavenly principle bright. At no place does he make even the slightest effort, yet at no place is even the slightest effort left unmade."[29]

The fiasco in the bamboo grove suggests that Wang Yangming was trying to concentrate meditatively on the bamboo, and failing because there was no problem to focus his mind. Zhu's meditation is this focused concentration—purposive, seeking the breakthrough expressed in *wu wei* efficacy. But that is "quiet sitting," not investigation, which requires studying up on things, finding out, sorting and weighing. This investigation of *things* is a therapy for recovering the original *mind*. Only after that recovery can we really begin to *know* things, that is, know how best to respond to them. You start investigating things, to prepare for knowledge of the original mind, but it is only with the breakthrough to original mind that knowledge of things becomes wise. "Complete yourself and only then will you be able to complete other things—the completion of things lies in the completion of the self." A perfected person is able to complete things because "once you understand the big moral principle clearly, when imperfections exist, you'll be able to transform them naturally, without even being aware of it. You won't have to make any effort."[30]

Reflections on Things at Hand (*Jin Si Lu*) is a compilation Zhu edited with Lü Zuqian, collecting important passages from earlier Neoconfucians and including many comments of his own. The result is a vade mecum of the

Confucian renaissance. A prominent theme is the esteem due to knowledge of the subtle and incipient. The value of investigation is to "know [the] processes of transformation" (Ye Cai). Cheng Yi alludes to the *Yijing,* which by then had become a classic: "The superior man . . . knows the subtle beginning of things." Then he says, "To know the ultimate point to be reached and to reach it is to extend knowledge. . . . Thus one knows [the end] from the start and is therefore able to know the subtle beginning of things. . . . This is the beginning and the end of learning." Zhu adds a remark of his own: "To know the subtle beginning of things means to know beforehand . . . a subtle beginning means foreknowledge." Such is the knowledge of the wise. "The man of wisdom knows how the subtle and incipient forces work" (Cheng Yi).[31]

This knowledge is valued because it is effective, more so than alternatives, especially violence. "The evil of the world cannot be suppressed by force. Therefore [a perfected person] examines its subtle origins, gets hold of the essential element, and stops up its source" (Cheng Yi). Effectiveness is another name for the unity of knowledge and action (*zhi xing he yi*). Knowledge is not wise until it bears the fruit of wise action. We will see Wang Yangming insist on this point too, as Xunzi did earlier. The unity of knowledge and action is confirmed all around in Zhu's collection: "Knowledge and action require each other" (Ye Cai); "Thought and action cannot be spoken of separately" (Zhu); "If a person really knows that a thing should be done, when he sees anything that should be done, he does not need to wait for his will to be aroused" (Cheng Yi); "When one truly knows that a thing should be done, he cannot help doing it" (Shi Huang).[32]

A second theme in Zhu's anthology is the value of impartiality (*gong*), and the need to overcome selfish desire. The utmost impartiality is required for wise knowledge and for the action that extends or completes the knowledge, proving its wisdom with a ceremonially appropriate response. "The extension of knowledge depends on nourishing our knowing faculty, and to nourish our knowing faculty there is nothing better than having few desires"—a condition Zhu correlates with impartiality. Selfish desire throws one off balance. We nourish knowledge by getting past desire, because the source of wise knowledge is the original mind, which is clotted by desire and fails to function. "The operation of the principle of the mind penetrates all as blood circulates and reaches the entire body . . . [whereas] selfishness separates and obstructs" (Zhu). Cheng Yi says, "The way of humanity may be expressed in one word, namely, impartiality," and, referring to Chan "no

mind," says, "The absence of mind is wrong. We should say only the absence
of a selfish mind." "Become broad and extremely impartial [and] respond
spontaneously to all things as they come" (Cheng Hao). "To have no selfish
subjectivity . . . means to be impartial. If a thing is good, love it. If it is evil,
hate it. . . . To have no selfish subjectivity is to be like the universe" (Zhu).[33]

Disburdened of everything that limits us to a "self" and obstructs our
response with perspective, we vanish into things, the consummate achievement of mastery. Consciousness is not extinguished. We remain perceptive,
and have not lost emotions. Instead, our perceptions and emotions respond
to what is eventlike or becoming (*ziran*) in what happens. In the words of
Cheng Hao, "For the exemplary person, nothing is better than being impersonal and impartial, and responding to events as they come." The sage
has the same emotions as anyone else because there is nothing wrong with
emotions. The only thing wrong is their occasion when they are untimely.
It is not that sages are never angry, for instance; rather, they are never angry
at the wrong time. "The normality of the sage is that his emotion follows
the nature of events. . . . When the sage is pleased, it is because the thing is
there which is rightly the object of pleasure. When the sage is angry, it is
because the thing is there which is rightly the object of anger. Therefore,
the pleasure and anger of the sage are not connected with his thinking and
feeling (*xin*) but with events." The less there is of self, which Cheng and Zhu
(like Kant) identify with material desires and purposes, the more disinterested the knowledge. This impartiality assures both the effectiveness of
knowledge and the righteousness of the action that extends or actualizes
it. Integrity and understanding become one.[34]

The value of impartiality coincides with what François Jullien calls the
globality of Chinese thought. Globality is what objectivity becomes when
there is no object (no finished form) and no supernatural transcendence.
Instead of transcending phenomena to know the thing in itself, these Chinese want to flow with the world, to enter the stream of transformation and
not get stuck. Unbound by egocentric perspective you become like water
and flow irresistibly around obstacles. It is not that you rise above perspectives but that you cannot be confined to one. Jullien reads the allusiveness
of Chinese literature, eschewing the explicit and definitive, as homage to
globality. Something said has not much value unless it works in many
contexts.[35]

The Mohist demand to make meaning explicit is aberrant. The more explicit words are the less allusive power they have, hence the less you can do

with them, the fewer contexts in which they are wise. Spell everything out, as Mohists want to, and once you have said it you are stuck. Mohists apart, Chinese thinkers prefer statements to resonate and admit of endless recontextualization, endlessly expanding the original wisdom. "The sage's remarks," Jullien says, "are continuously modified and never come to a standstill." *Zhuangzi* likens such words to a spillover goblet, referring to a vessel that tips and empties when it gets too full. "These spillover-goblet words give forth [new meanings] constantly. . . . They extend on without break and thus can remain in force to the end of one's years" (Z 107, Ziporyn).[36]

A third theme in Zhu's compendium is odium for the clever, cunning, calculated, and manipulating. Such behavior is a travesty at once moral and methodological. "Being cunning one cannot be at home with enlightenment" (Cheng Hao); "If one acts with any calculation, he is thinking of success first of all" (Cheng Yi); "If he devotes his mind to accomplishment and merits, his purpose will fall into cunning and making plans and manipulation" (Ye Cai). Zhu's contributors deplore the effort to force things. "To force anything will fail in the end. . . . Those who understand the *dao* . . . succeed in what they do without any artificial effort." "There is a natural pace in things. There is no room for compulsion" (Cheng Yi). "To understand spirit to the highest degree and to understand the process of transformation is the natural result of profound cultivation and cannot be achieved in any forced manner through thought or physical effort" (Zhang Zai). I do not think these remarks are necessarily directed against technics. The offensively artificial is not merely artifactual; it is marked by calculated purposiveness, deliberation, one almost wants to say malice aforethought, because for these thinkers anything cunningly purposive is unbalanced, excessive, and therefore malicious rather than impartial. "If it is manipulated it ceases to be the mean" (Cheng Yi).[37]

The more narrowly goal-directed an artifact (or intervention), the more it belongs to a limited perspective and to the desires that differentiate people rather than the heart that unites them. We investigate things to know that heart. We seek principle in things as a way of finding principle in ourselves, which is our original mind. Why not go to the mind directly without the detour through things? Is not *any* investigation ultimately an investigation of the mind? For Hegel, "Spirit is . . . in its every act only apprehending itself, and the aim of all genuine science is just this, that Spirit shall recognize itself in everything in heaven and on earth. An out-and-out Other simply does not exist." But we do not have to go to Europe to find this argument.[38]

Wang Yangming

Wang Yangming holds the unity of knowledge and action thesis in its strongest form. It is not just that if you know something but do not act your knowledge is superficial, nor that those who know can be expected to act well too. These formulations take knowledge and action for two things, different but coordinated. Wang's thought is that knowledge simply *is* action. Without appropriate action the knowledge remains in process and might be interrupted and fail to form. There is no need to shift gears from cognition to the will. Knowledge and will are phases of the same heart and mind, and not so different that one cannot be a more developed form of the other. Here Wang recalls both Socrates and Spinoza, who eschew the distinction between practical and theoretical intellect. The action *is* the knowledge come to term, completed, fully realized. Knowledge "is the beginning of action, and action is the completion of knowledge"; knowledge "in its genuine and earnest aspect is action, and action in its intelligent and discriminating aspect is knowledge."[39]

The teaching on knowledge and action emerges during Wang's time at the Guiyang Academy (Guizhou), in a difficult period of internal exile. As a teacher Wang had to supervise students preparing for the imperial examinations. The idea that one might acquire a lot of knowledge and hold it in reserve for future application was attractive to students absorbed in study. What they learn makes no difference to their life right now, but they are stocking up knowledge for later action as officials. Wang urges his students to confront the issue of relevance from the beginning of study. He exhorts them to combine learning with commitment. To study rightly requires more than learning words; one is challenged to make the learning relevant, to show what one understands it to mean in everyday action all the time.[40]

Wang rings changes on the idea of principle he inherits from three hundred years of Neoconfucian thought. There is a principle in nature that patterns and harmonizes the myriad things. The pattern reaches through everything like veins in a piece of jade. For Zhu and Song dynasty Confucianism, principle in the human heart links us to principle in nature and brings all things to completion in benevolent usage. For Wang, our heart does not *have* a principle; rather, it *is* Principle itself, the one all-unifying heavenly Principle, in its conscious, knowable form. My knowing (when it is *liang zhi*, pure knowing) is a local expression of the Principle of Nature, like a mode of Spinoza's substance. Knowledge and action join in the heavenly process. The pure, innate knowledge we have of our heart and its nature ripens into action that is exactly right, ceremonially impeccable, exemplary virtue. That is how I read passages such as these:

> Mind and principle are identical. When the mind is free from the obscurations of selfish desires, it is the embodiment of the principle of nature.

> Knowledge is the original substance of the mind. The mind is naturally able to know.

> Knowledge is principle made intelligent. In terms of its position as master, it is called mind. In terms of its position as endowment, it is called our nature. . . . When the intelligent faculty is not obstructed by selfish human desire, but is developed and extended to the limit, it is then completely the original substance of the mind and can identify its character with that of heaven and earth.

> Mind is no other than heavenly, cosmic principle in its power of natural consciousness.[41]

Wang calls the knowledge belonging to the original mind "innate" or "pure" (*liang zhi*). Though an established translation, "innate knowledge" is perhaps not ideal, since the relevant connotation is not "in advance of experience," the innate knowledge postulated by Plato and Descartes, but in advance of desire and its wreckage. In Western thought, innate knowledge refers to concepts that have only to be awakened to function in cognition. What we know innately are rational concepts—equality, difference, cause, and the like. These concepts are not artifacts of experience; they are presuppositions of thought, given by nature in advance of experience. Wang does not cherish pure theory or its truth, and might be less impressed than Plato and Descartes with concepts that guarantee it. What he expects from innate knowledge is not demonstrable truth; it is the infallible differentiation of right and wrong *and* the motivation to do what you know is right. What this pure knowledge apprehends are not slumbering universals; they are the circumstantial evidences of value, what is right or wrong in a given situation. "Thoughts (*yi*) should clearly be distinguished from pure knowing (*liang zhi*). Whenever an idea arises in response to any thing or affair (*wu*), this is called a 'thought.' Thoughts can be either correct or incorrect. That which is able to know which thoughts are correct and which incorrect is called pure knowing. If one relies upon pure knowing, then one will never act incorrectly."[42]

The word *liang* has two relevant connotations: being good or right, and being innate or natural, something understood without learning and practiced without instruction. In modern Chinese, *liang zhi* describes a good person with a conscience, who is not selfish and does the right thing. Mengzi launched the term in philosophical discourse. "That which people are capable of without learning is their *liang neng,* genuine capability. That which they know without pondering is their *liang zhi,* genuine knowledge" (7A15). To have *liang zhi* is not to know anything in particular. The knowing is nonobjective the way art always is. To be a physician, say, is not to know anything in particular; the knowledge is virtual and productive, not exhausted by actualities or their representation.

Wang's explanation effortlessly mixes *Mengzi* and the *Book of Changes.* "Our capacity to know the good (*liang zhi*) is in the human heart, the same through all time and in the whole universe. It is the capacity for knowledge which does not depend on reflective thinking [*Mengzi* 7A15], which works with ease and knows where danger is [*Yijing*]. It is the ability for action which does not depend on learning [*Mengzi*], which works with simplicity and knows where obstruction is [*Yijing*]." He draws a subversive conclusion left latent in *Mengzi.* If our nature is good, how important can learning be? What is important is that we not ruin our nature. Learning comes close to ruination. Who needs the artificial difficulties of books? There are problems enough in life to make a sage of the attentive mind. In a verse Wang writes: "The thousand sages are all passing shadows, / *Liang zhi* alone is my teacher."[43]

One's own nature is the teacher, and one's character is what must be investigated or, as Wang prefers, rectified. That is not to say investigation is directed "within." He deplores the dualism of internal and external, as if mind were inside and nature out. For Wang, as for Darwin, our mind is as external as Heaven, our environment as internal as the heart. As an ethicist rather than an epistemologist, Wang is saying we should look to making the heart right, and not worry about getting *things* right. That does not mean looking "inside." It means attending to the heart you put into everything you do. That is where we must look to "investigate"—that is, rectify things. Get the heart right. "There is really nothing in the things of the world to investigate [rectify]. . . . The effort to investigate [rectify] things is only to be carried out in and with reference to one's body and mind."[44]

Zhu Xi thought we could learn something important about ourselves by broad empirical investigation. For Wang that is futile. Knowledge of good and bad, right and wrong, is not to be obtained from empirical inquiry. We saw what he thinks of *that* from the fiasco in the bamboo grove. The principle we need to know and do right is not found in the multiplicity of individuated things. Return to the self, seek the original mind. The extension or completion of *liang zhi* may require empirical knowledge; for instance, to care for parents may require a plan to keep them warm in the winter. But there is no value for anything we might learn about nonhuman nature save for the exercise of innate moral knowledge. The only reason to care about empirical knowledge is to facilitate doing the right thing.

I cited part of this passage on foreknowledge in my Introduction: "The sage does not value foreknowledge (*qian zhi*). When blessings and calamities come, even a sage cannot avoid them. He only knows the incipient activating force of things and handles it in accordance with the circumstance. To innate knowledge there is neither the past nor the future. It knows only the incipient activating force of the present moment, and once this succeeds everything else will succeed. If one has the desire to foreknow, it means selfishness and the intention to go after advantage and avoid disadvantage."[45] "Foreknowledge" seems to mean knowing future facts (perhaps by divination), so as to foretell calamity and evade it. Wang contrasts such foreknowledge with the discernment of incipient activating forces—Zhuangzi's great knowledge, Sunzi's strategic knowledge. Such knowledge is not a representational foreseeing of future facts. It is knowing how to improvise, collaborate, and vanish into what happens *ziran*. Empirical knowledge of incipience collaborates with innate moral knowledge to make innate knowledge effective and effective knowledge sagacious.

Getting to the point where something happens *ziran* can take a lot of doing. On the question of knowledge Wang is closer to Mozi than to other Confucians. Like Mozi, and in contrast to practically his whole tradition, Wang ignores the connection between knowledge and *wu wei* effectiveness, which he denigrates. "To maintain a policy of nonaction . . . is the approach and method of Buddhists and Daoists." The value of knowledge is not fully realized until we do what we know is right. Knowledge with that power is *liang zhi,* the pure knowledge of the original mind. Pure knowing is knowing without deliberation, spontaneous but not effortless. What is good about this knowledge, what makes it sagacious, is that it motivates right action. To know is not to act with effortless effectiveness; it is to act with irreproachable sincerity. As in Mozi, it is purity of motive (in his case impartial care) that is important, not *wu wei* effortlessness in the doing. The perfected person spontaneously knows what to do, but the doing, which is the completion of the knowledge, may be onerous, as Wang, with his experience as a military governor, must have appreciated.[46]

Wang became a controversial teacher in part because of his interpretation of the *Great Learning* and especially its chapters on the extension of knowledge and the investigation of things. He did not condone Zhu Xi's recension of the text, especially his "reconstruction" of the "missing" chapter. Wang's teaching returned to the older text, before Zhu's emendations. The result is a strikingly different reading of what to this point I have translated as "the investigation of things" (*ge wu*) and "the extension of knowledge" (*zhi zhi*). Scholars say there is evidence for reading the word *ge* in three ways: as *han*, to oppose, defend, stand against; as *zhi*, to arrive at; or as *zheng*, to correct, rectify. Song thinkers, including Cheng Yi and Zhu Xi, read *ge wu* in the second sense, "to arrive at things," meaning to understand their principle. Wang prefers the third reading, "to correct, rectify, make right." Since *wu* can mean either things (objects, phenomena) or affairs, philology alone is incapable of deciding whether the classical expression *ge wu* means the investigation of things or the rectification of affairs.[47]

Wang worries that people will read the classic Zhu's way and believe that to cultivate themselves "they have to understand all the knowledge and ability of the sage before they can succeed." That is a terrible mistake. When we assume that "every event and every object has its own peculiar and definite principle," or as Cheng Yi put it, that "every blade of grass and every tree have their own patterns, and these must be investigated," our mind "becomes concerned with fragmentary and isolated details and broken pieces." All the principle worth knowing is already in our heart. The more we ponder the multiplicity of individuated things the further we lose ourselves in details we can never master, which subverts earnest commitment and leaves people demoralized. That was Wang's experience, as the bamboo grove debacle suggests and biography confirms.[48]

Wang descends from a distinguished family of officials, and was himself an official in several posts civilian and military. On one occasion, an indelicate memorandum to the emperor affronted the chief eunuch. For the offense Wang was humiliatingly flogged before the court, then sent into internal exile in Guizhou, in the far south. It was a devastating blow to his ego, and he struggled with it in the early years of his exile. One evening insight came to him in a "sudden enlightenment" concerning the meaning of the expression *ge wu,* a problem he had wrestled with for twenty years. He awakens from unsettled sleep and thinks, "My own nature is, of course, sufficient for me to attain sagehood. And I have been mistaken in searching for *li* [principle] in external things and affairs (*shi wu*)."[49]

His struggle to understand the language of the classic and Zhu's explanation are proof of a sincere commitment to become a sage, and that commitment, not success in empirical investigation, is proof of innate knowledge, the only knowledge needed to be a sage. The heart is sufficient. The heart *is* principle, the only principle there is. We should concentrate there, on our heart's mind and the sincere commitment to do as sages do, and forget about investigating the ten thousand things. On Wang's reading, *ge wu* directs us to rectify affairs and do right by things, to correct and establish them in the collective. Provided only that we are sincere and committed, we extend, that is, use or make function, knowledge, meaning the pure knowledge of a heart unfettered by selfish material desire. The injunction to *ge wu* is not to investigate; it is to do the right thing. Every situation confronts us with the question of how to handle what clamors for a response. The best response flows from a sincere commitment to becoming a sage. Fallible though we are, a sincere commitment handles the situation as well as can be. "If one relies upon pure knowing, then one will never act incorrectly."[50]

The moral quality of life depends on the sincerity with which it is lived, and exemplary virtue proves the pure knowledge such a life expresses. To carry out the directive to *ge wu* we make ourselves sincere and work on our commitment to be a sage. Sincerity (*cheng*) should reactivate the original *dao*-mind, actualizing the *liang zhi* that infallibly motivates doing the right thing. "Extending knowledge" is extending *liang zhi,* which means drawing out *liang zhi* from its virtual condition in the heart to the action that actualizes the knowledge, doing the right thing. "Your *liang zhi* is your own criterion. As your thoughts and intentions arise, it knows what is right and what is wrong. You cannot deceive it at all. . . . Follow it faithfully in everything you do. Then good will be preserved and evil will be removed. How secure and joyful [one can be] with it! This is the true secret of *ge wu,* and the real effort of *zhi zhi.*"[51]

Wang transforms *ge wu* from investigating, looking into things, which to him is a futile episodic cognition of fragments, to a lifelong process of cultivating sincerity and commitment. The worry about fragmentation recalls *Zhuangzi*: "Life flows between confines, but knowledge has no confines. If we use the confined to follow after the unconfined, there is danger" (Z 62). Wang alludes to *Daodejing* 48: "Famous but mediocre scholars . . . advocate the study of isolated details . . . [whereas] we want to diminish everyday rather than to increase everyday." We may wonder whether this is a plausible criticism of Song empiricism. Why is it inevitably fragmentary and inconclusive? And why must these qualities (if it has them) be demoralizing? Song thinkers seem to anticipate at least part of Wang's criticism, to which they respond with rare reflections on inductive and analogical reasoning:

> In investigating things to apprehend fully their patterns, there is no question of completely exhausting all the phenomena in the world. If the pattern is fully apprehended in one matter only, inferences can be made about other matters of the same class. (Cheng Hao)

> To devote oneself to investigating principle to the utmost does not mean to investigate the principle of all things in the world to the utmost nor does it mean that principle can be understood merely by investigating one particular principle. It is necessary to accumulate much knowledge and then one will naturally come to understand principle. (Zhu Xi)[52]

Wang seems to think that for most people, especially officials, this attitude is too aloof from their urgent need to handle things well. They cannot spend years investigating things and hope for the breakthrough, so that they can then extend their knowledge in practice. Whatever *ge wu* and *zhi zhi* mean, they have to be something anyone can do right now. Wang does not allow *ge wu* to mean a specific activity we do at the cost of something else we might have done instead. *Ge wu* is something we are challenged to do every day and not just at school. It is not a specific, exclusive activity; it is doing any activity in the right way, namely, with utmost sincerity and a commitment to doing as sages do. "If one sincerely loves the good known by the innate faculty but does not in reality do the good as he comes into contact with the thing to which the will is directed, it means that the thing has not been [rectified] and that the will to love the good is not yet sincere." Wang objects not to the logic of induction but its ethics, living inductively, with its uncertainty and pluralism, which he denigrates as fragmentation.[53]

For Wang, the best or wisest knowledge is knowledge of right and wrong, good and bad, in a given situation. It is not implausible, then, to think that *ge wu* has nothing to do with factual description, causal explanation, or empiricism of any kind. *Ge wu* means not to investigate but to rectify, using innate knowledge of good and bad to put matters right. Wang returns to the older understanding of the *Great Learning* before Zhu Xi's redaction. First you establish the conditions under which pure knowledge can function, which calls for sincerity and commitment. Then you extend, that is, use, knowledge to rectify things to the utmost, to put your utmost effort into the moral government of the world.

This extension of knowledge has nothing to do with enhanced cognition or penetrating insight; it is "simply extending one's innate knowledge of the good to the utmost," that is, *doing* good in everything one handles. One who acts badly does not lack knowledge, as Socrates supposes, but sincerity and commitment, as Mengzi said. One has always had all the knowledge goodness requires. The way to sincerity is through impartiality, which requires overcoming selfish desires. The challenge of self-cultivation is "to get rid of selfish human desires from the mind and preserve the principle of nature in the mind." "In trying to master oneself every selfish desire must be thoroughly and completely wiped out without leaving even one iota. If an iota remains, many evils will come one leading the other." Wang's lively language recalls the Desert Fathers of Christian monasticism, for whom desire was no less malign:

> This effort [removing desires] must be carried out continuously. Like eradicating robbers and thieves, one must resolve to wipe them out completely. In idle moments one must search out and discover each and every selfish thought for sex, wealth, fame, and the rest. One must resolve to pluck out and cast away the root of the sickness, so that it can never arise again. Only then may one begin to feel at ease. One must, at all times, be like a cat catching mice—with eyes intently watching and ears intently listening. As soon as a single [selfish] thought begins to stir, one must conquer it and cast it out. Act as if you were cutting a nail in two or slicing though iron. Do not indulge or accommodate it in any way. Do not harbor it, and do not allow it to escape.[54]

The desire to be eradicated is qualified as selfish, though it may be unclear what an unselfish desire is. We met this problem in the *Daodejing*, which seems to say that we have to get rid of desire before we can vanish into the *dao*. I suggested that we read the reference to desire as implicitly qualified, meaning something like selfish, material desires. The language seems more clear in Wang. He speaks of selfish desires (*ren yu*), material desires (*wu yu*), and private desires (*si yu*). He says that while a sage "makes no specific effort to like or dislike," that "does not mean not to like or dislike at all"; instead, "one's likes and dislikes completely follow the principle of nature." We saw this argument in Cheng Hao. It is also Xunzi's way of reconciling desire and sagacity: "The sage follows his desires and embraces all his dispositions, and the things dependent on these simply turn out well ordered."[55]

A sage helps what he handles to become what it is, "assists in and completes the universal process of production and reproduction," and in that sense vanishes into the becoming of things. One is free from desire in the relevant sense when one is sincerely committed to harmony. You may still have desires, for instance the desire for harmony and to be a sage, or the second-order desire not to be limited by selfish desires. The *Daodejing* seems to argue that getting to that point clears the way for action of effortless efficacy. For Wang there remains the challenge of determining how to put a commitment to sagehood into practice in every moment of life.[56]

A question commentators writing for a Western readership often raise is whether Wang is a metaphysical "idealist." There are passages that suggest there may be something to this reading:

> The original mind is vacuous, intelligent, and not beclouded. All principles are contained therein and all events proceed from it. There is no principle outside the mind; there is no event outside the mind.

> The master of the body is the mind. What emanates from the mind is the will. The original substance of the will is knowledge, and wherever the will is directed is a thing.... Therefore I say that there are neither principles nor things outside the mind.

> Wherever the will is applied, there cannot be nothing. Where there is a particular will, there is a particular thing corresponding to it, and where there is no particular will, there will be no particular thing corresponding to it. Is a thing, then, not the function of the will?

> Separated from my luminous spirit, there will be no heaven, earth, spiritual beings, or myriad things, and separated from these, there will not be my luminous spirit.[57]

Is this metaphysical idealism? In metaphysics, idealism is an ontological thesis, a thesis about being. The Greek version identifies the real with the rational, meaning the intelligible, logical, and infallibly knowable. What most veritably *is,* what is most fully *in being* about a being, is that for which there is a rational account, an intelligible form, an Idea. In Greek idealism nature is a system of such ideas. To know the truth of nature is to defy the siren song of the senses and turn one's mind toward these incorruptible forms, the soul's true home. The new idealism of modern philosophy is subjectivism, putting the individual subject and its representations at the center. Modern idealism is a philosophy of consciousness based on the fiction of a solitary subject reasoning with itself. Beings are ideas, ideas exist only for consciousness, to be is to be perceived.

Angus Graham does not mince words when it comes to Chinese "ontology." "It is important to keep Chinese concepts as far as possible free from contamination by the Being of Western philosophy." We must therefore be wary of the suggestion that Wang is any kind of ontologist, to say nothing of an idealist. Is he really talking about *Being?* Yet contemporaries seem to have detected something paradoxical in his thinking. We have a record of this exchange: "The Teacher was roaming in Nanchen. A friend pointed to flowering trees on a cliff and said, 'You say there is nothing under heaven external to the mind. These flowering trees on the high mountain flower and drop their blossoms of themselves. What have they to do with my mind?' The Teacher said, 'Before you look at these flowers, they and your mind are in the state of silent vacancy (*tong gui yu ji*). As you come to look at them, their colors at once show up clearly. From this you can know that these flowers are not external to your mind.' "[58]

To say the flowers are not external does not have to mean they are *internal,* in your mind, the way Bishop Berkeley thought trees and clouds are in one's mind (or rather, in God's mind). It can mean that your seeing is out there with the flowers; perception happens "out there," not "in here." It is an ecological transaction, not a monological moment of pure subjectivity. Before you look, you and the flowers are silently vacant to each other. There is as yet no resonance, no incitation and response, no history, memory, karma as it were, between you and those hitherto unnoticed flowers—until you begin to look. The seeing is an interaction, a relay, or exchange, each pole responding to the other, each changing the other. Does seeing the flowers change you? Surely it does. You are not a disembodied Cartesian subject contemplating a decontextualized representation. There is no flower in itself waiting for vision to disclose it. What we recognize as anything (a flower, its color) is a differentiation worked out in the typically unconscious transactions that precede recognition. It may seem a simple thing to open your eyes and see the flowering tree. But if we examine this act in any depth (for instance, neurologically or quantum mechanically) it is a very complex exchange and cannot be analyzed with appropriate nuance in the impoverished terms of a conscious subject representing an objective thing.

But does your looking change the flowers? I take the reference to "vacancy"—Wang's language (*tong gui yu ji*) is quite different from Daoist *xü* or Buddhist *kong*—to mean that perception activates a resonance that did not *actually* exist (exist as an actuality) before that exchange. An eye is not a monistic entity complete in itself. It cannot be what it is unless it is (virtually, vacantly, vanishingly) responding to another. Elsewhere he says that "the eye has no substance (*ti*) of its own. It regards as substance the color of all things. The ear has no substance of its own. It regards as substance the sound of all things." The organs vanish into the processes they perceive. A perception is a response; its qualities are intensive durations of interworldly resonance, becomings with a past, and not simply present "instantiations." Such qualities have no nonrelational existence, neither in the subject nor in the object. They do not exist until they arise from the exchange between vision and the visible. Every quality that defines the visible flower is a potential of which the perception of the eye is a condition of actuality. For Wang as for Henri Bergson, "Every attentive perception . . . is a *circuit*, in which all the elements, including the perceived object itself, hold each other in a state of mutual tension as in an electric circuit, so that no disturbance starting from the object can stop on its way and remain in the depths of the mind [as a mere secondary quality]: it must always find its way back to the object whence it proceeds."[59]

Wang is not equating being and idea. If we must have metaphysical terms, he is saying (like Bergson) that there is no thing-in-itself and no purely subjective Cartesian idea to represent it. Perception is a resonant response, not the passive reception of a fully present form. He is rightly untroubled by the so-called epistemological paradox of Neoconfucianism: how, just by knowing my heart, can I know anything about the world? There is a problem only if "know" means "adequately represent," which it never does in Chinese thought. If, however, "know" means (as it does in Wang) "know the right thing *and do it*," then the supposed paradox turns into the Socratic thesis that knowledge is virtue and inherently motivating. Wang's thought, as I understand it, is not that by attending to the heart we acquire objective, factual knowledge of things. It is that by attending to the heart *instead of* attending to objective, factual things we acquire effective ethical knowledge of what to do about the disorder of things.[60]

Another text savoring of idealism says, "Without the innate knowledge inherent in man, there cannot be plants and trees, tiles and stones. This is not true of them only. Even heaven and earth cannot exist without the innate knowledge that is inherent in man. For at bottom, heaven, earth, the myriad things, and man form one body. The point at which this unity is manifested in its most refined and excellent form is the clear intelligence of the human mind." For Wang, mind and principle are not merely inseparable (as they are for Zhu Xi); they are the same, two words for one reality. "The mind is the nature, heaven's imperative, the one, pervading man and things, reaching out to the four seas, and filling heaven and earth." We know that Wang studied Chan for many years. The *Platform Sutra* says, "Self-nature (*zi xing neng*) contains the ten thousand things—this is great. The ten thousand things are all in self-nature"; "All things (*wan fa*) are included in your own natures (*zi xing*)." Before we read Wang as a crypto-Buddhist, however, we should consider once more what Chan might take from earlier Chinese thought, in this case Mengzi: "The ten-thousand things are all complete within me" (7A4).[61]

Of course they are not all saying the same thing. The Buddhist probably means that any object is no more than a dream. Once we realize that all things are self-nature, we are halfway to realizing that there is nothing except mind alone, which is halfway to realizing that mind alone is empty. Mengzi, no less than Wang, is unlikely to envision anything so abstruse. If for Wang the only "things" that matter are affairs, concerns, or problems, that is not an ontological thesis about being; it is an ethics of attention, of sincerity and moral seriousness, which defines (as it confines) the wisdom of wise knowledge.

Luo Qinshun and the Question of Chinese Empiricism

A contemporary of Wang, Luo Qinshun is a Ming dynasty adherent of Song dynasty Neoconfucianism. His evocatively titled *Knowledge Painfully Acquired* (*Kun Zhi Ji*) repeatedly cites Cheng Yi's statement, "Principle is one; its particularizations are diverse." "Not a single word to be added," he says. This unity of principle regulates the immanent economy of the world, sustaining its unity from within rather than beyond. The difference from Buddhism is palpable. Distinctions among things are not delusions of karmic consciousness. They are *ziran* differentiations, fluctuating coagulations of *qi* that owe their coherence to the economy where they find their norm or principle.[62]

This *qi* is an energetic mass that completely fills the world, somewhat like the Stoic *pneuma*. Luo traces the genesis of *qi* to the primordial interaction of the empty and the full. Concentration disperses, the dispersed coalesces, phases of empty and full spontaneously transform into each other, the empty tending to actuality, the actual decaying into virtual emptiness. The oscillations locally synchronize and quasi materialize in the energetic ether of *qi*, whose passage through an endless series of *yin-yang* transformations defines our actuality. Luo cites with approval the words of the Song dynasty Confucian Zhang Zai: "As the *yin* and *yang qi* revolve through their cycle of alternation, they react upon one another through integration and disintegration . . . they include and determine one another. . . . There being no agent which causes this, it can only be called the coherence of nature and destiny (*xingming zhi li*)."[63]

This primordial movement, rendering all things resonant and coherent, defines the reality Luo calls "principle." "Whether in the immediacy of a single day or in the remoteness of a millennium, emptiness and fullness, concentration and dispersal, mutually create the cycle of interaction which is principle." Principle is the endlessly reticulated network whose resonant ripples reach everywhere, like veins coursing through jade. There is nowhere they do not lead, nothing they do not weave into an economy with others and ultimately with everything. This principle makes things not *what they are* (metaphysical essence) but *what they are good for*, what they can do, which establishes the norm of their adaptation in the fabric of the world. The *li* are pattern, yes, and coherence, but not a finished pattern suitable for contemplating whole, and more the *becoming* of coherence than the finality of its attainment. Principles are not actualities. In this respect they are unlike Platonic Ideas. Principle is the tendency to actuality, the plan or line of virtual becoming. To investigate principle is to study the tendencies of things, their adaptation and economy. With such knowledge comes enhanced response, right use, harmonious interaction. "To say that the sage regulates and brings [things] to completion means that he follows their seasons, accords with their principles, and establishes regulations and measures so as to further human interests."[64]

Luo sees in Wang Yangming a baleful subjectivism that Buddhism also encourages, even among Confucians, undermining their commitment to investigate things and extend their knowledge. Wang and the Buddhists make the same mistake. Wang identifies mind and principle, which is perhaps his major divergence from Song Confucianism. He concentrates everything on the mind, securing its commitment, and working on sincerity. Chan too concentrates on the mind, though the point is to derealize objects and empty the mind. A Buddhist might think Wang's innate knowledge were better called innate delusion, which is to say karma. Luo's point is that, differences aside, the concentration on mind in Wang and Buddhism rationalizes indifference to nature. For him it is our whole nature (*xing*), not specifically mind (*xin*), that embodies and expresses principle, and this nature is one with the nature and principle of all things. The priority of nature over mind is the priority of life over consciousness. We should not expect to know anything about the heart except by knowing about the whole economy of human and nonhuman nature. Luo cites the eleventh-century philosophical poet Shao Yong:

> You must explore the crevices of the moon
> If you would know things.
> Before having tracked the root of nature
> How can you know man?[65]

For Luo the investigation of things is an empiricism, unlike Wang's introspective recovery of pure knowledge. We have to look beyond consciousness, putting mind back into nature. Mind is not given; it is a process arising within the given. The point of investigating things is to bring to bear upon action an understanding of how *one* principle penetrates everywhere, organizes everything under heaven in an economy that includes us. Wang looks subjective to critics, including Luo, whose own approach is a kind of naturalism, reading mind back into nature. The heart is already outside, its principle already implicated in everything else, its responses adapted to the environing actuality of things. The further we investigate, the more ecstatically we vanish in the unity of heaven and earth. In a letter to Wang he writes, "What is of value in the investigation of things is precisely one's desire to perceive the unity of principle in all of its diverse particularizations. Only when there is neither subject nor object, neither deficiency nor surplus, and one has truly achieved unity and convergence, does one speak of knowledge being complete. This is also called knowing where to rest." Or vanishing into things.[66]

For Luo as for Zhu Xi the investigation of things is a program of self-cultivation. By investigating things and extending knowledge we subdue the self and return to propriety. The self needs subduing because we have lost the *dao* originally given with our *xing*-nature. What stands between us and the clarity of this *dao* is habitual selfishness, which is, as it were, the Confucian karma. Consciousness of self grows stronger by the day. Empiricism's inductive ethics are an antidote. "When things are investigated, it is no longer things but only principle that is perceived, and when the self has been subdued, it is no longer the ego but only the principle that one follows." A subdued self is a vanishing self. Luo explains the *ge* ("investigation") of *ge wu* as "penetrating everywhere with no separation," that is, becoming imperceptible. "When my endeavor approaches completion, it will involve penetration with no separation. Then things are myself and I am things, altogether unified without any differentiation." To arrive at (know, act upon) the unity of principle in all things you have to overcome the limitation of a standpoint, not by transcendence, but through an untrammeled immanence, at ease in any perspective and stuck in none.[67]

The unity Luo infers in nature is not monadic or incompatible with plurality. Nature is not a finished unity permanently present on the plane of essences, like the Platonic system of Ideas closed under the Good. Nature's unity is a tendency, a virtual unity whose actuality has to be creatively extended every moment. That is what we do, and what perfected people do perfectly. This understanding of unity has no close parallel in Western thought, which tends to think unity monistically, as a closed, eternally present being. Parmenides is the paradigm. The monad brooks no development, tolerating no internal complexity, differentiation, or multiplicity, all of which Luo views as appropriate to a well-orchestrated unity. Exceptionally in Western thought, Gilles Deleuze formulates an understanding of unity and multiplicity that better fits the phase of Chinese thought we are considering. Multiplicity, he says, is always "the inseparable manifestation, essential transformation, and constant symptom of unity. Multiplicity is the affirmation of unity . . . [and] the affirmation of multiplicity is itself one." He has a subtle view of what might be called original multiplicity, meaning a multiplicity that is not merely the multiplication of a monad but an aboriginal matrix antecedent to countable units. "A multiplicity is only in the *and*, which does not have the same nature as the elements, the sets, or even their relations." This *and* is not a specific relation, but rather "that which subtends all relations, the path of all relations, which makes relations shoot out their terms." "A quite extraordinary thought, and yet it is life."[68]

For Luo, unity is what Bruno Latour calls a "matter of concern" rather than a "matter of fact." It is not presumed to be already accomplished in things by themselves. It is the work of the perfected person to collaborate in this completion. Do we already know what entities there are? No, otherwise investigation would be superfluous. Do we already know the conditions of their unity in the common world? No. Otherwise the extension of knowledge would be superfluous. Investigation reveals new situations, which extension must then normalize, unify, adapt to the commonwealth of human and nonhuman things. Knowledge is never more finished than its objects, which are not things in themselves but tendencies and problems of collective adaptation. The work is endless, but so is life. A Chinese author of the second century CE writes, "The astronomical regularities are demanding in their subtlety. . . . Success and failure take their turns, and no technique can be correct forever. . . . When the technical experts trace them through computation, they can do no more than accord with their own time."[69]

Multiplicity and unity, the One and the Many, are not formidable metaphysical alternatives between which we must choose; they virtually coexist in the two tasks of knowledge. What Confucians call "the investigation of things" is for Latour the task of "making the deployment of actors visible," or in other words, exposing latent multiplicity. What Confucians call "the extension of knowledge" is the task of "making the unification of the collective acceptable to the unified," or in other words adjusting their interdependence, mutual adaptation, or symbiosis. Employing inquiry to extend the range of entities acknowledged to be at work in the world is not ethically disinterested research. Such knowledge is vital for what Latour calls "the task of cohabitation." Confucians call it "completing things."[70]

Is the Confucian "investigation of things" seriously an empiricism? Naturally something depends on how we understand that word. The first philosophical empiricists may have been the Sophists or at least Protagoras, who invented an empirical concept of proof. The evidence of the senses is all the evidence there is; all theory, argument, demonstration, and proof come down to sensory evidence. Protagoras reduces the world to sensory apprehension, a flat phenomenal surface without depth or "beyond." A legacy of this empiricism is the Epicurean thesis, "All perceptions are true." Taken in their bare givenness, perceptions have an evidence, an *enargeia,* or force of clarity, which Epicurus explains as the immediate awareness of a present object, unbiased by opinions. This irrefragable evidence is the Epicurean foundation of scientific knowledge, and the beginning of the idea of experience (*emperia*) as such a "foundation." Empiricism becomes a quasi-scientific theory of scientific knowledge (epistemology).[71]

There may be resonance between Protagoras's ideas on proof and themes in Mohist thought. Consider for instance the Mohist treatise on ghosts. It begins by establishing the urgency of its subject. The primary cause of disorder in the world is the reliance on might over right. It ought not to happen. It is partial, therefore contrary to Heaven's will. So why do people, rulers especially, resort to force? Master Mo says, "It is all because people have developed doubts concerning ghosts and spirits." The unexpected diagnosis has immediate policy implications. "If we could just persuade the people of the world to believe that ghosts and spirits can reward the worthy and punish the wicked, then how could the world ever become disordered?" He then raises the eminently logical question of method. How does one impartially decide a question of existence? What is the standard? He tells his disciples, "You proceed in the same way as in any other case of determining whether anything exists or does not exist; you must take as your standard the evidence provided by the eyes and ears of the people. If there really are people who have heard and seen something, then you must accept that such things exist." Merely to frame the question is exemplary epistemology, and to answer it as he does seems like a kind of empiricism. Epicurus, Locke, Mill, and Russell might applaud Mozi's procedure, though it is without a future in China, and is soon forgotten.[72]

Another strand in the fabric of empiricism compares the soul to a wax tablet, receiving impressions from outside through the senses. The Stoics are the classical advocates of this idea, even though Plato invented it. Zeno, founder of the Stoic school, supposedly explained *phantasia* (conscious awareness) as "an impression (*typos*) on the soul . . . involving depression and protrusion, just as does the impression made in wax by signet rings." This impressible soul, a concept of empiricist epistemology down to Locke, is without analogue in China, where philosophers did not pose questions to which a wax-tablet mind could be an answer. Even the Mohists appreciate that there is no knowledge in the senses without supplementary cognitive processing. "Knowing is different from having a pictorial idea. . . . When one knows, it is not by means of the five senses." It takes intelligence (*zhī*) to make the senses wise (*zhì*), and in this view the Mohists are silently followed by Xunzi and it seems most of later tradition.[73]

Experiments and experimental knowledge, for instance in the work of Galileo, Boyle, Newton, Lavoisier, and Faraday, define a distinctly modern empiricism to which comparison with Confucianism again seems inappropriate. Not only does this muscular empiricism aggressively search out and even orchestrate its experience; its most productive procedures have little value without the mathematization of problems (quantification) that remained undeveloped in traditional China. Western empiricism in all these varieties tends to be critical, skeptical, deflationary, a reaction to rationalism. China lacked this rationalism to react to, except perhaps for the Mohists, who were instead privately appropriated and publically ignored. Another modern empiricism may better support comparison with the Confucian investigation of things. Francis Bacon emphasizes careful observation rather than laboratory-style manipulation. The goal of natural knowledge is not theoretic truth but fruitful application, or what Confucians call the completion of things. Of course the comparison is imperfect. For Zhu Xi the classics are as natural as bamboo and no less worth investigating, whereas Bacon, an ideologist of modernity, aspires to purify natural philosophy of its lumbering traditions, which he blames for the sterility of natural knowledge.[74]

The first self-consciously "empiricist" theory of knowledge comes from writers in the Greek medical tradition. The art of medicine in Greece was originally a traditional skill, especially in surgery and drugs, without theory. However, from the fifth century BCE (the epoch of Anaximander and Empedocles) a new medicine appears, allied with the rising prestige of *logos,* having reasons, knowing causes. These new doctors are called Rationalists (*logikoi*), the first use of this expression in Western tradition. Medicine should be a field of accurate, systematic knowledge. A good physician not only cures; he also knows the explanation, the cause of the disease. Mere experience and healing competence are not enough. Experience is a source of facts, but explanation requires concepts and reasoning about nonapparent causes. There has to be a place for theory. That decision threw the doors open to speculation. Incommensurable theories proliferated, sparking a reaction by the self-named Empiricists. These physicians respect experience (*emperia*), and are hostile to the idea that a physician must have theoretical knowledge of causes. They denounce the Rationalists' effort to hijack the healing arts and make them "philosophical." The knowledge of the physician is an art, a *techne,* and not a theory or *logos.* All the knowledge healing requires comes from medical experience. No knowledge (if it *is* knowledge) of theory matters to what physicians know to do in cases.[75]

To be quite anachronistic about it, this empiricism is less a theory of knowledge (its foundation) than a metaphilosophical thesis to the effect that medicine does not need this so-called foundation. Rather than an alternative theory about the foundation of knowledge, the point is that neither the physicians' art (*techne*), nor their observation (*autopsia*), nor their ability to heal is enhanced by the detour through theory. That is the empiricism Galen knows. "He will be the most reliable exponent of empiricism who refrains, in whatever he says, from claiming any of those things which are thought to be found out only by indicative inference," which Galen explains as knowledge "based on rational consequence." This empiricist does not dogmatically claim that experience is the sole source of knowledge. He merely says "I do not know anything that goes beyond what is apparent, nor do I profess anything more wise than what I have seen oftentimes." Thus, as Galen says, "the empiricist's attitude toward medical matters is like the skeptic's attitude toward the whole of life. . . . One has to show one's art by what one does, rather than by one's reasoning, and to avoid dialectic."[76]

One again detects resonance between this medical empiricism and Mohist ideas; for instance, the empiricists' determination to hold medical discourse to a standard founded on consequences and the priority of benefit. But this empiricism is so much a reaction to rationalism in medicine that it strains comparison where there is no comparable polemic, which the Mohists seem not to have incited. Critics of Mohism like Mengzi and Xunzi object to the priority of economic efficiency, and denounce the idea of "impartial care" (*jian'ai*). But they tend merely to ignore the Mohists' determination to make reasoning explicit and subject to a fixed standard, and sometimes silently appropriate results of Mohist analysis, as Xunzi does in both his theory of perceptual knowledge and of names. These retooled themes from the Mohists may perhaps inform the context in which the *Great Learning* and the teaching on the investigation of things emerge. The empiricism of Confucian investigation might in part be a development of originally Mohist ideas about empirical knowledge and how it benefits the people, and another example of Confucians learning from their critics. This empiricism looks into things and searches out subtle differences in the phenomena of nature, somewhat as Francis Bacon required. Bacon's empiricism seems closer to the Mohists, though, than to Confucians. Benefit for the people is the highest good and the point of knowledge. The rites and ceremonies Confucians treasure are to be discarded as primitive relics of an age when knowledge was rudimentary.

We could advance the comparative argument if we could go beyond suggestive similarities to a comparison of philosophical principles. Deleuze suggests that the fundamental proposition of empiricism (he is thinking especially of Hume) is that relations are external to ideas. "Ideas do not account for the nature of the operations we perform on them, and especially of the relations that we establish among them," he writes. "When James calls himself a pluralist, he does not say, in principle, anything else. This is also the case when Russell calls himself a realist. We see in this statement the point common to all empiricisms." With this one idea, a thesis on external relations, the real empiricist world is "laid out for the first time to the fullest." It is a world "of exteriority, a world in which thought itself exists in a fundamental relationship with the Outside, a world in which terms are veritable atoms and relations veritable external passages; a world in which the conjunction 'and' dethrones the interiority of the verb 'is'; a harlequin world of multicolored patterns and nontotalizable fragments where communication takes place through external relations."[77]

If this perspective on empiricism seems unwonted, consider what external relations have to do with empiricism as we usually understand it. When relations (including sameness and difference) are external to ideas, nothing can be known about things a priori, by reasoning from concepts alone. That undercuts the usual argument for innate ideas, and eliminates a priori knowledge of nature, which are textbook polemics of empiricism. What makes relations external to ideas is precisely that they cannot be deduced from an adequate concept of their terms. To know what is related to what, one must examine external relations, which requires observation and investigation, and cannot be known by the reasoning mind alone. Thus we deduce a textbook profile of empiricism from Deleuze's point about external relations.

A further implication of external relations, though one seldom made explicit in empiricist theories of knowledge, is that when relations are external to ideas, no relations—no actual relations—transcend the collective economy of human and nonhuman things. I can explain what I mean, although the argument may not sound very Chinese. Here is a question to think about. Is it possible that two stones might lie in some precise though unknown relation to one another on the bottom of the sea, or on the moon, or somewhere else where they remain undetected by our sapient species? Does that seem possible, even obvious, "common sense"? If so, then relations (such as differences of shape or position) belong to a reality that transcends the collective economy and cannot be completely external, as empiricism dictates. But do the scenario and its implicit ontology really make sense?

We can indeed suppose that seabed relations obtain regardless of actual knowledge. Nobody goes down in a submarine and measures. But the seeming transcendence of relations breaks down when we consider not actual measurement but its possibility, which depends on us. Concepts like shape, size, and distance are inventions, artifacts, tools, or works of art. To imagine undetected shapes and distance we imagine detecting them. However, if we remove that possibility, which depends on the contingency of our practice, there remains nothing "real" about such relations among things in themselves. The *reality* of the relations is not indifferent to the contingent practice of measurement. Relation is artificial, an artifact, and therefore external to everything it touches. The truth value of statements concerning relations does not depend on actual measurement, but the actuality, the actual existence of relations, depends on virtual commensurability with what is actually measured, and that depends on us and all we depend on.[78]

That conclusion is not subjectivism, not even anthropocentrism. To be included is not to be at the center. It is to be part of the circumstances, a partner with Heaven and Earth. For Luo Qinshun, "Heaven and man, things and the self, inner and outer, beginning and end, darkness and light, the lessons of birth and death, and the conditions of positive and negative spiritual forces should form an all-pervading unity with nothing left behind. Thus, when we speak of the myriad things, is there any that is after all external to our own nature?" To say that nothing is external to our nature means that there is nothing whose being and identity are radically independent of the natural history that includes us. All these relations are *logically* external to their terms (not inherent or a priori), but they are also coevolving with our life and practice.[79]

From a logical point of view, nothing *has* to be related to anything else. Hume is right about that. However, actual things become related not by logic, or internally through concepts, but because they evolve together, contingently coming to share conditions of existence. What is external for logic may be internal for evolutionary ecology. For example, honeybees and flowers are logically external. No deduction from the concept of one leads to the concept of the other. Nevertheless, the bees do not actually exist apart from the actual existence of flowers and vice versa. Logically external, ecologically internal. External in concept, internal in evolution and actual existence. If empiricism implies the externality of relations, that is a logical externality. Should the empiricist also reject ecologically internal relations? Luo and other Confucians seem to think not. Perhaps no relation is finally, fully, logically internal. But there is a *becoming internal* of relations that is just as real and empirical as external relations among actual things.

For Hume, all relations are logically external and therefore really, actually external. He says, "The contrary of every matter of fact is still possible, because it can never imply a contradiction and is conceived by the mind with the same facility and distinctness as if ever so conformable to reality." A logical possibility is an ontological possibility. What can be *thought* apart can *be* apart too. "The mind never perceives any real connection among distinct existences." Any appearance of connection must be a mistake, a projection, a fiction of the mind. Which is an elegant deduction, but so much for logic! The eco-logic of every actual development entangles contingencies in conditions of existence. Because time is real and nature evolves, every actual existing external relation is *becoming* ecologically internal, and every such internal relation has a past of externality for its terms.[80]

"Becoming internal" means diminishing externality, displaced by an evolutionary tendency to adapt to existence with environing others. A thing is becoming internally related to others when it enters into their economy and begins to share their conditions of existence. That is evolution. Things that formerly shared relatively few conditions of existence come to share more, becoming more closely adapted to each other. What is evolving among externally related terms is precisely this ecological internality. Evolving relations are internal in the sense that the existence of their terms depends on actual relation to others. These same relations are external in the sense that what holds their terms together is not a *logos* of essences but a contingently evolved adaptation. Symbiosis, synergy, development, growth, adaptation, and evolution are all so many words for the becoming ecologically internal of logically external relations.

The empirical reality of relations is not that of a finished, fully present fact. It is the reality of a becoming, things becoming related. It is this becoming related, a dynamic, creative process, that makes our life a partner with Heaven and Earth. Relations do not depend on us in the sense that fully present relational facts would fail to obtain apart from the fully present fact of our consciousness. However, these terms "fact" and "fully present" indicate a presumed priority of being over becoming, as if it went without saying that being is first and becoming (and relation) antecedent accidents that happen to beings. That is an old assumption in Western thought; however, it *is* an assumption, and seldom (if ever) subject to reasoned proof from truly independent premises, which may not even be possible. It is possible, however, to think differently.

The empirical reality of relations is fundamentally the reality of becoming, not finished fact. It is the reality of evolution, an evolution not limited to the organic, and that continues unabated. What was less internally related to anything becomes more internally related to others. No actual, natural, physical relation will ever be logically internal, but in a world of real evolution the externality of relation is ever vanishing, and so are the externalities that seem to segregate human and nonhuman things. Beside the *logical* externality and contingency of relations there is a natural, physical, evolutionary, *empirical* becoming-internal of relations, in which externality vanishes into the ecology of things. The nearest parallel to this empiricism with Chinese characteristics is not the antiquated inductivism of Francis Bacon but the radical empiricism of William James. The usual empiricism tends, as we have seen, to accentuate disjunction and neglect conjunction. For James, "the conjunctive relations found in experience are faultlessly real," real and *growing,* not because of logic, but because of life.[81]

If the epitome of empiricism is that relations are external to their terms, its antithesis, rationalism, assumes that such relations are internal, meaning that if we thoroughly understand an idea, we know its relations, including its truth, its causes, and its effects. The first rationalists thought they could attain knowledge of the cause of disease through *logos* and dialectic. Spinoza is the summit of this rationalism, and Hume the most intense reaction. "All events," he says, "seem entirely loose and separate. One event follows another, but we never can observe any tie between them. They seem *conjoined* but never *connected.*" Loose and separate does not mean unrelated. It means not *internally* related, subverting Spinoza's thought that "nothing in nature is contingent, but all things are from the necessity of the divine nature determined to exist and to act in a definite way."[82]

Without exactly wanting to disagree with Hume, Confucians like Zhang Zai, Cheng Yi, or Luo Qinshun might find his argument puzzling. What is the difference between conjunction and connection? For their tradition, correlation is the connection par excellence. Marcel Granet writes, "Instead of observing successions of phenomena, the Chinese registered alternations of aspects. If two aspects seemed to them to be connected, it was not by means of a cause and effect relationship, but rather 'paired' like the obverse and reverse of something, or to use a metaphor from the *Book of Changes,* like echo and sound, or shadow and light." The relations of things are phenomena of contingent, evolutionary entanglement, not much like cause determining effect, even less like premise determining conclusion.[83]

Unity is a kind of artifice and not an intrinsic, subsistent reality. That is Hume's rebuke to Plato. But for Hume artificial unity is imaginary, fictional unity. The given is loose and separate; unity has to be assembled, and the results are mere fictions (about which people may nevertheless be passionate). Nothing complex is really unified, a real unity. This is an implication of the logical externality of relations, but only on the assumption that relations do not *become.* They either are or are not. Hume is right about the *being* of relations, which is logically external, but he overlooks what they are *becoming,* which is internal in a way that is at once empirical and real, meaning entwined and efficacious, as systems become entangled with systems in nature, and especially at the interface with technology. There is nothing fictional about the becoming that makes logically external relations ecologically internal. This becoming is a phenomenon, empirically accessible to investigation provided one's philosophy does not, as Hume's did, preclude the priority of becoming over being. *Ecologically internal* is not something a relation *is.* It is something relations are becoming.

This becoming means adaptively entering into shared conditions of existence with others, human and nonhuman. Guo Xiang's *Zhuangzi* commentary has a nice image for such becoming. "Although the hand and foot have their different duties and the five internal organs their varying offices, never taking part in one another's tasks, nonetheless the hundred parts all harmonize into a unity. This is being together in not being together. They have never deliberately done anything for the sake of one another, and yet both internally and externally they accomplish what needs to be done. This is doing things for one another without doing things for one another." It is also logically external relations becoming ecologically internal. Another image, this from an important Song dynasty Neoconfucian, likens ecological unity to stampeding horses: "Ultimate harmony is what is called *dao.* . . . Unless it is like wild horses, fusing and intermingling, it does not deserve the name 'ultimate harmony'" (Zhang Zai).[84]

What could be more dynamic than stampeding horses, each one charging, changing fast, with a great deal of energy, close together, running hard? Each horse is separate, logically external to the rest, though were one to quiver in a single footfall the surging mass would collapse into a writhing heap of broken animals. Instead, they flow unstoppably around any obstacle. There is nothing fictional about their unity or its efficacy. It is real, that is, effective; a potentially destructive power that will kill you if you try to interact with it inappropriately. Unity is nowhere simply given (Hume is right about that), but all things at all scales in space and time are constantly becoming entangled, more interdependent, less indifferent or extrinsic. Locally, the processes interfere and collapse before anything finally *is* internally related to anything else. However, the whole movement of time is this becoming. That is the *dao*: time, evolution, the becoming that entangles the adventitious, their externality vanishing into the evolution of things.

Confucians tend to assume that right action belongs to wise knowledge, whereas for Hume knowledge has nothing to do with "ought." Who is the better empiricist? Confucian thought is unimpressed by the supposed dichotomy between *is* and *ought*. The relations that make things what they become also create the norm by which they ought to affect others—ought, that is, if they would avoid untimely destruction. Neoconfucians identify this norm as *li*, principle, a rule of peaceful coexistence among circumstantially related things. There is a (not necessarily unique) optimal way for contingent things to coexist, a condition of mutual becoming by which they avoid provoking a destructive response, at least for the duration. In the words of *Zhongyong*, "All things are produced and develop without injuring one another . . . the courses of the seasons, the sun, and moon are pursued without conflict." The right way to interact with things is not deduced from their concept, it is induced from their synergy, their mutual vitality, which has to be investigated, and we successfully "extend" this knowledge when we *respond* righteously, *doing* the right. The Neoconfucian concept of *li*, principle, implies that the circumstances of human-nonhuman interaction can and should be harmonious, and that their being so or not depends on the subtlety and comprehensiveness (or vicious stupidity) of our response. To make the best of it we have to investigate things and extend the knowledge and never let up.[85]

Hume looks to the imagination for the source of relations. Any seeming interiority or connection among things is imaginary, a fiction. Yet this imagination, this power to imagine the unity of a heterogeneous ensemble—where does *that* come from? It cannot be more imagination. At this point Hume abandons his argument: "These ultimate springs and principles are totally shut up from human curiosity and inquiries." Luo Qinshun may be the more consistent empiricist. The real relations in nature are becomings and processes, neither finished, fully present facts nor imaginary fictions. Hume asks what a real relation could *be*. The answer is, nothing. Not because no relations are real, but because the reality of relations is the reality of a becoming, not a being. And the reason for *that* is quite simply that time is real. What is the reality of time, what is real about time? Interval, duration, multiplicity becoming related.[86]

Hume shares Plato's dichotomy between knowledge and belief, and comes down against Plato in favor of *doxa*. "Philosophical decisions are nothing but the reflections of common life, methodized and corrected." The Chinese operate with an idea of more or less sagacious praxis, which evades Plato's tendentious distinction between *episteme* and *doxa*. They admire penetrating subtlety over ontological truth, and esteem the acuity that turns inconspicuous indices into unstoppable effects over suppliant mimesis. The better one is at that efficacious apperception the more one's practice qualifies as knowledge and one's knowledge as wise.[87]

The Neoconfucian teaching is that the key to this synergy of perception and praxis is the investigation of things. Investigation entails more than inquiry, being also, even first of all, a discipline for the self-restraint requisite to a perfected person's virtue. These two lines—cultivation of self, investigation of things—are inseparable and function best as their distinction disappears. As Cheng Yi said, "Integrity and understanding are one." The "extension" of the knowledge investigation affords is action that, by advancing the evolutionary becoming-harmoniously-internal of external relations, tends to vanish into things. Who is acting? Humans? Nonhumans? One? Many? Art or Nature? It is impossible to say.

— 6 —

Resonance

"What is the really fundamental idea of the *Book of Changes?*"
The Daoist replied, "The fundamental idea of the *Book of Changes*
can be expressed in one single word, *resonance.*"
—*A NEW ACCOUNT OF THE TALES OF THE WORLD*

Huainanzi, The Book of the Huainan Masters, is an early Han compendium traditionally attributed to Liu An, King of Huainan (modern Anhui), in collaboration with the scholars for which his court was famous. According to a modern editor, the central concept of the work is resonance (*ganying*), or mutual response (*xiangying*). "All things in the universe are interrelated and influence each other according to pre-set patterns, so that interaction appears as spontaneous and not caused by an external agent." This is not simply the idea that everything is related to everything else. Patterns are concealed among these relations, "most subtle essences" that link things inconspicuously and make them resonate. "Mountain clouds are like grassy hummocks; river clouds are like fish scales; dryland clouds are like smoky fire; cataract clouds are like billowing water. All resemble their form and provoke responses according to their class." "The burning mirror can draw fire; the loadstone can draw iron; crabs spoil lacquer; and sunflowers incline to the sun." You cannot guess these things, or learn them from the classics. They have to be investigated.[1]

"That things in their categories (*lei*) are mutually responsive is dark, mysterious, deep, and subtle. Knowledge (*zhi*) is not capable of assessing it; argument (*bian*) is not capable of explaining it." "Knowledge" here means perceptual recognition and knowledge of names. "Investigations by ear and eye are not adequate to discern the [resonance] of things; discussions employing the mind and its conceptions are not adequate to distinguish true and false." Resonance can be known, however, when approached in the right way, which is diligent investigation. "Correlative categories cannot necessarily be inferred." You have to look and see. "The resemblances between things and categories that cannot be externally assessed are numerous and difficult to recognize. For this reason they cannot but be investigated." Obvious inferences can be completely wrong. "Tile is made in fire but you cannot get fire from it; bamboo grows in water but you cannot get water from it." If you are willing to investigate, however, the resonance of things can be discerned. "Lead and cinnabar are of different categories and have separate colors. Yet if one can use [both of] them to produce scarlet, it is because one has grasped the technique. Thus intricate formulas and elegant phrases are of no aid to persuasion. Investigate what they take as the basis; that is all." Carry investigation to the end, and you reach the point at which "from what is within the palm of one's hand, one can trace [correlative] categories to beyond the extreme endpoint [of the cosmos]." Then there is nothing that cannot be known. "Heaven and Earth revolve and interpenetrate; the myriad things bustle about yet form a unity. If one is able to know this unity, then there is nothing that cannot be known; if one cannot know this unity, then there is not even one thing that can truly be known."[2]

Resonance cannot be known well or deeply in any of the obvious, easy ways. Nor can it be explained in terms of obvious agencies. Investigation must go to the root, which lies in the primordial oscillation of the *qi*. *Huainanzi* gives an early version of ideas we saw in Luo Qinshun. The energy of the *qi* begins in the oscillation of the empty and full, which I gloss as virtual and actual, or becoming and being. Becoming is empty of being, and being—fully actual, fully present—is empty of becoming. Ceaselessly fluctuating tendencies of each to become the other create flows laminar and turbulent, keeping the *qi* far from equilibrium, and expressed in the world as the alternations of *yin* and *yang*. Remember that *yin-yang* implies nonantagonistic gradients on a scale, not diametrical opposition. Phenomena analyze into infinitely integrated responsive proportions; a predominantly *yin* phenomenon always has a germ of *yang*, and vice versa. Everything is made of *qi*, everything bears a distinctive *yin-yang* signature, and everything interacts, becomes correlated, and resonates. Everything that moves is a stimulus somewhere, and all things communicate, though in furtive patterns. If the *dao* is a flow, no one should think it is without turbulence.[3]

It was Joseph Needham who first proposed to translate *ganying* as "resonance," acknowledging China's tradition of experimental acoustics. The *Huainanzi* is an early expression of what he calls their preference for ideas of "wave-motion through a continuum, rather than direct mechanical impulsion of particles." Technically, resonance is a rise in the amplitude of an oscillation that occurs when a system is exposed to a periodic force whose frequency matches its own. Resonance arises everywhere, because at some level every physical system interacts with every other (for example, every proton in the universe has at some point interacted and become entangled), which makes all things virtually responsive, and introduces diffusion, uncertainty, and irreversible nonlinearity into every environment. Hence, as Ilya Prigogine observes, "It is difficult to identify an important problem in classical or quantum physics where resonances do not play a significant part." Taking resonance seriously implies a connection of things that is not exhausted by logic and experience, or even by logic and causation. Things are connected through their becoming, the mere fact that they come to be. From this becoming they receive a duration, a temporality, and cannot fail to resonate with, ultimately, everything.[4]

Resonance promises large returns from relatively small inputs, because the right effort at the right time can nudge a system the way it is already tending, but only tending, amid many contrary tendencies, to go. Resonance couples all kinds of processes, just like harmonics in music, and because resonant systems oscillate at their maximum amplitude, even small forces can induce large effects. A stiff breeze can bring down a steel bridge, as happened at Tacoma Narrows. The circadian sleep-awake cycle, which is technically an oscillator, and the rotation of the earth (another oscillator) resonate and have become entrained, creating an adaptive coordination of metabolic rhythms and seasonally changing daylight. A highly effective (adaptive) result arises from a very weak cause, hardly a cause at all, the coupling energies being so slight. That small forces have only small effects is an assumption of classical physics that is now refuted. The Chinese never made it. On the contrary, it was a proverb: An infinitesimal misstep at the beginning leads to infinite error later on. We now say "sensitive dependence on initial conditions."[5]

Chinese thought on resonance seems to begin with Zou Yan, of the so-called Jixia Academy in the third century BCE. The innovation appears in the context of a new discourse on *qi*. Causes and conditions formerly attributed to local, ancestral, and heavenly spirits begin to be explained in terms of the harmony, balance, and resonance of *qi*. This line of thought eventually incorporates the *yin-yang* and Five Phase theories, and music becomes a favored metaphor of harmonious process. An early example is the *Xunzi* "Discourse on Music": "When depraved sounds influence (*gan*) a person, a wayward *qi* responds (*ying*) to them." An innovation of the *Huai-nanzi* is to interpret *wu wei* in these new terms. Effortless efficacy becomes an art of resonances. "When the Quintessential Spirit is abundant and the vital energy is not dispersed, then you are functioning according to the Underlying Patterns. When you function according to the Underlying Patterns, you attain equanimity. When you attain equanimity, you develop penetrating awareness. When you develop penetrating awareness, you become spiritlike. When you are spiritlike, with vision, there is nothing unseen; with hearing, there is nothing unheard; with actions, there is nothing incomplete."[6]

That is the efficacy of genuine, genuinely sagacious knowledge. "Only when there is a genuine person (*zhen ren*) is there genuine knowledge (*zhen zhi*)." Genuine is the knowledge of those "who can return to that from which they were born, as if they had not yet acquired a physical form." People of genuine knowledge "are those who have not yet begun to differentiate from the Great One." They are vanished into things. Which is not nirvana. Nothing is extinguished. On the contrary, everything becomes concentrated, intense, large with transformation. We fold into the virtual landscape, "the dwelling place of Total Darkness," and contemplate "the lodging place of Total Brightness." We "roam in the fields of the Nebulous," plunge "into the Fathomless," take rest "in the realms of the Unfettered," and "enter the Nonexistent," the Great Beginning (*tai shi*), the phase space of the world, where the chaotic *huntun,* a body without organs, subsists as a purely virtual whole (*tai yi*).[7]

By the Song dynasty (if not earlier) Confucians are thinking in these terms too. A leader in bringing these ideas to their thought is the early Song Confucian Zhang Zai. "That which resonates to all is emptiness (*xü*)." "The potency of nature is empty (*xü*) and responds efficaciously." "The vast emptiness cannot be devoid of *qi, qi* cannot but condense and become the myriad things, and the myriad things cannot but dissolve and become the vast emptiness." I read that last remark to say that emptiness cannot be devoid of myriad tendencies to fullness, or becoming not *coming to be.* Every *yin* is pregnant with something *yang,* and vice versa. Actual opposition, *yin* meets *yang,* actualizes the virtuality that contains both as tendencies. Actualization, which is to say becoming, or the passing of the present, is precisely this differentiation of the virtual and its tendencies. The empty tends to become full through the differential actualization of virtual tendencies.[8]

Emptiness is "nothing" or "nothingness" only in the sense that it is not a being and lacks all the classical qualifications of being, according to which *to be* is to be substantial, self-identical, fully present, Plato's *auto kath auto,* Aristotle's *ousia,* Hindu *svabhava,* the *Ding an sich.* Tang Junyi, elucidating Zhang Zai, writes, "The passing from being (*you*) to nothingness (*wu*) is not really entering into nothingness but entering into the hidden (*you*), and similarly arriving from nothingness to being is but emerging from the hidden to what is manifest (*ming*)." What seems like "nothingness" from the perspective of being (whatever is not a being must accordingly be not-a-being, that is, nothing) is from the perspective of becoming merely the nascent virtuality from which beings ceaselessly birth.[9]

What is empty is the becoming or, if you like, the passing of the present. The *passing* of the present is empty of presence. Becoming is void of presence and therefore empty. Presence commences as becoming abates and a thing simply *is.* Becoming is empty, never finished or fully present, but from it comes the presence of the present; anything that moves, any change, any becoming is a flower of emptiness. This emptiness is not an abstract deduction (as void is for Democritus). We have an account of its genesis from qualitative multiplicity. "Only after resonance (*gan*) is there interpenetration; therefore if there are no polarities there is no unity." If we have polarities, if these polarities are truly polar—qualitative, intense, really different—then between them is the emptiness, the virtual tending, of one becoming the other, the phase space, as it were, of their *yin-yang* interaction.[10]

An empty, virtual becoming contains these differences virtually, without negation or opposition, as a multiplicity of originally different tendencies, some selection of which eventually shed the vestiges of virtuality to assume the differentiated forms of the somewhere sometime present. Becoming is empty of actuality, empty of form, empty of presence, the present, and opposition. This same emptiness is a teeming manifold, a multiplicity without number, pullulating with differential tendencies that are "older" than the beings and relations of beings that they are becoming. This becoming—original, older than being, never present, enfolding differences (of tendency) older than identity, and multiplicity older than unity—is the emptiness that Bergson calls duration and Daoists call the *dao.*[11]

Becoming touches all things and sets the new into resonance with the established. The passing of the present is a wave of empty becoming passing between qualitative polarities, as each rushes to meet the other like air to a vacuum. What is merely tending may never come to be, but that transformation (actualization, becoming present) is the tendency established by resonance. This tendency to actual ecological unity through multiplicity and

difference is the trend of all becoming. Earlier I called it "becoming internal."
It is this infinitely complex, infinitely resonant *yin-yang* fluctuation of *qi*
that the sage must tune to, sagaciously to see the little things, and act without
the semblance of action. "If polarities are not established, unity cannot be
seen, and if unity cannot be seen, the functioning of polarities will cease."
To keep a way open is an empirical work, the investigation of things, which
investigates latent or virtual coherence, probing the inklings of resonance.
"The sage," Zhang says, "makes the most of his course of nature in between,
by merging both dimensions [empty and full, being and becoming, virtual
and actual], and is not obstructed."[12]

These ideas were powerfully developed, first by the brothers Cheng, who
were friends of Zhang Zai's, and later by Zhu Xi, whose *Reflections on Things
at Hand* is a major source of what we have from Zhang Zai's writings. "Whatever moves stimulates, and what is stimulated must respond. That to which
it responds again stimulates it, and when stimulated it again responds, so
that the process is endless" (Cheng Yi). Or as we say, nonlinear. People
dampen resonance with selfishness, which makes their response labored and
calculating. If we overcome the damping, response becomes more intensely
resonant, which means more effective with less initiative. "What 'all under
heaven' (*tianxia*) means is that the things and events are responsive (*gan*)
to me, and I accommodate and adapt to them, thus achieving good fortune,
bad fortune, gain, and loss" (Wang Fuzhi). Sages see through the full to the
emptiness it responds to. They see not frozen fact or actual relation, but virtual tendency. Incipient actualizing admits multiple futures, with opportunities for effortless intervention at points of potential bifurcation that are
in themselves chaotic. Such action is easy, almost nothing, provided one has
penetrating insight into opportunity and can really see the little things.[13]

Despite their supposed attraction to organic models, the Chinese never
dreamed the Western dream of teleology, in which all nature is one system
organized by a transcendent purpose. This is humanity's most flattering
cosmos, suffused with intentionality, *logos*, rationality, presence, and purpose, all qualities intellect recognizes as its own. The Chinese cosmos is au-
tistic by comparison. There is no intentionality behind transformation, which
is *ziran*, from itself, an unregulated regularity, immanently orderly but tran-
scendently lawless. It seems unlikely that the thinkers I have considered
would balk at the idea of evolution. To say that nature has a history, that
species transmute, that the contours of the earth were once quite different,
the land and sea populated by different species, most of which are extinct,

and finally that these changes are unplanned contingencies that just happen to happen—none of that has to be received as sterile paradox, and might even sound attractive, especially to Daoists. They might agree with Spinoza and Darwin that there is no design or purpose in nature. Natural events happen not from agency or intentionality but *ziran,* from themselves, by a virtual potency things inherit with *qi.* The absence of purposiveness is recognized, even idealized in the *wu wei* eclipse of purpose, when intentionality vanishes into the evolution of things.[14]

Philosophical reflection on knowledge in China may begin with the art of war, even if *Sunzi bingfa* is not the Spring and Autumn text tradition says. This art of war discovers the first problems of knowledge when it discovers knowledge of position (*shi*), strategic knowledge, and the difference it makes to military effectiveness. The Confucians, literati scholars and ritual specialists, did not have to approve of what the new art-of-war commanders did to appreciate that they had grasped something important about knowledge. There are better ways to make knowledge wise than training for war. Humanity needs the discipline of classical learning and ceremonies. It takes decades of preparation before spontaneous reaction flawlessly accords with ceremonial appropriateness, but the result makes a righteous king more powerful than any army. Sage King Yu, founder of the Xia dynasty, subdued the barbarian Miao people by sheer charisma without a fight. The Confucian *Book of Rites* says, "The army has ritual propriety (*li*), therefore it accomplishes military merit," and the *Zuo Commentary* adds, "Having ritual propriety there will be no defeat."[15]

For Mengzi, "Those who are good at war deserve the greatest punishment" (4A14). He allows there is something to the art: "Heavenly omens are not as good as advantages of terrain." But something else is superior: "Advantages of terrain are not as good as harmony with the people" (2B1). Harmony comes from charismatic virtue, not cunning strategy. An art of war is superfluous for a true king. "If the ruler of a state is fond of benevolence, he will have no enemies in the world" (7B4). That is also Xunzi's argument. Chapter 15 of the *Xunzi* is a Confucian rebuttal of the military philosophy, presented as a debate between Xunzi and Lord Linwu, a master of strategy, whose first point is to praise strategic knowledge of position. Xunzi replies that the best rule in war is the same as in kingship, namely, humanity and righteousness. Strategic advantage is a byproduct of benevolent government.

Only when the king is virtuous and the officials sincere will rulers have the strategic disposition to overcome all enemies.

The strategic value of knowledge is the efficacy the wise derive from knowing the disposition or situation of things. They really see the little things, see the beginning and know the end, and so on. Transposed to the civilian realm, this understanding of wise knowledge is received differently. Some believe that the basis of civilization is political, a matter of relationships, appearances, and perceptions, and love what holds civilization together (a love rooted in fear). Others love what civilization makes possible, which is to escape relationships, to forget about politics, and create perceptions. To Confucians, this wandering mind is irresponsibly anarchic. For them, as Robert Cummings Neville observes, "the Daoists are not realistic at all about what is important in the human cultural sphere because they do not easily recognize or register a cultural reality whose rhythms require long beats of intentionally driven effort that are blind to many of mere nature's transformative openings."[16]

That was Xunzi's argument. However, we have seen that Daoists may be more alert to the problems of artifice than Xunzi was, with his fixation on ritual and the disdain of a literatus for artisanal skill and technics. What may look like Daoist aversion to knowledge is better seen as contempt for its deformation under an economy of short-sighted efficiency and artless ineptitude. We are challenged to sublimate technical mastery, to make it life-enhancing and not just narrowly profitable. The Confucian program is hopeless. To make knowledge wise requires a fundamental break with the Confucians' values, which only defeat the effectiveness they want to cultivate. Instead of caring for the self one should forget about the self, abandon it to chaos, and practice artful inactivity, undamped by names and fastidious ceremony.

Buddhism decrees the immanently virtual ontologically vacant. There is no incipience, no *ziran* transformation, no latency in positions. There is nothing more to becoming than actual concomitance: first this, then that. "The learned and noble disciple, O monks, attentively considers dependent origination: 'this exists when that exists, this originates from the origination of that; this does not exist when that does not exist, this ceases from the cessation of that.'" The conviction that life is good and can be enhanced by art and knowledge distinguishes classical Chinese thought from the Buddhism of later centuries. Might there not also be, in this optimistic evaluation of art and knowledge, an Occidental resonance? Western technology has proved effective in ways that might impress even the ancient Chinese, who tend to dismiss anything foreigners do. Paradoxically though, the drift of Western philosophy has not followed but, on the contrary, baffled the comprehension of technical competence in the labyrinth of epistemology. As a result, we have a technology that evades what our philosophy thinks knowledge is, and the Chinese have an understanding of efficacious knowledge for a technology they never imagined.[17]

The unity of knowledge and action is associated with Neoconfucian thought. However, all the thinkers we have considered (Buddhists apart) want to operate, however exactly they understand that: for example, ceremonially, or with disdain for ceremonies, with or without effort, on the battlefield or in the chambers of state; and even Buddhists value a Bodhisattva's skillful means. Since all sides understand the value of knowledge to lie in amplifying such effectiveness, all take the quality of practice, however evaluated, as the criterion of knowledge. Knowledge is not complete until it enhances practice; if practice turns out badly, then it never was knowledge. Such knowledge is an expressive quality of acts and their artifacts, which are the primary way knowledge becomes actual, and not secondary effects of a pure knowledge lodged elsewhere. There is no actual knowledge until there is actual expression, a performative effect, or artifact. These artifacts are the original expression of knowledge. Anything further back in their genesis (perception, belief, representation) is knowledge only in an indirect, secondary sense.

The philosophers of American pragmatism made a related argument, thinking of knowledge in terms of engineering instrumentality, an efficient response to a problem. However, the Chinese expect more than efficiency or a profitable proportion between cost and benefit. They aspire to a sublime and artful effectiveness out of all proportion to the instigating force. A pragmatist like John Dewey wants more technology—more rational, more efficient, more consistently applied; not a different technology, one that forgets about economy and substitutes the artful intensity of engineering *ziran* effectiveness. The genesis of knowledge in Chinese tradition does not unfold as Dewey thinks it should, from a problem consciously apprehended as a need or want, to the engineered efficiency of inquiry-guided action. Instead, knowledge emerges in the response to what affects me, a response the more sagacious the more subtly it achieves all that is required, however defined, with near-invisible cost. The less it does (while leaving nothing undone), and the less conspicuously problematic the stimulus to which it responds, the more sagacious. That defines the wisdom of wise knowledge, which is good, not at solving obvious problems, but avoiding them in the first place.

When Neoconfucians subordinate the particularity of things to "principle" they subordinate things to relationships. Perhaps it is confidence in the efficacy of ceremonies that encourages them in this course. Without those now-long-forgotten proprieties they would have nothing to distinguish wisdom from cleverness or knowledge from sophistry. Must that dampen their resonance for us? Or is there something comparable to the ancient *li* that might stand in their place and do what they were expected to do for knowledge, which is to make it at once efficacious and wise? Justice, perhaps. Could the proof of wise knowledge be the justice it does to things human and nonhuman? Before we can take this idea seriously we require an understanding of justice undeterred by the difference between human and nonhuman things.[18]

In Western tradition the knowledge most worth knowing has to be true. It may seem obvious that knowledge has to be true, yet it *is* an assumption, and not without difficulty. For instance, it requires that the principal expression of knowledge be a *truth,* which postclassical philosophy understands in terms of true propositions. So nothing that resists translation into propositions can fully count as knowledge, especially not the philosophically most important knowledge. In one blow, the knowledge of arts and *techne* drops under the horizon. "The speculative mind does not think of what is practical," says Aristotle, "and says nothing about what is to be avoided or pursued." For Plato we only get to the point of application after contemplative truth is attained. "All the great arts require idle speculation and natural philosophy." Plotinus depicts action as the shadow of contemplation; doing and making are either a weak contemplation or the concomitants of contemplation. Excellent practice presupposes excellent theory; we have to have a reason and it has to be true. Otherwise virtue is incomplete or, worse, merely apparent. By contrast, the knowledge Chinese thought esteems as wise creates not just efficiency but good use, at once righteous and aesthetically satisfying, to be enjoyed as we do orchestral music or a blended flavor.[19]

Why did the philosophers insist on truth? It is a question they are curiously incurious about. It seems to go without saying that of course philosophers want *the truth*. G. E. R. Lloyd thinks this claim on *the truth* begins as a rhetorical strategy appropriate to contentious, *agon*-admiring Greeks. "Greek intellectuals sought and claimed incontrovertibility chiefly in a bid to outdo their rivals and downgrade their merely plausible arguments." And their merely practical virtue. The disagreement between the "philosopher" Socrates and the "sophist" Protagoras is purely theoretical. In their lives, their virtue, these men are both exemplary. According to Lloyd, "attempting in public to undermine what others believed was a peculiarly Greek phenomenon." All the philosophers were out to impress. They made their reputation by wowing peers in public, not winning favor at court. "Their chief constraint was the need to succeed in the fiercely competitive environment of those claiming special knowledge." By contrast, "no Chinese group attempted to mark itself out as different from and superior to all others on the grounds that it could deliver what no one else could, more than just what is persuasive, namely, the incontestably true."[20]

Features of institutional inquiry in traditional China include official posts (for example, court astronomer or physician), rulers and ministers as the primary audience, and the authority of the ancient canons. Expertise combines tested knowledge that traces back to legendary sages with a secure lineage of transmission. At no point, however, must knowledge detour through dialectic. Knowledge requires subtlety and effectiveness, not reasons or truth. After the eclipse of Mao Zedong Thought in the latter twentieth century, Chinese intellectuals enthusiastically took up Western works of postmodern theory, although they proved to be exquisitely selective readers, cheerfully ignoring what the Western authors might think are their most important arguments. How could they do otherwise? Having never made dichotomies of appearance and reality or matter and spirit, understanding truthfulness as authenticity and objectivity as impartiality, what have the Chinese to learn about overcoming metaphysics, the incredulity of metanarratives, or the deconstruction of phallogocentrism? Not even the authority they accord the past is ontological, being a harmony that has constantly to be renewed.[21]

China never experimented with alternative political constitutions. Benevolent rule by a wise king is the only model. By contrast, a volatile experience with politics (the variety of constitutions and experiments in government) may have primed Greek thinkers to explore dramatically different solutions in other matters too. For instance, during the lifetime of Zeno the Stoic, a resident alien of Athens in the early third century BCE, there were seven constitutional changes, three unsuccessful revolts, and four sieges, two of which resulted in the fall of the city. Constitutions in the Hellenistic period oscillated between democracy, oligarchy, and monarchy. Paradoxically, however, this diversity and experimentation did not affect the *theoretical* content of ancient political thought, which is no less monotonous than in China, if in a different key, preoccupied by the urgency of order, avoidance of conflict, and a patrician orientation to aristocracy or oligarchy.[22]

These philosophers were also isolated from experience with power. The ambition to advise a ruler is normal in China and unusual in Greece. Greco-Roman rulers did not gather intellectuals to legitimate their rule with cosmology. Greeks had no emperor to persuade, no orthodoxy to defend, no advisory position to protect. Reputation and livelihood depended instead on conspicuously confrontational debate. Teachers had to attract pupils and win arguments with rivals. Differences of opinion were not minimized but amplified and inventively explored in debates that could be intense and bitter. Strident adversariality, the pluralism of perspectives, and the inhibition of orthodoxy were the result. Philosophy is still like that.

I would like to anticipate a misunderstanding. A reader might think I am saying the Chinese are good at "knowing how" and favor effectiveness, while Western philosophy favors theoretical truth and propositional "knowing that." This distinction between "knowing how" and "knowing that" is amazingly popular. I have to say I do not like it and do not use it in a philosophical theory of knowledge. Perhaps I should explain my reservations.[23]

What is the distinction supposed to distinguish? Meanings for the word *know,* or different concepts of knowledge, or different forms or types of knowledge? There are problems with each alternative. If the point of the distinction is to analyze the meaning of the word *know,* what is the evidence of semantic difference, despite our blameless use of one word? Grammatical intuitions about "what we would say" seem unconvincing. Why should we respect them? How could they show that the knowledge we refer to when we say someone knows the truth is different *as knowledge* from what we refer to when we say that someone knows how to play the flute? And even if there were a difference of meaning (whatever that means!), it would not explain why knowledge of truth merits one-sided philosophical attention more than any other sense of *know.*

Is there perhaps some conceptual difference between knowing the truth and knowing how? Or a difference of logical type, essence, or noetic nature? There are indeed many varieties of knowledge that do something valuable without much talk or explanation. I take my broken shoe to a shoemaker and he returns it repaired. He could be mute for all it matters to his knowledge or its expression. But if you turn to face others and say, "I *know* that such and such" and expect them to take you seriously, you have to be able to explain your claim rationally. Knowledge that, knowing the truth, is knowing sufficient reasons. And knowing those reasons implies mastery of the skills required to justify claims with arguments others take seriously, which is not unlike knowing how to dance. The difference between performances that are evaluated by mute effectiveness and those whose value depends on a dancelike articulation of reasons therefore falls entirely on the side of *praxis* and *techne*. They are different skills of different arts, not one a practical how-to knowledge of technique and the other something entirely different.

Plato tried to say that only someone who understands the explanation really knows, knowing the highest, best, most godlike knowledge. This argument was his contribution to the old rivalry between philosophy and *techne*, meaning art or technical knowledge. Apart from this antiquated polemic, though, why does knowledge *have* to divide along the lines of *episteme* and *techne*, art and science, truth and technique? Why does knowledge of truth *have* to stand out as uniquely valuable and admitting of dedicated study? Why is "knowing the truth" not a practical kind of knowing how? Some people certainly seem better at it than others. The knowledge propositions express is not different as knowledge from that expressed in knowing how, knowing who, knowing when, even knowing not. Insofar as it is knowledge, it is all pretty much the same thing.

And what thing is that? It is a mistake to equate knowledge with knowing the truth and to forget about art. It is also a mistake to overgeneralize in the other direction and think that know-how is the essence of knowledge. It is not. Lots of so-called know-how is not knowledge at all. If I use a paper clip as a trigger, and rig a mousetrap from the contents of your desk drawer, that is art and knowledge. But the usual use of a paper clip is not. One "knows how" to use it, but the "knowing" is no more than right use, normative habit, the praxeological equivalent of opinion, and not knowledge at all. The reason is that the usual use of a paper clip does not admit the superlative. There is nothing artful about it. No one uses a paper clip as a paper clip to notably better effect than anyone else, unlike, say, the use of a violin.

The fact that an ordinary person with ordinary abilities can be described as "knowing" how to use a paper clip should not detain a philosophy of knowledge. There is more to understand about knowledge than the use of these or any words. There is history, experience, and human evolution; there are the arts, sciences, and technologies. If we consider more context, I think we find that knowledge is basically a quality of artifacts. What makes knowledge desirable and worth cultivating is the enhancement it brings to the effectiveness with which we act in an artifactual environment. There is knowledge wherever artifacts are designed and made, where they withstand trials of strength, some performing better than others. Every artifact expresses the knowledge that invented it, and the knowledge it takes (if it does, and not all do) to use it well. Whether we speak of knowing how or knowing that, we are qualifying artifacts, evaluating their performance. Knowing how and knowing that are not different kinds of knowledge or different logical senses or concepts. They are different ways of performing well with different artifacts.

Knowing how and knowing that have more in common as knowledge than distinguishes them as varieties, and the distinction is not a helpful epitome of Chinese and Western ideas. It seems better to think in terms of value. What value do the Chinese distinguish as knowledge? For what accomplishment do they select or prefer it? When we approach the material in this way, I think we see broad agreement across a spectrum of traditional Chinese thought. Distinctions emerge when we ask how knowledge so understood is to be acquired and trained for wisdom. That seems most to differentiate thinking about knowledge among Confucians, Mohists, Daoists, and so on.

Chinese tradition understands knowledge to pose a problem to wisdom. What makes knowledge problematic is its effectiveness, which confronts the wise with the problem of the relationship between being effective in that way and virtue, humanity, education, longevity, ritual, rulership, and war. How is such effectiveness best cultivated and regulated? Under what conditions is it harmonious or calamitous? Western thought, by contrast, tends to see knowledge not as a problem but as a solution, indeed, a panacea. That is the Socratic legacy. Everything bad comes from ignorance. Let knowledge overcome ignorance and the Good falls into your lap.

The Socratic expectation for knowledge, the idea that knowledge suffices for wisdom, turned out to be a mistake. We know that now because knowledge abounds while wisdom remains as rare as ever. We should not blame

Socrates. It must have seemed like a good idea at the time. But it is wrong, a dead end, a refuted hypothesis. We are only now making a discovery the Chinese made much earlier. Knowledge does not make people wise, just as truth does not make us free. We are challenged, as Chinese thinkers were, to reflect on the ethos or ethics of sagacious sapience. The question is ethical, a question of good use, the wise way to go about the endless work Confucians call extending knowledge and completing things.

We still tend to see knowledge as a solution rather than a problem, though in a modern mode that forgets about wisdom. Solutions are good or bad in a "technical" way that experts understand. Good solutions are technical, problems of expertise. Use knowledge, apply a formula, calculate. What ought to be a problem of wisdom—the ethical life of knowledge—shatters into endless technical problems for specialists. Unfortunately, that too does not work. Instead of solving problems, the effort to manage them scientifically tends to make them multiply, and the worst become frustratingly entrenched. We have not entirely recovered from Socrates's poison. We expect knowledge to determine solutions and solve technical problems, when the genius of knowledge is to avoid problems in the first place.

Knowledge is the tool of tools and the art of arts. We ought to cultivate it religiously. Instead, the good use of knowledge is counterproductively dampened by the ethical indifference of those who pursue the work of inquiry, including you and me. We do not care as we should about the ethical use of knowledge. We do not know how to care, how to express such care, to whom, or with what arguments. We tend either to think, like idealists, that knowledge is intrinsically good. Put it out there! That is good and sufficient. Or we think like bureaucrats, T. H. Huxley's administrative nihilists. Ethical life? Good use? Not *my* job! Of course it seems too much, too late, to ask those who humbly (or not!) take their place in the economy of knowledge for a commitment to wisdom in the investigation of things. The masters of modern knowledge are professional experts, specialists, the best and brightest, disciplinary superstars. But do not expect wisdom. They are not trained for that. It is not their job (though, it turns out, no one else's either). Consider the words of J. Robert Oppenheimer, director of the Los Alamos atomic bomb project, when in November, 1945, he spoke at the ceremony closing the wartime facility: "It is good to turn over to mankind at large the greatest possible power to control the world and to deal with it according to its lights and its values." Ethical use? Not *my* job. Take up your concerns with mankind at large![24]

That is our new "problem of knowledge" in a nutshell. Where knowledge really is a problem (in ethics) we do not see it, and where we *do* see a problem (in epistemology), we have made a scholarly labyrinth with nothing to show for itself. Preoccupied with epistemological scruples, we overlook the ethical problem, which turns out to be the really serious one. Modern research and experimental knowledge have for centuries been indifferent to ethics, indifferent to the wise use of knowledge. We are told that this must be. No *is* determines *ought,* and knowledge is all *is.* So inquiry drifts on currents of conventional wisdom and winds of whimsy. Oppenheimer again: "When you see something that is technically sweet, you go ahead and do it and argue about what to do about it only after you have had your technical success. That is the way it was with the atomic bomb." The fortress of modern moral logic sheltered a garden where knowledge proliferated undisturbed by ethical scruples. Follow the sweetness! Eventually, the negligent growth crept over the ivory towers to wrap potentially suffocating tendrils around the common world. Philosophers hardly see this. We have no experience with knowledge as a problem except in epistemology, which distracts us from the *other* problem, how to enhance the ethical intelligence of our knowledge. The most challenging thing today to be wise about is the wise, the ethical use of knowledge.[25]

That is unquestionably a change in perspective, and not at all how classical philosophy understood the relationship between knowledge and wisdom. The classical challenge to wisdom is imperturbability, which was the philosophers' idea of happiness. Most of what happens to people is uncontrollable, but it is up to us whether we are truly harmed, and nothing harms the wise. That is Socrates again, and all the philosophers of antiquity reprise and confirm his idealism. So little is really up to us (especially back then) that we do better to husband our power and minimize the agitating impact of everything before which we are helpless. For Epicureans and Stoics, the shrewder one is at that (the boon of knowledge), the less vulnerable, the more serene. Platonists and Aristotelians expect contemplative philosophical knowledge to translate the soul to a placid plane of true being, whose supernal sanctity compensates for contingency and the distress of life's accidents.

Looking at it today, we see how innocent these arguments are of modern technoscience. What is external? What is not up to us? Michel Serres raises this question in conversation with Bruno Latour. He thinks the new mixed scientific disciplines (biochemistry, medical physics, genetic engineering, and so on) have practically eliminated the category of the "not up to us." "Our wisdom is shaken by the tearing down of those objective tendencies that were formerly irremediable and unforgiving. . . . We have become the tragic deciders of life or death, masters of the greatest aspects of our former dependence: Earth, life and matter, time and history, good and evil." He thinks the alliance of science and technology "[makes] us responsible for the generations to come, for their number and their health, as well as the real conditions that we will leave them—this or that kind of world, depending on our decisions and our acts."[26]

That is a call not for more knowledge, but more responsibility, wiser knowledge, a more consistently ethical use of knowledge. We are like sailors—this was Otto Neurath's simile—who must rebuild their ship at sea. Except that the ship is not merely an apt image for science and the sailors for scientists. It is a figure for humanity, the image of our ecology, a metaphor of the species and its future. The good ship Gaia. Sailors cannot dominate the sea, or manage it, or "apply" a knowledge gained elsewhere to the challenge of sailing the oceans. Knowledge better used, wiser knowledge suited to the unprecedented challenge, would work with environing forces the way a navigator works with tides, currents, and wind. The work would be softer, more synergetic, like Daoist engineering, good at evading problems petty knowledge cannot see coming, rather than expecting to use knowledge to solve obvious problems everyone sees.

The environmental crises at the beginning of the third millennium share the quality of being unintended, unforeseen, often ironic side effects of human action. In other words, design failure, negligence in knowing the not known. We were undeterred in a possibly irreversible commitment to fossil fuels by how little we know of the implications for climate change. Nations committed their economies to nuclear energy without caring how little we know about problems of waste and safety. We cannot reliably foresee the reaction of complex natural systems to human-initiated changes, so insurance agencies hire accounting firms to persuade administrators to agree it does not matter, and duly report to investors who care only about the bottom line, not how it got there ("Not *my* job!"). The specialist organization of knowledge limits our capacity to know whole-system effects, so specialist modeling assumes, however unrealistically, that the knowledge is superfluous. It seems obvious that rapid, inexpensive communication is a good thing, and we ask no justification from technology that makes it faster. Yet beyond a relatively low threshold, rapid communication becomes an obstacle to timely action, and things that really *need* to happen quickly, like sustainable agriculture, provision against climate change, preservation of biodiversity, and population control, cannot happen at all.[27]

What psychological literature calls the Dunning-Kruger effect occurs when people's incompetence masks their ability to recognize their incompetence. We suffer from an ironic variation in which our competence masks our stupidity. One can be wise without knowing a lot, in the sense of scientific understanding and advanced technology. But having that understanding and technology is no substitute for wisdom. The petty knowledge Zhuangzi belittled was mostly pedantry, harming only those who take it seriously. However, the global alignment of science, technology, and capitalism has made our petty knowledge—ordinary, passing, actually applied, ethically indifferent knowledge—a new kind of stupidity, more dangerous than stupidity has ever been.[28]

We stand at the onset of a new geological epoch, the Anthropocene, a technical name for an age when the environment begins to change on a planetary scale in response to things people do. Stupidity has become geological. Under these conditions it seems obvious that wisdom cannot remain confined to private perfection or "happiness." The trials against which wisdom is tested have invaded the common world, challenging the "friends of wisdom" to make a necessarily collective practice of knowledge wise. The ethical subject—the ethical "us" or "we"—is no longer humanity but includes nonhuman species, artifacts, technological systems, geological systems, the planetary ecology. These are all enmeshed, having grown internal with each other to various degrees, and cannot be addressed effectively except as a collective. "The subject," especially the ethical subject, is ontologically multiple, a polymorphous, polyvocal, planetary commonwealth.

The priority of being is lodged deep in Western thought, as is the complementary idea of becoming as change, something that contingently happens to beings: first there are beings, determinate and self-identical; then comes change. Becoming and change are not the same, however. What is becoming does not change; on the contrary, it maintains itself (it *is*, is *the same, endures*) only by ceaseless difference. Only what constantly differs is becoming; never having been, neither does it change. To change is to stop being one thing and start being another, an uncanny transition Lucretius likens to death. "Whatever by being changed passes outside its own boundaries, at once this is the death of that which was before." Hence the mortuary logic of our *logos*. "A man should make all haste to escape from earth to heaven," Socrates tells his friends. "It seems likely that we shall attain that which we desire and of which we claim to be lovers, namely, wisdom, only when we are dead. . . . Either we can never attain knowledge or we can do so only after death."[29]

Chinese thought observes an originality for becoming that Western thought reserves for being. What to Western understanding is a self-identical thing looks more like a phase in a relatively slow and local process. Individuals at any level are multiplicities one level down. Imminent transformation shadows actual form. Hence, as François Jullien observes, the impossibility of a Chinese nude. "That nudes were neither painted nor sculpted in China can ultimately be attributed to 'theoretical' reasons: namely, that China never conceived, singled out, and put forward a cohesive plane of essences, and that the Chinese imagination therefore found no gratification in the embodiments of essences that the mythological figures represent to us." For Chinese painting it is numinous latency, spectral potency, the difficulty looming transformation poses for forms fixed on paper, that make the depiction of rock or bamboo a greater technical challenge than the idealized figure of a classical nude. In the words of the *Huainanzi*, "When one paints [a picture] of the face of Xi Shi, it is beautiful but cannot please; when one draws with a compass the eyes of Meng Ben, they are large but cannot inspire awe; what rules form (*junxing*) is missing from them." That challenge provoked experimentation in Chinese painting as exquisite and fecund as the challenge of perspective in Renaissance art. "All the great [Chinese] painters of landscapes," says a scholar of this art, "were acute perceivers of transformation," which they did not merely perceive but translated into ink. Contemporaries described Ming dynasty painter Dong Qichang as having "the powers of transformational creation at his brush tip."[30]

Change, inevitable for beings, is not inevitably viable. Once a being exists, it never stops changing, but some of those changes enhance power and prolong life while others do the opposite. The challenge ethical life poses to our wisdom is to minimize toxic changes and maximize those we can collectively live with. For human beings viable change depends on knowledge. That is not true for all beings, but it is true for us. The need for knowledge is the price people pay for release from the relatively inflexible adaptations of other organized beings from minerals to monkeys. For us, to do what comes naturally is not to rely on instinct but to interpose artifice, make a technical detour, perform a rite or calculation, hum a tune, reach for a tool. This interposition of art creates problems because it can be more or less artfully done, and there is no preestablished harmony—preestablished harmony is precisely what we have given up in return for the arts of freedom. Viability, adaptation, symbiosis—these are for us ethical and technical challenges, problems of art and ethos, not gifts of nature, as they are for other species. That fundamental fact of human evolution has gradually made our stupidity geological.

Symbiotic, enduringly viable works of art make the best use of knowledge in a world where so much depends on what people are technically able to do. In the real world, any form (any assemblage, organism, or economy) is a complex nonlinear system massively interacting with others. Soft form excels at interactive adaptation. The softer form is, the more conditions of existence it shares with the rest of its environment, and therefore the more resilient it is. A successfully soft form withstands the forces of its environment not by superior rigidity but by adaptation, deriving durability not indirectly, from the indomitable will that applies it, but directly, internally, ecologically, from its convivial synergy with an environment.

The obstacles to wise knowledge are not as Western philosophy traditionally assumes, namely, the body, especially the senses, imagination, pleasure, and desire. Whatever may have been the case in antiquity, it is not now reasonably denied that everything we think with—our neurology, our senses, the instruments contrived to enhance them, our cultural traditions, and languages—is corporeal and contingently evolved. Our mind is an outcome of millions of years of evolution without direction or design. Knowledge is what we make of reactions elicited from our neurology, reactions that reveal a contingent evolution and not a transcendent order of fact or being. To get things right is to get them right in our terms. There is no "pure" intellect, and self-identical "being" is a delusion of rationalism.

The obstacles to wise knowledge are obstacles to cooperation, communication, and the prevalence of long-term perspectives; in other words, political obstacles, obstacles of the collective and its habits. The economy of the disciplines and the specialist principle in research and teaching are examples. Knowledge cannot be wise when the agencies of inquiry are isolated and do not know or care what *others* want to know. Interdisciplinarity makes what others want to know common knowledge. It becomes difficult to act with indifference to knowledge others want. The practice of such interdisciplinarity would make everything about knowledge more realistically complicated. If as a result knowledge slows down a lot, well, are we sure that is a bad thing? It would depend on the quality of the slower knowledge.

That quality will not be "truth." The presumptive truth of knowledge (or the best, philosophically most significant knowledge) is another obstacle to making knowledge wise. We saw the original motivation for the philosophers' idealization of truth, which was a way of disqualifying competitors among the poets and sophists. "*We* have the truth," the philosophers say, "you have mere opinion. We *know*, you merely believe. *We* are in touch with reality, you are sunk in shadows." Enforcing this idea of truth today would be no more than a way to evade the responsibility to communicate, fending it off, and establishing barriers to the questions of others. There is still too much of that in philosophy. We should know better, because we should know that knowledge (including our own) flourishes under opportunistic mixing, not sanctimonious purity. Philosophy has always been fecundated by forces from outside, like Greek medicine and geometry, Christian revelation, Islamic scholarship, Galilean experimentation, mathematical logic, and perhaps too the globalization of our time.

Knowledge becomes effective though translation, in the literal sense of carrying over, transposing from one place or form to another, germinating hybrids, starting new conversations among new interlocutors, adding black boxes to black boxes, like contingent tiles in an improvised mosaic. This agitated articulation is inimical to classical Truth, which instead of succumbing to translation is a treasure to preserve and keep pure. To no avail. The value of knowledge lies in the efficacy of these transverse translations—what they connect or relate, the correlations they exploit, the networks they expand, the fecundity of their resonance.

Dao means "way," though the oldest, philosophically most relevant image is not a road or path but a river or canal, the way of flowing water. Method (Greek *methodos*) also means "way." Method, as we understand it since Descartes, means the geometrically straight path of light or falling bodies, the rational economy of means, a logical plan. This method belongs to the modern tradition of looking at systems locally, isolating mechanisms analytically, and optimistically aggregating. Method presupposes obstacles and promises to surmount them. It postulates control, and only works through constant control, whereas to change with the *dao* is to overcome the need for what control promises, which is solutions to obvious problems.[31]

Wisdom cannot be a matter of methods or expertise, because the efficacy of methods and expertise belongs to the problem knowledge poses to wisdom. The problem is to find its *dao,* its way of settling into our habitat and common future, the ecological principle of endurance for technoscientific knowledge and its works. The genius of wise knowledge is to see problems before they are problems, when they are still but tendencies, still virtual, and to evade them by that minimal intervention Chinese tradition lauds. The challenge to wisdom is to use this power wisely, which does not mean solving obvious problems but assisting the commonweal to evade problems before they become obvious, and to vanish into things instead of struggling for a method to control them.

To vanish into things is not the metaphysical dream of contemplative transparency before finally finished forms. To vanish is to mix. The sugar vanishes into the water, not gone, merely rendered invisible, while endowing its matrix with new tendency. To mix is to mix well; what does not mix well is not mixed at all. Obstinately immiscible, selfishly self-identical, it resists a tendency to soften up and become more consistently internal to its environment. In language I used earlier, vanishing means becoming (more) internally related. What becomes imperceptible offers no resistance to the mixing that redistributes it. Fluently translated, its form is a phase, its identity experimental. We vanish into things when what they do, their economy, becomes indistinguishable from what we do, our vitality. We vanish by synthesis, symbiosis, and synergistic evolution. We mix well, not losing ourselves, despite losing boundaries that seemed to separate us, and make us think we were subjects confronting objects. The only self to lose is one that was an obstacle to apprehending the incipient and virtually invisible, hindering a resonant rapport with the circumstances that ultimately determine our fate. Vanishing, we become more extensive, complex, integral, and integrally effective, but also softer, not more dramatically powerful, and better at avoiding problems than solving them. We vanish when our viability merges with the *ziran* productivity of things, something that can be intentional, even engineered, a work of art.

That is the art of wise knowledge. It knows how to soften whatever comes contingently in touch, how to orchestrate multiplicities without abolishing differences, how to turn analysis into synthesis, orthodoxy into unorthodoxy, and method into a way of viable evolution. We vanish into things with resonant forms that connect and endure, that enhance the commonwealth, and that make the artifact of knowledge a lasting work of art.

*   *   *

"Never ceasing for an instant, we find ourselves constantly thrown suddenly into newness. There is no moment when all things between heaven and earth are not moving along. The world is ever new but believes itself to be old." Thus Guo Xiang, in his classic commentary on *Zhuangzi*. Interaction between Western and Chinese philosophy is as old as Leibniz at the beginning of the eighteenth century. What is new in our time is the intensity, reciprocity, and potential fecundity of this interaction. More of it is inevitable, as is more interaction between Western and Chinese *anything*. You name it—trade, security, politics, industry, art, science, technology. In every way that Modernity tried to measure its own footprint, China's presence in the world is only going to grow. As teachers and students of philosophy, we are part of this change. Let us therefore *want to be* part of it, and seek the new questions that will ensure a future for philosophy in a world beyond the superannuated division of East and West.[32]

The philosophy that flourishes in a post-Western environment must invent hybrid concepts for hybrid contexts, and cultivate a sort of experimentation in philosophy which, in preferring aesthetic values (like the interesting, beautiful, and new) over "truth," has more in common with poetry than theory. Such *poiesis* is experimental, not because it tests a falsifiable hypothesis, but because no one can say where it might lead, what it might accomplish, provoke, or inspire, and because its success is not to express feelings but to create new experiences, new values, new ways to know ourselves, and never stop becoming who we are.

Chronology

Notes

Glossary

Acknowledgments

Index

Chronology

With the dates of major figures mentioned in the text.

Xia Dynasty
2205–1766 BCE

Shang Dynasty
1766–1045 BCE. Earliest written records

Zhou Dynasty
1045–256 BCE

Spring and Autumn Period (722–481 BCE)

Kongzi, 551–479 BCE
Sunzi, ca. 544–496 BCE
Mozi, ca. 480–390 BCE

Warring States Period (403–221 BCE)

Mengzi, ca. 385–312 BCE
Yang Zhu, ca. 350 BCE
Laozi, probably fourth century
Zhuangzi, ca. 320 BCE
Xunzi, ca. 310–219 BCE

Qin Dynasty
221–206 BCE. First Emperor

Han Dynasty
202 BCE–220
Liu An, ca. 180–122 BCE

Six Dynasties
222–589

Guo Xiang, d. 312
Bodhidharma, ca. 470–543

Sui Dynasty
589–618

Tang Dynasty
618–907

Huineng, 638–713

Five Dynasties
and Ten Kingdoms
907–960

Song Dynasty
960–1279

Zhang Zai, 1020–1077
Cheng Yi, 1033–1107
Zhu Xi, 1130–1200

Yuan Dynasty
1279–1368

Ming Dynasty
1368–1644

Luo Qinshun, 1465–1547
Wang Yangming, 1472–1529

Notes

Introduction: To Really See the Little Things

1. The story is told in several versions. I follow Zhai Jianyue, trans., *Guanzi* (Guilin, China: Guangxi Normal University Press, 2005), chap. 51. Duke Huan of Qi (d. 643 BCE) and Guan Zhong lived about a century before Confucius. Other versions are in *Hanfeizi*, 16.38 and *The Spring and Autumn of Lü Buwei*, chap. 18.2, where the story ends with the observation, "Sages can hear voiceless sounds and see shapeless things." Zhai Jianyue, trans., *The Spring and Autumn of Lü Buwei* (Guilin, China: Guangxi Normal University Press, 2005), 787.

2. *Daodejing*, chap. 52. In referring to this work I follow Philip J. Ivanhoe, trans., *The Daodejing of Laozi* (Indianapolis, IN: Hackett, 2003), though occasionally (as here) modifying the translation. For the Chinese text, I follow the bilingual edition of Roger T. Ames and David L. Hall, *Dao De Jing: A Philosophical Translation* (New York: Ballantine Books, 2003). All further references to the *Daodejing* are to chapter numbers and are parenthetically embedded as DDJ. John S. Major, Sarah A. Queen, Andrew Seth Meyer, and Harold D. Roth, trans. and eds., *The Huainanzi* (New York: Columbia University Press, 2010), 339, 399.

3. Confucius, *Analects, with Selections from Traditional Commentaries,* trans. Edward Slingerland (Indianapolis, IN: Hackett, 2003), 2.10. I follow this translation throughout with references to book and chapter parenthetically embedded as A. Wang Yangming, *Instructions for Practical Living*, trans. Wing-tsit Chan (New York: Columbia University Press, 1963), 225. The Chinese general's observations on dust are quoted from Ralph D. Sawyer, *The Tao of Spycraft: Intelligence Theory and Practice in Traditional China* (Boulder, CO: Westview Press, 2004), 451–452, 454.

4. *Huainanzi*, 612.

5. I develop this argument in *Knowledge and Civilization* (Boulder, CO: Westview Press, 2004).

6. Friedrich Nietzsche, *The Will to Power,* trans. Walter Kaufmann and R. J. Hollingdale (New York: Vintage Books, 1967), § 4. On "truth as correspondence" and its postmodern critics, see my *Truth in Philosophy* (Cambridge, MA: Harvard University Press, 1993).

7. On the perils of emic and etic in Chinese material, see Mark Csikszentmihalyi, "Ethics and Self Cultivation Practice in Early China," in *Early Chinese Religion, Part One: Shang Through Han,* ed. John Lagerwey and Marc Kalinowski (Leiden: Brill, 2009), 1:519. For an emic approach to my topic see Jana S. Rošker, *Searching for the Way: Theory of Knowledge in Pre-Modern and Modern China* (Hong Kong: Chinese University Press, 2008). For a balanced treatment of the debate over Chinese "philosophy," see Carine Defoort, "Is there Such a Thing as Chinese Philosophy?" *Philosophy East and West* 51 (2001): 393–413.

8. See Tang Yijie, "Constructing 'Chinese Philosophy' in Sino-European Cultural Exchange," in *New Interdisciplinary Perspectives in Chinese Philosophy,* ed. Karyn L. Lai (Oxford: Blackwell, 2007). On the potentially misleading artifice of "philosophical schools" in ancient China, see Mark Csikszentmihalyi and Michael Nylan, "Constructing Lineages and Inventing Traditions Through Exemplary Figures in Early China," *T'oung Pao* 89 (2003): 59–99.

9. A. C. Graham, *Disputers of the Tao* (Chicago: Open Court, 1989), 134, 146. Elsewhere he calls knowledge "the ultimately unchallengeable imperative" of Chinese thought. A. C. Graham, *Studies in Chinese Philosophy and Philosophical Literature* (Albany: State University of New York Press, 1990), 435.

10. Thomas Metzger, *A Cloud Across the Pacific: Essays on the Clash Between China and Western Political Theories Today* (Hong Kong: Chinese University of Hong Kong Press, 2005), 51, 673; Bruno Latour, *We Have Never Been Modern,* trans. Catherine Porter (Cambridge, MA: Harvard University Press, 1993). The limited truth in what Metzger says of Chinese "optimism" has nothing to do with epistemology. There is, as Roger Ames shows, a tendency in Confucian and therefore Chinese tradition to exaggerate the power of human purpose to transform the world. Roger Ames, *Confucian Role Ethics* (Honolulu: University of Hawaii Press, 2011), 264–265. Wills calls it "a Chinese optimism about what man could be that survived all experience of what man really was." John E. Wills, Jr., *Mountain of Fame: Portraits in Chinese History* (Princeton, NJ: Princeton University Press, 1994), 5.

1. Confucians

1. I draw from Lisa Raphels, *Knowing Words: Wisdom and Cunning in the Classical Traditions of China and Greece* (Ithaca, NY: Cornell University Press, 1992), 11–17.

2. *Xunzi*, chap. 22, in Jane Geaney, *The Epistemology of the Senses in Early Chinese Thought* (Honolulu: University of Hawaii Press, 2002), 194; Steven Shankman and Stephen W. Durrant, eds., *Early China/Ancient Greece* (Albany: State University of New York Press, 2002), 90n15.

3. *Book of Rites*, in Michael David Kaulana Ing, *The Dysfunction of Ritual in Early Confucianism* (Oxford: Oxford University Press, 2012), 107. For a philosophical appreciation of Confucian thought on ritual see Robert Cummings Neville, *Ritual and Deference* (Albany: State University of New York Press, 2008).

4. Lao An, trans., *Book of Rites* (Jinan, China: Shandong Friendship Press, 2000), 267, 269.

5. Randall Collins, *Interaction Ritual Chains* (Princeton, NJ: Princeton University Press, 2004), 7; *Zhongyong*, 27, in Tu Wei-Ming, *Centrality and Commonality* (Albany: State University of New York Press, 1989), 83–84.

6. *Book of Rites*, 29.1, in Ing, *Dysfunction*, 36.

7. Benjamin I. Schwartz, *The World of Thought in Ancient China* (Cambridge, MA: Harvard University Press, 1985), 46–48, 62–63.

8. The background of these Confucian innovations is explained in Yuri Pines, *Foundations of Confucian Thought: Intellectual Life in the Chunqiu Period 722–453 BCE* (Honolulu: University of Hawaii Press, 2002). For Kongzi's biography, see Annping Chin, *Confucius: A Life of Thought and Politics* (New Haven, CT: Yale University Press, 2008). On agriculture, see Christian Daniels and Nicholas K. Menzies, *Agro-Industries and Forestry, Science and Civilization in China*, vol. 6, pt. 3 (Cambridge: Cambridge University Press, 1996).

9. On the Confucian reduction of government to ceremony see A. C. Graham, *Disputers of the Tao* (Chicago: Open Court, 1989), chap. 1; and Tu, *Centrality and Commonality*, 48–54, who writes that for Kongzi, "governing a kingdom is no more than the political corollary of understanding proper sacrificial ceremonies" (48). Pines describes the concept of rule by ritual as the major achievement of the Spring and Autumn period (*Foundations*, 210). The *Zuozhuan Commentary* on the *Spring and Summer Annals* states, "When one uses ritual to fulfil one's government, the people will therefore enjoy rest." Cited in Erica Fox Brindley, *Music, Cosmology, and the Politics of Harmony in Early China* (Albany: State University of New York Press, 2012), 32.

10. Plato, *Phaedrus*, 229e–230a, in *Complete Works*, ed. John M. Cooper (Indianapolis, IN: Hackett, 1997). In citing works of Plato I follow this edition throughout. On Socratic esteem for knowledge, see *Protagoras*, 352c: "If someone knows what's good and what's bad, he would not be overpowered by anything so as to act contrary to what knowledge commands—wisdom is powerful enough to come to his aid." Also Aristotle: "Socrates thought it astonishing if knowledge, being present in a man, could be overpowered by something else." *Nicomachean Ethics*, 1145b, in *The Basic Works of Aristotle*, ed. Richard McKeon

(New York: Random House, 1941). In citing works of Aristotle I follow this edition throughout. On Confucian *gongfu*, see Peimin Ni, "*Gongfu*—A Vital Dimension of Confucian Thinking," in *Confucius Now: Contemporary Encounters with the "Analects,"* ed. David Jones (Chicago: Open Court, 2008); Ni, "Reading *Zhongyong* as a *Gongfu* Instruction," *Dao* 3 (2004): 189–203.

11. Aristotle, *Nicomachean Ethics*, 1178b.

12. *Mengzi, with Selections from Traditional Commentaries*, trans. Bryan W. Van Norden (Indianapolis, IN: Hackett, 2008), 7A13. I follow this translation throughout, and further references are parenthetically embedded.

13. *The Great Learning*, chap. 6, in Daniel K. Gardner, *The Four Books: The Basic Teachings of the Later Confucian Tradition* (Indianapolis, IN: Hackett, 2007), 6; *Book of Rites*, 211.

14. See also A 6.3, 11.7, 17.8. I follow the excellent treatment in Franklin Perkins, "Love of Learning in the *Lun Yu*," *Journal of Chinese Philosophy* 33 (2006): 505–515; and Philip J. Ivanhoe, "Thinking and Learning in Early Confucianism," *Journal of Chinese Philosophy* 17 (1990): 473–493.

15. Roger Ames, *Confucian Role Ethics* (Honolulu: University of Hawaii Press, 2011), 91.

16. Friedrich Nietzsche, *The Gay Science*, trans. Walter Kaufmann (New York: Vintage, 1974), 324.

17. *Book of Rites*, 32.7, in Ing, *Dysfunction of Ritual*, 144.

18. One should bear in mind the scope of these *li*, which are not limited to what modern English might consider obviously ceremonial occasions. Kongzi is reported as saying, "To speak, and then to perform what was spoken is *li*." *Book of Rites*, 29.5, in Ing, *Dysfunction of Ritual*, 23.

19. An authoritative study is Edward Slingerland, *Effortless Action: Wu-Wei as Conceptual Metaphor and Spiritual Ideal in Early China* (New York: Oxford University Press, 2003).

20. John S. Major, Sarah A. Queen, Andrew Seth Meyer, and Harold D. Roth, trans. and eds., *The Huainanzi* (New York: Columbia University Press, 2010), 59.

21. *Huainanzi*, 320, 360. The alternative translation is in Thomas Michael, *The Pristine Dao* (Albany: State University of New York Press, 2005), 75.

22. *Han Shu*, cited in Ralph D. Sawyer, *The Tao of Spycraft: Intelligence Theory and Practice in Traditional China* (Boulder, CO: Westview Press, 2004), 317–318.

23. The citations from the *Zhouyi* are from Lo Ch'in-shun (Luo Qinshun), *Knowledge Painfully Acquired*, trans. Irene Bloom (New York: Columbia University Press, 1987), 50; Yi Wu, *Chinese Philosophical Terms* (Lanham, MD: University Press of America, 1986), 96; and Ames, *Confucian Role Ethics*, 52.

24. *Wuxingpian*, 5, in Haiming Wen, *Confucian Pragmatism* (Lanham, MD: Lexington Books, 2009), 142; *Zhongyong*, 24, in Wu, *Chinese Philosophical Terms*, 114. Goldin suggests that the *Wuxingpian* derives "from a single tradition of

Confucianism and datable to around 300 BC." Paul R. Goldin, *After Confucius: Studies in Early Chinese Philosophy* (Honolulu: University of Hawaii Press, 2005), 36.

25. Zhai Jianyue, trans., *Guanzi* (Guilin, China: Guangxi Normal University Press, 2005), 251, 917; Zhai Jianyue, trans., *The Spring and Autumn of Lü Buwei* (Guilin, China: Guangxi Normal University Press, 2005), 671, 989, 721, 1093.

26. *Huainanzi*, 742; Dong Zhongshu, cited in David L. Hall and Roger T. Ames, *Thinking Through Confucius* (Albany: State University of New York Press, 1987), 50–51.

27. *Huainanzi*, 420; Sima Qian, *Shiji*, in Joseph Needham, *The Shorter Science and Civilization in China,* ed. Colin A. Ronan (Cambridge: Cambridge University Press, 1978), 142–143; Pheasant Cap Master, in Marnix Wells, *The Pheasant Cap Master and the End of History* (St. Petersburg, FL: Three Pines Press, 2013), 133, 136, 166.

28. Ralph D. Sawyer, ed. and trans., *The Seven Military Classics of Ancient China* (New York: Basic Books, 1993), 55, 69, 127, 206.

29. *Baopuzi*, in Jay Sailey, *The Master Who Embraces Simplicity: A Study of the Philosopher Ko Hung AD 283–343* (San Francisco: Chinese Materials Center, 1978), 70–71; *Shuowen*, in Shigehisa Kuriyama, *The Expressiveness of the Body and the Divergence of Greek and Chinese Medicine* (New York: Zone Books, 1999), 174; I also draw from 178.

30. *Yellow Emperor's Inner Classic*, in Kuriyama, *Expressiveness of the Body*, 179–180.

31. The story of Bian Que and Duke Huan is recounted in *Shiji*, chap. 105, and *Hanfeizi*, chap. 21; Kuriyama, *Expressiveness of the Body*, 154, 162–163.

32. Xu Gan, *Balanced Discourses*, trans. John Makeham (New Haven, CT: Yale University Press, 2002), 41; Ji Kang, in *Philosophy and Argumentation in Third-Century China: The Essays of Hsi K'ang*, trans. Robert G. Henricks (Princeton, NJ: Princeton University Press 1983), 38; Zhi Yu, in Howard L. Goodman, *Xun Xu and the Politics of Precision in Third Century AD China* (Leiden: Brill, 2010), 347; Sima Chengzhen, in Livia Kohn, *Sitting in Oblivion: The Heart of Daoist Meditation* (Dunedin, FL: Three Pines Press, 2010), 148–149; *Book of Balance and Harmony,* in Sun Tzu, *The Art of War,* trans. Thomas Cleary (Boston: Shambhala, 2003), 7.

33. "Yang Family Forty Chapters," in Douglas Wile, *Lost T'ai-chi Classics from the Late Ch'ing Dynasty* (Albany: State University of New York Press, 1996), 89, 81; Wang Yangming, *Instructions for Practical Living,* trans. Wing-tsit Chan (New York: Columbia University Press, 1963), 225; Fang Yizhi, in *Zhuangzi: The Essential Writings, with Selections from Traditional Commentaries,* trans. Brook Ziporyn (Indianapolis, IN: Hackett, 2009), 221. I explore connections between the Chinese idea of knowledge and Asian martial arts in *Striking*

Beauty: A Philosophical Look at the Asian Martial Arts (New York: Columbia University Press, 2015).

34. John Makeham, *Name and Actuality in Early Chinese Thought* (Albany: State University of New York Press, 1994), 46–48. On the rectification theme in Confucianism, see Sarah A. Mattice, "On Rectifying Rectification," *Asian Philosophy* 20 (2010): 247–260. There is a good discussion of the historical context of *Analects,* 13.3, including the identity and circumstances of Kongzi's interlocutor Zilu in Hui-chieh Loy, "*Analects* 13.3 and the Doctrine of 'Correcting Names,'" in Jones, ed., *Confucius Now.* Nietzsche appreciates the performative power of names to create the realities they designate; see *Gay Science* §§ 57–58.

35. The contrast between calendars and metrics is from May Sim, *Remastering Morals with Aristotle and Confucius* (Cambridge: Cambridge University Press, 2007), chap. 3.

36. Rudolf Carnap, "Intellectual Autobiography," in *The Philosophy of Rudolf Carnap,* ed. Paul A. Schilpp (La Salle, IL: Open Court, 1963), 67–71.

37. George Orwell, "The Principles of Newspeak," *Nineteen Eighty-Four* (Harmondsworth, UK: Penguin, 1983), 263, 266; and the words of Thomas Jefferson and Martin Heidegger, respectively. Carnap analyzes the Heidegger statement in his paper, "The Elimination of Metaphysics Through Logical Analysis of Language," (1932), in Sahotra Sarkar, ed., *Basic Works of Logical Empiricism* (New York: Garland, 1996), vol. 2, 10–31.

38. Carnap, "Replies and Expositions," *Philosophy of Rudolf Carnap,* 867; James C. Scott, *Seeing Like a State* (New Haven, CT: Yale University Press, 1998), 3–4. Neurath was fanatical about planning; see Nancy Cartwright, Jordi Cat, Lola Fleck, and Thomas Uebel, *Otto Neurath: Philosophy Between Science and Politics* (Cambridge: Cambridge University Press, 1996).

39. On the date and authorship of *Zhongyong* I follow Tu, *Centrality and Commonality,* 131–132 and Roger Ames and David Hall, *Focusing on the Familiar* (Honolulu: University of Hawaii Press, 2001).

40. *Maintaining Perfect Balance,* 25.3, in Gardner, *Four Books,* 126. On the collective economy of humans and nonhumans see Bruno Latour, *Politics of Nature: How to Bring the Sciences into Democracy,* trans. Catherine Porter (Cambridge, MA: Harvard University Press, 2004).

41. Zhang Zai, in Anne D. Birdwhistell, "The Concept of Experiential Knowledge in the Thought of Chang Tsai," *Philosophy East and West* 35 (1985), 43. This divergent concept of thing, as a transition rather than a form, is the theme of François Jullien, *The Silent Transformations,* trans. Michael Richardson and Krzysztof Fijalkowski (London: Seagull Books, 2011). *Dao,* he says, "if it must at any price be defined, is essentially *transition,* and this is why it is indefinable (and not for some 'mystical' reason, as we prefer to think in the West)" (34).

42. *Maintaining Perfect Balance*, 25, 22, 32, in Gardner, *Four Books*, 125, 124, 129.

43. Cheng Yi, in Chu Hsi (Zhu Xi), *Reflections on Things at Hand*, trans. Wing-tsit Chan (New York: Columbia University Press, 1967), 25; Jürgen Habermas, *The Theory of Communicative Action*, vol. 1, *Reason and the Rationalization of Society*, trans. Thomas McCarthy (Boston: Beacon Press, 1984).

44. Zhu Xi, comment on *Maintaining Perfect Balance*, 2.2, in Gardner, *Four Books*, 113. On the comparison with Aristotle, see Andrew Plaks, "Means and Means: A Comparative Reading of Aristotle's *Ethics* and the *Zhongyong*," *Early China/Ancient Greece*, 187–206; Kanaya Osamu, "The Mean in Original Confucianism," in *Chinese Language, Thought, and Culture*, ed. Philip J. Ivanhoe (Chicago: Open Court, 1996); and Sim, *Aristotle and Confucius*, chap. 4.

45. G. E. R. Lloyd, "Quotation in Greco-Roman Contexts," *Extrême-Orient Extrême Occident* 17 (1995), 144 and *The Ambitions of Curiosity: Understanding the World in Ancient Greece and China* (Cambridge: Cambridge University Press, 2002), 15. The idea of a *priscia sapientia*, an ancient, universal wisdom common to the Indians, Egyptians, Hebrews, and other peoples, of which Pythagoras was the earliest representative in Greece, is a late doctrine of the Neoplatonic school, from the third century CE.

46. A. C. Graham, "Mo tzu," in *Early Chinese Texts: A Bibliographical Guide*, ed. Michael Loewe (Berkeley, CA: Society for the Study of Early China, 1993).

47. *Mozi*, trans. Wang Rongpei and Wang Hong (Changsha, China: Hunan People's Publishing House, 2006), chap. 39. Citations from this volume are by chapter number, and parenthetically embedded. Few Western scholars seem to be aware of this bilingual edition. I had intended to replace my citations from this *Mozi* with references to the newer *The Mozi*, trans. Ian Johnston (New York: Columbia University Press, 2010). However, early reviews of this work are discouraging; see Carine Defoort, *Monumenta Serica* 59 (2011): 491–501, and Dan Robbins, *Dao* 10 (2011): 551–556, and when I compared the passages I cite from the Wang translation with Johnston's I could see no significant difference, so I have retained them.

48. This reference to the will of Heaven may have seemed reactionary to contemporaries, in light of a skeptical reappraisal of relations with divine powers in elite Chinese society from the early Spring and Autumn period. Pines, *Foundations of Confucian Thought*, 56–57, 78–80.

49. For the textual history of the *Canons*, see A. C. Graham, *Later Mohist Logic, Ethics and Science* (Hong Kong: Chinese University Press, 1978), 64–72. In addition to this invaluable source my account of Mohist epistemology draws from Christoph Harbsmeier, *Language and Logic, Science and Civilization in China*, vol. 7, pt. 1 (Cambridge: Cambridge University Press, 1998), 338–342; and Raphels, *Knowing Words*, 53–67.

50. *Mozi,* in Harbsmeier, *Language and Logic,* 349. The term translated as *wisdom* here is neither *zhī* nor *zhì* but the *zhì* character written above the "heart" radical *xin.* Though frequent in *Mozi* the usage is otherwise rare. Graham observes that the Mohist *Canons* are notorious for an abundance of otherwise unknown graphs. *Mohist Logic,* 76.

51. *Mozi,* in Harbsmeier, *Language and Logic,* 339.

52. Yang Zhu, in Fung Yu-Lan, *A Short History of Chinese Philosophy,* ed. Dirk Bodde (New York: Free Press, 1948), 63; and in He Zhaowu, *An Intellectual History of China* (Beijing: Foreign Languages Press, 1991), 46; *Mengzi,* 3B9.

53. A. C. Graham, "The Background of the Mencian Theory of Human Nature," in *Essays on the Moral Philosophy of Mengzi,* ed. Xiusheng Liu and Philip J. Ivanhoe (Indianapolis, IN: Hackett, 2002); Tang Junyi, in Ames, *Confucian Role Ethics,* 130; I also draw from 129. On developmental over innatist ideas in biology see Jason Robert, *Embryology, Epigenesis, and Evolution: Taking Development Seriously* (Cambridge: Cambridge University Press, 2004).

54. *Sayings of the States,* 431 BCE, in Zhang Dainian, *Key Concepts in Chinese Philosophy,* trans. Edmund Ryden (Beijing: Foreign Languages Press, 2002), 46; Manfred Porkert, *The Theoretical Foundations of Chinese Medicine* (Cambridge, MA: MIT Press, 1974), 167–168.

55. *Maintaining Perfect Balance,* 30.3, in Tu, *Centrality and Commonality,* 86.

56. Zhu Xi, in Joseph Needham, *History of Scientific Thought, Science and Civilization in China,* vol. 2 (Cambridge: Cambridge University Press, 1956), 492; Dai Zhen, in Zhang, *Key Concepts,* 348. It would be wrong to think Chinese cannot distinguish "is" and "ought" or that they were unaware of this distinction, which in their terms is the difference between *so yi ran zhi li* (pattern by which something is so) and *dang ran zhi li* (pattern by which something should be so). A. C. Graham, *Studies in Chinese Philosophy and Philosophical Literature* (Albany: State University of New York Press, 1990), 430.

57. Friedrich Nietzsche, *Beyond Good and Evil,* trans. Walter Kaufmann (New York: Vintage, 1966), § 9. We shall see further agreement between Nietzsche and Xunzi.

58. References to Xunzi are to chapter and section in the translation by John Knoblock, which I consult in the bilingual edition, *Xunzi* (Changsha, China: Hunan People's Publishing House, 1999). On Xunzi and Daoism, see also David S. Nivison, "Xunzi and Zhuangzi," in *Virtue, Nature, and Moral Agency in the Xunzi,* ed. T. C. Kline and Philip J. Ivanhoe (Indianapolis, IN: Hackett, 2000); and Aaron Stalnaker, "Aspects of Xunzi's Engagement with Early Daoism," *Philosophy East and West* 53 (2003): 87–129.

59. Plato, *Phaedo,* 66e. My discussion of sensory knowledge is indebted to Jane Geaney, *Epistemology of the Senses,* whom I follow on the main points, having also consulted Anne D. Birdwhistell, "Knowledge Heard and Seen: The Attempt

in Early Chinese Philosophy to Analyze Experiential Knowledge," *Journal Of Chinese Philosophy* 11 (1984): 67–82.

60. On Xunzi and Mohism, see Chris Fraser, "Knowledge and Error in Early Chinese Thought," *Dao* 10 (2010): 127–148.

61. François Jullien, *The Impossible Nude: Chinese Art and Western Aesthetics*, trans. Maev de la Guardia (Chicago: University of Chicago Press, 2007), 33; Makeham, *Name and Actuality*, 8. See also Anthony C. Yu, "*Cratylus* and *Xunzi* on Names," in *Early China/Ancient Greece*, 235–250. On Greek *ousia*, see Charles H. Kahn, *The Verb "Be" in Ancient Greek* (Dordrecht: Reidel, 1973).

62. Wilfrid Sellars, *Science, Perception, and Reality* (London: Routledge and Kegan Paul, 1963), 1.

63. Creating this second nature is a corporeal discipline, the desired alteration of character arising though moral commitment but also requiring strict attention to physical deportment and corporeal habits. Ori Tavor, "Xunzi's Theory of Ritual Revisited: Reading Ritual as Corporal Technology," *Dao* 12 (2013): 313–330.

64. Haun Saussy, *The Problem of a Chinese Aesthetic* (Stanford, CA: Stanford University Press, 1993), 102, 103.

65. Zi Chan, in Leo S. Chang and Yu Feng, *The Four Political Treatises of the Yellow Emperor* (Honolulu: University of Hawaii Press, 1998), 13.

66. *The Classic of Changes*, trans. Richard John Lynn (New York: Columbia University Press, 1994), 77.

67. While it is not a "Confucian" text, the *Huainanzi* confirms the prodigious investigations of the early sages. "They observed Earth's patterns"; "they investigated mountains and plains"; "they investigated human virtues"; "they clarified and outlined the natures of metal, wood, water, fire, and earth"; "they distinguished high and low sounds"; "they studied the order of the seasons" (805).

68. Hobbes (in *De Cive*) takes the side of Xunzi. People are "born unapt for society"; "Man is made fit for society not by nature, but by education." *Man and Citizen* (Indianapolis, IN: Hackett, 1991), 1.2. The Roman tradition that Rousseau inherits tends to sound more like Mengzi, for instance, Cicero: "Undoubtedly we carry the seeds of virtue at birth (*semina innata virtutum*)." *Tusculan Disputations*, trans. J. E. King (Cambridge, MA: Harvard University Press, 1966), 2.3.1.2. Likewise Seneca: "It is easy to encourage one's listener in the love of the good: nature has placed in every heart the foundation and first seed of the virtues (*semenque virtutum*)." *Epistles*, trans. Richard M. Gummere (Cambridge, MA: Harvard University Press, 1925), letter 108. See also Friedrich Nietzsche, *On the Genealogy of Morals*, trans. Walter Kaufmann (New York: Vintage, 1967); T. H. Huxley, "Evolution and Ethics," in Huxley, *Evolution and Ethics and Science and Morals* (Amherst, NY: Prometheus Books, 2004); Sigmund

Freud, *Civilization and Its Discontents* (1930; Harmondsworth, UK: Pelican Freud Library, 1985), vol. 12.

69. Darwin's theory of the evolution of morality is in *The Descent of Man,* chap. 4. See also Howard E. Gruber, *Darwin on Man* (New York: E. P. Dutton, 1974); and Robert J. Richards, *Darwin and the Emergence of Evolutionary Theories of Mind and Behavior* (Chicago: University of Chicago Press, 1987).

2. Daoists

1. The *Daodejing* seems to have reached its final form by the late third century BCE. See William G. Boltz, "Lao tzu Tao te ching," in *Early Chinese Texts: A Bibliographical Guide,* ed. Michael Loewe (Berkeley, CA: Society for the Study of Early China, 1993). An ancient bamboo text (Jingmen, Hubei, 1993) that seems to be an early *Daodejing* dates to the middle or late fourth century BCE, which may predate the oldest part of *Zhuangzi.* Early "Daoist" texts clearly do not constitute a self-conscious school or organized movement, though they display the consistent logic of a central idea and a pattern of convictions and procedures. N. J. Girardot, *Myth and Meaning in Early Taoism* (Berkeley: University of California Press, 1983). It has been argued that there is "much to recommend the view that the received text is an anthology of earlier (perhaps fifth and fourth century BCE) oral traditions, that were later (at least by 168 BCE) codified into a 'coherent' text." Louis Komjathy, *The Daoist Tradition* (London: Bloomsbury, 2013), 46. Attribution to a sage Laozi is conventional and almost certainly legendary. For a plausible explanation of how the work acquired this ascription, see A. C. Graham, "The Origins of the Legend of Lao Tan," *Studies in Chinese Philosophy and Philosophical Literature* (Albany: State University of New York Press, 1990).

2. "Certainly the audience to which *Lao-tzu* (unlike *Chuang-tzu*) is directly addressed is the ruler of a state." A. C. Graham, *Disputers of the Tao* (Chicago: Open Court, 1989), 234. A political *Daodejing* is also argued for by Michael LaFargue, *Tao and Method: A Reasoned Approach to the* Daodejing (Albany: State University of New York Press, 1994); and Bo Wang, *Zhuangzi: Thinking Through the Inner Chapters,* trans. Livia Kohn (St. Petersburg, FL: Three Pines Press, 2014), 14. The fifth century CE *Hanshu,* or dynastic history of the Han, classifies the *Daodejing* as a work on the "art of rulership" or "art of emperors and kings," but that seems less the conclusion of a close reading than a clerical library decision. Against a political *Daodejing,* see Thomas Michael, *The Pristine Dao* (Albany: State University of New York Press, 2005); and Harold D. Roth, *Original Tao* (New York: Columbia University Press, 1999).

3. Yi Wu, *Chinese Philosophical Terms* (Lanham, MD: University Press of America, 1986), 82. "What we call virtual is not something that lacks reality but some-

thing that is engaged in a process of actualization following the plane that gives it its particular reality." Gilles Deleuze, *Pure Immanence*, trans. Anne Boyman (New York: Zone Books, 2001), 31. Henri Bergson introduced the concept of the virtual in philosophy. It receives important development by Deleuze, beginning with *Bergsonism*, trans. Hugh Tomlinson and Barbara Habberjam (New York: Zone Books, 1988), and continued in *Difference and Repetition*, trans. Paul Patton (New York: Columbia University Press, 1994). A useful introduction to this difficult material is Manuel Delanda, *Intensive Science and Virtual Philosophy* (London: Continuum, 2002).

4. *Chuang-Tzu: The Inner Chapters*, trans. A. C. Graham (Indianapolis: Hackett, 2001), 110. Citations from *Zhuangzi* follow this translation, which includes a substantial part of the entire traditional text. References to *Zhuangzi* from this source are parenthetical page numbers abbreviated Z. Occasionally I prefer the translation of Paul Kjellberg, *Readings in Classical Chinese Philosophy*, ed. Philip J. Ivanhoe and Bryan W. Van Norden (Indianapolis, IN: Hackett, 2001), and indicate as much, though I reference the page on which the passage occurs in the Graham translation. For the Chinese text, as well as passages not included in either of these translations, I follow the Library of Chinese Classics bilingual edition: Wang Rongpei, trans., *Zhuangzi* (Changsha, China: Hunan People's Publishing House, 1999). Citations from *Zhuangzi* commentaries (and occasionally from the text) are from Brook Ziporyn, trans., *Zhuangzi: The Essential Writings, with Selections from Traditional Commentaries* (Indianapolis, IN: Hackett, 2009).

5. Cheng Yi, in Chu Hsi (Zhu Xi), *Reflections on Things at Hand*, trans. Wing-tsit Chan (New York: Columbia University Press, 1967), 13. Easing the assimilation of the *Daodejing* among Confucians is Kongzi's saying that "the gentleman has no predispositions for or against any person" (A 4.10), and "no preconceived notions of what is permissible and what is not" (A 18.8). This is Kongzi's "timeliness," his flexibility, and his greatest virtue according to Mengzi (5B1).

6. "If we had a keen vision and feeling of all ordinary life, it would be like hearing the grass grow and the squirrel's heartbeat, and we should die of that roar which lies on the other side of silence. As it is, the quickest of us walk around well wadded with stupidity." George Eliot, *Middlemarch* (London: Penguin, 1973), 226.

7. I am not implying an ancient connection between Daoist classics and taiji, which develops only much later, and becomes associated with Daoism later still. During taiji's maturation in the nineteenth and early twentieth centuries, to say something was "Daoist" was to say that it was *Chinese*, the Manchu rulers having coopted Buddhism and Confucianism. See Douglas Wile, "Taijiquan and Daoism," *Journal of Asian Martial Arts* 16 (2007): 8–45; and my *Striking Beauty:*

A Philosophical Look at the Asian Martial Arts (New York: Columbia University Press, 2015), chap. 1. The association with Chinese nationalism is ironical and misplaced because non-Chinese ethnic groups played a significant role in Daoism from the beginning and Daoism remains influential among ethnic minorities within and outside China. See Terry F. Kleeman, "Ethnic Identity and Daoist Identity in Traditional China," in *Daoist Identity,* ed. Livia Kohn and Harold D. Roth (Honolulu: University of Hawaii Press, 2002).

8. Chris Fraser, "*Wu Wei,* Background, and Intentionality," in *Searle's Philosophy and Chinese Philosophy,* ed. Bo Mou (Leiden: Brill, 2008), 81, 89. The criticism updates the argument of Herrlee Creel, *What Is Taoism?* (Chicago: University of Chicago Press, 1970). For a survey of criticism *wu wei* has attracted see David Loy, "*Wei-Wu-Wei:* Nondual Action," *Philosophy East and West* 35 (1985): 73–86.

9. Fraser, "*Wu Wei,* Background, and Intentionality," 89–90.

10. Zhuangzi does not describe Cook Ding's finesse as *wu wei,* a comparatively rare expression in this work. See Alan Fox, "Reflex and Reflexivity: *Wuwei* in the *Zhuangzi,*" in *Hiding the World in the World: Uneven Discourses on the* Zhuangzi, ed. Scott Cook (Albany: State University of New York Press, 2003). I do not think this point renders the passage unavailing for the interpretation of *wu wei.* Writing of the Sunzi *Art of War,* the respected sinologist Victor Mair says that what he calls the *wu wei* ethos is "plentifully evident throughout the text" despite not a single occurrence of the actual expression itself. Victor H. Mair, trans., *The Art of War: Sun Zi's Military Methods* (New York: Columbia University Press, 2007), 74n86. In a Ming dynasty *Zhuangzi* commentary, Shi Deqing writes of "the great functional effectiveness of nondeliberate action," and says "the whole meaning of the entire book is contained in this one phrase." Comment on *Zhuangzi,* 1.13; Ziporyn, *Zhuangzi,* 134.

11. Fraser describes *wu wei* in the *Daodejing* as "the absence of action motivated by the agent's desires," and as "unmotivated." Chris Fraser, "On *Wu-wei* as a Unifying Metaphor," *Philosophy East and West* 57 (2007), 99, 100. That we are dealing with a cultivated minimization of desire rather than an ideal absence is also suggested in *Mengzi:* "For cultivating the heart, nothing is better than having few desires" (7B35).

12. Second-order desires are desires to have particular desires, or desiring to have a certain desire be one's will. See Harry Frankfurt, "Freedom of the Will and the Concept of a Person," *Journal of Philosophy* 68 (1971): 5–20.

13. Fraser, "*Wu-wei* as Metaphor," 100, 103. On the theory of action under a description, see G. E. M. Anscombe, *Intention* (Oxford: Blackwell, 1963); and Donald Davidson, *Essays on Actions and Events* (Oxford: Oxford University Press, 1980).

14. Edward Slingerland, *Effortless Action: Wu-wei as Conceptual Metaphor and Spiritual Ideal in Early China* (New York: Oxford University Press, 2003), 7, 29–33; François Jullien, *A Treatise on Efficacy: Between Western and Chinese Thinking,* trans. Janet Lloyd (Honolulu: University of Hawaii Press, 2004), 91. Philip J. Ivanhoe thinks that rendering *wu wei* as effortless action is an elegant translation but that Slingerland's interpretation, which suggests that the ideal of *wu wei* is a kind of conundrum early Chinese thinkers wrestled with, is "very likely mistaken," even "simply not true." "The Paradox of *Wu Wei?*" *Journal of Chinese Philosophy* 34 (2007): 277–287. On the definition of purpose, see Immanuel Kant, *Critique of Judgment,* § 10.

15. Chris Fraser, "Distinctions, Judgment, and Reasoning in Classical Chinese Thought," *History and Philosophy of Logic* 34 (2013): 1–24.

16. See Gilles Deleuze and Félix Guattari, *A Thousand Plateaus: Capitalism and Schizophrenia,* trans. Brian Massumi (Minneapolis: University of Minnesota Press, 1987), especially what they say in Plateau 12, "Treatise on Nomadology," concerning the difference between minor and major or royal science.

17. Deleuze, *Difference and Repetition,* 180.

18. Gilles Deleuze, *Expressionism in Philosophy: Spinoza,* trans. Martin Joughin (New York: Zone Books, 1990), chap. 9; Isabelle Stengers, *Thinking with Whitehead,* trans. Michael Chase (Cambridge, MA: Harvard University Press, 2011), 3.

19. Parmenides, fragment 6, in Kathleen Freeman, *Ancilla to the Pre-Socratic Philosophers* (Cambridge, MA: Harvard University Press, 1948), 43; Plato, *Republic,* 477a, emphasis added. What is in this sense not known is not *unknowable,* and is neither what Nicholas of Cusa discusses in his famous treatise *On Learned Ignorance* (1440), nor what Nicholas Rescher discusses in *Unknowability* (Lanham, MD: Lexington Books, 2009). Both of these works concern what Rescher calls "those deeply intractable issues that no one can possibly resolve as a matter of principle rather than contingent circumstance" (6). For Cusanus, the intractability of the infinite, incommensurable to anything finite, instructs us in the insuperable barriers to knowledge of God.

20. Graham thinks substantial parts of chapters 23–26 are also likely to be by Zhuang Zhou. *Disputers of the Tao,* 173n. On Graham's analysis of *Zhuangzi* authorship, see Harold D. Roth, "An Appraisal of Angus Graham's Textual Scholarship on the *Chuang Tzu,*" in Harold D. Roth, ed., *A Companion to Angus C. Graham's Chuang Tzu* (Honolulu: University of Hawaii Press, 2003).

21. The translation of Z 45 is by Kjellberg. I also draw from Chris Jochim, "No Self in Zhuangzi," in *Wandering at Ease in the Zhuangzi,* ed. Roger T. Ames (Albany: State University of New York Press, 1998).

22. François Jullien, *Vital Nourishment,* trans. Arthur Goldhammer (New York: Zone Books, 2007), 31.

23. Graham, in Roth, *Companion*, 112; Plato, *Cratylus*, 386d-e.

24. Guo Xiang, in *A Source Book in Chinese Philosophy*, ed. Wing-tsit Chan (Princeton, NJ: Princeton University Press, 1963), 335.

25. Sextus Empiricus, *Outlines of Skepticism*, bk. 1, chap. 12, in *Selections From the Major Writings*, trans. Sanford G. Etheridge (Indianapolis, IN: Hackett, 1985), 41–42. The Platonic Academy under Arcesilaus (third century BCE) is called "skeptical" by modern scholars, though they did not use this term among themselves. On Zhuangzi and Skepticism, see also Paul Kjellberg, "*Dao* and Skepticism," *Dao* 6 (2007): 281–299; Lisa Raphels, "Skeptical Strategies in the *Zhuangzi* and *Theaetetus*," *Philosophy East and West* 44 (1994): 501–526; and Russell B. Goodman, "Skepticism and Realism in the Chuang Tzu," *Philosophy East and West* 35 (1985): 231–237.

26. Sextus, *Outlines of Skepticism*, bk. 1, chap. 14; *Major Writings*, 62.

27. Paul Kjellberg, "Sextus Empiricus, Zhuangzi, and Xunzi," in *Essays on Skepticism, Relativism, and Ethics in the* Zhuangzi, ed. Paul Kjellberg and Philip J. Ivanhoe (Albany: State University of New York Press, 1996), 9–10.

28. Philip J. Ivanhoe, "Zhuangzi on Skepticism, Skill, and the Ineffable Dao," *Journal of the American Academy of Religion* 61 (1993), 647. On "nihilism" in Zhuangzi, see Deborah H. Soles and David E. Soles, "Fish Traps and Rabbit Snares: Zhuangzi on Judgement, Truth and Knowledge," *Asian Philosophy* 8 (1998): 149–164.

29. Friedrich Nietzsche, *The Will to Power*, trans. Walter Kaufmann and R. J. Hollingdale (New York: Vintage Books, 1967), §§ 481, 477. The thought is not limited to Nietzsche's unpublished notes. "*There are no moral facts at all.* . . . Morality is just an interpretation of certain phenomena." *Twilight of the Idols*, trans. Richard Polt (Indianapolis, IN: Hackett, 1997), 38.

30. Nietzsche, *Will to Power*, § 481.

31. Arthur Schopenhauer, *The World As Will and Presentation*, trans. Richard E. Aquila (New York: Pearson Longman, 2008), 1:485, 48; Friedrich Nietzsche, *The Gay Science*, trans. Josefine Nauckhoff (Cambridge: Cambridge University Press, 2001), § 54. Leibniz denies that dreams inevitably violate the Cartesian continuities: "What prevents the course of our life from being a long, well-ordered dream, a dream from which we could be wakened in a moment?" (to Simon Foucher, 1675); "It would not be impossible for a creature to have long or orderly dreams resembling our life, such that everything it believed it perceived by the senses was nothing but mere appearance" (to Queen Sophie Charlotte of Prussia, 1702). G. W. Leibniz, *Philosophical Essays*, trans. R. Ariew and D. Garber (Indianapolis, IN: Hackett, 1989), 4, 188.

32. Gilles Deleuze, *The Logic of Sense*, trans. Mark Lester (New York: Columbia University Press, 1990), 148.

33. The *Secret Transmission of Acupuncture Point's Hand Combat Formulas* and *Hand Combat Classic* are cited from Meir Shahar, *Shaolin Monastery: History, Religion, and the Chinese Martial Arts* (Honolulu: University of Hawaii Press, 2008), 118, 126.

34. On *daoyin,* see Livia Kohn, *Chinese Healing Exercises: The Tradition of Daoyin* (Honolulu: University of Hawaii Press, 2008). On Zhuangzi and inner cultivation practices, see Harold D. Roth, "Bimodal Mystical Experience in the *Qiwulun* Chapter of the *Zhuangzi,*" in *Hiding the World in the World,* 15–32. On Ancestor Peng and his Warring States–period association with the quest for longevity, see Ori Tavor, "Xunzi's Theory of Ritual Revisited: Reading Ritual as Corporeal Technology," *Dao* 12 (2013): 313–330.

35. The *Inward Training (Nei ye)* is translated in Roth, *Original Tao,* from which I cite verses 66, 86, 82. Zhao Shouzheng, *Guanzi* (Beijing, 1989), cited in Roth, *Original Tao,* 12. The earliest source for an "inner" martial art dates from the seventeenth century. See Douglas Wile, *Ta'i Chi's Ancestors: The Making of an Internal Martial Art* (New City, NY: Sweet Ch'i Press, 1999), 52. For an example of contemporary practice, see Robert W. Smith, *Hsing-I: Chinese Mind-Body Boxing* (Berkeley, CA: North Atlantic Books, 2003). I discuss the affiliations of Chinese philosophy and martial arts in *Striking Beauty,* chap. 1. See also Peter A. Lorge, *Chinese Martial Arts: From Antiquity to the Twenty-First Century* (Cambridge: Cambridge University Press, 2011).

36. Jullien, *Vital Nourishment,* 77.

37. Epictetus, *Enchiridion,* 11, in *Moral Discourses of Epictetus,* trans. Elizabeth Carter (London: J. M. Dent and Sons, 1937), 258; Stoic fragments, cited from A. A. Long, *Hellenistic Philosophy* (Berkeley: University of California Press, 1986), 199, 200; and Cicero *De finibus,* 4.14, in Margaret Reesor, *The Nature of Man in Early Stoic Philosophy* (New York: St Martin's, 1989), 109. I also draw from William O. Stephens, *Stoic Ethics* (London: Continuum, 2007); and David B. Wong, "The Meaning of Detachment in Daoism, Buddhism, and Stoicism," *Dao* 5 (2006): 207–219.

38. Epictetus, *Discourses,* 4.1.13. On the Stoic invention of the "problem of the freedom of the will," see Michael Frede, *A Free Will: Origins of the Notion in Ancient Thought,* ed. A. A. Long (Berkeley: University of California Press, 2011).

39. Epictetus, *Discourses,* 4.1.13.

40. J. M. Rist explains *proharesis* in Epictetus as personality, moral character, and one's entire spiritual being, equating it with the *hegemonikon* of the Old Stoa. *Stoic Philosophy* (Cambridge: Cambridge University Press, 1969), 229.

41. My reading of this passage is influenced by Robert E. Allinson, *Chuang-tzu for Spiritual Transformation* (Albany: State University of New York Press, 1989), chap. 11.

42. Quoting Cheng Xuanying, a prominent Tang dynasty Daoist, commenting on *Zhuangzi*, 4.19, in Ziporyn, *Zhuangzi*, 177.

43. Guo Xiang, in Brook Ziporyn, *The Penumbra Unbound: The Neo-Taoist Philosophy of Guo Xiang* (Albany: State University of New York Press, 2003), 117.

44. Cheng Xuanying, cited in Livia Kohn, *Sitting in Oblivion: The Heart of Daoist Meditation* (Dunedin, FL: Three Pines Press, 2010), 38; Sima Chengzhen, "Sitting in Oblivion," in ibid., 143. "Twofold mystery" also alludes to the *Daodejing's* allusion to the *dao*: "mysterious and again mysterious—the gateway to all that is wondrous" (DDJ 1).

45. "To be brief, in all these matters I base my attitude upon one principle: had Nature condemned sodomy's pleasures, incestuous correspondences, pollutions, and so forth, would she have allowed us to find so much delight in them? That she may tolerate what outrages her is unthinkable." Marquis de Sade, *Philosophy in the Bedroom* (1795), in *Justine and Other Writings*, trans. R. Seaver and A. Wainhouse (New York: Grove Weidenfeld, 1965), 237.

46. The passage from chapter 32 is not included in Graham; I cite from the Wang translation, 573. It may not be whimsy for the *Zhuangzi* author to put this argument in Kongzi's mouth, for, as Roger Ames writes, "what is most fundamentally and significantly human in Confucian tradition is the seemingly indeterminate possibilities for creative change—for growth, cultivation, and refinement. . . . It is the transformability of the human being both physically and psychically that makes one most spiritual." "On Body as Ritual Practice," in *Self As Body in Asian Theory and Practice*, ed. Thomas P. Kasulis (Albany: State University of New York Press, 1993), 154.

47. Tang Junyi, cited in Roger Ames, *Confucian Role Ethics* (Honolulu: University of Hawaii Press, 2011), 131; Shi Deqing, commenting on *Zhuangzi* 6.2, cited in Ziporyn, *Zhuangzi*, 188; Benjamin I. Schwartz, *The World of Thought in Ancient China* (Cambridge, MA: Harvard University Press, 1985), 229; Livia Kohn, *Zhuangzi: Text and Context* (St. Petersburg, FL: Three Pines Press, 2014), 57–58.

48. John S. Major, Sarah A. Queen, Andrew Seth Meyer, and Harold D. Roth, trans. and ed., *The Huainanzi* (New York: Columbia University Press, 2010), 536–537.

49. *Huainanzi*, 425, 401.

50. According to Graham's ideas on authorial strata, most of what I call the know-nothing polemic (chaps. 8–11) is the work of his Primitivist (209–202 BCE), and two chapters (12–13) he assigns to a later Synchretist (second century BCE).

51. *Zhuangzi*, chap. 25. This passage is not included in Graham. I cite from the Wang translation, 451.

52. Guo Xiang is responsible for the received thirty-three chapter *Zhuangzi*. He explains that in editing the text he cut some nineteen chapters, all now lost, which he considered spurious. That implies that he considered the rest to be one "Zhuangzi." According to Livia Kohn, no Chinese scholar ex-

pressed doubt regarding the single authorship of the work before the Song dynasty, and such doubts are still novelties in Ming and Qing times. *Zhuangzi*, 6–7.

53. Guo Xiang, in Ziporyn, *Penumbra Unbound,* 41, 45; and comment on *Zhuangzi,* 2.48, in Ziporyn, *Zhuangzi,* 162.

54. See Friedrich Nietzsche, "On Truth and Lying in a Nonmoral Sense," in *The Birth of Tragedy and Other Writings,* trans. Ronald Speirs (Cambridge: Cambridge University Press, 1999).

55. Guo, in Ziporyn, *Penumbra Unbound,* 73.

56. Ibid., 127, 71.

57. Ibid., 73.

58. Ibid, 40; and Guo, comment on *Zhuangzi,* 3.2, in Ziporyn, *Zhuangzi,* 166.

59. Guo, comment on *Zhuangzi,* 6.3, in Ziporyn, *Zhuangzi,* 188; Su Shi (Su Dongpo), "Painting Bamboo," in *Early Chinese Texts on Painting,* ed. Susan Bush and Hsio-yen Shi (Cambridge, MA: Harvard University Press, 1985), 212.

60. Haiming Wen, *Confucian Pragmatism* (Lanham, MD: Lexington Books, 2009), 167; Deleuze and Guattari, *A Thousand Plateaus,* 280; John Dewey, *Art as Experience* (New York: G. P. Putnam's Sons, 1934), 249; Nietzsche, *On the Genealogy of Morals,* trans. Walter Kaufmann (New York: Vintage, 1967), Second Essay.

61. Carine Defoort, *The Pheasant Cap Master* (Albany: State University of New York Press, 1997), 215–216.

62. Joseph Needham, *Mechanical Engineering, Science and Civilization in China,* vol. 4, pt. 2 (Cambridge: Cambridge University Press, 1965), 20–23, 41, 170. I also draw from Needham, *The Great Titration: Science and Society in East and West* (London: George Allen and Unwin, 1969), 181. From the Eastern Han onward, learned members of the administrative elite sometimes practice artisanal skills, for example, lacquerware and smithing. See Howard L. Goodman, *Xun Xu and the Politics of Precision in Third Century AD China* (Leiden: Brill, 2010); and Anthony J. Barbieri-Low, *Artisans in Early Imperial China* (Seattle: University of Washington Press, 2007). Printing from wood blocks was fully developed from the early Song (latter tenth century). Tsien Tsuen-Hsuin, *Paper and Printing, Science and Civilization in China,* vol. 5, pt. 1 (Cambridge: Cambridge University Press, 1985), 159. When print eventually came to the West, how-to books on technical secrets were again the first best-sellers. See William Eamon, *Science and the Secrets of Nature: Books of Secrets in Medieval and Early Modern Culture* (Princeton, NJ: Princeton University Press, 1994); and Pamela O. Long, *Openness, Secrecy, Authorship: Technical Arts and the Culture of Knowledge from Antiquity to the Renaissance* (Baltimore: Johns Hopkins University Press, 2001).

63. The citation from *Huainanzi* is from 767. There is a Western echo in Zhuangzi's approximate contemporary Diogenes the Cynic. "When Hegesias asked to

borrow one of his writings, Diogenes said, 'You're a fool, Hegesias; you wouldn't choose painted figs over real ones, but you're overlooking the real discipline in your eagerness for a written version.'" Diogenes Laertius, *Lives of the Philosophers*, 6.48, cited in *The Cynics*, ed. R. Bracht Branham and Marie-Odile Goulet-Cazé (Berkeley: University of California Press, 1996), 83n8.

64. Xu Gan, *Balanced Discourses*, trans. John Makeham (New Haven, CT: Yale University Press, 2002), 87. The *Book of Artisans*, originally part of the *Zhou Li*, which modern scholarship dates to mid-third-century BCE, is cited from Needham, *Mechanical Engineering*, 12.

65. *Huainanzi*, 55. Other citations in this paragraph are from Joseph Needham, *Civil Engineering and Nautics, Science and Civilization in China*, vol. 4, pt. 3 (Cambridge: Cambridge University Press, 1971), iii.

66. Joseph Needham, *Physiological Alchemy, Science and Civilization in China*, vol. 5, pt. 5 (Cambridge: Cambridge University Press, 1983), 293; and *Apparatus, Theories, and Gifts, Science and Civilization in China*, vol. 5, pt. 4 (Cambridge: Cambridge University Press, 1980), 261, 243; Michael Puett, *To Become a God: Cosmology, Sacrifice, and Self-Divinization in Early China* (Cambridge, MA: Harvard University Press, 2002), 115–116. On the relationship between Chinese cosmology and their advanced metallurgy, see Ursula Franklin, John Berthrong, and Alan Chan, "Metallurgy, Cosmology, Knowledge: The Chinese Experience," *Journal of Chinese Philosophy* 12 (1985): 333–369.

67. *Huainanzi*, 269, 268; Joseph Needham, *History of Scientific Thought, Science and Civilization in China*, vol. 2 (Cambridge: Cambridge University Press, 1956), 125, 126. On this putative animosity to technics see also Kristofer Schipper, *The Taoist Body*, trans. Karen C. Duval (Berkeley: University of California Press, 1993), 197; and Roth, *Original Tao*, 56, 58.

68. *Huainanzi*, 304, 205–206, 303.

69. Ibid., 326, 751. According to Needham, Chinese bronze crossbow triggers are "among the greatest triumphs of ancient metallurgical and engineering practice in any civilization." *Military Technology, Science and Civilization in China*, vol. 5, pt. 7 (Cambridge: Cambridge University Press, 1986), 121. They were produced under conditions of secrecy in imperial workshops and classified as restricted, "forbidden instruments" (Needham, *Mechanical Engineering*, 18).

70. I develop this argument about tools and machines in *Artifice and Design* (Ithaca, NY: Cornell University Press, 2008), chap. 2. See also Abbott Payson Usher, *A History of Mechanical Inventions* (Boston: Beacon, 1959).

71. On Zigong, see Ralph D. Sawyer, *The Tao of Spycraft: Intelligence Theory and Practice in Traditional China* (Boulder, CO: Westview Press, 2004), 20–26.

72. *Zhuangzi*, chap. 14; I cite from the Wang translation, 233.

73. *Huainanzi*, 770–771.

74. Needham, *History of Scientific Thought,* 443, 447; Needham, *Civil Engineering,* 256.

75. *Huainanzi,* 770; Zhai Jianyue, trans., *The Spring and Autumn of Lü Buwei* (Guilin, China: Guangxi Normal University Press, 2005), 707; Needham, *History of Scientific Thought,* 69, 71.

76. On reinforced concrete and its use in design, see *Artifice and Design,* 132–133, and the technical sources cited there.

77. Deleuze and Guattari, *A Thousand Plateaus,* 329. G. E. R. Lloyd observes how Chinese technical interest lies less in mastering materials than in getting materials to work for them. Li Bing did not overcome the floodwater, but succeeded in getting it to cooperate with his aims. *The Ambitions of Curiosity: Understanding the World in Ancient Greece and China* (Cambridge: Cambridge University Press, 2002), 97.

78. *Daodejing,* chap. 5, trans. Robert Temple, in *The Genius of China: 3000 Years of Science, Discovery, and Invention* (Rochester, VT: Inner Traditions, 2007), 46. Ivanhoe's translation, from which I usually cite, reads: "Is not the space between heaven and earth like a bellows? Empty yet inexhaustible! Work it and more will come forth."

79. Temple, *Genius of China,* 79. The span is forty meters. A segmented arch bridge is unattested in Europe before the Ponte Vecchio, Florence, 1345. The idea of removing material from the side of an arch in a way that makes it both stronger and lighter did not enter European engineering until Swiss designer Robert Maillart in the early twentieth century. See David P. Billington, *Robert Maillart's Bridges: The Art of Engineering* (Princeton, NJ: Princeton University Press, 1979).

80. Temple, *Genius of China,* 204–205.

3. The Art of War

1. According to an early tradition, a work by Sun Wu on warfare in thirteen *pian* (the division of the *Sunzi* as we have it) was read by He Lü, King of Wu (reigned 514–495 BCE). Archaeological evidence seems to confirm that our *Sunzi* had its form by the end of the Spring and Autumn period, circa 496–453 BCE. See Krzysztof Gawlikowski and Michael Loewe, "Sun tzu ping fa," in *Early Chinese Texts: A Bibliographical Guide,* ed. Michael Loewe (Berkeley, CA: Society for the Study of Early China, 1993). Ralph Sawyer (with the concurrence of Robin Yates) prefers a half-century-later date of 453–403 BCE. Ralph D. Sawyer, ed. and trans., *The Seven Military Classics of Ancient China* (New York: Basic Books, 1993), 422. Victor Mair rejects these early dates ("completely impossible"), and dates the work to after 350 BCE. Victor H. Mair, trans., *The Art of War: Sun Zi's Military Methods* (New York: Columbia University Press, 2007),

28. Mark Edward Lewis concurs, arguing that prophecies and historical references suggest that the work was begun in the fourth century BCE, with later chapters compiled in the early third century. Mark Edward Lewis, "Writings on Warfare Found in Ancient Chinese Tombs," *Sino-Platonic Papers*, no. 158 (Philadelphia: Department of Asian Languages and Civilizations, University of Pennsylvania, 2005), 5–7. The *Daodejing* obviously knows about the military philosophy, which it alludes to twice in consecutive chapters (68–69). On Daoism and the art of war, see Christopher C. Rand, "Chinese Military Thought and Philosophical Taoism," *Monumenta Serica* 34 (1979–1980): 171–218. My references follow Philip J. Ivanhoe, trans., *Master Sun's Art of War* (Indianapolis, IN: Hackett, 2011), abbreviated SZ, with chapter numbers parenthetically embedded. Occasionally I prefer the translation by Mair or that in Sawyer, *Military Classics*. For the Chinese text, I consult the bilingual edition, edited by Wu Rusong (Beijing: Foreign Languages Press, 2005).

2. Andrew Meyer and Andrew Wilson, "Inventing the General: A Re-appraisal of the *Sunzi Bingfa*," in *War, Virtual War, and Society*, ed. Andrew R. Wilson and Mark L. Perry (Amsterdam: Rodopi, 2008); and Mark Edward Lewis, *Sanctioned Violence in Early China* (Albany: State University of New York Press, 1990), 98.

3. Taigong, *Six Secret Teachings*, in Sawyer, *Military Classics*, 69.

4. Lewis, *Sanctioned Violence*, 124. On *qi* (unconventional, unorthodox, special forces) in the military philosophy, see Ralph D. Sawyer, *The Tao of Deception* (New York: Basic Books, 2007). The discrepancy of forces may grow in the memory of victors. A modern authority estimates the Shang army at Mu Yeh (when the dynasty was defeated by the Zhou) at seventy thousand and the Zhou army at about half that. Ralph D. Sawyer, *Ancient Chinese Warfare* (New York: Basic Books, 2011), 219.

5. *Wuzi*, in Sawyer, *Military Classics*, 220; Sun Bin, in Sawyer, *Ancient Chinese Warfare*, 371–372. An example in *Sunzi* is in chap. 11. On the mysterious authorship of the *Sun Bin Bingfa*, see Jens Ostergard Petersen, "What's in a Name? On the Sources Concerning Sun Wu," *Asia Major* 5 (1992): 1–31. For another view of these dialogues as a genre in the military texts, see Lewis, "Writings on Warfare," 12.

6. *Six Secret Teachings*, chap. 26, in Sawyer, *Military Classics*, 69; Ming dynasty commentator in Sawyer, *Tao of Deception*, 308; Ghost Valley Master in François Jullien, *A Treatise on Efficacy: Between Western and Chinese Thinking*, trans. Janet Lloyd (Honolulu: University of Hawaii Press, 2004), 181.

7. *Six Secret Teachings*, in Sawyer, *Military Classics*, 69; *Sin Bin*, chap. 30, in Sawyer, *Tao of Deception*, 84–85, modified after Sun Tzu, *The Art of War*, trans. Thomas Cleary (Boston: Shambhala, 2003), 404; Song commentary in Sawyer, *Tao of Deception*, 290.

8. Sawyer, *Tao of Deception*, 3–6.

9. Zhuge Liang (181–234 CE) is the unique example of a military strategist who is also a hero to Confucians. John E. Wills, Jr., *Mountain of Fame: Portraits in Chinese History* (Princeton, NJ: Princeton University Press, 1994), 100–113. His legendary cleverness made him the figure most associated with knowledge in Chinese literature. Lisa Raphels, *Knowing Words: Wisdom and Cunning in the Classical Traditions of China and Greece* (Ithaca, NY: Cornell University Press, 1992), 133.

10. *Li Wei Gong Bing Fa*, in Ralph D. Sawyer, *The Tao of Spycraft: Intelligence Theory and Practice in Traditional China* (Boulder, CO: Westview Press, 2004), 130.

11. The *Strategies of Huang-shih Kung* is cited from Sawyer, *Military Classics*, 297–298. On these planning exercises see also Sawyer, *Tao of Spycraft*, 123. The rationality of the procedure recommended it to the civilian arm in works of administrative philosophy like the *Spring and Autumn of Lü Buwei*: "Planning to gain some advantage but instead suffering harm stems from not investigating properly" (Sawyer, *Tao of Spycraft*, 391). Already in the Shang dynasty threats were assessed, options evaluated, forces chosen, and commanders appointed based on an extensive intelligence system transmitting economic and military information from all quarters. Sawyer, *Ancient Chinese Warfare*, 230.

12. Shi Zimei, in Sawyer, *Tao of Spycraft*, 146–147.

13. Carl von Clausewitz, *On War*, cited in Michael Howard, *Clausewitz* (Oxford: Oxford University Press, 1983), 73; Raymond Aron, *Clausewitz: Philosopher of War*, trans. Christine Booker and Norman Stone (Englewood Cliffs, NJ: Prentice-Hall, 1985), 128–129, 131–132.

14. Henry Lloyd, in Howard, *Clausewitz*, 13; and Clausewitz, *On War*, cited in ibid, 42.

15. General Carl von Clausewitz, *On War*, trans. J. J. Graham (1909; Project Gutenberg, 2006), vol. 1, bk. 1, chap. 10. Project Gutenberg Ebook no. 1946 (2006) (unpaginated), available from www.gutenberg.org.//enottxt//.

16. Howard, *Clausewitz*, 14, 61; John Keegan, *Intelligence in War: Knowledge of the Enemy from Napoleon to Al-Qaeda* (Toronto: Key Porter, 2003), 369.

17. Clausewitz, *On War*, bk. 1, chap. 3.

18. Ibid.

19. Ibid.

20. Ibid.

21. Ibid., bk. 4, chap. 11; and Howard, *Clausewitz*, 41. On Western indifference to the history and theory of warfare in Asia, see David Graff, *Medieval Chinese Warfare, 300–900* (New York: Routledge, 2001). *Sunzi* was translated into French in 1772 by a Jesuit who served under Qing emperor Qian Long. Napoleon was rumored to have studied this translation, though Mair thinks that is unlikely. The work was also translated into Russian (1860) and English (1905), but not

into German before the mid-twentieth century. Victor H. Mair, "Soldierly Methods: Vade Mecum for an Iconoclastic Translation of Sun Zi bingfa," *Sino-Platonic Papers,* no. 178 (Philadelphia: Department of Asian Languages and Civilizations, University of Pennsylvania, 2008).

22. Lewis, *Sanctified Violence,* 223–224; *Six Secret Teachings,* in Sawyer, *Military Classics,* 353; Mao Zedong, in Mair, *Miliary Methods,* 53; Han dictionary in Lewis, *Sanctified Violence,* 228; *Wuzi,* chap. 4, in Sawyer, *Military Classics,* 217.

23. Ferdinand Foch, *Principles of War* (1903), in Howard, *Clausewitz,* 62–63.

24. Alastair Iain Johnston, *Cultural Realism: Strategic Culture and Grand Strategy in Chinese History* (Princeton, NJ: Princeton University Press, 1995), 62, 107n, 71n, 69, 70, 71, 151; Nicola Di Cosmo, ed., *Military Culture in Imperial China* (Cambridge, MA: Harvard University Press, 2009), 3; see also Yu Kam-por, "Confucian Views on War," *Dao* 9 (2010): 97–111.

25. Basil Henry Liddell Hart, *Strategy: The Indirect Approach,* 5th ed. (London: Faber and Faber, 1967), 356, 224–225.

26. Ibid., 353, 357.

27. Ibid., 340–341, 25.

28. Ibid., 236, 219, 164; Lewis, *Sanctified Violence,* 116.

29. Hart, *Strategy,* 338, 339. A Chinese example of victory "without bloody blades" is Pei Xingjian's amazingly elaborate ruse against the Western Turks, 679 CE. See Jonathan Karam Skaff, "Tang Military Culture," in Di Cosmo, *Military Culture,* 185–186.

30. Hart, *Strategy,* 344, 346, 350.

31. Ming dynasty minister of war cited in Johnston, *Cultural Realism,* 212. The *Military Classics* commentator is Shi Zimei, in Johnston, *Cultural Realism,* 151.

32. *Huangdi Neijing: Synopsis with Commentaries,* trans. Y. C. Kong (Hong Kong: Chinese University of Hong Kong Press, 2010), 302n1.

33. Clausewitz, *On War,* bk. 2, chap. 2, pt. 45.

34. Ibid., bk. 1, chap. 6.

35. Ibid., bk. 4, chap. 14; bk. 1, chaps. 3, 6.

36. Clausewitz's unique reference to spies is *On War,* bk. 4, chap. 14.

37. For the Confucian view of the military philosophy, see *Analects* 14.5, 15.1; *Mengzi* 4A14, 2B1, 7B4; and *Xunzi,* chap. 15. Their hostility is not to violence or the martial per se, but to the assumption that an art of command obviates the need for a morally potent ruler. Lewis, *Sanctified Violence,* 235–239.

4. Chan Buddhism

1. Yoshito S. Hakeda, trans., *The Awakening of Faith Sutra* (Berkeley, CA: Numata Center for Buddhist Translation and Research, 2005), 71; Mark Siderits, *Buddhism As Philosophy* (Indianapolis, IN: Hackett, 2007), 23–26. On paradoxes

of knowledge in Buddhism, see David Burton, "Knowledge and Liberation: Philosophical Ruminations on a Buddhist Conundrum," *Philosophy East and West* 52 (2002): 326–345.

2. John R. McRae, *Seeing Through Zen* (Berkeley: University of California Press, 2003), 115. I mean large public temples (*shi fang cong lin*), not small, so-called hereditary temples (*zi sun miao*). Holmes Welch, *The Practice of Chinese Buddhism* (Cambridge, MA: Harvard University Press, 1967), 3–4, 395–400 (on the idea of "sect" (*zong*) in Chinese Buddhism).

3. D. T. Suzuki, trans., *The Lankavatara Sutra* (Clear Lake, CA: Dawn Horse Press, 1983), 107, 71, 123, 114. Early Chan identifies itself with this work, which was believed to have been transmitted from Bodhidharma to his Chinese successor Huike. Henrik H. Sorensen, "History and Practice of Early Chan," in *Readings of the* Platform Sutra, ed. Morton Schlütter and Stephen F. Teiser (New York: Columbia University Press, 2012).

4. Kristofer Schipper, *The Taoist Body*, trans. Karen C. Duval (Berkeley: University of California Press, 1993), 13. What I say of Chan-Daoist relations draws from Kenneth Inada, "Zen and Taoism: Common and Uncommon Grounds of Discourse," *Journal of Chinese Philosophy* 15 (1988): 51–65; Livia Knaul, "Chuangtzu and the Chinese Ancestry of Ch'an Buddhism," *Journal of Chinese Philosophy* 13 (1986): 411–428; Livia Kohn, *Daoism and Chinese Culture* (Cambridge, MA: Three Pines Press, 2004); Henri Maspero, *Taoism and Chinese Religion*, trans. Frank A. Kierman, Jr. (Amherst: University of Massachusetts Press, 1981); Hans-Georg Moeller, *Daoism Explained* (Chicago: Open Court, 2004); Joseph Needham, *History of Scientific Thought, Science and Civilization in China*, vol. 2 (Cambridge: Cambridge University Press, 1956); and Wu Yi, "On Chinese Ch'an in Relation to Taoism," *Journal of Chinese Philosophy* 12 (1985): 131–154.

5. Bernard Faure, *Chan Insights and Oversights: An Epistemological Critique of the Chan Tradition* (Princeton, NJ: Princeton University Press, 1993), 162–163; Meir Shahar, *Shaolin Monastery: History, Religion, and the Chinese Martial Arts* (Honolulu: University of Hawaii Press, 2008), 12–13. On Bodhidharma, see McRae, *Seeing Through Zen*, chap. 2. Bodhidharma is not associated with Shaolin Temple until the early eighth century, and not associated with martial arts until the twentieth century. See Stanley E. Hemming, "Academic Encounters with the Chinese Martial Arts," *China Review International* 6 (1999): 319–332. It is often claimed that Buddhists brought monasticism to China and bequeathed it to Daoists; see, for example, Louis Komjathy, *The Daoist Tradition* (London: Bloomsbury, 2013), 73. However, early religious communities in India were not monasteries but avasas, loose collections of monks living within fixed boundaries, only sometimes enclosed. Religious practice remained individual, without collective worship or meditation (Welch, *Chinese Buddhism*, 143). Daoists, by

contrast, enjoyed a long history of eremitic and cenobitic communities prior to the rise of Buddhism.

6. Maspero, *Taoism*, 411; Isabelle Robinet, *The World Upside Down: Essays on Taoist Internal Alchemy*, trans. Fabrizio Pregadio (Mountain View, CA: Golden Elixir Press, 2011); Gil Raz, *The Emergence of Daoism* (Milton Park, UK: Routledge, 2012). The expression "Laozi look-alikes" comes from Alan Cole, *Fathering Your Father: The Zen of Fabrication in Tang Buddhism* (Berkeley: University of California Press, 2009), 21.

7. Michael Loewe, *Faith, Myth, and Reason in Han China* (Indianapolis, IN: Hackett, 2005), 115. Unlike Japan, China has no special Chan ordination; monks are ordained into the general Buddhist order and not a particular sect. Morten Schlütter, *How Zen Became Zen* (Honolulu: University of Hawaii Press, 2008), 15. On Sinitic reaction to Buddhist Indocentrism, see Dale S. Wright, *Philosophical Meditations on Zen Buddhism* (Cambridge: Cambridge University Press, 1999), 20; Brook Ziporyn, "The Platform Sutra and Chinese Philosophy," in *Readings of the* Platform Sutra; and Cole, *Fathering*, for whom it is a major point.

8. John R. McRae, *The Northern School and the Formation of Early Ch'an Buddhism* (Honolulu: University of Hawaii Press, 1986), 18–19, 117, 252; Bernard Faure, *The Will to Orthodoxy: A Critical Genealogy of Northern Chan Buddhism*, trans. Phyllis Brooks (Stanford, CA: Stanford University Press, 1997); Mario Poceski, *Ordinary Mind As the Way: The Hongzhou School and the Growth of Chan Buddhism* (Oxford: Oxford University Press, 2007).

9. Cole describes the legend of Northern and Southern schools, supposedly divided on the question whether enlightenment is sudden or gradual, as "a polemical invention that has bedeviled Chan Studies for decades" (*Fathering*, 210). There were no "Northern" or "Southern" schools until Shenhui invented them for his polemic, and no controversy over sudden or gradual enlightenment, theory and practice in all the early Chan communities being much the same (McRae, *Northern School*, 246–247). On the extraordinary violence of the An Lushan rebellion, see Steven Pinker, *The Better Angels of Our Nature: Why Violence has Declined* (New York: Penguin, 2011).

10. Antoine Panaïoti, *Nietzsche and Buddhist Philosophy* (Cambridge: Cambridge University Press, 2013), 46n143. I also draw from Jan Westerhoff, *Nagarjuna's Madhyamaka: A Philosophical Introduction* (Oxford: Oxford University Press, 2009), 12–13, 25, 49. For examples of this *auto kath auto*, see Plato, *Phaedo*, 78d, 100b; *Parmenides*, 128e–129a; *Timaeus*, 51d; and the analysis in Gregory Vlastos, *Socrates, Ironist and Moral Philosopher* (Ithaca, NY: Cornell University Press, 1991), 72–76. On Chan and Mahayana, see Hsueh-li Cheng, "The Roots of Zen Buddhism," *Journal of Chinese Philosophy* 8 (1981): 451–478; and Chen-Chi Chang, "The Nature of Ch'an (Zen) Buddhism," *Philosophy East and*

West 6 (1957): 333–355. The line along which Nagarjuna penetrated China is the life-vector of the Buddhist translator Kumarajiva (344–413), who introduced Madhyamaka into China in the early fifth century and first exposed the Chinese to Mahayana systematic philosophy. Richard H. Robinson, *Early Madhyamaka in India and China* (Madison: University of Wisconsin Press, 1967), chap. 3.

11. Robinson, *Early Madhyamaka,* 40, 58; Westerhoff, *Nagarjuna,* 47.

12. Nagarjuna, in Kamaleswar Bhattacharya, *The Dialectical Method of Nagarjuna* (Delhi: Motilal Banarsidass, 1978), 23.

13. Nagarjuna, in Panaïoti, *Nietzsche and Buddhist Philosophy,* 148–149; Ueda Shizuteru, "Emptiness and Fullness: Sunyata in Mahayana Buddhism," *The Eastern Buddhist* 15 (1983): 9–37.

14. Nagarjuna, in Westerhoff, *Nagarjuna,* 18. I also draw from Robinson, *Early Madhyamaka,* 43, 49. "Not-Being is as real as Being." Democritus, in Kathleen Freeman, *Ancilla to the Pre-Socratic Philosophers* (Cambridge, MA: Harvard University Press, 1948), fragment 156.

15. Nagarjuna, in Robinson, *Early Madhyamaka,* 43; and Siderits, *Buddhism As Philosophy,* 204. On "passing for true" see my *Truth and Philosophy* (Cambridge, MA: Harvard University Press, 1993), chap. 7, where I develop the comparison between truth values and money.

16. Parmenides, fragment 6, in Freeman, *Ancilla,* 43. Nagarjuna, cited from Siderits, *Buddhism As Philosophy,* 204. I also draw from Westerhoff, *Nagarjuna,* 73.

17. McRae, *Northern School,* 76–78, 95; Wright, *Zen Buddhism,* 86–89.

18. Urs App, ed. and trans., *Master Yunmen* (New York: Kodansha International, 1994), 152, 111, 97; and McRae, *Seeing Through Zen,* 76–78, 86, 173n16.

19. Huangbo, *Transmission of Mind,* in *Zen Sourcebook,* ed. Stephen Addiss (Indianapolis, IN: Hackett, 2008), 39; Dahui Zonggao, in McRae, *Seeing Through Zen,* 127; and in Schlütter, *How Zen Became Zen,* 108.

20. Philip Yampolsky, trans., *The Platform Sutra of the Sixth Patriarch* (New York: Columbia University Press, 1967), 175.

21. *Platform Sutra,* 138, 153. "No-thought" neither distinguishes Chinese from Indian Buddhism, nor is unique to Chan. See Yun-hua Jan, "A Comparative Study of 'No-Thought' (*wu-nien*) in Some Indian and Chinese Buddhist Texts," *Journal of Chinese Philosophy* 16 (1989): 37–58.

22. Franz Brentano, *Psychology from an Empirical Standpoint,* trans. Antos C. Rancurello, D. B. Terrell, and Linda L. McAlister (London: Routledge, 1995), 88; Edmund Husserl, *Ideas,* trans. W. R. Boyce Gibson (London: George Allen and Unwin, 1931), 243. Perception without an object, for instance sensing not sensing (sensing the absence of sight in a dark room, for example), is a theme in Aristotlean psychology. See Daniel Heller-Roazen, *The Inner Touch: Archaeology of a Sensation* (New York: Zone Books, 2007).

23. Surangama Sutra Translation Committee, trans., *The Surangama Sutra* (Burlingame, CA: Buddhist Text Translation Society, 2009), 74, 193, 46, 327–328. This sutra directly concerns the value of knowledge, being spoken in response to a lapse by the disciple Ananda, who was seduced by a prostitute while begging alms. Ananda, famous for his erudition, paid too much attention to learning and not enough to meditation, which left him with inadequate concentration to resist the prostitute's spell. Erudition merely led him into idle speculation; all his knowledge is not equal to a single day of correct practice (165). See also Jiang Wu, "Knowledge for What? The Buddhist Concept of Learning in the *Surangama Sutra*," *Journal of Chinese Philosophy* 33 (2006): 491–503.

24. *Platform Sutra*, 138, 147; Huangbo, *Transmission of Mind*, 35.

25. *Blue Cliff Record*, in App, *Master Yunmen*, 68; *Lankavatara Sutra*, 86, 143, 112–113.

26. Bankei Yotaku and So Sahn, in *Zen Sourcebook*, 239, 213.

27. *Xian Zong Ji*, in Robert B. Zeuschner, "The Hsien Tsung Chi: An Early Ch'an (Zen) Buddhist Text," *Journal of Chinese Philosophy* 3 (1976), 258; Ruth Fuller Sasaki, trans., *The Recorded Sayings of Ch'an Master Lin-chi Hui-chao* (Kyoto: Institute for Zen Studies, 1975), 20, 21, 33 (emphasis added). "On meeting a buddha slay the buddha. . . . By not cleaving to things, you freely pass through" (25).

28. *Platform Sutra*, 139.

29. Ibid., 180, 142.

30. Huangbo, in Poceski, *Ordinary Mind*, 185, 170, and Wright, *Zen Buddhism*, 192; Mazu, in Poceski, *Ordinary Mind*, 183; Chandrakirti, *Lucid Exposition of the Middle Way*, trans. Mervyn Sprung (Boulder, CO: Prajna Press, 1979), 259.

31. *Surangama Sutra*, 164; *Record of Baizhang*, in Poceski, *Ordinary Mind*, 131–132, 137–138.

32. Bodhidharma, "Bloodstream Sermon," in Red Pine, trans., *The Zen Teaching of Bodhidharma* (San Francisco: North Point Press, 1989), 35; "Wake-Up Sermon," ibid., 57. There is little chance these texts derive from Bodhidharma, but as McRae observes, "[this] material may be used as a key to the subsequent development of Ch'an" (Northern School, 117).

33. "Wake-Up Sermon," *Zen Teaching of Bodhidharma*, 47.

34. "Breakthrough Sermon," *Zen Teaching of Bodhidharma*, 97; *Heart Sutra*, *Zen Sourcebook*, 5; Yue Xu, "Buddhism and the Justification of War with Focus on Chinese Buddhist History," in *Buddhism and Violence*, ed. Vladimir Tikhonov and Terkel Brekke (New York: Routledge, 2013).

35. The *Treatise on Military Affairs* and *Exposition of the Original Shaolin Staff Method* are cited from Shahar, *Shaolin Monastery*, 77, 62. See also Douglas Wile, "Taijiquan and Daoism," *Journal of Asian Martial Arts* 16 (2007): 8–45; and Nikolas Broy, "Martial Monks in Medieval Chinese Buddhism," *Journal of Chi-*

nese Religions, no. 40 (2012): 45–89, who observes that obedience to (ultimately Indic) monastic rules was increasingly questioned as Buddhism spread across China.

36. Takuan Soho, "The Mysterious Record of Immovable Wisdom," in William Scott Wilson, trans., *The Unfettered Mind* (Tokyo: Kodansha International, 1986), 26, 32. Compare the *Platform Sutra:* "Being apart from the environment and putting an end to birth and destruction is like going along with the flow of water" (147).

37. Soho, "Mysterious Record," 26–27, 24.

38. Buddha, in John W. Schroeder, *Skillful Means* (Honolulu: University of Hawaii Press, 2001), 25.

39. *Prajnaparamita Sutra,* in Michael Pye, *Skillful Means: A Concept in Mahayana Buddhism* (London: Routledge, 2003), 104, 108; and John Schroeder, "Truth, Deception, and Skillful Means in the Lotus Sutra," *Asian Philosophy* 21 (2011): 35–52.

40. *Lotus Sutra,* in Pye, *Skillful Means,* 39. Paul J. Griffiths cites Augustine's words to a skeptical Jerome: "[It must be] unshakably believed and defended that those who wrote sacred Scripture—and most especially the canonical books—were completely free from the lie." *Lying: An Augustinian Theology of Duplicity* (Grand Rapids, MI: Brazos Press, 2004), 150.

41. *Record of Baizhang,* in Poceski, *Ordinary Mind,* 165.

42. Zeuschner, "Hsien Tsung Chi," 258, 259, 260. On Shenhui as probable author of the *Platform Sutra,* see Yampolsky, *Platform Sutra,* 114; for doubts and qualifications, Sorensen, "Early Chan," 68–69. According to Robinson, "The skillful Buddhist essayist could at once gain entrée to literary circles and cast unwelcome ideas in a welcome form by contriving his essay so that it would seem Taoist to the Taoist, Buddhist to those who understood, and aesthetically pleasing to everyone." *Early Madhyamaka,* 17.

43. Zeuschner, "Hsien Tsung Chi," 259, 258, 261.

44. A. F. Price and Wong Mou-lam, trans., *The Diamond Sutra* (Boulder, CO: Shambhala, 1974), 21.

45. Which is not to say that rituals cannot fail. See Michael David Kaulana Ing, *The Dysfunction of Ritual in Early Confucianism* (Oxford: Oxford University Press, 2012).

46. Nagarjuna, in Robinson, *Early Madhyamaka,* 41.

47. Yu Yan, *Explanation of the Token for Joining the Three in Accordance with the Book of Changes,* in Robinet, *The World Upside Down,* 27; Liu Zianxin, comment on *Zhuangzi,* 2.1, in Brook Ziporyn, trans., *Zhuangzi: The Essential Writings, with Selections from Traditional Commentaries* (Indianapolis, IN: Hackett, 2009), 137; Robinet, *The World Upside Down,* 18; Chong Tojon, *Criticism of Buddhism,* in Youngin Choi, "History of Confucianism in Korea," *Confucianism*

in Context, ed. Wonsuk Chang and Leah Kalmanson (Albany: State University of New York Press, 2010), 38.

48. Wang Yangming, in Julia Ching, *To Acquire Wisdom: The Way of Wang Yangming* (New York: Columbia University Press, 1976), 224.

5. The Investigation of Things

1. *The Great Learning,* in Daniel K. Gardner, trans., *The Four Books: The Basic Teachings of the Later Confucian Tradition* (Indianapolis, IN: Hackett, 2007), 4–5. Tradition attributes the *Great Learning* to Kongzi as recorded by Zeng Shen, though it may be the work of Yuezheng Ke, a student under Mengzi, circa 260 BCE. Joseph Needham, *Botany, Science and Civilization in China,* vol. 6, pt. 1 (Cambridge: Cambridge University Press, 1986), 214.

2. *Great Learning,* 7–8, emphasis added.

3. Cheng Yi, in A. C. Graham, *Two Chinese Philosophers: Ch'eng Ming-Tao and Ch'eng Yi-Ch'uan* (London: Lund Humphries, 1958), 75. Graham argues that Cheng is "the truly creative figure in the movement" and "the greatest Confucian thinker of the last two thousand years" (xix).

4. Needham, *Botany,* 214. *Ge wu* is not how the Chinese translate modern "science," which is *ke xue,* an expression associated with classification. However, for Needham it is certain that "for the past thousand years Chinese scholars concerned with the investigation of nature have taken the words to apply to scientific studies more or less in our modern sense" (ibid.). For an assessment of this claim see Willard J. Peterson, "Chinese Scientific Philosophy and Some Chinese Attitudes Towards Knowledge," *Past and Present* 87 (1980): 20–30.

5. Graham, *Two Philosophers,* 18; Chen Shun, in Joseph Needham, *History of Scientific Thought, Science and Civilization in China,* vol. 2 (Cambridge: Cambridge University Press, 1956), 566. "The word *li* [ceremony] has the same import as *li* [principle]." Wang Yangming, *Instructions for Practical Living,* trans. Wing-tsit Chan (New York: Columbia University Press, 1963), 16. In a gloss by A. C. Cua, ceremony is the manifest order of principle, and principle is the hidden order of ceremony. *The Unity of Knowledge and Action: A Study in Wang Yangming's Moral Psychology* (Honolulu: University of Hawaii Press, 1982), 47.

6. Philip J. Ivanhoe, *Confucian Moral Self Cultivation* (Indianapolis, IN: Hackett, 2000), 50–52.

7. I draw from William Theodore de Bary, *The Message of the Mind in Neoconfucianism* (New York: Columbia University Press, 1989), 5–6, 17–18, 51.

8. Chu Hsi (Zhu Xi), *Learning to Be A Sage: Selections from the Conversations of Master Chu, Arranged Topically,* trans. Daniel K. Gardner (Berkeley: University of California Press, 1990), 89. I also draw from Daniel K. Gardner, "Chu

Hsi's Reading of the *Da-hsueh:* A Neoconfucian's Quest for Truth," *Journal of Chinese Philosophy* 10 (1983): 183–204.

9. *Institutions of Emperor Yao,* in Geoffrey Lloyd and Nathan Sivin, *The Way and the Word: Science and Medicine in Early China and Greece* (New Haven, CT: Yale University Press, 2002), 190.

10. *Book of History,* Counsels of Yu, in de Bary, *Neoconfucianism,* 9. The part about keeping to the mean is also in *Analects,* 20.1, which omits reference to *renxin* and *daoxin.* Compare the *Nei ye* book of *Guanzi:* "Within the mind there is yet another mind." *Guanzi,* 13.11, in Livia Kohn, *Sitting in Oblivion: The Heart of Daoist Meditation* (Dunedin, FL: Three Pines Press, 2010), 26.

11. Chu Hsi (Zhu Xi), citing Cheng Yi, *Learning to Be a Sage,* 66.

12. Zhu Xi, in Ivanhoe, *Self Cultivation,* 52–53.

13. Chu Hsi (Zhu Xi), *Reflections on Things at Hand,* trans. Wing-tsit Chan (New York: Columbia University Press, 1967), 119, 92; *Learning to Be a Sage,* 148, 159, 149, 182.

14. *Mengzi,* 10B1. See also Kirill O. Thompson, "The Archery of Wisdom in the Stream of Life: Wisdom in the Four Books with Zhu Xi's Reflections," *Philosophy East and West* 57 (2007): 330–344; and Chungying Cheng, "Method, Knowledge and Truth in Chu Hsi," *Journal of Chinese Philosophy* 14 (1987): 129–160. Zhu Xi's explanation of the value of study may have been more bold than one thinks. See David S. Nivison, "'Knowledge' and 'Action' in Chinese Thought Since Wang Yang-ming," in *Studies in Chinese Thought,* ed. Arthur F. Wright (Chicago: University of Chicago Press, 1953).

15. *Book of Rites,* in Yi Wu, *Chinese Philosophical Terms* (Lanham, MD: University Press of America, 1986), 85–86.

16. *The Spring and Autumn of Lü Buwei,* in A. C. Graham, *Later Mohist Logic, Ethics and Science* (Hong Kong: Chinese University Press, 1978), 192; *Hanfeizi,* 6.20, in A. C. Graham, *Disputers of the Tao* (Chicago: Open Court, 1989), 286.

17. Wang Bi, in Zhang Dainian, *Key Concepts in Chinese Philosophy,* trans. Edmund Ryden (Beijing: Foreign Languages Press, 2002), 230; Brook Ziporyn, *Zhuangzi: The Essential Writings, with Selections from Traditional Commentaries* (Indianapolis, IN: Hackett, 2009), 215. My discussion of *li* also benefits from Ziporyn, "Form, Principle, Pattern, or Coherence? *Li* in Chinese Philosophy," *Philosophy Compass* 3 (2008): 401–422; and Ziporyn, "Li (Principle, Coherence) in Chinese Buddhism," *Journal of Chinese Philosophy* 30 (2003): 501–524.

18. Cheng Yi, in Graham, *Two Philosophers,* 81.

19. Ibid., 9–10.

20. Ibid., 23.

21. Zhu Xi, *Learning to Be a Sage,* 53.

22. Cheng Yi, in Graham, *Two Philosophers,* 76.

23. Aristotle, *De Anima*, 429b, 431b. "The ordering (*kosmon*), the same for all, no god nor man has made, but it ever was and is and will be: fire everliving, kindled in measures and in measures going out." Heraclitus, in Charles H. Kahn, *The Art and Thought of Heraclitus* (Cambridge: Cambridge University Press, 1979), 132.

24. *Maintaining Perfect Balance*, 25.3, in Gardner, *Four Books*, 126.

25. Wang, *Instructions for Practical Living*, 249. For a scandalized reaction see Needham, *History of Scientific Thought*, 510.

26. Li Kan, *Zhu Pu Xiang Lu* (Ji Nan, China: Shangdong Hua Bao, 2006). Song literati painters carried out comparably probing investigations, especially of plants and animals. Li Zehou, *The Path of Beauty: A Study of Chinese Aesthetics*, trans. Gong Lizeng (Hong Kong: Oxford University Press, 1994), 185–186, 190.

27. Zhu Xi, *Learning to Be a Sage*, 124, 181.

28. Allen Wittenborn, "Some Aspects of Mind and the Problem of Knowledge in Chu Hsi's Philosophy," *Journal of Chinese Philosophy* 9 (1982): 11–43.

29. Zhu Xi, *Learning to Be a Sage*, 174, 171; on the difference from Chan, 176, 178. I also draw from Ivanhoe, *Self Cultivation*, 49.

30. Zhu Xi, *Learning to Be a Sage*, 101–102.

31. Zhu Xi, *Reflections*, 72 (Ye Cai); 43n38 (*Yijing*); 42–43, 188 (Cheng Yi); 43 (Zhu Xi).

32. Zhu Xi, *Reflections*, 208 (Cheng Yi); 46 (Ye Cai); 47 (Zhu); 63 (Cheng Yi, Shi Huang); also *Xunzi*, 8.19.

33. Zhu Xi, *Reflections*, 150, 75 (Zhu); 71 (Cheng Yi); 62 (Zhu, Cheng Yi); 40 (Cheng Hao); 45 (Zhu).

34. Cheng Hao, in Fung Yu-Lan, *A Short History of Chinese Philosophy*, trans. Dirk Bodde (New York: Free Press, 1948), 287.

35. François Jullien, *Detour and Access: Strategies of Meaning in China and Greece*, trans. Sophie Hawkes (New York: Zone Books, 2000), 311.

36. Ibid., 298.

37. Zhu, *Reflections*, 40 (Cheng Hao); 67, 253, 8, 24 (Cheng Yi); 275 (Ye Cai); 72 (Zhang Zai).

38. G. W. F. Hegel, *Enzyklopädie der Philosophischen Wissenschaften* (Frankfurt: Suhrkamp, 1970), § 377 (Zusatz).

39. Wang, *Instructions for Practical Living*, 11, 93. It is usual to link Wang to Lu Xiangshan, a younger contemporary of Zhu Xi, and speak of a Lu-Wang school. However, Tu Wei-Ming shows that Lu "was virtually irrelevant as an alternative to Zhu Xi in Yang-ming's formative years," and that a dichotomy between Cheng-Zhu and Lu-Wang is "not only oversimplified but also misleading." Tu Wei-Ming, *Neoconfucian Thought in Action: Wang Yang-ming's Youth (1472–1509)* (Berkeley: University of California Press, 1976), 161.

40. Tu, *Neoconfucian Thought*, 151.

41. Wang, *Instructions for Practical Living,* 7, 15, 76, 176.

42. Wang, "Reply to Wei Shiyue," in Philip J. Ivanhoe, trans., *Readings From the Lu-Wang School of Neo-Confucianism* (Indianapolis, IN: Hackett, 2009), 127. Compare Mengzi: "The function of the heart is to reflect. If it reflects, then it will get it. If it does not reflect, then it will not get it" (6A15).

43. Wang, *Instructions for Practical Living,* 156; and his poem "Longevity," in Ivanhoe, *Self Cultivation,* 68. On *liang zhi* I draw from Stephen C. Angle, "Sagely Ease and Moral Perception," *Dao* 5 (2005): 31–55; Julia Ching, *To Acquire Wisdom: The Way of Wang Yang-ming* (New York: Columbia University Press, 1976), 62–65; Yong Huang, "A Neoconfucian Conception of Wisdom: Wang Yangming on Innate Moral Knowledge," *Journal of Chinese Philosophy* 33 (2006): 393–408; Ivanhoe, *Self Cultivation,* 65–69; and Shu-hsien Liu, "On Chu Hsi as an Important Source for the Development of the Philosophy of Wang Yang-Ming," *Journal of Chinese Philosophy* 11 (1984): 83–107.

44. Wang, *Instructions for Practical Living,* 249.

45. Ibid., 225.

46. Wang, *Record For Practice,* § 11, in *Lu-Wang School,* 156. For an analysis of Wang's philosophy in action during his campaign to crush an uprising, see Larry Israel, "The Prince and the Sage: Concerning Wang Yangming's 'Effortless' Suppression of the Ning Princely Establishment Rebellion," *Late Imperial China* 29 (2008): 68–128; and Leo K. Shin, "The Last Campaigns of Wang Yangming," *T'oung Pao* 92 (2006): 101–128.

47. Tu, *Neoconfucian Thought,* 164.

48. Wang, *Inquiry on the "Great Learning,"* in *Instructions for Practical Living,* 274; Cheng Yi, in Zhu, *Reflections,* 93.

49. Wang, in Tu, *Neoconfucian Thought,* 120. The bamboo fiasco occurred in 1492, when Wang was 22. Tu thinks he was "much disturbed by his failure to put *ge wu* into practice. He sincerely believed that there was something basically inadequate in himself" (50). The experience led to redoubled effort to understand Zhu's teaching. He decides that his mistake in the bamboo grove was to "stubbornly force himself to understand the inner structure of a thing as if his life depended on it" (51); instead he should "let the thing gradually sink into his mind so that he could appreciate its vicissitudes from a multidimensional point of view" (52). It was repeated frustration in these redoubled efforts that supposedly motivated Wang's research into *daoyin.*

50. Wang, "Reply to Wei Shiyue," *Lu-Wang School,* 127.

51. Wang, *Instructions for Practical Living,* 150.

52. Ibid., 62; Cheng Hao, in Needham, *Mathematics and the Sciences of the Heavens and the Earth, Science and Civilization in China,* vol. 3 (Cambridge: Cambridge University Press, 1959), 165; Zhu, *Reflections,* 92.

53. Wang, *Inquiry on the "Great Learning,"* 279–280.

54. Wang, *Instructions for Practical Living*, 278, 70, 44, 45. On the problem of desire in early Christian monasticism, see Peter Brown, *The Body and Society: Men, Women and Sexual Renunciation in Early Christianity* (New York: Columbia University Press, 1988), chap. 11.

55. *Xunzi*, 21.12.

56. Wang, *Instructions for Practical Living*, 64; Ching, *To Acquire Wisdom*, 105, 115.

57. Wang, *Instructions for Practical Living*, 33, 14, 104, 257. "His conclusion [is] that to be is to be perceived—a Berkelean proposition that predated Berkeley." He Zhaowu, *An Intellectual History of China* (Beijing: Foreign Languages Press, 1991), 362. For another example of this reading, see Jana S. Rošker, *Searching for the Way: Theory of Knowledge in Pre-modern and Modern China* (Hong Kong: Chinese University Press, 2008), 85. For criticism see Ching, *To Acquire Wisdom*, 191–193; Amy Ihlan, "Wang Yang-Ming: A Philosopher of Practical Action," *Journal of Chinese Philosophy* 20 (1993): 451–463; and Shu-hsien Liu, "How Idealistic is Wang Yang-Ming?," *Journal of Chinese Philosophy* 10 (1983): 147–168.

58. Wang, *Instructions for Practical Living*, 222. Graham, *Disputers of the Tao*, 99. On "idealism" in Western philosophy, see Jeremy Dunham, Iain Hamilton Grant, and Sean Watson, *Idealism: The History of a Philosophy* (Montreal and Kingston, ON: McGill-Queen's University Press, 2011).

59. Wang, *Instructions for Practical Living*, 223; Henri Bergson, *Matter and Memory*, trans. Nancy Margaret Paul and W. Scott Palmer (Mineola, NY: Dover, 2004), 124, 127.

60. Haiming Wen advances the "epistemological paradox" of Neoconfucianism in *Confucian Pragmatism* (Lanham, MD: Lexington Books, 2009), 102.

61. Wang, *Instructions for Practical Living*, 221–222; *The Platform Sutra of the Sixth Patriarch*, trans. Philip Yampolsky (New York: Columbia University Press, 1967), 146, 171. On Wang's involvement with Chan, see Tu, *Neoconfucian Thought*, 63–72.

62. Lo Ch'in-shun (Luo Qinshun), *Knowledge Painfully Acquired*, trans. Irene Bloom (New York: Columbia University Press, 1987), 172.

63. Ibid., 128–129.

64. Ibid., 98, 115.

65. Shao Yong, in Luo, *Knowledge Painfully Acquired*, 80. Compare Cheng Hao (writing against Buddhists): "When they strive only to understand the high without studying the low, how can their understanding of the high be right?" and the locus classicus in *Analects*, "I study what is below in order to comprehend what is above" (A 14.35). Cheng is cited in Needham, *The Great Titration: Science and Society in East and West* (London: George Allen and Unwin, 1969), 64.

66. Luo, Letter to Wang Yangming, 1520, in *Knowledge Painfully Acquired,* 177.

67. Luo, *Knowledge Painfully Acquired,* 74, 58.

68. Gilles Deleuze, *Nietzsche and Philosophy,* trans. Hugh Tomlinson (New York: Columbia University Press, 2006), 24; Gilles Deleuze with Claire Parnet, *Dialogues,* trans. Hugh Tomlinson and Barbara Habberjam (New York: Columbia University Press, 1987), 57.

69. Bruno Latour, *Politics of Nature: How to Bring the Sciences into Democracy,* trans. Catherine Porter (Cambridge, MA: Harvard University Press, 2004); Cai Yong, in Lloyd and Sivin, *Way and the Word,* 192.

70. Bruno Latour, *Reassembling the Social* (Oxford: Oxford University Press, 2005), 256, 257, 262.

71. On the Epicurean thesis "all perceptions are true," see Lucretius, *De Rerum Natura,* trans. W. H. D. Rouse, rev. Martin Ferguson Smith (Cambridge, MA: Harvard University Press, 1975), bk. 4, l. 499; C. C. W. Taylor, "'All Perceptions are True,'" *Pleasure, Mind, and Soul: Selected Papers in Ancient Philosophy* (Oxford: Clarendon Press, 2008); and Elizabeth Asmis, "Epicurean Empiricism," *The Cambridge Companion to Epicureanism,* ed. James Warren (Cambridge: Cambridge University Press, 2009). On Protagoras's empiricism, see James I. Porter, *The Origins of Aesthetic Thought in Ancient Greece: Matter, Sensation, and Experience* (Cambridge: Cambridge University Press, 2010), 201.

72. *Mozi,* chap. 31, in *Readings in Classical Chinese Philosophy,* ed. Philip J. Ivanhoe and Bryan W. Van Norden (Indianapolis, IN: Hackett, 2001), 94, 95.

73. Mohist *Canons,* in Christoph Harbsmeier, *Language and Logic, Science and Civilization in China,* vol. 7, pt. 1 (Cambridge: Cambridge University Press, 1998), 339; also *Xunzi,* 17.4, 21.8. Zeno is cited from Samuel Sambursky, *Physics of the Stoics* (London: Routledge and Kegen Paul, 1959), 125. The wax-tablet trope begins with Plato, *Theaetetus,* 191c-d, and recurs in Aristotle, *De Anima,* 424a, and *On Memory and Reminiscence,* 450b. On the appropriation of Mohist thought about perception, see Anne D. Birdwhistell, "The Concept of Experiential Knowledge in the Thought of Chang Tsai," *Philosophy East and West* 35 (1985): 67–82; and Donald J. Munro, "A Villain in the *Xunzi,*" in *Chinese Language, Thought, and Culture,* ed. Philip J. Ivanhoe (Chicago: Open Court, 1996). There is a parallel appropriation of Mohist thought on names; see A. C. Graham, *Later Mohist Logic, Ethics and Science* (Hong Kong: Chinese University Press, 1978), 63; and John Makeham, *Name and Actuality in Early Chinese Thought* (Albany: State University of New York Press, 1994), 57.

74. On Bacon's empiricism, see Paolo Rossi, *Francis Bacon: From Magic to Science,* trans. Sacha Rabinovitch (London: Routledge and Kegan Paul, 1968); and Hans Blumenberg, *The Legitimacy of the Modern Age,* trans. Robert M. Wallace (Cambridge, MA: MIT Press, 1983). On the purification of nature and society in the

self-image of modernity, see Bruno Latour, *We Have Never Been Modern,* trans. Catherine Porter (Cambridge, MA: Harvard University Press, 1993).

75. Michael Frede, "The Ancient Empiricists," *Essays in Ancient Philosophy* (Minneapolis: University of Minnesota Press, 1987).

76. Galen, *Three Treatises on the Nature of Science,* trans. Richard Walzer and Michael Frede (Indianapolis, IN: Hackett, 1985), 23, 24, 42, 13.

77. Gilles Deleuze, *Empiricism and Subjectivity,* trans. Constantin V. Boundas (New York: Columbia University Press, 1991), 98–99; and "Hume," in *Pure Immanence,* trans. Anne Boyman (New York: Zone Books, 2001), 38.

78. I elaborate on this argument in *Truth in Philosophy* (Cambridge, MA: Harvard University Press, 1993), chap. 7; and *Knowledge and Civilization* (Boulder, CO: Westview, 2004), chap. 1.

79. Luo, *Knowledge Painfully Acquired,* 55.

80. David Hume, *An Enquiry Concerning Human Understanding,* ed. Charles W. Hendel (Indianapolis, IN: Bobbs-Merrill, 1955), 41; *A Treatise of Human Nature,* ed. L. A. Selby-Bigge, rev. P. H. Nidditch (Oxford: Oxford University Press, 1978), 636.

81. William James, *Essays in Radical Empiricism,* ed. Ralph Barton Perry (New York: E. P. Dutton, 1971), 103.

82. Hume, *Enquiry,* 85; Baruch Spinoza, *Ethics,* I, proposition 29, in *Ethics and Selected Letters,* trans. Samuel Shirley (Indianapolis, IN: Hackett, 1982), 51.

83. Marcel Granet, *La pensée Chinoise,* in Roger Ames, *Confucian Role Ethics* (Honolulu: University of Hawaii Press, 2011), 63.

84. Guo Xiang, comment on *Zhuangzi,* 6.45, in Ziporyn, *Zhuangzi,* 202; Zhang Zai, in Zhang, *Key Concepts,* 22. The image occurs earlier in *Zhuangzi,* "A thing's life is like a stampede, a gallop, at every prompting it alters; there is never a time when it does not shift" (Z 148). A related point distinguishes *he,* a harmony that includes multiplicity, and *tong,* a monotonous sameness; see *Analects* 13.23.

85. *Zhongyong,* 30.3, in Tu Wei-Ming, *Centrality and Commonality* (Albany: State University of New York Press, 1989), 86; see also *Mengzi* 6A6. On "is" and "ought," see Hume, *Treatise of Human Nature,* 469–470. As Graham pointed out, the Chinese have no trouble formulating this distinction; A. C. Graham, *Studies in Chinese Philosophy and Philosophical Literature* (Albany: State University of New York Press, 1990), 430. Needham emphasizes the difference between *li* and "law of nature," *Great Titration,* 325. Graham concurs: "For the Sung philosophers, a principle is a line which it is natural to follow, not a law which one is bound to obey" (*Two Philosophers,* 12–13).

86. Hume, *Enquiry,* 45.

87. Ibid., 170.

6. Resonance

1. Charles Le Blanc, *Huai-Nan-Tzu. Philosophical Synthesis in Early Han Thought* (Hong Kong: Hong Kong University Press, 1985), 8; *The Huainanzi*, John S. Major, Sarah A. Queen, Andrew Seth Meyer, and Harold D. Roth, trans. and eds. (New York: Columbia University Press, 2010), 217, 219. Shellfish produce an enzyme that prevents lacquer from drying, and they were carefully kept away wherever lacquer was manufactured. On the historical context of *Huainanzi*, its composition, presentation to the emperor, and the aftermath, see Griet Vankeerberghen, *The* Huainanzi *and Liu An's Claim to Moral Authority* (Albany: State University of New York Press, 2001). The expression *ganying* does not actually appear in *Huainanzi*, though *gan* (influence, stimulus) and *ying* (respond, response) appear many times and "conform exactly to the meaning of resonance that one expects from the concept of *ganying*." John Major, in *The Huainanzi*, 210.

2. *Huainanzi*, 216, 219, 685, 755, 686, 753, 217, 245.

3. John S. Major, *Heaven and Earth in Early Han Thought* (Albany: State University of New York Press, 1993), 28–29, 30, 32.

4. Joseph Needham, *The Great Titration: Science and Society in East and West* (London: George Allen and Unwin, 1969), 75; Ilya Prigogine, *The End of Certainty: Time, Chaos, and the New Laws of Nature* (New York: Free Press, 1997), 42; also David L. Hall and Roger Ames, *Anticipating China* (Albany: State University of New York Press, 1995): "The vocabulary of *qi* and *yin-yang* emphasizes acoustic resonance and response" (260).

5. Prigogine, *End of Certainty*, 42, 44, 122–127; John Gribbin, *Deep Simplicity* (London: Penguin, 2004), 61; Manuel Delanda, *Intensive Science and Virtual Philosophy* (London: Continuum, 2002), 114.

6. *Xunzi*, chap. 20, in Erica Fox Brindley, *Music, Cosmology, and the Politics of Harmony in Early China* (Albany: State University of New York Press, 2012), 141; also 3–7; *Huainanzi*, 243; Major, *Heaven and Earth*, 44; Michael Puett, *To Become a God: Cosmology, Sacrifice, and Self-Divinization in Early China* (Cambridge, MA: Harvard University Press, 2002), 115–116. I have also consulted John B. Henderson, *The Development and Decline of Chinese Cosmology* (New York: Columbia University Press, 1984); and Geoffrey Lloyd and Nathan Sivin, *The Way and the Word: Science and Medicine in Early China and Greece* (New Haven, CT: Yale University Press, 2002), chap. 5.

7. *Huainanzi*, 96, 537, 250. Also *Zhuangzi*: "There can be true knowledge only when there is a true man" (Z 84).

8. Translations from Zhang Zai are in Jung-Yeup Kim, "A Revisionist Understanding of Zhang Zai's Development of *Qi* in the Context of his Critique of the Buddhist," *Asian Philosophy* 20 (2010), 119, 121, 114.

9. Tang Junyi, "Zhang Zai's Theory of Experience" (1956), cited in in Kim, "Revisionist Understanding," 119.

10. Zhang Zai, in Kim, "Revisionist Understanding," 114.

11. See Gilles Deleuze, "Bergson's Conception of Difference," in *Desert Islands and Other Texts*, ed. David Lapoujade, trans. Michael Taormina (Los Angeles: Semiotext(e), 2004).

12. Zhang Zai, cited in Kim, "Revisionist Understanding," 114, 121.

13. Cheng Yi, in A. C. Graham, *Two Chinese Philosophers: Ch'eng Ming-Tao and Ch'eng Yi-Ch'uan* (London: Lund Humphries, 1958), 38–39; Wang Fuzhi, in Haiming Wen, *Confucian Pragmatism* (Lanham, MD: Lexington Books, 2009), 102.

14. The fantastic transformations depicted in chapter 18 of the *Zhuangzi*, which may have inspired the less whimsical variation in *Huainanzi*, 4.18, and reappear in *Liezi*, 1.4, make an interesting comparison to the evolutionary vision of Diderot's *Dream of D'Alembert*. I noted (Chapter 1) resistance to Darwinism in Xunzi, though evolution and Darwinism are not the same thing.

15. *Book of Rites* and *Zuo Commentary*, in Victor H. Mair, trans., *The Art of War: Sun Zi's Military Methods* (New York: Columbia University Press, 2007), 48.

16. Robert Cummings Neville, *Ritual and Deference* (Albany: State University of New York Press, 2008), 57–58.

17. Buddha, in Mark Siderits, *Buddhism As Philosophy* (Indianapolis, IN: Hackett, 2007), 41.

18. On justice to nonhumans see Bruno Latour, "Morality and Technology: The End of the Means," *Theory, Culture & Society* 19 (2002): 247–260; and *Politics of Nature: How to Bring the Sciences into Democracy*, trans. Catherine Porter (Cambridge, MA: Harvard University Press, 2004); Michel Serres, *The Natural Contract*, trans. Elizabeth MacArthur and William Paulson (Ann Arbor: University of Michigan Press, 1995); and my paper "The Cultural Politics of Nonhuman Things," *Contemporary Pragmatism* 8 (2011): 3–19.

19. Aristotle, *De Anima*, 432b; Plato, *Phaedrus*, 270a; Plotinus, *Enneads*, 3.8.4.

20. G. E. R. Lloyd, *Adversaries and Authorities: Investigations into Ancient Greek and Chinese Science* (Cambridge: Cambridge University Press, 1996), 219, 90; and *The Ambitions of Curiosity: Understanding the World in Ancient Greece and China* (Cambridge: Cambridge University Press, 2002), 43, 14, 20. The question of truth's value surfaces in Western thought with Nietzsche. See my *Truth in Philosophy* (Cambridge, MA: Harvard University Press, 1993), chap. 3; and François Jullien, "Did Philosophers Have to Become Fixated on Truth?," *Critical Inquiry* 28 (2002): 803–824.

21. Lloyd and Sivin, *Way and Word*, 193, 205, 208; Howard L. Goodman, "Chinese Polymaths 100–300 AD," *Asia Major* 18 (2005): 101–174; Gloria Davies, *Worrying About China: The Language of Chinese Critical Inquiry* (Cambridge,

MA: Harvard University Press, 2007); Haun Saussy, *Great Walls of Discourse and Other Adventures in Cultural China* (Cambridge, MA: Harvard University Asia Center, 2001).

22. Lloyd and Sivin, *Way and Word*, 111, 116–117, 138, 180, 185–187, 241; Page Du-Bois, *Out of Athens: The New Ancient Greeks* (Cambridge, MA: Harvard University Press, 2010), 125, 173.

23. The distinction between knowing how and knowing that was popularized by Gilbert Ryle, "Knowing How and Knowing That" (1945), *Collected Papers*, vol. 2 (London: Hutchinson, 1971), and *The Concept of Mind* (London: Hutchinson, 1949). Ryle favored different senses of "to know." Michael Polanyi thinks in terms of different kinds of knowledge. "Human knowledge is of two kinds. What is usually described as knowledge, as set out in written words or maps, or mathematical formulae, is only one kind of knowledge; while unformulated knowledge, such as we have of something we are in the act of doing, is another form of knowledge." *The Study of Man* (Chicago: University of Chicago Press, 1959), 12. I elaborate on my animadversions about this distinction in *Knowledge and Civilization* (Boulder, CO: Westview Press, 2004), and *Artifice and Design* (Ithaca, NY: Cornell University Press, 2008).

24. J. Robert Oppenheimer, in Jeremy Bernstein, *Oppenheimer: Portrait of an Enigma* (London: Duckworth, 2004), 89.

25. Oppenheimer, in Bernstein, *Oppenheimer*, 121–122.

26. Michel Serres with Bruno Latour, *Conversations on Science, Culture, and Time*, trans. Roxanne Lapidus (Ann Arbor: University of Michigan Press, 2006), 170–171.

27. David W. Orr, *The Nature of Design: Ecology, Culture, and Human Intention* (New York: Oxford University Press, 2002), 37–51. Bruno Latour also writes of the need to slow down technoscientific change, and has some ideas about how to do it in *We Have Never Been Modern*, trans. Catherine Porter (Cambridge, MA: Harvard University Press, 1993). On the penchant of modern technics for paradoxical counterproductivity see Ivan Illich, *Toward a History of Needs* (Berkeley, CA: Heyday, 1978), and Edward Tenner, *Why Things Bite Back: Technology and the Revenge of Unintended Consequences* (New York, Vintage, 1997).

28. Justin Kruger and David Dunning, "Unskilled and Unaware of It: How Difficulties of Recognizing One's Own Incompetence Lead to Inflated Self-Assessments," *Journal of Personality and Social Psychology* 77 (1999): 1121–1134.

29. Lucretius, *De Rerum Natura*, trans. W. H. D. Rouse, rev. M. F. Smith (Cambridge, MA: Harvard University Press, 1975), bk. 1, ll. 670–671; Plato, *Theaetetus*, 176a-b; *Phaedrus*, 66e.

30. François Jullien, *The Impossible Nude: Chinese Art and Western Aesthetics*, trans. Maev de la Guardia (Chicago: University of Chicago Press, 2007), 129;

Huainanzi, 649; John Hay, "The Human Body as a Microcosmic Source of Macrocosmic Values in Calligraphy," in *Self As Body in Asian Theory and Practice,* ed. Thomas P. Kasulis (Albany: State University of New York Press, 1993), 203. The observation holds for calligraphy no less than painting. "The most potent function of calligraphy [is] its transformational flow of energy" (205).

31. The oldest use of the term *dao* seems to occur in the *Book of History,* where it refers to cutting a channel and leading a river to prevent the overflow of banks. For a study of Western thinking about "method" see Neal W. Gilbert, *Renaissance Concepts of Method* (New York: Columbia University Press, 1960).

32. Guo Xiang, on *Zhuangzi* 6.27; in Brook Ziporyn, trans., *Zhuangzi: The Essential Writings, with Selections from Traditional Commentaries* (Indianapolis, IN: Hackett, 2009), 195.

Glossary

Every transliterated Chinese word or expression I use is given here in Chinese characters, listed according to their *pinyin* spelling.

Ai 礙 (obstructed)

Bagua 八卦 (eight trigrams of the *Yijing*)

Baopuzi《抱朴子》(*Book of the Master Who Embraces Simplicity*)

Bei 備 (to be provided for)

Bian 辯 (discrimination, argument, disputation)

Bingfa 兵法 (military methods, art of war)

Bu zhan 不戰 (without fighting)

Bu zheng 不爭 (do not contend)

Bu zhi 不知 (no knowledge)

Cai 才 (capability)

Chan 禪 (Japanese, *Zen*)

Cheng 誠 (truthfulness, sincerity)

Cheng wu 成物 (the completion of things)

Chengxin 成心 (fixed mind, prejudiced mind)

Chun bai 純白 (pure and simple)

Da li 大理 (great principle)

Dang ran zhi li 當然之理 (pattern by which something should be so)

Dao 道 (way, path)

Daodejing《道德經》(*Classic of the Way and Its Power*)

Daojia 道家 (Daoist, Daoism)

Daoxin 道心 (mind of the *dao*)

Daoxue 道學 (learning of the *dao*)

Daoyin 導引 (guided stretching; art of making joints flexible)

Datong 大同 (grand unity)

Da Xue《大學》(*The Great Learning*)

Da zhi 大知 (great knowledge)

De 德 (power, virtue)

De zui 得罪 (give offense)

Di 禘 (a ritual sacrifice)

E 惡 (bad, evil)

Erya《爾雅》

Fa 法 (standards)

275

Fang bian 方 便 (skillful means; Sanskrit, *upaya kausalya*)

Fei 非 (not so, wrong)

Fu 富 (rich, wealth)

Gan 感 (responsive)

Ganying 感 應 (resonance)

Ge wu 格 物 (investigation of things)

Gong 工 (artisanal work)

Gong 公 (impartial)

Gong'an 公 案 (a case; Japanese, *koan*)

Gongfu 功 夫 (effort, exertion, practice, work)

Guanzi 《 管 子 》

Gui 詭 (deception)

Gui Gu Zi 《 鬼 穀 子 》 (*Ghost Valley Master*)

Gun fa 棍 法 (staff fighting method)

Han 捍 (to oppose, defend, stand against)

Hanfeizi 《 韓 非 子 》

Hao xue 好 學 (love of learning)

He 和 (harmony)

Heguanzi 《 鶡 冠 子 》 (*Pheasant Cap Master*)

Hu 瑚 (a ritual vessel)

Huainanzi 《 淮 南 子 》 (*Book of the Huainan Masters*)

Huangdi Neijing 《 黃 帝 內 經 》 (*The Yellow Emperor's Classic of Medicine*)

Huatou 話 頭 (the key phrase in a *gong'an*)

Hui wu hui 慧 無 慧 (wisdom that is not wisdom)

Huntun 混 沌 (chaos)

Ji 機 / 幾 (incipient)

Ji 紀 (knot)

Ji 幾 (pivot)

Ji 計 (planning)

Ji 蹟 (trace)

Jian 見 (see, sight, vision)

Jian 間 (spy)

Jian 奸 (trickery)

Jian'ai 兼 愛 (impartial care)

Jiang 匠 (artisanal work, worker)

Jiang 將 (commander, general)

Jian ren suo bu jian wei zhi ming 見 人 所 不 見 謂 之 明 (To see what others do not is called enlightenment)

Jian xiao yue ming 見 小 曰 明 (To really see the little things is called enlightenment)

Ji er zhi zhi tian ye 幾 而 知 之 天 也 (knowing it by observing its inchoate beginnings is heaven/ nature)

Jing 靜 (still)

Jin Si Lu 《 近 思 錄 》 (*Reflections on Things at Hand*)

Ji xie 機 械 (ingenious machines)

Ji xin 機 心 (ingenious minds)

Junxing 君 形 (that which rules form)

Junzi 君 子 (son of the prince, gentleman, perfected person)

Kao Gong Ji 《 考 工 記 》 (*Book of Artisans*)

Ke xue 科 學 (science)

Ke xue de zhen li 科 學 的 真 理 (scientific truth)

Kong 空 (empty)

Kou 口 (mouth)

Kuang chan 狂禪 (mad Zen)

Kun Zhi Ji《困知記》(*Knowledge Painfully Acquired*)

Laozi《老子》

Lei 類 (category)

Li 裏 (measure of distance, about half a kilometer)

Li 理 (principle, pattern)

Li 禮 (rite, ritual, ceremony)

Lian 璉 (a ritual vessel)

Liang neng 良能 (innate ability)

Liang zhi 良知 (innate knowledge, pure knowing)

Liji《禮記》(*Book of Rites*)

Ling 靈 (efficacious)

Lingxing 靈性 (spiritual nature)

Li ren 利人 (beneficial to people)

Liu 流 (to flow)

Liu Tao《六韜》(*Six Secret Teachings*)

Li Wei Gong Bing Fa《李衛公兵法》

Lixue 理學 (study of principle)

Lü 慮 (thinking)

Mengzi《孟子》

Min 民 (the people)

Ming 冥 (dark, darkening, "vanishing into things")

Ming 明 (illumination, enlightenment, manifest)

Ming 名 (name)

Mou 謀 (planning)

Mozi《墨子》

Nei li 內力 (inner strength)

Nei ye 內業 (inner training)

Pian 篇 (book chapter)

Ping chang xin 平常心 (ordinary mind)

Qi 氣 (energy, breath)

Qi 奇 (strange, unorthodox)

Qi 器 (a vessel)

Qian shi 前識 (ability to predict what is to come)

Qian zhi 前知 (foreknow)

Qiao 巧 (device, skill)

Qing 情 (emotion, sentiment, love, essence)

Qiwulun《齊物論》(*Discourse on Equalizing Things*)

Qü 屈 (collapse)

Quan bian 權變 (weighing changes)

Ren 仁 (humane, human-hearted, benevolence)

Ren 人 (person)

Renqing 人情 (untaught dispositions)

Renren 仁人 (humane man)

Renxin 人心 (human heart, ordinary human mind)

Renxing 人性 (human nature)

Ren yu 人欲 (selfish desires)

Ren zhi 人知 (knowing people)

Ru 儒 (Confucian scholar)

Se 色 (color, hue, face, mien)

Shan 善 (good)

Shen 身 ((living) body)

Shen 神 (spirit)

Shengren 聖人 (sage)

Shen sheng bu ding 神生不定 (restless mind)

Shi 矢 (arrow)

Shi 是 (so, good)

Shi 勢 (strategic situation, position)

Shi 實 (thing, actual, real, solid; opposite of *xu*)

Shi fang cong lin 十方叢林 (Buddhist public temples)

Shijing 《詩經》 (*Book of Songs*)

Shi wu 事物 (external things and affairs)

Shu 樞 (pivot, axis)

Shu 恕 (sympathetic understanding)

Shuo 說 (explanation)

Shuo Wen Jie Zi 《說文解字》 (*Annotated Explanation of Characters and Interpretation of Phrases*)

Si 思 (thinking, reflection)

Si yu 私欲 (private desires)

Sun Bin Bingfa 《孫臏兵法》 (Sun Bin *Art of War*)

Sunzi Bingfa 《孫子兵法》 (Sunzi *Art of War*)

Suo yi 所以 (reasons)

Suo yi ran zhi li 所以然之理 (pattern by which something is so)

Taiji 太極 (supreme ultimate; also the name of a martial art)

Tai shi 太始 (Great Beginning)

Tai yi 太一 (Great One)

Ti 體 (body, substance)

Tian 天 (heaven, nature)

Tian li 天理 (heavenly patterns/principles)

Tianxia 天下 (all under heaven)

Tong 同 (sameness, agreement)

Tong de 同德 (uniform integrity)

Tong gui yu ji 同歸於寂 (state of silent vacancy)

Tui 推 (inference, extension, push)

Wan fa 萬法 (all things)

Wang er zhi zhi 望而知之 (know things at a glance)

Wei 為 (act, deed, deliberate effort)

Wei 微 (subtle)

Wei shi 为实 (contrived affirmation)

Wei wu wei 為無為 (do "not doing")

Wen 文 (culture, civilian)

Wu 舞 (dance)

Wu 武 (martial, military)

Wu 無 (nothing)

Wu 物 (thing)

Wu bu wei 無不為 (nothing not done)

Wu bu zhi 無不治 (nothing not ordered/managed)

Wu ci 無辭 (without words, without reasons)

Wu gong 無功 (without accomplishment)

Wu ji 無己 (without self)

Wu ming 無名 (without name)

Wu nian 無念 (no thought)

Wu wei 無為 (non-action, effortless action)

Wu xin 無心 (no mind)

Wuxingpian 《五行篇》 (*Chapter on the Five Forms*)

Wu yu 物欲 (material desires)

Wu zhi 無治 (not ordered/managed)

Wuzi 《吳子》

Xi 希 (rarified)

Xiangying 響應 (mutual response)

Xian zhi 先知 (foreknowledge)

Xian Zong Ji 《顯宗記》 (*Illuminating Essential Doctrine*)

Xiao zhi 小知 (little, petty knowledge)

Xiashi 俠士 (freelance martial artist)

Xin 心 (heart, mind)

Xing 行 (action, practice)

Xing 形 (form, body)

Xing 性 (nature)

Xingming zhi li 性命之理 (the coherence of nature and destiny)

Xinxue 心學 (learning of the mind)

Xiushen 修身 (self-cultivation)

Xü 虛 (empty, tenuous; opposite of *shi,* solid, full)

Xue 學 (learning)

Xunzi 《荀子》

Yi 夷 (minute)

Yi 一 (one, unity, unified)

Yi 意 (thought)

Yijing 《易經》 (*Book of Changes*)

Ying 應 (respond, response)

Yin shi 應是 (adaptive affirmation)

Yin yang 陰陽 (shady/sunny, female/male, stillness/movement, cold/hot, etc.)

Yiquan 意拳 (inner boxing)

Yi wei she ming 以微射明 (From the inconspicuous he hits upon brightness)

Yong 用 (function)

You 有 (being)

You 幽 (hidden)

You wei 有為 (taking deliberate action)

Yu 欲 (desire)

Yu 愚 (ignorance, stupid)

Yu bu yu 欲不欲 (desire no desire)

Yu de 欲得 (desire to acquire)

Yu ying 欲盈 (desire fullness)

Zao hua zhe 造化者 (shaping forces of nature)

Zhen 真 (genuine, real, true)

Zheng 正 (to correct, rectify)

Zheng bi 爭彼 (contending arguments)

Zheng ming 正名 (rectification of names)

Zhengqi 正氣 (righteous *qi*)

Zhen ren 真人 (genuine person)

Zhen zhi 真知 (genuine knowledge)

Zhexue 哲學 (philosophy)

Zhi 致 (to arrive)

Zhì 智 (noun: knowledge, wisdom)

Zhī 知 (verb: to know; noun: knowledge, wisdom)

Zhi 治 (manage, direct)

Zhi 志 (will, commitment, resolution)

Zhi bu zhi zhi zhi 知不知之知 (knowing the knowledge of knowing-not)

Zhihui 智慧 (wisdom; Sanskrit, *prajna*)

Zhili 知禮 (knowing ritual)

Zhi ren 知人 (knowing people)

Zhi xing he yi 知行合一 (unity of knowledge and action)

Zhi zhi 致知 (extension of knowledge)

Zhong 忠 (conscientiousness)

Zhong 中 (middle, balance)

Zhong He Ji《中和集》(*Book of Balance and Harmony*)

Zhongyong《中庸》(*Maintaining Perfect Balance*)

Zhou Li《周禮》

Zhouyi《周易》

Zhuangzi《莊子》

Zhu Pu Xiang Lu《竹譜詳錄》 (*Detailed Record of Bamboo*)

Zi 子 (master)

Ziran 自然 (natural, spontaneous, so of itself)

Zi sun miao 子孫廟 (Buddhist hereditary temples)

Zi xing 自性 (own nature)

Zi xing neng 自性能 (self-nature)

Zong 宗 (sect)

Zu kao lai ge 祖考來格 (the ancestors arrive)

Acknowledgments

My most profound debt is to Weng Haizhen 翁 海 贞. Were it not for her unfailingly patient and resourceful assistance with the Chinese language, I would not have dared even to begin this project, and could never have brought it to completion in the form I envisioned. To safeguard her generosity requires me to insist on responsibility for any errors of fact or usage classical or modern that may have crept into the work despite her diligent vigilance.

I am grateful to Brook Ziporyn for the inspired translation that supplied my title; to Roger Ames, Hans-Georg Mueller, and Yong Huang for generously encouraging an interloping neophyte in fields they have long cultivated; to Michael Ruse for reminding me how a book like this one should begin; and to Jeffrey Perl for encouraging interest and support from an early point.

Several of my earlier articles were stepping-stones to developing themes and ideas explored in this book: "A Dao of Technology," *Dao* 9 (2010); "War as a Problem of Knowledge," *Philosophy East and West* 65 (2015); "The Virtual and the Vacant: Emptiness and Knowledge in Chan and Daoism," *Journal of Chinese Philosophy* 37 (2010); and "The Cloud of Knowing: Blurring the Difference with China," *Common Knowledge* 17 (2011).

Index